HIDDEN®

Idaho

Including Boise, Sun Valley & Yellowstone National Park

Richard Harris

FIFTH EDITION

Ulysses Press®

BERKELEY, CALIFORNIA

Published by:
ULYSSES PRESS
P.O. Box 3440
Berkeley, CA 94703
www.ulyssespress.com

ISSN 1521-7833
ISBN 1-56975-397-0

Printed in Canada by Transcontinental Printing

10 9 8 7 6 5

MANAGING EDITOR: Claire Chun
PROJECT DIRECTOR: Kate Allen
COPY EDITOR: Lily Chou
EDITORIAL ASSOCIATES: Leona Benten, Kaori Takee
TYPESETTERS: Lisa Kester, James Meetze
CARTOGRAPHY: Pease Press
HIDDEN BOOKS DESIGN: Sarah Levin
COVER DESIGN: Sarah Levin, Leslie Henriques
INDEXER: Sayre Van Young
FRONT COVER PHOTOGRAPHY: Steve Bly
ILLUSTRATOR: Claudine Gossett

Distributed in the United States by Publishers Group West and in Canada by Raincoast Books

Write to us!

If in your travels you discover a spot that captures the spirit of Idaho, or if you live in the region and have a favorite place to share, or if you just feel like expressing your views, write to us and we'll pass your note along to the author.

We can't guarantee that the author will add your personal find to the next edition, but if the writer does use the suggestion, we'll acknowledge you in the credits and send you a free copy of the new edition.

ULYSSES PRESS
P.O. Box 3440
Berkeley, CA 94703
E-mail: readermail@ulyssespress.com

*

What's Hidden?

At different points throughout this book, you'll find special listings marked with a hidden symbol:

◄ HIDDEN

This means that you have come upon a place off the beaten tourist track, a spot that will carry you a step closer to the local people and natural environment of Idaho.

The goal of this guide is to lead you beyond the realm of everyday tourist facilities. While we include traditional sightseeing listings and popular attractions, we also offer alternative sights and adventure activities. Instead of filling this guide with reviews of standard hotels and chain restaurants, we concentrate on one-of-a-kind places and locally owned establishments.

Our authors seek out locales that are popular with residents but usually overlooked by visitors. Some are more hidden than others (and are marked accordingly), but all the listings in this book are intended to help you discover the true nature of Idaho and put you on the path of adventure.

Contents

Maps

OUTDOOR ADVENTURE SYMBOLS

The following symbols accompany national, state and regional park listings, as well as beach descriptions throughout the text.

▲	Camping			Waterskiing
	Hiking			Windsurfing
	Biking			Canoeing or Kayaking
	Horseback Riding			Boating
	Downhill Skiing			Boat Ramps
	Cross-country Skiing			Fishing
	Swimming			

ONE

Idaho

There's no New York City in Idaho, no San Francisco, not even a Seattle. The state doesn't offer many urban pleasures (although Boise, the increasingly sophisticated state capital, tries hard to provide them). Idaho lures visitors with other sorts of attractions. And because this is such an amazingly diverse state, that isn't difficult.

Come to Idaho for spectacular scenery. Hells Canyon, which envelops the Snake River for some 60 miles along the Oregon border, is the deepest in North America, its gorge half again deeper than the Grand Canyon of the Colorado River. Craters of the Moon National Monument preserves a striking volcanic region where American astronauts have trained for otherworldly experiences. The Bruneau Dunes are taller than those of Death Valley; Shoshone Falls are higher than Niagara; the Thousand Springs burst from sheer canyon walls in the Hagerman Valley. The jagged Sawtooth Range is a magnificent climax to Idaho's Rocky Mountain region, which is crisscrossed by wilderness rivers and punctuated by hot springs. The northern Panhandle is dominated by some of the largest unspoiled lakes in the United States, including Pend Oreille.

Come to Idaho for outdoor recreation. None of the other 48 contiguous states come close to Idaho as a whitewater-rafting destination: its 3250 miles of navigable whitewater is more than those found in Colorado and Utah combined. America's first destination ski resort was built at Sun Valley in 1936, still one of the great mountains in the United States; alpinists have since discovered the joys of other peaks throughout the state. Fly-fishermen consider Idaho a paradise on earth, especially when they snare steelhead in the Salmon River and trophy-size trout in Henry's Fork and other streams. Backpackers and horseback riders can disappear for weeks at a time in the state's huge central wilderness areas, havens for a diverse and truly "wild" wildlife.

Come to Idaho for its rich history, dating back tens of thousands of years. Hagerman Fossil Beds National Monument preserves one of the world's richest lodes of early mammal fossils; the animal civilization was doomed by the Ice Age and the great Bonneville Flood, which dramatically altered southern Idaho landscapes about 15,000 years ago. Volcanic fury further reshaped the Snake River Plain, so that by the time pioneers crossed this arid region 150 years ago, it tested their mettle like no other section of the Oregon Trail. Subsequent settlers made and squandered fortunes in gold and silver; their legacies are the ghost towns that speckle many of the state's mountainsides. The heritage of Idaho's native tribes is not forgotten today; August's Shoshone-Bannock Indian Festival is one of the nation's largest, and Nez Perce National Historical Park recalls the colorful and tragic history of one of the West's preeminent peoples.

There are many more reasons to visit Idaho. There are its resorts: in particular, Sun Valley and the lakeside communities of Coeur d'Alene and McCall. There are its birds: just outside Boise are the World Center for Birds of Prey and the federally mandated Birds of Prey National Conservation Area. There are its people: hardworking, independent, generally conservative, but friendly and respectful toward those who offer them and their state the same respect.

Hidden Idaho is designed to help you explore this marvelous state in comprehensive fashion. It covers popular, "must-see" places, offering advice on how best to enjoy them. It also tells you about many off-the-beaten-path spots, the kind you would find by talking with folks at the local café or with someone who has lived in the area all of his or her life. It describes the region's history, its natural areas and its residents, both human and animal. It suggests places to eat, to lodge, to play, to camp. Taking into account the varying interests, budgets and tastes of travelers, the book provides the information you need whether you enjoy backpacking, golf, museum browsing, shopping or all of the above.

The traveling part of this book begins in Chapter Two with Boise. The university town of 186,000 people, established in the 1860s after a mining boom in the nearby Boise Basin, has its head in the future (high-tech computer and engineering industries pad the local economy) but its heart in the adjacent outdoors.

Chapter Three looks at Southwestern Idaho surrounding Boise. The Treasure Valley, to the capital's west, is one of Idaho's richest agricultural regions. South is the Birds of Prey reserve on the Snake River and, beyond that, the forbidding near-badlands of the Owyhee Plateau. Southeast are the Bruneau Dunes and the town of Mountain Home, where the U.S. Air Force has its only air intervention wing known as the 366th Fighter Wing.

Chapter Four follows the Snake River east through the lush Hagerman Valley to Twin Falls and South Central Idaho. Don't miss the Snake River Canyon, its sheer cliffs as high as 600 feet: Highlights in the canyon include Shoshone Falls, the "Niagara of the West," and the Thousand Springs, which weep from its walls. Here also are Hagerman Fossil Beds National Monument, Shoshone Ice Caves and the striking City of Rocks.

Chapter Five covers Southeastern Idaho, richer in pioneer history than any other part of Idaho. Oregon Trail ruts bypass the site of Fort Hall, a replica of which stands in Pocatello's Ross Park. Mountain men rendezvoused on the shores of turquoise Bear Lake, on the Utah border; Idaho's earliest white communities were founded by Mormon refugees from Salt Lake City. Geysers, hot springs, cave systems and other natural features add to regional intrigue.

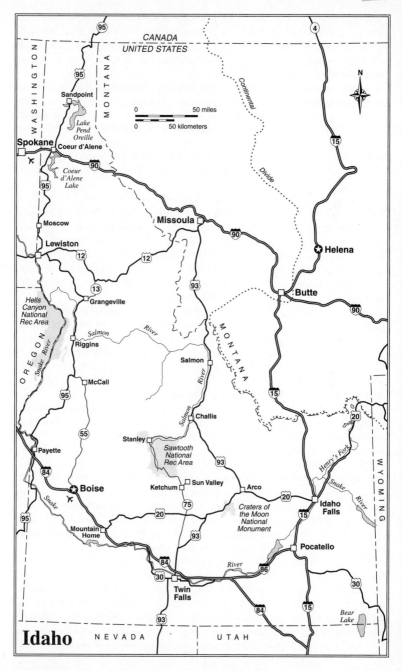

Idaho

Chapter Six explores Eastern Idaho, focusing on Idaho Falls. Besides being the state's best potato farmland, the area is famous for its world-class trout fishing on Henry's Fork of the Snake River; for majestic Upper and Lower Mesa Falls and the nearby St. Anthony Sand Dunes; for the glorious views of the Teton Valley and nearby Grand Targhee resort.

Chapter Seven visits Yellowstone National Park, the world's preeminent natural wonderland, located mainly in Wyoming but extending into eastern Idaho. Here people make way for bisons, time is told by Old Faithful and elk prance around the thermal vents, geysers and fumaroles that have attracted curiosity seekers for over a century. Initially discovered by trappers, the area boasts the largest concentration of mammals in the contiguous United States. The animals now roam free, protected on the park's 2.2 million acres. Humans also roam the park on its 1200 miles of hiking trails.

Chapter Eight, Central Idaho, includes some of the state's prime attractions, including the resort area of Sun Valley, the soaring peaks of Sawtooth National Recreation Area and the spatter cones and lava flows of Craters of the Moon National Monument. The Salmon River, longest in any single state outside Alaska, meanders north from the Sawtooth through the massive Frank Church–River of No Return Wilderness.

Geysers, hot springs, fumaroles and boiling mud appear in Yellowstone National Park in greater concentrations than anywhere else on earth.

Chapter Nine focuses on Hells Canyon National Recreation Area and the lakes and resorts of the McCall region. Remarkable Hells Canyon is a favorite of rafters and jet boaters; its Seven Devils uplands are favored by hikers, and a series of reservoirs above the canyon draw anglers. McCall, on the shore of pristine Payette Lake, is as popular with water-sports enthusiasts as it is with skiers at nearby Brundage Mountain.

Chapter Ten pays attention to the southern half of Idaho's Panhandle, primarily the Clearwater River basin. This is the homeland of the Nez Perce tribe, which assisted Lewis and Clark in their early-19th-century journey of discovery; today, you can visit Nez Perce National Historical Park and trace the Lewis and Clark Trail. Lewiston is a major inland seaport, and the university town of Moscow is surrounded by the ripple and wave of wheat and barley in the undulating Palouse Hills.

Chapter Eleven surveys the northern Panhandle, a region of dense forests, mineral-laden slopes and huge lakes with waters as pristine as any in North America. Coeur d'Alene is a burgeoning resort town on conifer-shrouded Coeur d'Alene Lake. The fulcrum of activity on deep Lake Pend Oreille is Sandpoint, an artists' community near the foot of popular Schweitzer Mountain ski resort. A string of historic silver-mining towns extends east of Coeur d'Alene to the Montana border.

There's so much to experience in Idaho that even most lifelong residents can count on making new discoveries once in a while. First-time vacation visitors are hard-pressed just to make brief stops at the best-known highlights of the state, while seasoned travelers often prefer to explore a more limited area in depth and then return on later trips to different spots, perhaps in different seasons. Either way, people generally come back, often to stay. *Hidden Idaho* will help you experience a wealth of exciting places and adventures.

The Rocky Mountains of Idaho consist mainly of granite, an igneous rock. That means it is made up of several different minerals—quartz, feldspar and granite, along with traces and veins of metals such as gold, silver, lead and zinc—blended deep within the earth countless millennia ago under conditions of great heat. Long after the other major mountain chains in the United States had already been formed, the massive layer of granite that would become the Rocky Mountains lay under the sandy floor of a great sea. For a period of about 700 million years, Idaho's western border was the continental coast of North America.

The Story of Idaho

GEOLOGY

Very slowly, inexorably, two tectonic plates that make up most of the North American continent—the Canadian Shield and the Pacific Plate—drifted toward each other, floating on molten rock far beneath the earth's surface. In a slow collision, the plates crushed against each other and started to crumple, pushing the granite layer upward. Dinosaurs, which were abundant in the area at that time, would have experienced the phenomenon as occasional earthquakes.

The collision of tectonic plates and the uplifting of the granite rock continues even now, though the process is so slow that the mountains have gained only a few inches in height during the time humankind has walked the earth. In Idaho the granite is exposed in the most rugged and inaccessible areas of the state: the Frank Church–River of No Return Wilderness and the Sawtooth, Pioneer and White Cloud ranges of central Idaho; the Selway-Bitterroot Wilderness on the Continental Divide; and the Selkirks of the northern panhandle.

The mountains as we see them today were shaped by glaciers. A series of ice ages, the last of which ended 10,000 years ago (a mere eyeblink in geological time), covered the high country in accumulations of snow and ice. These glaciers flowed down the mountainsides slowly, in solid frozen rivers that gouged deep valleys called moraines, creating steep mountain faces and marking the courses for the turbulent rivers that would slice canyons hundreds of feet deep.

The lofty mountains attract storm clouds like a magnet, making for rainfall and snowfall many times greater than in the deserts and arid prairies at their feet. Runoff from the melting snowpack in spring and the thunderstorms of summer is the source of Idaho's great rivers: the Snake, the Salmon and the Clearwater. The Snake River drains all of Idaho except for the rivers of the northern Panhandle, and, like all the state's rivers (except the Bear, which flows into the Great Salt Lake), is part of the larger Columbia River Basin that drains into the Pacific Ocean. The Snake River Canyon, extending across southern Idaho, was carved by a months-long flood of biblical proportions—nearly 1000 times the river's present volume—when Lake Bonneville, covering much of Utah and Nevada, drained suddenly 15,000 years ago. In Hells Canyon, the Snake has carved the deepest canyon on the continent. The second- and third-deepest canyons were cut by the main Salmon River and its Middle Fork through the granitic plug at Idaho's center.

Volcanism has had a profound effect in the formation of southern Idaho. The earth remains especially restless in and around Yellowstone National Park, on the border of eastern Idaho and western Wyoming, which encompasses a giant ancient caldera. The area weathers more earthquakes than anywhere in the lower 48 states outside California. Geologists believe that this ancient caldera is a particularly hot spot of the earth's mantle and that the Snake River Plain was formed as the North American continental crust passed westward over it. The plain is dotted with the remains of extinct volcanoes that are the skeletons of earlier "Yellowstones," and it is marked as well with cracks in the earth's crust where volcanic magma has seeped out and covered vast areas—even as recently as 2000 years ago. Craters of the Moon National Monument near Arco is part of this great rift where Idaho's volcanism can be seen at its most spectacular.

HISTORY   Idaho is so alive with history that we can still see and feel its Western character, its hopes and successes, and its bitter failures and discouragements. Children of pioneer families are still living and can remember arriving in Conestogas to homestead a patch of ground. Tracks left by wagon wheels still scar the fragile and brutally dry deserts; grave markers punctuate stories of expectation with hardship. Buildings thrown hurriedly together in a gold and silver fever still stand—gray with weather, crumbling and leaning. Mostly, though, there is still a look of rawness to the land that has not gone away. The history of white settlement here is short—a mere hundred-plus years—but others can trace theirs for many thousands of years in tribal stories. Their history is here, too, longer and deeply resonant in the land.

THE FIRST PEOPLE   American Indians touched Idaho lightly and with reverence. The people of the mountains—Utes, Shoshone and Bannocks in southern Idaho, Nez Perce and Coeur d'Alene in northern Idaho—lived as nomads, huddling around fires in bison-leather tents through thousands of long, brutal winters along the foothills of the Rockies, waiting to follow the spring snowmelt into hidden canyons and ancient forests of the high country. The American Indian population of Idaho was never large. With such a vast territory to roam, the mountain tribes rarely came into conflict. In fact, they rarely encountered one another except on purpose, in intertribal powwows held at traditional times and places for purposes of trade, social contests, spiritual ceremonies and political diplomacy.

Warfare among the tribes took place mainly along the eastern edge of the mountains. Before the arrival of whites, intertribal battles bore little resemblance to the bloodbaths that would come later. War parties were generally small and had no firearms, steel or horses. The limited supply of arrows a warrior could carry did not last long in battle, and it was better to save them for hunting if possible, since each handmade arrow represented many hours of work.

> Idaho is known for its potatoes—but it's also the number-one producer of Austrian winter peas and wrinkled seed peas.

At least two non-Indian influences—horses and guns—began to change the tribal way of life long before the first white man set foot in Idaho at the beginning of the 19th century. Horses first came into Indian hands in northern New Mexico in 1680, when Pueblo people revolted against their Spanish oppressors, looting and burning every settler's home. Navajo and Apache groups decided to help the Pueblos drive out the Spaniards; in exchange, they could keep all the livestock they could round up from the Spanish ranches and farms— including thousands of horses. Many more horses driven off from the ranches were never captured but instead went wild to spawn the herds of mustangs that inhabit remote areas of the Owyhee Mountains even today. As neighbors of the Navajo, the Ute people got their first horses around 1700, and within the next 60 years virtually every tribe in the Rocky Mountain West had bought, captured or stolen enough horses to breed its own herd. Horses let the Indians travel much farther and faster, bringing more frequent contact—whether friendly or hostile— between tribes.

Guns spread more slowly among American Indians. In the British and French settlements along America's east coast, armies of both colonial powers gave rifles to tribes that helped fight the Seven Years War (1756–63). Guns meant power to conquer other tribes. Fur traders on what was then the American frontier found that the self-defense needs of the tribes made guns extremely valuable as items of exchange, as well as empowering the tribes to hunt more efficiently and trade larger quantities of valuable furs for more guns. As a tribe got guns by trading with whites from the east, it often turned them against rival tribes to the west in order to expand its hunting territory. In this way, firearms often made their way westward ahead of the first white explorers.

EXPLORERS AND MOUNTAIN MEN A vast area of North America, from the Mississippi River to the Pacific Northwest coast, including all of Idaho, was claimed as Spanish territory in 1769, even though no Spanish settlement was ever established beyond the port city of New Orleans. France acquired the Louisiana Territory from Spain by treaty in 1800, but except for small trading expeditions up the river, the French found it impossible to occupy, or even explore and map, the territory. In 1803 they sold it to the United States for $12 million. Two years later, the first French trappers and traders reached the Rocky Mountains; they had been in the wilderness so long that they did not know the region had been sold to America. Nor did it matter much, since virtually all the estimated 150 French frontiersmen who went West found homes among the tribes and never returned east.

No American expedition reached Idaho until the summer of 1805, when 45 men led by Captain Meriwether Lewis and William Clark made their way up the Missouri River and across Montana and Idaho. They found willing guides in the Shoshone interpreter Sacajawea and her French fur-trader husband, who led them all the way to the mouth of the Columbia River on the Pacific coast.

Lewis and Clark recorded the incredible numbers of fur-bearing animals in the territory, and soon thereafter the exploitation began. On Lewis and Clark's return trip in 1806, expedition member John Colter left the party to seek his fortune as a trapper and trader on the new frontier. He returned to St. Louis, Missouri, four years later with stories of boiling springs and smoke spewing from the earth. Although most people dismissed Colter's tales as the product of an imagination gone mad in the wilderness, no one ignored the fact that he had also brought back a fortune in beaver pelts.

John Colter was the first white man to see the strange landscape that would become Yellowstone National Park.

David Thompson, working for the Hudson's Bay Company in 1809, was the first to establish a fort and to trade in valuable pelts. Kullyspell House, as Thompson named the fort, was situated on the banks of Lake Pend Oreille. In 1811, less than a year after John Colter's return from the wilderness, John Jacob Astor's American Fur Company sent its first expedition into the northern Rocky Mountains and Idaho. There followed a seesaw contest to control the lucrative trade, but for almost 40 years the Hudson's Bay Company—often abbreviated HBC and then mockingly referred to as Here Before Christ—maintained an iron grip on the fur trade from Puget Sound to the eastern slope of the Rocky Mountains. Efforts to expand trapping led to explorations farther south and the establishment of Fort Boise and Fort Hall, which played an essential role as a resupply center at the crossroads of several frontier byways, particularly the Oregon Trail.

As large international fur-trading companies built posts on the Rockies' eastern scarp, hundreds of freelance adventurers set off to probe deeper into the mountains in search of pelts. These "mountain men," as they were called—men like Jim Bridger, Jedediah Smith and Jeremiah "Liver Eatin' " Johnston—explored virtually every valley in the Rockies during the next 30 years, bringing back more than half a million beaver pelts each year. In order to kill animals in such phenomenal numbers, the mountain men not only set their own traps but also traded gunpowder and bullets to the Indians for more furs. By the close of the 1840s, beavers had become nearly extinct in most of the Rockies, and during the next decade, dwindled to almost nothing in Idaho. The last of the old-time fur trappers either became guides for army expeditions and pioneer wagon trains or established their own trading posts, where they continued to sell ammunition to the tribes—a practice that would soon become controversial and then illegal.

PIONEERS AND PROSPECTORS   The first wagon train crossed the Continental Divide in 1842. It was made up of 100 frontier families from Iowa, Kentucky, Illinois and Missouri, traveling in Conestoga wagons with a herd of cattle, bound for Oregon's fertile Willamette Valley. The route they blazed, which came to be known as the Oregon Trail, would be used by virtually all pioneers en route to the western territories for the next 27 years. From 1842 to 1847, about 5000 people made the journey west—a mere trickle compared to the great migration to come. Although pioneers passed along the trail in growing numbers each year, they all continued to the West Coast. Hardly anyone stayed to settle Idaho until 1860 when a band of Mormons pushed north and established the town of Franklin in what they believed was northern Utah; in fact, it was southeastern Idaho. That same year gold was discovered in the Clearwater Valley and then in the Salmon River drainage near the town of Florence, north and east of Payette Lake. People now came to stay—at least as long as the rich veins held—and boomtowns sprouted to take the miner's dust and provide him with necessary supplies. When the ore played out, the miners took their Pulaskis and shovels and went looking for the next big strike, which came in the Boise Basin and the Owyhees. Other strikes in the forested north brought miners to Coeur d'Alene, Kellogg and Wallace.

Over the next three decades, the mines that continued to operate became large established outfits and the surviving mining towns became settled by merchants, farmers and ranchers; the money-mad and lusty miners were now a minority. During those years, Oregon-bound pioneers carved deep ruts across southern Idaho in their hurry to cross its terrible and hot scrub plains. But Oregon began to "fill up," and early irrigation projects proved the Idaho "wastelands" to be fantastically fertile and the native grasses to provide good forage. Crops were planted, and as the bison were slaughtered, almost disappearing from Idaho's range-land, they were replaced by cattle. Cowboys drove these to the railroad terminus in Cheyenne, Wyoming, before a spur line came to Pocatello. By 1884, the Union Pacific had laid tracks across southern Idaho; two years before, the Northern Pacific had reached Idaho's Panhandle, fueling the mining boom and making possible large-scale logging of what was then the nation's most extensive virgin stand of white pine.

More waves of pioneers came to settle, leading inevitably to conflict between homesteaders and American Indians. Two important Indian wars occurred in Idaho, against the Nez Perce (see "I Will Fight No More, Forever" in Chapter Ten) and the Bannocks, who rose against emigrants determined to plow under and farm the historic camas gathering grounds near Fairfield. Full-scale irrigation came to the Snake River Plain after the turn of the century under federal reclamation efforts, such as the Minidoka, Boise and King Hill projects. Dry-land farming of wheat, barley and other grains thus became possible in lands distant from the canals.

MODERN TIMES Agriculture, timber and mining fueled Idaho's economic growth, but even before Idaho became a state in 1890, tourism tagged along behind. Yellowstone became the world's first national park in 1872, and with the coming of the railroads, the first tourists were able to see the fantastic sights of the Western frontier they had been hearing about since Lewis and Clark's return from the Pacific. Still, in those days, Idaho was more remote than the African veldt or the Australian outback is today—the exclusive destination of adventurers, tycoons and wealthy dilettantes. It was not until the 1920s, when many Americans bought automobiles and the first main highways were paved, that tourists began heading toward Idaho in great numbers. In Sun Valley, the nation's first destination ski resort was built in 1936. Tourism has since become ever more important in Idaho's economic picture and is predicted to be the state's largest industry shortly after the millennium.

But just as tourists have been enticed to Idaho's wild, remote and pristine environment, so have timber and mining companies. Recreation has expanded into the open deserts and canyons of southern and central Idaho—lands once the sole province of cattle ranchers—and battles and tempers have flared there too. Underlying these tensions is the migration away from overcrowded and expensive coastal cities to the West, supported by new technologies that make it possible to conduct business remotely, by computer. As modern cowboys and cowgirls have ridden onto the range, Idaho's population has grown faster than most western states, primarily near Boise and Coeur d'Alene.

Growth has been both welcomed and scorned. Few Idahoans complain about rising property values, but many abhor the impact of a larger population on their cherished quality of life—the wide open spaces, the outdoor sports, the abundance of wildlife, the lack of crowds, traffic and crime. The irony is that newcomers seek the same quality of life too. Exploding urban populations and expanding tourism are forcing a pronounced shift in Western values. The Western way of life—ranching, timber and mining, for so long the backbone of Idaho—is changing. Extraction of resources is no longer assumed to be the best use of Idaho's natural bounty. Recreationists and tourists don't want to see clear-cut forests, sediment choked streams and overgrazed range. Many of Idaho's small rural communities understand that their traditional economic base is shifting, but haven't yet seen the full benefit of the growing tourist economy. Visitors can make a difference by treading lightly and letting their dollars vote for the Idaho and the West they want to see in 20, 50 or 100 years.

> Idaho's arid prairies are so sparse that it takes 25 to 40 acres to graze a single cow.

FLORA

Altitude makes all the difference when it comes to plant life in Idaho. At lower elevations—"low" in this region meaning about a mile above sea level—the environment consists of arid prairies with sparse vegetation. The reason is that the Rocky Mountains cast a "rain shadow"; as weather patterns move from west to east, clouds dump most of their rain or snow on the high, cool mountains, leaving little moisture to fall on the prairies. The closer the land is to the base of the mountains, the drier it is, with natural vegetation that consists mainly of thin veneers of grass punctuated by prickly pear cactus. In southern Idaho, farmers have transformed this seeming wasteland into fields of wheat, potatoes, sugar beets and other crops made possible by irrigation wells that tap into huge underground aquifers fed by the moisture that falls in the mountains and then seeps into the earth.

Mountain forests, too, change with elevation, forming three distinct bands. On the lower slopes of the mountains, ponderosa pine stand 50 feet tall and more. Douglas fir and blue spruce dominate the higher reaches of the mountains. Between the two bands of evergreen forest, shimmering stands of aspen trees fill the mountainsides and paint them bright yellow in early October. The aspen, perhaps the most intriguing and distinctive tree in Idaho, is what forestry experts call an "opportunistic species": stands grow wherever clearings appear in the evergreen woods—usually because of forest fires or pine beetle infestations. Gradually, over a span of centuries, the taller evergreens will crowd out old aspen stands as new ones appear elsewhere. The aspen is a delicate tree that cannot tolerate high- or low-altitude extremes.

The upper boundary of the deep green forests of spirelike Douglas fir is known as "timberline," the elevation above which temperatures drop below freezing at night year-round and trees can't grow. Timberline is around 8000 to 9000 feet in southern Idaho and lower the farther north you go—around 6000 feet in the Selkirk Range. Above timberline lies the alpine tundra, a delicate world of short grasses and other green plants rooted in permafrost, where tiny flowers appear for brief moments each summer.

At the highest elevations—12,000-foot summits in the Lemhi and Pioneer ranges, 7000 feet near the Canadian border—summer freezing prevents even small plants of the tundra from growing. Up there, clinging to the granite cliffs and boulders, grows lichen, a symbiotic combination of two plants that survive in partnership: a type of moss forms a leathery, sheltering shell that protects an alga, which in turn provides nutrients by photosynthesis to feed the moss. This ingenious arrangement is perhaps the ultimate tribute to life's amazing capacity for adapting to even the harshest environments.

FAUNA   One of Idaho's greatest attractions is its abundance of wildlife. You are most likely to get a good look at large animals in national parks, where long-standing prohibitions against hunting have helped them lose their fear of humans. Wildlife populations are about the same in national forests, but sightings are much less common because animals generally keep their distance from roads, trails and any human scent.

The Snake River and high plains and mountain parks (not the kind with rangers, but flat grasslands surrounded by mountain ranges) are a favorite habitat of jackrabbits, coyotes and pronghorn antelope, as well as prairie birds such as hawks, grouse and pheasants. Coyote populations are on the increase just about everywhere in the West. They are commonly seen not only in open grasslands but also on the outskirts of urban areas, including Boise. Intelligent and curious, coyotes can often be spotted observing people from a distance. They are rarely dangerous to humans, though they may sometimes attack small pets.

Pronghorn antelope, once hunted nearly to extinction and until recently listed as a threatened species under the federal Endangered Species Act, have multiplied to the point that they are now a familiar sight on Idaho's central and southern plains. Although these tan, black and white deerlike creatures with short legs and large heads are commonly called antelope, they are not related to the true antelope of Africa and Asia. In fact, they are not related to any other living species.

American bison, more often called buffalo although they are unrelated to Asian buffalo, once roamed throughout the Snake River Plain. Today they are found only in Yellowstone National

Park and in parts of other northern Rocky Mountain states. There are also rattlesnakes in the foothills and high plains. The good news is that they rarely venture into the mountains. Snakes and other reptiles are cold-blooded and cannot function in low temperatures, so they are hardly ever found at elevations above about 7000 feet. When hiking at lower elevations, walk loudly and never put your hand or foot where you can't see it.

Deer, mountain lions and bobcats inhabit Idaho's mountains, and are sighted regularly near Boise. While mule deer and white-tailed deer may be spotted anywhere in the mountains, they prefer to graze in areas where scrub oak grows. Mountain lions hunt deer and prefer areas with high rocks, where they can spot both dangers and prey a long way away. Since mountain lions are nocturnal and reclusive, it's a stroke of luck to glimpse one darting across the road in your headlights at night. They have not been known to attack humans in Idaho, though several recent incidents in California and Colorado have proved that they can be dangerous. Wild horses also graze on Idaho's Owyhee Plateau.

In forests and meadows, common small mammals include squirrels, chipmunks, raccoons, foxes, porcupines and skunks. Large animals include elk and black bears. Since elk prefer high mountain meadows in the warm months, they are usually seen outside of national parks by serious hikers who venture deep into the wilderness. Sightings are more common in winter, when they descend to lower elevations where grass is easier to reach under the snow. In some areas, usually marked by signs and sometimes observation areas, herds of elk can often be spotted from the road in winter; they are especially common in the Mammoth Hot Springs area of Yellowstone National Park. Moose are found in the northern Rockies of Idaho. Most frequently found in marshy areas around dawn or dusk, these herbivores are hard to spot because of their ability to blend into forest surroundings.

As for black bears, they are elusive but more common than most hikers realize. In times of drought, when food becomes scarce, it's not unusual for a bear to raid trash cans along the fringes of civilization. Black bears rarely attack people, but they are unpredict-

WHO'S AFRAID OF THE BIG GRAY WOLF?

Wolves were virtually extinct in Idaho until 1995, when in a highly controversial move the first gray (timber) wolves were reintroduced to the Frank Church–River of No Return Wilderness and to the backcountry of Yellowstone National Park. Initial reports are that the several dozen canine relatives are flourishing—much to the chagrin of area ranchers, whose forebears paid bounty hunters for their slaughter.

able and can be dangerous because of their size. Most injuries involving bears happen because campers store their food inside tents with them at night. When camping in the forest, one should leave all food inside a closed vehicle or suspended from a tree limb. Grizzly bears, larger and more aggressive cousins of black bears, live in the backcountry of Yellowstone and are found in the northern Panhandle close to the Canadian border and in remote areas of the Continental Divide in central Idaho.

Beavers once inhabited virtually every stream in Idaho. Trapped by the millions for their pelts in the early 19th century, these largest of North American rodents once stood on the brink of extinction. In more recent times, they have too often been considered pests because their habit of damming streams (to create ponds surrounding their dome-shaped sticks-and-mud lodges) floods the most desirable areas of mountain valleys. Landowners persisted for many years in poisoning the beavers or dynamiting their dams and putting up low electric fences to keep them away. They have been enough of a problem in downtown Boise that trees along the Greenbelt have been wrapped with wire fencing for protection. Now a protected species in Idaho, beavers seem to be making a slow comeback. It's not unusual to discover beaver ponds on backcountry streams, and if you watch a pond near sunset, you may get a look at the animals themselves.

Above timberline, Rocky Mountain bighorn sheep are common and easy to spot in alpine meadows. Herds of ewes are protected by a single ram, while other males lead a solitary existence elsewhere until mating season, when the high crags echo with the crash of horns as young rams challenge their elders for dominance over the female herd. Mountain goats—shaggy, snow white and solitary—may also be seen in some high mountain areas, especially Sawtooth National Recreation Area. The smaller animals most commonly seen above timberline are golden marmots, large, chubby rodents nicknamed "whistlepigs" because they communicate with shrill whistles. Smaller rodents called pikas colonize high-altitude rock piles, where swarms of hundreds are sometimes seen.

Where to Go

Travel anywhere in Idaho and you will be taken by the number of rivers and by the mountains that feed them. They represent more exciting and challenging exploration than can be accomplished in a lifetime. Few native Idahoans have climbed even half the state's peaks, fished through half its streams and lakes or floated half its rivers. If you try to see it all in a single trip, you may find yourself so focused on covering large distances that you sacrifice quiet moments to appreciate the natural beauty you came to see. Deciding what to see and where to go is a tough choice. The good news is that, no matter how many times you visit, there will always be more places to discover the next time you come.

Chances are, if you fly into Idaho you will land in **Boise**, the rapidly growing state capital and largest city in the state, located where the Great Basin meets the Snake River Plain and the Rocky Mountain foothills. This surprising city ranks consistently high in national polls rating livability and quality of life—to the chagrin of growth-weary residents. Take a moment to walk, bike or skate the city's extensive riverside parks and Greenbelt where you can also catch trout, watch eagles soar or float the gentle Boise River in rafts and inner tubes all summer long. Join residents as they enjoy long summer evenings in the outdoor cafés and bistros that dot Boise's commercial district, where you can also tour the Capitol and historic Old Town.

Lake Pend Oreille is so deep that the United States Navy uses it for sonar experiments.

Arcing around Boise, in **Southwestern Idaho**, the Snake River courses through the Snake River Birds of Prey National Conservation Area, home of North America's highest concentration of raptors, and then irrigates the fertile Treasure Valley. South of the Snake are the forbidding and beautiful Owyhee Mountains and Plateau and its deeply carved river canyons. Less than an hour north of the state capital, whitewater boaters can take on the challenge of the famous Payette River: There is more raft-ready whitewater surrounding Boise than any other city in the United States. Wild West enthusiasts can explore abandoned mining towns in the upper Boise Basin. The Bruneau Dunes, outside Mountain Home, are America's tallest sand dunes.

Following the Snake River through **Twin Falls and South Central Idaho** toward its headwaters in Yellowstone National Park, the river has carved 600-foot canyons through the volcanic soils that cover all of southern Idaho. Here are the horseshoe-shaped Shoshone Falls, which are higher than Niagara, and the Thousand Springs, which burst from sheer canyon walls. Nearby ice caves contrast with steaming hot springs. Hagerman Fossil Beds National Monument harbors Idaho's most extensive paleontological site and City of Rocks National Reserve attracts modern-day rock-climbers. The region's common treads are the wagon ruts of the Oregon Trail along the banks of the Snake.

The geologic drama reaches even greater heights in **Pocatello and Southeastern Idaho**. Ancient Lake Bonneville, the size of the five Great Lakes combined and covering vast areas of Utah and Nevada, drained in a massive flood that raged down the Portneuf Valley to the Snake River Plain and on through southern Idaho. Frontier trappers took beaver by the mule-load from the Rockies and, near lakes and hot springs in the gentle mountains above

Pocatello, rendezvoused with local tribes and fellow frontiersmen to celebrate their hardy way of life. Those gatherings are restaged here annually, and the area's resort hot springs may be Idaho's finest. Pocatello was an important stopping place on the way west for many pioneers seeking supplies at Fort Hall. Today's travelers can stretch their legs by strolling a full-size replica of the fort.

Idaho Falls and Eastern Idaho serve as a gateway to Yellowstone and Teton national parks. Here the Snake enters Idaho, nourishing the state's famous potato fields, visible along the Swan Valley, and supporting trout fisheries that draw anglers from around the world. The focus is on wildlife, with some of Idaho's densest populations and best viewing. Winter skiing at the Grand Targhee resort and in the Caribou–Targhee National Forest is considered world-class.

Yellowstone National Park is the world's first national park (it was established in 1872) and undoubtedly its most famous. A remarkable thermal wonderland of more than 10,000 geysers, hot springs and boiling mud caldrons, as well as impressive canyons, waterfalls and high-elevation lakes, Yellowstone sits on the crest of an ancient volcanic crater. It also has perhaps the Rocky Mountain's most varied and accessible wildlife, from elk and moose to bison and grizzly bears. The western entrance, at the bustling gateway community of West Yellowstone, provides easy access to the park for visitors coming from Idaho.

In **Sun Valley and Central Idaho,** north of the Snake River Plain is the world-famous resort area of Sun Valley and the Sawtooth National Recreation Area, encompassing high, craggy peaks and the headwaters of the wilderness Salmon River, the broadest river system within any one state outside Alaska. This country is often called the "Heart of Idaho," and with reason; it is stunningly beautiful. The town of Salmon is a gateway to river running on the Salmon River, which will take boaters through the largest wilderness area in the lower 48. Idaho's tallest mountain, 12,662-foot Borah Peak, looms over a vast central lava plain best seen at Craters of the Moon National Monument.

In **West Central Idaho** the resort town of McCall is a major gateway to the Frank Church–River of No Return Wilderness surrounding the Salmon River, while through Hells Canyon the Snake River has carved the deepest canyon on the continent. Hells Canyon's steeply sloping sides are just this side of heaven for hunters, and its waters are plied by anglers fishing for trout, steelhead, sturgeon and even catfish, and by whitewater rafters and jetboaters. McCall is built on the shore of high, clear and cold Payette Lake—very refreshing to Boiseans in the heat of summer. The town is surrounded by mountains sprinkled with yet more lakes and streams that offer superb fishing and hiking. The town of Riggins, 2000 feet lower in elevation, provides access to more fishing and whitewater on the Salmon River.

The historic Lewis and Clark Trail follows the Lochsa and Clearwater rivers through **Lewiston and the Lower Panhandle.** Here the two famous explorers met with the Nez Perce, who assisted them on their journey to the Pacific Ocean. The Nez Perce National Historical Park memorializes dozens of sites associated with this remarkable native tribe. Lewiston, at Idaho's lowest point of elevation, is sometimes called the state's "banana belt." The city was Idaho's second permanent settlement and many of its historic buildings still are standing. Here, too, are the rolling hills of the grain-rich Palouse country and the University of Idaho in Moscow, located at its heart. On the Continental Divide, along the eastern border with Montana, are vast stretches of remote wilderness.

Pristine lakes and wild-and-scenic rivers are trademarks of **Coeur d'Alene and the Upper Panhandle.** The nationally acclaimed resort town of Coeur d'Alene rests on the shore of an evergreen-shrouded lake of the same name. Located an easy drive away are deep blue Lake Pend Oreille and remote Priest Lake. The artists community of Sandpoint is located on the shores of Lake Pend Oreille, and way up in the surrounding mountains, which offer magnificent hiking and fishing, are Idaho's remaining stands of giant old-growth cedar and pine. The towns of Kellogg and Wallace tell the colorful history of some of the nation's most productive gold and silver mines. And skiing at the area's several resorts attracts visitors in winter who ride the world's longest gondola.

LET IT SNOW

Snowfall amounts, as well as winter temperatures in the mountains, can vary a lot from year to year, so, despite the official Thanksgiving-through-March Idaho ski season, the actual dates of operation at various ski areas are somewhat unpredictable. These days, the huge artificial snowmaking capacity of most ski areas almost always assures a Thanksgiving opening day. While snowmaking usually ceases after March when advance-reservation business slows down, skiing continues until spring temperatures rise enough to erode the snow base. In some years, at some ski areas, late-season skiing may continue well into April. Uncrowded ski trails, discount lift tickets and lots of sunshine make the late season a favorite time for many local ski enthusiasts.

▼ ▼ ▼ ▼ ▼ ▼ ▼ ▼ ▼ ▼
When to Go

SEASONS

Though it may sound romantic, springtime in Idaho is less than appealing in reality. Cold winds, occasional avalanches, brown vegetation and plenty of mud are a few of the reasons most people in the tourist business here shut down their shops and motels in April and take their own vacations to more southerly climes. Just about any other time of year, however, the climate is ideal for one kind of outdoor recreation or another, giving rise to Idaho's distinctive summer-and-winter double tourist season.

The traditional summer tourist season, which runs from Memorial Day to Labor Day, is characterized by cool nights, mild days, colorful wildflowers and sudden, brief afternoon rainstorms. In most parts of Idaho, it's a good idea to start outdoor activities early and carry a wind or rain shell on all-day hikes. In a common, peculiar phenomenon, wind currents called "waves" can carry precipitation for long distances from clouds hidden behind the mountains, causing "sun showers." Old-timers say that if it rains while the sun is shining, it will rain again tomorrow. This adage almost always holds true—but then, if it doesn't rain in the sunshine, it's still likely to rain tomorrow. The good news is that summer rains rarely last more than an hour, and skies generally clear well before sunset.

In the mountains, clouds typically build in the early afternoon and then burst into thunder, lightning and sometimes hail. Storms tend to be small, scattered and frequent. An exception to this rule is the Snake River Plain, which can be barbarously hot and dry in midsummer, its 90° to 100°F temperatures only rarely broken by thunderstorms, which tend not to descend from the adjacent foothills.

Above timberline, temperatures fall below freezing at night all summer and typically reach only 40° to 50°F at midday. It is not unusual for high mountain roads to be closed by blizzards even in August, sometimes stranding motorists for an hour or two before snowplows clear the road.

Early fall—around the end of September—is one of the most delightful times to visit Idaho, as the turning of the aspens paints the mountainsides in yellow with splashes of orange and red, brilliant against a deep green background of evergreen forests. Mountain highways tend to be crowded with carloads of leaf-gawkers on weekends but not on weekdays, while hiking and biking traffic on forest trails is much lighter than during the summer. The weather is generally dry and cool in early fall, making it a great time to take a long wilderness hike or mountain-bike excursion. The first light snowfall can be expected in the high country around the first week of October (national parks usually close about this time) and in the low country around the third week; the first heavy snow typically comes around Halloween. November is hunting season, a good time to stay out of the mountains unless you're armed and dangerous.

The official ski season in Idaho runs from Thanksgiving through March, the period in which all ski areas expect a reliable snow base and within which all ski events and package tours are scheduled. If you're planning ahead for a major ski vacation, you will want to schedule it between those dates, too.

CALENDAR OF EVENTS

JANUARY

Hells Canyon and the McCall Area   The ten-day **McCall Winter Carnival** is highlighted by its world-class snow-sculpting contest near the shores of Payette Lake; there are also snowmobile and ski races, parades, fireworks and an evening ball.

Coeur d'Alene and the Upper Panhandle   The **Sandpoint Winter Carnival** includes ten days of festivities near Lake Pend Oreille, including snow sculptures, snowshoe softball, a torchlight parade and a Christmas tree–burning ritual.

FEBRUARY

Boise   The **Winter Games of Idaho** offer winter- sports competition for weekend athletes at Bogus Basin and other venues throughout the month.

Lewiston and the Lower Panhandle   Some of the world's best-known musicians are featured at the four-day **Lionel Hampton Jazz Festival** on the University of Idaho campus in Moscow.

MARCH

Pocatello and Southeastern Idaho   The **Dodge National Circuit Finals Rodeo** in Pocatello is the second-largest points-qualifying rodeo in the U.S.

Yellowstone National Park   West Yellowstone hosts the **Yellowstone Rendezvous Ski Race**, including 25- and 50-kilometer cross-country ski competitions.

Lewiston and the Lower Panhandle   The **Moscow Mardi Gras Festival** includes a Mardi Gras parade, art gallery showings and celebrity bands.

APRIL

Boise   **Earth Day** is observed with a variety of events in the Boise area.

Lewiston and the Lower Panhandle   Garden tours and an arts-and-crafts fair highlight Lewiston's **Dogwood Festival**, a ten-day rite of spring that also includes a rodeo, concerts and plays.

Hells Canyon and the McCall Area   Entrants from as far away as New Zealand compete at Riggins in the **Salmon River Jet Boat Races**, the first leg of the U.S. championship series.

MAY

Southwestern Idaho   Payette celebrates its **Apple Blossom Festival** with a parade, carnival and crafts show.

Twin Falls and South Central Idaho   **Western Days** in Twin Falls offers a full week of events, including a parade, dances, a barbecue, a chili cook-off and an Old West shootout. The high point of **Hagerman Fossil Days** is the opportunity to tour remote reaches of Hagerman Fossil Beds National Monument.

Idaho Falls and Eastern Idaho   The free **St. Anthony Fishermen's Breakfast** marks the beginning of fishing season on Henry's Fork of the Snake River.

Hells Canyon and the McCall Area   A parade kicks off the **Riggins Rodeo**, staged within a natural stadium contained by steep Salmon River canyon walls.

Lewiston and the Lower Panhandle   Dragons and wizards abound at Moscow's **Renaissance Faire**, which includes free concerts of medieval to modern music.

JUNE

Boise   Boise's skies fill with soaring dirigibles in late June with the **Hot Air Balloon Festival**.

Hells Canyon and the McCall Area   Weiser hosts the **National Old-Time Fiddlers Contest**, during which the best country fiddlers in America play in competition and informal jam sessions.

Coeur d'Alene and the Upper Panhandle   Sandpoint's **Timberfest**, a celebration of the logging industry, includes competition in such events as pole climbing, ax throwing and log rolling; there are exhibits of logging equipment, a concert and a dance.

JULY

Boise   The **San Inazio Basque Festival** in Boise features traditional food and dancing from Europe's Basque country.

Southwestern Idaho   Nampa's **Snake River Stampede** is one of the top 25 rodeos in the country; there are also parades and nightly concerts by leading country-and-western stars.

Pocatello and Southeastern Idaho   Montpelier's **Oregon Trail Rendezvous Pageant** takes place on the trail itself, with actors re-enacting the drama of the pioneer movement west.

Idaho Falls and Eastern Idaho   At Driggs, the **Teton Valley Hot Air Balloon Races** offers splashes of color in the sky.

Sun Valley and Central Idaho   The **Sun Valley Summer Symphony** kicks off three weeks of performances by classical and jazz musicians from throughout the country. The **Sawtooth Mountain Mamas Arts and Crafts Fair** in Stanley brings as many as 100 artisans together, and includes a barbecue dinner and a performance by old-time fiddlers.

Hells Canyon and the McCall Area   The **Summer Music Festival** in McCall features blues, Latin and a variety of fusion mixes for a weekend of music.

Coeur d'Alene and the Upper Panhandle   In Moscow, well-known jazz, folk, blues and classical musicians perform under a canopy of trees during the nine-day **Rendezvous in the Park**. Kamiah celebrates its **Riverfest** with a bluegrass concert the weekend following July 4th. Old Mission State Park at Cataldo hosts a **Historic Skills Fair**, featuring such pioneer activities as spinning, quilting and black-powder shooting.

AUGUST

Boise   The **Western Idaho Fair**, the largest fair in the state, offers livestock and crafts exhibits, a carnival and top-name entertainment.
Southwestern Idaho   Horses and riders re-enact a fording of the Snake River by a pioneer wagon train during **Three Island Crossing**, a weekend-long event on a portion of the original Oregon Trail at Glenns Ferry.
Pocatello and Southeastern Idaho   The **Shoshone-Bannock Indian Festival** at Fort Hall features dances and games in traditional native costume, tribal arts and crafts and the All-Indian Old Timers Rodeo.
Idaho Falls and Eastern Idaho   Rexburg's **Idaho International Folk Dance Festival** draws dance troupes from around the world for eight days of traditional dancing and music, kicked off by a colorful street fair. Top-name talent performs in the **Bluegrass Festival** at nearby Grand Targhee Resort.
Sun Valley and Central Idaho   The town of Hailey features a **Northern Rockies Folk Festival** and Sun Valley has the **Sun Summer Symphony**, putting on with 12 free outdoor concerts.
Lewiston and the Lower Panhandle   There's Nez Perce dancing during **Chief Looking Glass Days** in Kamiah, a traditional pow-wow celebrated by descendants of the chief.
Coeur d'Alene and the Upper Panhandle   The **Festival at Sandpoint** is an evening series of classical, pop, jazz and ragtime concerts along the shore of Lake Pend Oreille.

SEPTEMBER

Boise   Artists from all over the United States display their works during Boise's **Art in the Park**, a three-day event featuring music, food and kids' events.
Southwestern Idaho   Mountain Home celebrates **Air Force Appreciation Day** with a parade, barbecue, street fair and a fly-by of jet aircraft based just outside of the city.
Pocatello and Southeastern Idaho   Country stars appear at the **Eastern Idaho State Fair** in Blackfoot.
Idaho Falls and Eastern Idaho   The Great Potato Giveaway and the World Spud Picking Championships are among highlights of **Idaho Spud Day** in Shelley, a family-style fête of the Idaho potato celebrated since 1927.
Sun Valley and Central Idaho   Near Sun Valley, the **Ketchum Wagon Days Celebration** is highlighted by the largest nonmotorized parade in the West, a procession of giant ore wagons used in past mining days; other events include band concerts, dances, a carnival and a car auction.

Lewiston and the Lower Panhandle The **Lewiston Roundup** features a top-class rodeo and a cowboy breakfast. In Orofino, the **Clearwater County Fair and Lumberjack Days** includes a parade, a carnival and a logging competition that attracts timbermen from all over the world.

Coeur d'Alene and the Upper Panhandle The **Idaho Draft Horse International** in Sandpoint offers exhibits and contests demonstrating the speed and strength of such great working horses as the Clydesdale and the Percheron.

OCTOBER **Sun Valley and Central Idaho** The **Sun Valley Jazz Jamboree** features four nights of Big Band–era dancing and five days of groovin' to traditional jazz, swing and ragtime music, performed by more than 20 North American bands at the Sun Valley Resort.

NOVEMBER **Boise** The "City of Trees" observes a **Festival of Trees** over Thanksgiving weekend with a display of lavishly decorated Christmas trees and holiday wreaths. Well over 300 artisans display their works for sale during the **Beaux Arts Holiday Sale** at the Boise Art Museum.

Pocatello and Southeastern Idaho Preston's **Festival of Lights** begins with a Veterans Day parade and continues until Christmas with parades and a musical show; the town's lighting display is considered the state's best.

Yellowstone National Park The **U.S. Nordic and Biathlon Training Camps** open at West Yellowstone, where Olympic-hopeful winter athletes come for early-season training.

Lewiston and the Lower Panhandle Lewiston anglers cast their lines on the Snake and Clearwater rivers for the anadromous steelhead trout during the **Great Snake Lake Steelhead Derby** during Thanksgiving week.

DECEMBER **Idaho Falls and Eastern Idaho** The **Holiday Art Show** displays the work of regional artists.

Sun Valley and Central Idaho Sun Valley has a **Christmas Eve Torch Light Parade and Celebration** at the Sun Valley Lodge.

▼ ▼ ▼ ▼ ▼ ▼ ▼ ▼ ▼ ▼
Before You Go

VISITORS CENTERS

For free visitor information packages including maps and current details on special events, accommodations and camping, contact the **Idaho Department of Commerce and Travel Council.** ~ 700 West State Street, Boise, ID 83720; 208-334-2470, 800-842-5858, fax 208-334-2631; www. visitid.org. Or you may try the **Wyoming Division of Tourism** for information on Yellowstone National Park. ~ Route 25 at College Drive, Cheyenne, WY 82002; 307-777-7777, 800-225-5996, fax 307-777-2877; www.wyomingtourism.org, e-mail tourism@state. wy.us. In addition, most towns have chambers of commerce or visitor information centers. Tourist information centers are usually not open on weekends.

The old adage that you should take along twice as much money and half as much stuff as you think you'll need is sound advice as far as it goes. In the more remote reaches of Idaho, however, stores selling something more substantial than beef jerky and country-and-western cassettes are few and far between.

When packing clothes, plan to dress in layers. Temperatures can turn hot or cold in a flash. During the course of a single summer day in the mountains, you can expect to start with a heavy jacket, a sweater or flannel shirt and a pair of jeans, peeling down to a T-shirt and shorts as the day warms up, then putting the extra layers back on as the late-afternoon shadows set in.

Other essentials to pack or buy along the way include a good sunscreen and high-quality sunglasses. Cool temperatures often lull newcomers into forgetting that thin high-altitude air filters out far less of the sun's ultraviolet rays; above timberline, exposed skin will sunburn faster than it would on a Florida beach. If you are planning to camp in the mountains during the summer months, you'll be glad you brought mosquito repellent. Umbrellas are considered an oddity in the western states. You'll hardly ever see one, and you'll get funny looks from the locals if you carry one. Outside Boise, the approved means of keeping chilly afternoon rain from running down the back of your neck is a cowboy hat.

For outdoor activities, tough-soled hiking boots are more comfortable than running shoes on rocky terrain. Even RV travelers and those who prefer to spend most nights in motels may want to take along a backpacking tent and sleeping bag when the urge to stay out under star-spangled western skies becomes irresistible. A canteen, first-aid kit, flashlight and other routine camping gear are also likely to come in handy. Both cross-country and downhill ski rentals are available everywhere you look during the winter, though serious skiers may find that the quality and condition of rental skis leave something to be desired. In the summer, mountain bikes can be rented in just about any small town. Other outdoor-recreation equipment—kayaks, fishing tackle, golf clubs and gold pans—generally cannot be rented, so you'll want to bring the right gear for your special sporting passion.

A camera, of course, is essential for capturing your travel experience; of equal importance is a good pair of binoculars, which let you explore distant landscapes from scenic overlooks and bring wildlife up close. And don't, for heaven's sake, forget your copy of *Hidden Idaho*.

Lodgings in Idaho run the gamut from tiny one-room cabins to luxury hotels that blend traditional alpine-lodge ambience with contemporary elegance. The Old Faithful Inn at Yellowstone National Park ranks high among the region's most memorable historic inns. (This is among the most sought-after accommodations, so travelers need to make reservations several months ahead of time.) Bed and breakfasts can be found in many towns you're likely to visit—not only chic destinations like Sun Valley and Coeur d'Alene. They come in all types, sizes and price ranges. Typical of the genre are lovingly restored Victorian-era mansions comfortably furnished with period decor, usually with fewer than a dozen rooms. Some bed and breakfasts, however, are guest cottages or rooms in nice suburban homes, while others are larger establishments, approaching motel size, of the type sometimes referred to as country inns.

The abundance of motels in towns along all major highway routes presents a range of choices, from name-brand motor inns to traditional mom-and-pop establishments that have endured for the half century since motels were invented. While rather ordinary motels in the vicinity of major tourist destinations can be pricey, lodging in small towns away from major resorts and interstate routes can offer friendliness, quiet and comfort at ridiculously affordable rates.

At the other end of the price spectrum, peak-season rates at leading ski resorts can be incredibly costly. To save money, consider staying in more affordable lodging as much as an hour away and commuting to the ski slopes during the day, or plan your vacation during "shoulder seasons," before and after the peak seasons. Even though the summer is a lively time in many ski towns, accommodations are in surplus and room rates often drop to less than half the winter rates.

In Boise you'll find lavishly restored historic hotels that date back to the gold-boom days of the late 19th century. Many combine affordable rates with plenty of antique decor and authentic personality.

WHERE CITY SLICKERS GATHER

Guest ranches are located throughout Idaho. Horseback riding, fishing and river rafting are common activities offered; some offer luxury lodging, spa facilities and a full range of activities that may include fishing, boating, swimming and even tennis. Others operate as working ranches, providing lodging in comfortably rustic cabins and offering the opportunity to participate in roundups and other ranching activities. Rates at most guest ranches are comparatively expensive but include all meals and use of recreational facilities. Most guest ranches have minimum-stay requirements ranging from three days to a week.

Whatever your preference and budget, you can probably find something to suit your taste with the help of this book. Remember, rooms can be scarce and prices may rise during peak season, which is summer throughout most of the region and winter in ski resorts. Travelers planning to visit a place in peak season should either make advance reservations or arrive early in the day, before the "No Vacancy" signs start lighting up.

Lodging prices listed in this book are high-season rates. If you are looking for off-season bargains, it's good to inquire. *Budget* lodgings generally run less than $50 per night for two people and are satisfactory and clean but modest. *Moderate* hotels range from $50 to $90; what they have to offer in the way of luxury will depend on where they are located, but they generally offer larger rooms and more attractive surroundings than budget lodgings. At *deluxe*-priced accommodations, you can expect to spend between $90 and $130 for a homey bed and breakfast or a double in a hotel or resort. In hotels of this price you'll generally find spacious rooms, a fashionable lobby, a restaurant and often a bar or nightclub. *Ultra-deluxe* facilities, priced above $130, are the finest in the region, offering all the amenities of a deluxe hotel plus plenty of extras.

Room rates vary as much with locale as with quality. Some of the trendier destinations have no rooms at all in the budget price range. In other communities—those where rates are set with truck drivers in mind and those in out-of-the-way small towns— every motel falls into the budget category, even though accommodations may range from $19.95 at rundown, spartan places to $45 or so at the classiest motor inn in town. The price categories listed in this book are relative, designed to show you where to get the most out of your travel budget, however large or small it may be.

DINING

Fine dining in Idaho tends to focus on the region's traditional cuisine—beef and trout. Competition for restaurant business is fierce in the more exclusive resort areas, such as Sun Valley, and it's there you'll find menus featuring everything from duck *à l'orange* to grilled elk. If your idea of an ideal vacation includes savoring epicurean delights, then by all means seize opportunities whenever they arise. When traveling in Idaho, you can go for days between gourmet meals.

Restaurants listed in this book offer lunch and dinner unless otherwise noted. Dinner entrées at *budget* restaurants usually cost $7 or less. The ambience is informal, service usually speedy and the crowd often a local one. *Moderate*-priced restaurant entrées range between $7 and $12 at dinner; surroundings are casual but pleasant; the menu offers more variety and the pace is usually slower than at budget restaurants. *Deluxe* establishments tab their entrées from $12 to $20; cuisines may be simple or sophisticated, depending on the location, but the decor is plusher and the service more personalized than at moderate-priced restaurants.

Ultra-deluxe dining rooms, where entrées begin at $20, are often the gourmet places; here cooking has become a fine art and the service should be impeccable.

Some restaurants change hands often and are occasionally closed in low seasons. Efforts have been made in this book to include places with established reputations for good eating. Compared to evening dinners, breakfast and lunch menus vary less in price from restaurant to restaurant.

DRIVING   Some first-time visitors to the Rocky Mountains wonder why so many mountain roads do not have guard rails to separate motorists from thousand-foot drop-offs. The fact is, highway safety studies have found that far fewer accidents occur where there are no guard rails. Statistically, edgy, winding mountain roads are much safer than straight, fast interstate highways. Unpaved roads are another story. While many are wide and well-graded, weather conditions or the wear and tear of heavy seasonal use can create unexpected road hazards. Some U.S. Forest Service and Bureau of Land Management roads are designated for four-wheel-drive or high-clearance vehicles only. If you see a sign indicating four-wheel-drive only, believe it. These roads can be very dangerous in a standard passenger car without the high ground clearance and extra traction afforded by four-wheel drive—and there may be no safe place to turn around if you get stuck.

Some side roads will take you far from civilization, so be sure to have a full radiator and tank of gas. Carry spare fuel, water and food. Should you become stuck, local people are usually helpful about offering assistance to stranded vehicles, but in case no one else is around, for extended backcountry driving, a CB radio or cell phone would not be a bad idea.

In the winter months, mountain passes frequently become snowpacked, and under these conditions tire chains are advised. At the very least, studded tires—legal in this state from November to April—are recommended. In winter it is wise to travel with a shovel, gravel or cat litter for traction, and blankets in your car.

The air at Rocky Mountain altitudes is "thin"—that is, it contains considerably less oxygen in a given volume than air at lower altitudes. If your car is not running well at high altitudes, the carburetor or fuel injection unit should be set leaner to achieve an efficient fuel-to-air mixture. Another common problem when climbing mountain passes is vapor lock, a condition in which low atmospheric pressure combined with high engine temperatures causes gasoline to evaporate in the fuel lines, making bubbles that prevent the fuel pump from functioning. The result is that your car's engine coughs and soon stops dead. If this occurs, pull over to the side of the road and wait until the fuel system cools down. A damp rag held against the fuel line will speed up the process and get you back on the road more quickly.

You can get full information on statewide road conditions for Idaho at any time of year by calling 208-336-6600; for conditions in Yellowstone National Park, call 307-344-7381.

TRAVELING WITH CHILDREN

Any place that has wild animals, cowboys and Indians, rocks to climb and limitless room to run is bound to be a hit with youngsters. Plenty of family adventures are available in Idaho, from man-made attractions to experiences in the wilderness. A few simple guidelines will help make traveling with children a pleasure.

Book reservations in advance, making sure that the places you stay accept children. Many bed and breakfasts do not. If you need a crib or extra cot, arrange for it ahead of time. A travel agent can be of help here, as well as with almost all other travel plans.

If you are traveling by air, try to reserve bulkhead seats where there is plenty of room. Take along extras you may need such as diapers, changes of clothing, snacks, toys and small games. When traveling by car, be sure to take along the extras, too. Make sure you have plenty of water and juices to drink; dehydration can be a subtle but serious problem. Larger towns have all-night convenience stores that carry diapers, baby food, snacks and other essentials; national parks and some state parks also have such stores, though they usually close early.

If your car is not fuel-injected and does not seem to run well at high elevations, you should probably have the carburetor adjusted at the next service station.

A first-aid kit is a must for any trip. Along with adhesive bandages, antiseptic cream and something to stop itching, include any medicines your pediatrician might recommend to treat allergies, colds, diarrhea or any chronic problems your child may have. Mountain sunshine is intense, so take extra care for the first few days. Children's skin is usually more tender than adult skin, and severe sunburn can happen before you realize. A hat is a good idea, along with a reliable sunblock.

Often, national parks and monuments offer special activities designed just for children. Visitors center film presentations and rangers' campfire slide shows can help inform children about the natural history of the Rocky Mountains and head off some questions. Still, kids tend to find a lot more things to wonder about than adults have answers for. To be as prepared as possible, seize every opportunity to learn more—particularly about wildlife, a constant curiosity for young minds.

TRAVELING WITH PETS

Idaho is big dog country, and you'll probably notice more recreationers traveling with their pets than in other regions. Pets are permitted on leashes in virtually all campgrounds, but few B&Bs or guest ranches will accept them, and more run-of-the-mill motels seem to be adopting "No Pets" policies each year. Otherwise, the main limitation of traveling with a canine companion is that national parks and monuments prohibit pets on trails or in the backcountry. You are supposed to walk your dog on the roadside, then leave it in the car while you hike in the woods. Make sure the dog gets adequate ventilation and water. Fortunately, dogs are free to run everywhere in national forests, and leashes are required only in designated camping and picnic areas.

While traveling through Idaho, perhaps you'll recognize scenes from *Dante's Peak*, *Pale Rider* and *Heaven's Gate*—they were all filmed in the Gem State.

Wildlife can pose special hazards for pets in the backcountry. At lower elevations in the plains and foothills, campers should not leave a cat or small dog outside at night because coyotes may attack it. In remote forest areas, it's especially important to keep an eye on your dog at all times. Bears are upset by dogs barking at them and may attack even very large dogs. Porcupines, common in pine forests, are tempting to chase and slow enough to catch; if your dog catches one, a mouthful of quills means painfully pulling them out one by one with a pair of pliers or making an emergency visit to a veterinary clinic in the nearest town.

WOMEN TRAVELING ALONE

Traveling solo grants an independence and freedom different from that of traveling with a partner, but single travelers are more vulnerable to crime and should take additional precautions. Although Idaho is reasonably safe compared to more urbanized states, it's entirely unwise to hitchhike and probably wise to avoid inexpensive accommodations on the outskirts of towns; the money saved does not outweigh the risk. B&Bs, youth hostels, and more deluxe hotels and motor inns are generally your safest bets for lodging.

Keep all valuables well-hidden and hold onto cameras and purses. Avoid late-night treks or strolls through undesirable parts of town, but if you find yourself in this situation, continue walking with a confident air until you reach a safe haven. A fierce scowl never hurts.

If you are hassled or threatened in some way, never be afraid to yell for assistance. It's a good idea to carry change for a phone call and to know the number to call in case of emergency. Most areas have 24-hour hotlines for victims of rape and violent crime. In Boise, call the **Women's Crisis Center**. ~ 720 West Washington Street, Boise; 208-343-7025.

For more helpful hints, get a copy of *Safety and Security for Women Who Travel* (Travelers' Tales).

GAY & LESBIAN TRAVELERS

Idaho is a conservative state, and is not among the more sympathetic to sexual minorities. Nonetheless, you'll find social and support groups in a handful of towns. Boise, the state capital, has a visible gay community as do the year-round resort area of Sun Valley, the University of Idaho campus in Moscow and the Idaho State University campus in Pocatello.

For information on everything from lodging to HIV/AIDS resources in Boise and elsewhere in Idaho, call the **Treasure Valley Gay and Lesbian Community Center**. ~ 919 North 27th Street, Boise; 208-336-3870. You can normally reach someone there evenings or weekends.

You can find out about gay- and lesbian-oriented activities by reading *Diversity*, a community newspaper available free at gay-friendly establishments. ~ www.gayidaho.com/diversity/.

SENIOR TRAVELERS

Idaho is a hospitable place for older vacationers, many of whom migrate from hotter climates to enjoy the cool summers. Persons 62 and older can save considerable money with a Golden Age Passport, which allows free lifetime admission to national parks and monuments. Apply for one in person at any national-park unit that charges an entrance fee. The passports are also good for a 50 percent discount on fees at most national-forest campgrounds. Many private sightseeing attractions also offer significant discounts for seniors.

The **American Association of Retired Persons** (AARP) offers membership to anyone 50 and over. AARP's benefits include travel discounts with a number of firms. ~ 601 E Street NW, Washington, DC 20049; 800-424-3410; www.aarp.org.

Elderhostel offers all-inclusive packages with educational courses at colleges and universities. Call for information on specific programs in Idaho. ~ 11 Avenue de Lafayette, Boston, MA 02111; 877-426-8056, fax 617-426-0701; www.elderhostel.org.

Be especially careful with your health. High altitude is the biggest risk factor. Since many driving routes through Idaho cross mountain passes at 7000 to 9000 feet above sea level, it's advisable to ask your physician if high altitude is a problem for you. People with heart problems are commonly advised to avoid all physical exertion above 10,000 feet, and those with respiratory conditions such as emphysema may not be able to visit high altitudes at all. In the changeable climate of the mountains, seniors are more at risk of suffering hypothermia. Many tourist destinations in the region are a long way from any hospital or other health-care facility.

In addition to the medications you ordinarily use, it's a good idea to bring along your prescriptions in case you need replacements. Consider carrying a medical record with you, including your history and current medical status as well as your doctor's name, phone number and address. Make sure that your insurance covers you while you are away from home.

DISABLED TRAVELERS   Idaho is striving to make public areas fully accessible to persons with disabilities. Parking spaces and restroom facilities for the physically challenged are provided according to both state law and national-park regulations. National parks and monuments also post signs that tell which trails are wheelchair accessible. Some recreation areas even have Braille nature trails with marked points of interest appealing to the senses of touch and smell.

Golden Access Passports, good for free lifetime admission to all national parks and monuments as well as discounts at most federal public campgrounds, are available at no charge to persons who are blind or have a permanent disability. You may apply in person at any national park unit that charges an entrance fee.

Information sources for travelers with disabilities include the **Society for Accessible Travel & Hospitality**. ~ 347 5th Avenue, Suite 610, New York, NY 10016; 212-447-7284; www.sath.org, e-mail sathtravel@aol.com. You may want to also contact the **MossRehab Resource Net**. ~ MossRehab Hospital, 1200 West Tabor Road, Philadelphia, PA 19141; 215-456-5995; www.moss resourcenet.org. For general travel advice, contact **Travelin' Talk**, a networking organization. ~ P.O. Box 1796, Wheatridge, CO 80034; 303-232-2979; www.travelintalk.net, e-mail info@travel intalk.net. Its sister organization, **Access-Able Travel Service**, has worldwide information online. ~ www.access-able.com.

FOREIGN TRAVELERS   **Passports and Visas**   Most foreign visitors, other than Canadian citizens, need a passport and tourist visa to enter the United States. Contact your nearest U.S. embassy or consulate well in advance to obtain a visa and to check on any other entry requirements.

Customs Requirements   Foreign travelers are allowed to carry in the following: 200 cigarettes (1 carton), 50 cigars, or 2 kilograms (4.4 pounds) of smoking tobacco; one liter of alcohol for personal use only (you must be 21 years of age to bring in alcohol); and US$100 worth of duty-free gifts that can include an additional quantity of 100 cigars. You may bring in any amount of currency, but must fill out a form if you bring in over US$10,000. Carry any prescription drugs in clearly marked containers. (You may have to produce a written prescription or doctor's statement for the customs officer.) Meat or meat products, seeds, plants, fruits and narcotics are not allowed to be brought into the United States. Contact the **United States Customs Service** for further information. ~ 1300 Pennsylvania Avenue NW, Washington, DC 20229; 202-927-6724; www.customs.treas.gov.

Driving   If you plan to rent a car, you should obtain an international driver's license before arriving in the United States. Some car-rental agencies require both a foreign license and an international driver's license. Virtually all agencies require a lessee to be at least 25 years of age and to present a major credit card.

Currency   U.S. money is based on the dollar. Bills generally come in denominations of $1, $5, $10, $20, $50 and $100. Every dollar is divided into 100 cents. Coins are the penny (one cent), nickel (five cents), dime (ten cents) and quarter (25 cents). Half-dollar and dollar coins exist but are rarely used. You may not use foreign currency to purchase goods and services in the United States. Consider buying traveler's checks in dollar amounts. You may also use credit cards affiliated with an American company such as Interbank, Barclay Card, VISA and American Express.

Idaho has two time zones: the area north of the Salmon River lies in the Pacific Time Zone, while the region to the south is in the Mountain Time Zone.

Electricity and Electronics   Electric outlets use currents of 110 volts, 60 cycles. For appliances made for other electrical systems, you need a transformer or other adapter. Travelers who use laptop computers for telecommunication should be aware that modem configurations for U.S. telephone systems may be different from their European counterparts. Similarly, the U.S. format for videotapes is different from that in Europe; U.S. Park Service visitor centers and other stores that sell souvenir videos often have them available in European format.

Weights and Measures   The United States uses the English system of weights and measures. American units and their metric equivalents are: 1 inch = 2.5 centimeters; 1 foot (12 inches) = 0.3 meter; 1 yard (3 feet) = 0.9 meter; 1 mile (5280 feet) = 1.6 kilometers; 1 ounce = 28 grams; 1 pound (16 ounces) = 0.45 kilogram; 1 quart (liquid) = 0.9 liter.

Outdoor Adventures

CAMPING

RV or tent camping is a great way to tour Idaho during the summer months. Besides saving substantial sums of money, campers enjoy the freedom to watch sunsets from beautiful places, spend nights under spectacularly starry skies and wake up to find themselves in lovely surroundings that few hotels can match.

Most towns have commercial RV parks of some sort, and long-term mobile home parks often rent spaces to RVers by the night. But unless you absolutely need cable television, none of these places can compete with the wide array of public campgrounds available in national and state parks, monuments and forests. Federal campground sites are typically less developed: You won't find electric, water or sewer hookups in campgrounds at national forests, national monuments or national recreation areas. However, Yellowstone National Park has more than 300 hookups. Idaho is well-adapted for RVs: Half of its 22 state parks offer hookups. The largest public campgrounds, such as those in Yellowstone National Park, offer tent camping loops separate from RV loops, as well as hike-in backcountry camping by permit. There is no charge in national forests for primitive camping.

You won't find much in the way of sophisticated reservation systems in Idaho. In July and August, the largest campgrounds in Yellowstone National Park require reservations by calling 800-365-2267, or contacting http://reservations.nps.gov (credit card required); however, reservations are not accepted for most Yellowstone campgrounds. The general rule in public campgrounds is still first-come, first-served, even though they fill up practically every night during peak season. For campers, this means traveling in the morning and reaching your intended campground by early afternoon—or, during peak season at Yellowstone, by late morning. In many areas, campers may find it more convenient to keep a single location for as much as a week and explore surrounding areas on daytrips.

If you're planning to camp in the mountains during the summer months, don't forget to pack lots of mosquito repellent.

For a listing of state parks with camping facilities and reservation information, contact **Idaho State Parks & Recreation.** ~ P.O. Box 83720, Boise, ID 83720; 208-334-4199; www.idahoparks.org.

Information on camping in national forests is available by calling 877-444-6777, or from U.S. Forest Service regional offices. In southern Idaho, call **U.S. Forest Service–Intermountain Region.** ~ 324 25th Street, Ogden, UT 84401; 801-625-5306. In northern Idaho, call **U.S. Forest Service–Northern Region.** ~ P.O. Box 7669, Missoula, MT 59807; 406-329-3511. For information on camping in Yellowstone National Park, call 307-344-7381; www.nps.gov/yell.

PERMITS The passage of the Wilderness Act of 1964 represented a major expansion of federal wilderness protection. Today, more than 4.2 million acres of national-forest and Bureau of Land Management (BLM) land in Idaho has been designated as wilderness. To be considered for federal wilderness protection, an area must consist of at least five contiguous square miles without a road of any kind. At the time it has been declared a wilderness area, the land is limited to uses that existed as of that date. Since most wilderness areas in Idaho were created quite recently—from 1964 to 1980—it is generally the highest peaks, where roads are few and far between, that qualify for wilderness status. Besides protecting ancient forests from timber cutting by newly developed methods like skylining or helicopter airlifting, federal wilderness designation prohibits all mechanized transportation—no jeeps, motorcycles or all-terrain vehicles and, after years of heated controversy, no mountain bikes. Wilderness areas usually have well-developed trail networks for hiking, cross-country skiing and pack trips using horses or llamas.

You no longer need a permit to hike or camp in wilderness areas, but plan to stop at a ranger station anyway for trail maps and advice on current conditions and fire regulations.

Tent camping is allowed without restriction in wilderness areas and almost all other backcountry areas of national forests, except where posted signs prohibit it. Throughout the national forests in dry season and in certain wilderness areas at all times, regulations may prohibit campfires and sometimes ban cigarette smoking, with stiff enforcement penalties.

For backcountry hiking in most national parks and monuments, you must first obtain a permit from the ranger at the front desk in the visitors center. The permit procedure is simple and free. It helps park administrators measure the impact of hiking on sensitive ecosystems and distribute use evenly among the major trails.

BOATING & RAFTING

Many large artificial lakes in and around Idaho are administered as state parks, while others are national recreation areas, some of them supervised by the U.S. Army Corps of Engineers. Federal boating safety regulations may vary slightly from state regulations. Indian reservations have separate rules for boating on tribal lakes. More significant than any differences between federal, state and tribal regulations are the local rules in force for any particular lake, which are posted near boat ramps. Ask for applicable boating regulations at a local marina or fishing supply store or use the addresses and phone numbers listed in "Parks" or other sections of each chapter in this book to contact the headquarters for lakes where you plan to use a boat.

Boats, from small motorized skiffs to big, fast bass boats and sometimes even houseboats, can be rented by the half-day, day, week or longer at marinas on many of the larger lakes. At most marinas, you can get a boat on short notice on a weekday, since much of their business comes from local weekend recreation.

Rafting is a very popular sport in many areas of Idaho, notably the Payette River north of Boise; the Lochsa River along Route 12 below Lolo Pass; the St. Joe River, which drains into Lake Coeur d'Alene; and day-use sections of the Salmon River near Salmon and Riggins. For week-long backcountry float trips, there are the Salmon River through the Frank Church–River of No Return Wilderness; the Selway River, which joins the Lochsa to form the Middle Fork of the Clearwater River; and the Snake River through Hells Canyon National Recreation Area along the Idaho–Oregon border. Permits are required for extended Salmon and Selway river trips (see "Outdoor Adventures" in Chapter Seven and Chapter Nine). Independent rafters are welcome, but because of the bulky equipment and specialized knowledge of river hazards involved, most adventurous souls stick with group tours offered by the many rafting companies located throughout the region. State and federal regulations require rafters, as well as people using canoes, kayaks, sailboards or inner tubes, to wear life jackets.

FISHING   Idaho is justly famous for the fishing found in its 2700 miles of stream and 2000 lakes. The more accessible a shoreline is, the more anglers you're likely to find there, especially in summer. You can beat the crowds by hiking a few miles into the backcountry or, to some extent, by planning to fish on weekdays.

Fish hatcheries stock streams with trout, particularly rainbows. Many cold-water mountain lakes also offer fishing for cutthroat and golden trout, kokanee salmon and mountain whitefish. In the Snake River and its tributaries, the autumn spawning run of anadromous steelhead trout is the highlight of the angler's year; spawning salmon, however, have become rare this far inland.

Idaho's various runs of chinook and sockeye salmon and steelhead have been severely reduced in recent years, due largely to a series of hydroelectric dams on the Snake and lower Columbia rivers that the fish must negotiate en route to and from the Pacific Ocean. In Idaho, the salmon have been supplanted by thriving bass and crappie fisheries in Snake River reservoirs above Hells Canyon. Below the canyon, smaller salmon and steelhead runs still travel up the Clearwater and undammed Salmon river systems. The various government agencies and power companies that own and operate the dams are working with environmental activist groups, tribal councils and other concerned conservationists to reestablish strong salmon runs. Restoring habitats and improving water quality through land management are the preferred solutions, but removal of the dams themselves looms as a more radical prospect.

Although rainbow trout is Idaho's most popular game fish, the official state fish is the cutthroat trout.

Catch-and-release flyfishing is the rule in some popular areas, allowing more anglers a chance at bigger fish. Be sure to inquire locally about eating the fish you catch, since some seemingly remote streams and rivers have been contaminated by old mines and mills.

The larger reservoirs, especially those at lower elevations, offer an assortment of sport fish, including carp, crappie, channel catfish, largemouth bass, smallmouth bass, white bass, bluegill, bullhead, perch, walleye and northern pike.

For copies of the state's fishing regulations, inquire at a local fishing supply or marina, or contact the **Idaho Department of Fish and Game**. ~ 600 South Walnut Street, Boise, ID 83701; 208-334-3700.

State fishing licenses are required for fishing in national forests and national recreation areas, but not on Indian reservations, where daily permits are sold by the tribal governments. Yellowstone National Park has a ten-day fishing license, which is sold at any of the parks visitors centers for $10, as well as a seasonal license.

Nonresidents may pay $74.50 for a one-year Idaho fishing license, about three times the resident fee. But less costly, short-term licenses (for one to three days) are also available to non-resident visitors. Nonresident children normally fish free with a licensed adult. High-lake and stream fishing seasons normally begin in late spring and run through the fall; lower-elevation lakes and reservoirs may be open year-round for fishing.

WINTER SPORTS

Idaho has a winter "hotline," updated daily with current weather and snow conditions at downhill ski resorts throughout the state. ~ 800-243-2754. You should also call for road conditions; see "Driving," above.

All state parks and recreation departments (see the listing under "Camping," above) administer snow park areas that provide cross-country skiers and snowmobilers with access to extensive networks of groomed trails. The fee charged for season parking is much less than the fine you must pay if you park without a permit.

GUIDES

The best way to assure the reliability of the folks guiding you into the wilderness by horse, raft or cross-country skis is to choose someone who has met the standards of a statewide organization of their peers. For membership lists, contact the **Idaho Outfitters and Guides Association**. ~ P.O. Box 95, Boise, ID 83701; 208-342-1919; www.ioga.org, e-mail ioga@ioga.org. For guides and out-fitters in Yellowstone National Park, contact **Xanterra Parks & Resorts**. ~ 307-344-7311.

TWO

Boise

Listen to locals say, "Boise's not on the way to anywhere else," and you'll hear both their major grievance—perhaps their only grievance—with Idaho's capital city and their joy of living here. As recently as the mid-1980s, Boise (pronounced "BOY-see") was a smallish city of 100,000 souls camped at the edge of North America's Great Outback. Its distance from the hustle of American commerce was also its greatest asset. Sitting hard by the foothills of the northern Rocky Mountains and at a soft edge of the harsh but intoxicating Great Basin deserts, the city appealed to those drawn to a life outdoors.

Boise is still barely more than a way station to other locales, and its accessibility to the outdoors remains a prized asset, but the city has been discovered. Despite its out-of-the-way location and feeling, which visitors can sense immediately, Boise is the largest city between Portland and Minneapolis, between Salt Lake and the Canadian border. Its population has grown to nearly 186,000, attracted by booming high-tech computer and engineering industries and the quality of life. In an expanse of open Western space, there is more "here" here than most any place else. And although Boiseans appreciate their burgeoning cultural scene, you are just as likely to find them casting hand-tied caddis flies for rainbow trout in the Boise River as you are to find them offering polite applause at the Boise Symphony. In fact, during intermission, symphony goers can watch anglers stand waist-deep in the river trying their luck.

The river is a good place to be during a Boise summer, and Boiseans spend a lot of time in it and on it, as temperatures can be fiercely hot. But the city boasts many outdoor restaurants and cafés for enjoying the long, cooler and very gracious evenings. Even biting insects stay, mostly, blissfully away.

Boise's mild winters make it possible for commuters, and students at downtown's Boise State University, to hop on their bikes year-round. During lunch breaks and after work, bikers, joggers, skaters—and sometimes winter skiers—take to the Boise River Greenbelt to enjoy its 20 miles of lush trails, shade and wildlife.

Boise is Idaho's commercial and political center. Downtown is dotted with banks and the corporate offices of Idaho's largest companies. For two months in late winter, Idaho's citizen-politicians descend to make legislative hay and then de-part—and the city and the state breathe an almost palpable sigh of relief. Parks are everywhere in this small and tidy metropolis, often dressed with a widening collection of public art—another sign that the city is growing up.

Boise was named by French Canadian trappers in the early 19th century. Accord-ing to local legend, the men crested a nearby hill after a hot, dry crossing of the desert and, gazing down upon the vegetation surrounding the Boise River, exclaimed: "*Les bois! Les bois!*" ("Woods! Woods!"). The city, established in 1863 as a service cen-ter for miners in the Rocky Mountain foothills, takes its name seriously: Its founders turned the banks of the river into a verdant greenbelt and planted so many species around their community that today Boise is known as "the City of Trees."

Within a year of its establishment, Boise was made the territorial capital. The seat of government remained here when Idaho achieved statehood in 1890. The **State Capitol**, built between 1905 and 1920, was constructed of native sandstone quarried at nearby Table Rock; the marble in its interior comes from Alaska, Georgia, Vermont and Italy. Patterned after the U.S. Capitol in Washington, D.C., this neoclassical building is America's only geothermally heated statehouse. Self-guided tours of the 200,000-square-foot building take in four floors of fine art and historical exhibits, as well as the Senate and House chambers. ~ 700 West Jefferson Street; 208-332-1007; e-mail asims@adm.state.id.us.

SIGHTS

Surrounding the capitol are more than eight square blocks of additional government buildings. Many of them house offices, but on consecutive blocks to its east are the county courthouse, the state supreme court and the state historical library. Across State Street from the library is the 1897 Queen Anne–style **Alexander House**. ~ 304 West State Street; 208-332-1900, fax 208-334-4031.

South of the Alexander House, $75 million worth of silver and gold over a period of 60 years passed through the two-foot-thick walls of the 1872 **U.S. Assay Office**. (The building now houses state historical society offices and is listed on the National Register of Historic Places.) Closed Saturday and Sunday. ~ 210 West Main Street; 208-334-3861, 877-653-4367, fax 208-334-2775.

Head west to Capitol Boulevard and south to Grove Street. Step around Boise's Grove Hotel to reach **The Grove,** a broad pub-lic plaza and pedestrian mall built around an open fountain at 8th and Grove streets. In the 1970s, during a frenzy of urban renewal, Boise city planners saw fit to raze the downtown area south of Main. The loss of many architectural treasures notwithstanding, creation of The Grove was one of the benefits of this enterprise. Every week from mid-May to mid-September, this plaza attracts thousands of Boiseans to a free Wednesday-evening musical bash called "Alive After Five."

At the plaza's southwest corner is **Boise Centre on the Grove**, the city's primary convention hall. ~ 850 West Front Street; 208-336-8900. A **visitor information center** adjoining the convention center offers maps and other information. Closed Sunday. ~ On The Grove plaza; 208-344-5338.

At the plaza's southeast corner is the luxurious **Grove Hotel**. The property is adjacent to an events center that features big-name concerts and the opening season of the Idaho Steelheads, a Western Hockey League franchise. ~ 245 South Capitol Boulevard; 208-333-8000, 800-426-0670, fax 208-333-8800; www.grovehotelboise.com.

Farther east is the **Basque Museum and Cultural Center**, a tribute to the colorful heritage and unique language of one of America's most invisible ethnic minorities. An anomaly even in their traditional homeland along the Bay of Biscay coast of Spain and France, the Basques (who call themselves *Euskaldunak*) found the northern Great Basin region conducive to raising sheep and other livestock more than a century ago. Today Boise is home to the largest concentration of Basques in the United States. The adjacent cultural center sponsors performances by the Oinkari Basque Dancers and other events. Closed Sunday and Monday. ~ 611 Grove Street; 208-343-2671, fax 208-336-4801; www.basquemuseum.com, e-mail mail@basquemuseum.com.

The little **C. W. Moore Park** integrates architectural artifacts from early Boise buildings since demolished, among them a century-old waterwheel. ~ 5th and Grove streets.

South of The Grove is the **8th Street Market Place**, a turn-of-the-20th-century warehouse block that has been renovated for shops, restaurants, offices, and a comedy club. ~ 405 South 8th Street.

Just past the Market Place and the **Boise Public Library** (715 South Capitol Boulevard; 208-384-4238, fax 208-384-4025), on the east side of Capitol Boulevard and the north bank of the Boise River, is 90-acre **Julia Davis Park**, where many of Boise's visitor attractions are concentrated. ~ 1000 Americana Boulevard; 208-384-4240, fax 208-384-4127.

Housed in a historic African-American church, the **Idaho Black History Museum** is one of the many museums in Julia Davis Park. The building was constructed in 1921 by the church's first pastor and is listed on the National Register of Historic Places. Photo exhibits recount the history of the state's black population

---

The Basque Museum and Cultural Center—the only one devoted to the Basque culture in the U.S.—occupies Boise's oldest brick building (the 1864 Cyrus Jacobs-Uberuaga House, which was once a boarding house for Basque immigrants).

—including the migration of black Mormons in the 1870s and the career of George Washington Blackman, the miner whose name graces Blackman Peak in the White Cloud Mountains. Closed Sunday through Tuesday. ~ 508 North Julia Davis Drive; 208-433-0017, fax 208-433-0048; www.ibhm.org, e-mail ibhm@mind spring.com.

The Boise Tour Train trolley stop is adjacent to the **Idaho State Historical Museum**, which recounts Idaho's colorful history from prehistoric times through the early days of white settlement. Displays focus on American Indian culture, the fur-trading and gold-rush eras and establishment of modern cities. On the last Saturday in September, volunteers bring to life such exhibits as an Old West saloon, a blacksmith's forge, a turn-of-the-20th-century kitchen and a Chinese apothecary shop. A neighboring Pioneer Village preserves a log, adobe and wood-frame dwelling dating from the 1860s. Closed Monday. Admission. ~ 610 North Julia Davis Drive; 208-334-2120, fax 208-334-4059.

The nearby **Boise Art Museum** contains 16 galleries, including an expansive sculpture court. The museum also features a rotating calendar of 20 or more touring exhibitions of regional and national work representing a wide range of themes. Closed Monday from September through May. Admission. ~ 670 South Julia Davis Drive; 208-345-8330, fax 208-345-2247; www.boiseart museum.org.

In the middle of Julia Davis Park is **Zoo Boise**, which features over 200 animals from 83 species. You'll find elk, deer, moose, bighorn sheep and birds as well as the more exotic collection of monkeys, zebras and two Amur tigers. Large, open aviaries house numerous species of birds of prey. There's a gift shop. Admission. ~ 355 North Julia Davis Drive; 208-384-4260, fax 208-384-4194; www.cityofboise.org/parks/zoo.

The **Discovery Center of Idaho** is at the northern edge of the park. A participatory science museum for children and adults alike, it contains nearly 150 permanent exhibits that encourage personal involvement and hands-on manipulation. Visitors learn about motion, magnetism, electricity and much, much more. Hours change seasonally; call ahead. Admission. ~ 131 Myrtle Street; 208-343-9895, fax 208-343-0105; www.scidaho.org, e-mail dis cover@scidaho.org.

A footbridge connects Julia Davis Park with the 110-acre campus of **Boise State University**, which stretches from Capitol Boulevard to Broadway Avenue on the south side of the Boise River. Over 18,000 students attend this institution, the state's largest. The campus includes the beautiful Morrison Center for the Performing Arts (2201 Campus Lane). Campus tours are offered on a regular schedule. ~ 1910 University Drive; 208-426-

1820, 800-824-7017, fax 208-426-4253; www.boisestate.edu, e-mail bsuinfo@boisestate.edu.

South of BSU via Capitol Boulevard is the Mission-style **Boise Depot**. Built in 1925 by Union Pacific Railroad, it's now used as an event center. ~ 2603 Eastover Terrace; 208-384-4014, fax 208-384-4118.

BSU and Julia Davis Park are an integral part of the **Boise River Greenbelt**, a network of walking and biking paths, mostly paved, that extends more than 20 miles through the heart of the city, from southeast to northwest. A focal point for the city, the Greenbelt links parks and community facilities and provides access to the river for everyone from businessmen-anglers (some of whom spend their lunch hours flyfishing for trout) to summer floaters. ~ 1104 Royal Boulevard; 208-384-4240, fax 208-384-4127.

Traveling west, the Greenbelt passes through Boise's largest park, **Ann Morrison Memorial Park**, with sports fields and extensive facilities. ~ Ann Morrison Park Drive; 208-384-4240. You'll also see the tranquil **Kathryn Albertson Park**, an urban wildlife refuge. ~ Americana Boulevard; 208-384-4240. Two miles farther northwest is **Veterans Memorial State Park**, dedicated to Idahoans who gave their lives in Vietnam, Korea and the World Wars. ~ 930 Veterans Way; www.cityofboise.org/parks.

Traveling east along the Greenbelt, just past Julia Davis Park on the north bank of the Boise River, you'll see the world headquarters of the **Morrison-Knudsen Co.**, one of the most prominent construction firms in North America. Morrison-Knudsen's projects have included the Manned Spacecraft Center in Houston, the locks on the St. Lawrence Seaway, the old Defense Early Warning (DEW) radar system and some 100 dams around the world, including those on Hells Canyon. ~ 720 Park Boulevard; 208-386-5000, fax 208-386-7186; www.wgint.com.

HIDDEN ►

Virtually next door to the east is the **Morrison-Knudsen Nature Center**. This unique exhibit re-creates, in compact scale, the life cycle of a mountain stream. Through underwater windows, visitors can observe the growth and behavior of trout and other fish from developing eggs to full-size adults. The stream flows into a wetland pond where such species as mink and muskrat find a wild home in an urban environment. Interpretive signs assist self-guided tours. The center also offers changing exhibits on Idaho's fish and wildlife. Closed Monday from mid-March to late October; closed Saturday through Monday from November to mid-March. ~ 600 South Walnut Street; 208-334-2225, fax 208-287-2905. The Nature Center is located behind the state **Department of Fish & Game** headquarters. ~ 600 South Walnut Street; 208-334-3700. Both are adjacent to **Municipal Park**, a popular site for group picnics. ~ 500 South Walnut Street; 208-384-4240.

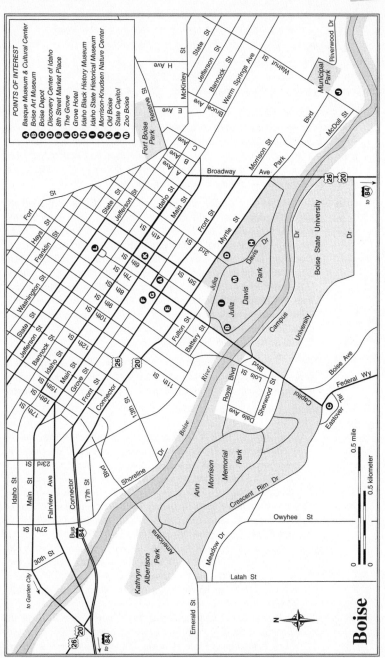

POINTS OF INTEREST

- **A** Basque Museum & Cultural Center
- **B** Boise Art Museum
- **C** Boise Depot
- **D** Discovery Center of Idaho
- **E** 8th Street Market Place
- **F** The Grove
- **G** Grove Hotel
- **H** Idaho Black History Museum
- **I** Idaho State Historical Museum
- **J** Morrison-Knudsen Nature Center
- **K** Old Boise
- **L** State Capitol
- **M** Zoo Boise

Boise

Heart of Boise

The State Capitol (see page 37) is in the heart of downtown Boise and is a fine place to begin a walking tour. From the front steps of the capitol you can look straight down Capitol Boulevard, which runs in a southerly direction for one and a quarter miles across the Boise River to the train station and effectively divides downtown Boise in two. Follow the boulevard three blocks to Main Street and what may be the most intriguing urban corner in Idaho.

HISTORIC BUILDINGS On your left is the modern **Boise City Hall**, its streetside plaza boasting the flags of all 50 states. ~ 150 North Capitol Boulevard; 208-384-3710. On your right is the 1926 **Egyptian Theater**, with Egyptian-revival architecture that was inspired by the discovery of King Tutankhamen's tomb. ~ 700 West Main Street; 208-342-1441. Opposite the theater, on the southwest corner of Main, is the 19-story **U.S. Bank Plaza**, an office building and the tallest structure in the state. ~ 101 South Capitol Boulevard. On the southeast corner is the **Fritchman-Perrault Building**; built in 1878 of locally quarried sandstone, it is the oldest commercial building in Old Boise. ~ 104 South Capitol Boulevard; 208-342-6320.

OLD BOISE The lovingly restored Old Boise historical district provides a glimpse of the capital city's colorful past. Brick facades shelter bustling restaurants, bars, coffeehouses and quaint shops, many of them housed

Municipal Park is just a quarter mile south of Warm Springs Avenue, old Boise's original upper-class residential district. This neighborhood's Victorian mansions were beneficiaries of the modern world's first urban geothermal heating system. Since 1892, 700,000 gallons of 172°F water have been pumped each day from a rhyolite aquifer beneath **Quarry View Park**. The park's restored pump house can still be viewed. ~ Bacon Drive and Old Penitentiary Road; 208-384-4240, fax 208-384-4127.

About 400 homes—including the Warm Springs district's oldest residence, the 1868 **G. W. Russell House**—and eight government buildings, the State Capitol among them, are still heated in this way, at about half the cost of natural-gas heating. ~ 1035 Warm Springs Avenue.

Quarry View Park nestles at the foot of Castle Rock at the east end of the Warm Springs residential district, beside the **Old Idaho Penitentiary State Historic Site** about two miles east of downtown. More than 13,000 prisoners did time here between in buildings that date from the late 19th century. ~ Bounded by Main, 5th, 10th and Bannock streets. Turning south (left) down Main Street to 5th Street will bring you to **The Belgravia** building, whose medieval-looking sandstone walls contain offices and a fine-dining restaurant. ~ 5th and Main streets.

BOISE'S SHOPPING & FINANCIAL DISTRICT Retrace the way you came and continue to 9th and Main streets, where you'll find yourself in Boise's shopping and financial district. Perhaps the most intriguing building in this part of the city is the six-story, French château–style **Idanha Hotel**, which opened on New Year's Day 1901 with Idaho's first elevator. The hotel has been converted into apartments, but it's worth a visit for a glimpse of the outside. ~ 928 West Main Street. The high-rise opposite is **One Capital Center**, world headquarters of the J. R. Simplot Company, one of the nation's agricultural (potatoes—Simplot gained his fame providing french fries to McDonald's) and mining (phosphate) giants. ~ 999 West Main Street; 208-336-2110.

BOISE CASCADE CORPORATION Looping back towards the capitol via 11th Street you'll pass the Boise Cascade Corporation, a national leader in the wood-products industry. Its ground floor is a veritable arboretum. Closed weekends. ~ 1111 West Jefferson Street; 208-384-6161, fax 208-384-7199; www.bc.com. Turn east on Jefferson and continue four blocks back to the capitol.

1870, when the prison was built as a single-cell jail, and 1973, when state authorities opened a new facility (on Pleasant Valley Road in south Boise).

The Old Pen, as locals know it, was placed on the National Register of Historic Places in 1974. Today this foreboding complex—whose sandstone buildings and high turreted stone walls were quarried, hand-cut and constructed by the prisoners themselves—is an intriguing museum. A walking tour begins with an 18-minute video presentation that recalls lowlights of prison history and some of its most notorious residents, like Lady Bluebeard, who was convicted of poisoning her fifth husband; oddly enough, her first four husbands had also died unexpected deaths. Lady Bluebeard escaped from her cell, and by the time the authorities caught up with her she had married again! Luckily, her sixth husband was still alive, and Lady Bluebeard was returned to the penitentiary to serve her final ten years. Visitors can experience the claustrophobic women's ward and the desperation of solitary confinement, meditate in the inmates' rose garden and view the gallows that performed only one hanging (in 1957); Idaho's previous nine hangings were enacted on temporary gallows. Museum exhibits include displays of contraband weapons and prison tattoo art (the only one of its kind, featuring photos of inmates' own skin designs). Admission. ~ 2445 Old Penitentiary Road; 208-334-2844, fax 208-334-3225; www.idahohistory.net/oldpen.html.

Housed within the Old Pen complex is the **J. Curtis Earl Arms Collection,** displaying weaponry from the Bronze Age to modern times, and the **Idaho Transportation Exhibit,** featuring numerous turn-of-the-20th-century vehicles.

Adjacent to the Old Pen is the **Museum of Mining & Geology,** where exhibits describe geological features and show archival photographs and artifacts from the early days of mining in the state. Closed Monday and Tuesday in the summer; closed Monday through Friday the rest of the year. ~ 2455 Old Penitentiary Road; 208-368-9876. Adjacent on the other side of the Old Pen is the historic **Bishops' House,** moved from downtown Boise in 1975 and now used for private receptions. ~ 2420 Old Penitentiary Road; 208-342-3279.

On the east side of the Old Pen, the 33-acre **Idaho Botanical Garden** comprises 13 separate theme and display gardens in bloom from late April to mid-October: gardens of heirloom roses and historical irises; gardens to inspire meditation and to attract butterflies and hummingbirds; an herb garden and a garden planted especially for children. The three-quarter-mile nature trail winds through an area abundant in native plant life. See the winter garden aglow with 150,000 lights during the holiday season. Closed weekends from November through March. Admission. ~ 2355 North Penitentiary Road; 208-343-8649, 877-527-8233, fax 208-343-3601; www.idahobotanicalgarden.org, e-mail idbotgrd@idaho botanicalgarden.org.

Warm Springs Avenue continues southeast some three and a half miles to its junction with Route 21 outside the Boise city lim-

AUTHOR FAVORITE

sights

In Julia Davis Park is the depot of the **Boise Tour Train,** which operates two trains. Each motorized 1890s-replica locomotive pulls a pair of trolley cars on one-hour tours of the streets of historic Boise as a guide points out landmarks and tells punny stories. In addition to train tours, you can also take a river float down the Boise River. Tour times vary seasonally; call ahead. Reservations recommended. Closed November through April. Admission. ~ 600 North Julia Davis Drive; 208-342-4796, fax 208-336-9498; www.boisetours.net, e-mail boisetourtrain@ aol.com.

its. One-half mile south of the junction is **Barber Park**, the "put-in" point for most of the quarter-million rafters and inner-tubers who float the Boise River each year. ~ Healy Road; 208-343-1328.

Route 21 continues southeast another five miles to **Lucky Peak State Park**, then turns north to Boise National Forest, the old mining boom town of Idaho City (see Chapter Three) and the Sawtooth National Recreation Area at Stanley (see Chapter Seven). ~ Route 21; 208-334-2679, fax 208-334-3741.

North from downtown Boise, parallel routes extend up stately **Harrison Boulevard**, lined with early-20th-century manors of many architectural styles, and through the hip Hyde Park neighborhood, four blocks to its east. They come together near the intersection of Bogus Basin Road, which wends its way past Boise's best-known private residence—the palatial hilltop estate of industrialist J. R. Simplot (4000 North Simplot Lane), its giant Stars and Stripes always waving in the wind—to the **Bogus Basin Recreational Area**. This midsize ski resort is located just 16 miles from and not quite a mile above downtown Boise.

Bogus Creek Outfitters offers winter sleigh rides here; in summer, the runners are replaced by wheels for horse-drawn wagon trips. ~ 7355 South Eagle Road; 208-887-7880, 888-264-8727, fax 208-855-2550; www.boguscreek.com.

Located five miles from central Boise, straddling the Boise–Garden City border, is the **Western Idaho Fairgrounds**. ~ 5610 Glenwood Street; 208-287-5650, fax 208-375-9972; www.idaho fair.com. The facility is also used by **Les Bois Park** horse-racing track. ~ 5610 Glenwood Street; 208-376-7223; www.lesboispark. org. **Hawks Memorial Stadium**, home of the Boise Hawks baseball team is also in this area. ~ 5600 Glenwood Street; 208-322-5000 or 208-322-6846; www.boisehawks.com.

Northwest of downtown Boise, Chinden Boulevard (Route 20/26) transits **Garden City**, an enclave town almost completely surrounded by Boise. Originally, Garden City was the home of Chinese gardeners who supplied Boise with fresh produce from well-tended plots along the river, hence the town's name; its central thoroughfare, Chinden Boulevard, is a contraction of "Chinese garden." Today, Garden City is mainly known for its light industrial and commercial strip, budget motels and lower-income housing.

Beyond Garden City, Route 44 (State Street) extends four miles to Eagle, a country town that retains its separate identity from Boise, and four miles farther west, **Eagle Island State Park**. ~ Hatchery Road, Eagle; 208-939-0696, phone/fax 208-939-0704.

On the south side of Boise, near the bustling Boise Municipal Airport, is the **National Interagency Fire Center**—the logistics   ◄ HIDDEN
support center for the thousands of firefighters who battle forest fires, grassland blazes and other wildfires in the United States each year. Tours, arranged in advance depending on fire activity, take

in an infrared mapping system, radio communication systems and other high-technology equipment such as a warehouse and smoke jumper loft. Closed Saturday and Sunday. ~ 3833 South Development Avenue; 208-387-5512, fax 208-387-5386; www.nifc.org.

Founded in 1994, the **World Sports Humanitarian Hall of Fame** inducts three new members each year. Inductees include tennis player Arthur Ashe, baseball star Roberto Clemente, speedskater Bonnie Blair, basketball star David Robinson and many others. Call for location and hours. ~ 208-343-7224, fax 208-343-0831; www.sportshumanitarian.com.

Southwest of the airport is the Peregrine Fund's **World Center for Birds of Prey**, six miles off Route 84 via South Cole Road. (See "An Eagle's-eye View of the Snake" in Chapter Three.) Admission. ~ 5668 West Flying Hawk Lane; 208-362-8687, 800-377-3716, fax 208-362-2376; www.peregrinefund.org. The World Center provides a perfect introduction to raptors for travelers continuing to the **Snake River Birds of Prey National Conservation Area**, 15 miles southwest of the capital. The conservation area covers 81 miles of land along the Snake River and hosts the largest population of nesting raptors in North America. ~ Swan Falls Road, Kuna; 208-384-3300, 800-377-3716, fax 208-384-3326; www.birdsofprey.blm.gov.

LODGING   The **Grove Hotel** is a luxury accommodation. The richly decorated lobby is accented with cherry-wood paneling while the 254 rooms, suites and condominiums feature cherry-wood furnishings, marble bathrooms and a host of niceties such as fluffy bathrobes, two phones and hairdryers. Aside from the standard restaurants, lounges and fitness facilities, the hotel is connected to a multi-use arena that is home to the Idaho Steelheads professional hockey team. ~ 245 South Capitol Boulevard; 208-333-8000, 800-961-5000, fax 208-333-8800; www.grovehotelboise.com, e-mail sales@grovehotelboise.com. DELUXE TO ULTRA-DELUXE.

AUTHOR FAVORITE

On the north side of downtown is the **J. J. Shaw House Bed & Breakfast Inn**, another National Historic Register property that now welcomes guests. A fully restored 1907 Queen Anne Victorian home on a quiet street a few blocks from the city center, it has five nonsmoking rooms with private baths, phones and air conditioning. A full breakfast is served each morning, and homemade refreshments are offered in late afternoon. ~ 1411 West Franklin Street; 208-344-8899, 877-344-8899, fax 208-344-6677; www.jjshaw.com, e-mail jjshaw@earthlink.net. MODERATE TO DELUXE.

For something completely different, try the kitschy **Anniversary Inn**. Its name aptly reflects the clientele—couples hoping to capture the romance of Romeo and Juliet's Veronese love nest or the mysteries of Pharaonic Egypt, sans the steep airfare. This place is an elaborate theme hotel with impressive, creative rooms: the Mammoth Ice Cave Suite features stalactites and stalagmites, for instance, while the Hay Loft Suite houses an actual barn with cedar wood walls. Attention to detail is a high priority and you're sure to find a theme that piques your interest. After all, there are more than 20 available. ~ 1575 South Lusk Place; 208-387-4900, 877-386-4900; www.anniversaryinn.com. DELUXE TO ULTRA-DELUXE.

The one-story **State Motel** houses 12 moderately sized rooms, some with kitchenettes. Definitely not glamorous, but it's still a comfortable and cheap place to rest your head. ~ 1115 North 28th Street; 208-344-7254. BUDGET.

The 100-room **Owyhee Plaza Hotel** is the home of an elegant restaurant as well as a piano lounge and coffee shop. Standard rooms are small but pleasant; executive-level third-floor rooms are considerably more spacious and cost only a few dollars more. Facilities include a swimming pool. ~ 1109 West Main Street; 208-343-4611, 800-233-4611, fax 208-336-3860; www.owyhee plaza.com, e-mail reservations@owyheeplaza.com. MODERATE TO DELUXE.

Another reliable downtown hotel is the **Statehouse Inn**, located almost directly opposite the convention center. The inn offers 112 comfortable rooms with standard decor, including seven suites with jacuzzis. All rooms have VCR attachments to cable TVs and modem hookups. There's also a restaurant and lounge, a fitness facility and spa, and free covered parking. ~ 981 Grove Street; 208-342-4622, 800-243-4622, fax 208-344-5751; www.statehouse-inn.com, e-mail info@statehouse-inn.com. DELUXE TO ULTRA-DELUXE.

The **Boise Centre GuestLodge** is within walking distance of the Capitol building and other downtown attractions. Clean and modest, it features a swimming pool and offers free continental breakfast. ~ 1314 Grove Street; 208-342-9351, fax 208-336-5828; www.guestlodge.com, e-mail guestlodge@qwest.net. BUDGET TO MODERATE.

A few blocks east of downtown, the **Cabana Inn** offers convenient and inexpensive lodging. Its 50 rooms are modest but serviceable. For those traveling with pets, it's a welcoming spot. ~ 1600 Main Street; 208-343-6000. DELUXE.

Boise's most centrally located bed and breakfast is the **Idaho Heritage Inn**, built in 1904 and listed on the National Register of Historic Places. The former residence of Governor Chase Clark (1941–43) and Senator Frank Church (1957–81), the geothermally heated mansion was sold in 1987 and restored as a six-bedroom B&B. There's a sunroom off the living room, which is large enough to have hosted many a political reception, and a dining room with an outdoor patio where breakfast is served in summer. Each guest room is decorated with antique furnishings and has a private bath. ~ 109 West Idaho Street; 208-342-8066, fax 208-343-2325; www.idheritageinn.com, e-mail info@idheritageinn.com. MODERATE TO DELUXE.

> Boise is one of only three state capitals (the others are Helena, Montana, and Juneau, Alaska) where nesting bald eagles can be found.

South of downtown, bordering the Boise State University campus, the two-story **University Inn** has 84 cozy but nicely decorated rooms with wood furnishings and botanical-print decor. All rooms have spacious private baths. Located at the corner of Capitol Boulevard, the motel has a large swimming pool, a deck with hot tub and a lounge. A continental breakfast is included. ~ 2360 University Drive; 208-345-7170, 800-345-7170, fax 208-345-5118; www.universityinnboise.com, e-mail info@universityinnboise.com. BUDGET.

Business travelers guarantee high occupancy and high weekday rates at the six-story **Doubletree Club Hotel**. But on Friday through Sunday nights, the rates are cut by half and drop almost into the budget price range—making it a real bargain. Catering to its business clientele, all rooms have two phones and dataports. On the ground floor are an elegant café and lounge, a large outdoor swimming pool and deck, and a workout room with adjoining spa. ~ 475 Park Center Boulevard; 208-345-2002, 800-222-8733, fax 208-345-8354; www.doubletree.com. MODERATE TO DELUXE.

Boise's largest hostelry is the **Doubletree Hotel Boise Riverside**, located on the Greenbelt beside the Boise River one and a half miles west of downtown. Its 304 spacious and brightly decorated guest rooms (including 35 suites) have oversized bathtubs and wet bars. Facilities include a restaurant, a lounge, an outdoor swimming pool, a large fitness center with a jacuzzi, and a gift shop. ~ 2900 Chinden Boulevard; 208-343-1871, 800-222-8733, fax 208-344-1079; www.doubletreeboise.com, e-mail boir_ds@hilton.com. MODERATE TO ULTRA-DELUXE.

Chain hotels dominate in the Boise Municipal Airport area. Perhaps the best value in this part of town is the **Shilo Inn–Boise Airport**. The inn has 125 rooms, "mini-suites" and executive suites with kitchenettes and private baths. Within the hotel are an outdoor swimming pool, a hot tub, a sauna, a steam room and a workout room. A full breakfast is included in the rate. ~ 4111 Broadway; 208-343-7662, 800-222-2244, fax 208-344-0318; www.shiloinns.com, e-mail boiseairport@shiloinns.com. MODERATE TO DELUXE.

Boise is the region's culinary capital, offering a wide variety of **DINING** excellent restaurants in all price ranges.

For lovers of ethnic cuisine, there are several excellent choices in the downtown area. **Cazba** wins more plaudits than any other restaurant for its treatment of such Greek and Middle Eastern dishes as kabobs and gyros, as well as gourmet moussaka, *spanikopita* and dolmades. ~ 211 North 8th Street; phone/fax 208-381-0222. DELUXE.

Yen Ching, Boise's preeminent Chinese restaurant, specializes in the cuisine of northern China. You won't find chop suey on the menu here, but you *will* find good Mandarin spicy beef, *kung pao* chicken and *mu shu* pork. ~ 305 North 9th Street; 208-384-0384, fax 208-336-0707. BUDGET TO MODERATE.

Another great place for Chinese food is the **Oriental Express.** Check out the full wok-fried meals of shrimp lo mein, volcano beef or General Tso's chicken. ~ 110 North 11th Street; 208-345-8868. BUDGET TO MODERATE.

Shige Japanese Cuisine has a fine sushi bar on the second floor of the Capitol Terrace shopping complex. You can also get noodle and tempura dishes, but the deft work and sharp blade of the resident raw-fish expert is the reason most folks visit. Closed Sunday. ~ 100 North 8th Street; 208-338-8423, fax 208-323-4980. MODERATE TO DELUXE.

In a prosaic strip mall you'll find **Aladdin,** an Egyptian restaurant that offers an array of savory Mediterranean dishes. The authentic cuisine will delight anyone who is seeking an alternative to meat and potatoes. For a delectable cross between the Northwest and the Middle East try the salmon. Shish kebabs and lamb stew are popular as well; there are also several flavorful and well-spiced vegetarian options. The restaurant is decorated with Egyptian cloths and paintings; it's all complemented with Egyptian music. ~ 111 Broadway Avenue; 208-368-0880. MODERATE TO DELUXE.

Gino's Italian Ristorante is known for its fresh ingredients and familial atmosphere. They serve fresh seafood daily and feature such specialties as lobster-stuffed ravioli and veal shanks. They also, of course, have standard Italian fare. Closed Sunday. ~ 150 North 8th Street; 208-331-3771. DELUXE TO ULTRA-DELUXE.

Lunch-hour lines often extend from The Grove into the front door of the **Brick Oven Bistro,** where generous portions of soups, salads, sandwiches and "blue-ribbon specials" like shepherd's pie and salmon loaf are dished up cafeteria-style. Seating is in a homey dining room or outside on the patio. ~ North 8th and West Main streets; 208-342-3456, fax 208-384-0266. MODERATE.

The old Idanha Hotel houses **Borton's,** whose menu features Continental dishes with New American flair, like beefsteak tomatoes with mozzarella and vinaigrette, and turkey schnitzel with lingonberries and lemon. ~ 928 West Main Street; 208-336-9100. DELUXE.

Angell's Bar and Grill, an upscale steak-and-seafood establishment on the ground floor of J. R. Simplot's One Capital Center building, is consistently among the best in Boise for food, service and atmosphere. Light eaters have a choice of excellent salads; there's also a full-service lounge. No lunch Saturday through Monday. ~ 999 West Main Street; 208-342-4900, fax 208-342-3971. DELUXE TO ULTRA-DELUXE.

The Gamekeeper, in the Owyhee Plaza Hotel, draws raves for its tableside service and flambées. The cuisine is best described as Continental with a French flair; the decor is simple but elegant. A piano lounge adjoins. No lunch. Closed Sunday. ~ 1109 Main Street; 208-343-4611, fax 208-336-3860; www.owyheeplaza.com, e-mail dining@owyheeplaza.com. DELUXE TO ULTRA-DELUXE.

HIDDEN ► Downtown Boise's funkiest diner (and, tellingly, the haunt of governors and legislators) is **Moon's Kitchen**, at the rear of a gift shop a block and a half from the capitol. Moon's is like an old-time soda fountain, with malts and milkshakes "to die for" and a wide choice of hearty sandwiches and burgers. Breakfast and lunch only. ~ 815 West Bannock Street; 208-385-0472; www.moonskitchen.com. BUDGET TO MODERATE.

Boise's widest selection of fresh seafood is offered by **Milford's Fish House**, next to the 8th Street Market Place. The handsome restaurant, whose decor features dark wood with brass accents, has Northwest salmon and halibut, prawns and Gulf snapper as well as a full oyster bar. Dinner only. ~ 405 South 8th Street; 208-342-8382, fax 208-345-6112; e-mail milfords1@mcleodusa.net. ULTRA-DELUXE.

Another good choice for seafood is **Murphy's**. An elegant restaurant located a couple of miles southeast of downtown, this is the place to come for coconut prawns, honey-roasted tuna and sesame-shiitake mahimahi. Service is excellent. Murphy's also offers Boise's best Sunday brunch, even for folks who don't like

AUTHOR FAVORITE

Boise has several restaurants famous for beef, but perhaps none with a greater following than **Lock, Stock & Barrel**. Thick slabs of prime rib, steaks and seafood are simply prepared and served in a casual downtown atmosphere. There's also a salad bar. Dinner only. ~ 1100 West Jefferson Street; 208-336-4266. DELUXE TO ULTRA-DELUXE.

fish. ~ 1555 Broadway Avenue; 208-344-3691, fax 208-344-9807; www.theram.com. DELUXE TO ULTRA-DELUXE.

There are several delightful restaurants in the quaint Hyde Park district in Boise's North End, not the least of which is **Richard's Across the Street**. Cuisine at this café is "contemporary country French" with a bistro touch. Try the grilled shrimp on risotto cakes with basil cream sauce as an appetizer, the garlic-roasted free-range chicken as a main course. ~ 1520 North 13th Street; 208-331-9855; www.rampartrestaurants.com. DELUXE TO ULTRA-DELUXE.

Heading west from downtown Boise on State Street, you might give more than a passing glance to the **Westside Drive-In**, a rarity among fast-food restaurants: It's owned by a gourmet chef who also runs his own catering firm. Sure, the menu at Lou Aaron's institution (in operation since 1957) features burgers and shakes, but you can also order the likes of beef stroganoff, lasagna or a prime rib dinner. No breakfast on Sunday. ~ 1939 West State Street; 208-342-2957, fax 208-386-9106; www.chef lou.com. MODERATE.

Idaho's only East Indian restaurant is located in the Northgate Shopping Center halfway between downtown Boise and the satellite community of Eagle. **Madhuban** serves up the rich Mughal flavors of northern India—tandoori chicken, shrimp *masala*, lamb *vindalu* and a wide variety of vegetarian curries—in a room enhanced by taped sitar music. Closed Tuesday. ~ 6930 West State Street; 208-853-8215, fax 208-853-8384. MODERATE.

For fast-food junkies, the selection in the **Boise Towne Square Food Court** offers a bit of everything. Within footsteps of one another are a dozen different counters, including such all-American favorites as McDonald's, A&W, Orange Julius and Italian, Mexican and Chinese fast food. There are another 14 restaurants and specialty-food outlets in and around the mall. ~ 350 North Milwaukee Street; 208-378-4400, fax 208-378-4933; www.myboisetownesquare.com. BUDGET.

Chapala II may be the most traditional Mexican café in town. Jaliscan regional specialties such as *sopitos* and *chile verde* highlight the menu, although tacos and enchiladas still get more takers. ~ 3447 Chinden Boulevard, Garden City; 208-342-5648, fax 208-342-5653. BUDGET TO MODERATE.

West of Garden City in Meridian, local crowds flock to **Epi's Basque Restaurant** for authentic preparations of lamb, steak, fish, chicken and pork, as well as beef tongue and inkfish. Desserts (rice pudding, *flana*, *gateau basque*) also get the Basque treatment. Tucked away in a small house, it's always packed; reservations are highly recommended. Dinner only. Closed Sunday and Monday. ~ 1115 North Main Street, Meridian; 208-884-0142. MODERATE TO DELUXE.

SHOPPING   When Boiseans get serious about shopping, they head to **Boise Towne Square**, a two-story, 185-shop mall on the west side of the city. Anchored by such department stores as JCPenney, Sears, The Bon-Macy's and Mervyn's, the mall (the region's largest) sells everything from apparel and jewelry to sporting goods, books and electronic equipment. **Made in Idaho or** USA (208-378-1188; www.idahomall.com) features handcrafted items, foods and wines exclusively produced within the state. Towne Square is located just north of Route 184 between Franklin and Milwaukee streets. ~ 350 North Milwaukee Street; 208-378-4400, fax 208-378-4933; www.myboisetownesquare.com.

The darlings of the discount shopping set are the **Boise Factory Outlets**, just off Route 84 at the east end of the city. The 30 or so name-brand stores offer clothing (Bugle Boy, Adidas, Levi's and the Dress Barn), housewares (Corning Revere and Kitchen Collection) and specialty foods (Rocky Mountain Chocolate Factory), to name just a few. ~ Eisenman and Gowen roads; 208-331-5000, fax 208-331-5002; www.boisefactoryoutlets.com.

Boise galleries and other businesses get together for a "First Thursday" event each month; call **208-472-5251** for information.

In downtown Boise, a small but intriguing shopping complex is the historic **8th Street Market Place**, which includes galleries, gift shops, restaurants, theaters and offices housed in a pair of turn-of-the-20th-century former warehouses. ~ 405 South 8th Street. The **Old Boise Shopping District** is heavy in art galleries and fashion outlets, bistros and bars. ~ West Main Street between Capitol Boulevard and North 4th Street. Downtown's single largest store is **The Bon Marché**, a mid-priced department store with five floors. ~ 918 West Idaho Street; 208-344-5521.

For gift and souvenir shopping, **Taters**, on The Grove, boasts such unique-to-the-state products as potato novelty items, huckleberry gift packs and T-shirts. ~ 249 South 8th Street; 208-338-1062; www.idahotaters.com. **Gibson & Lane** carries upscale imports and one-of-a-kind crafts, with inventories geared toward upcoming holidays. ~ 809 West Bannock Street; 208-336-4370. **Stewart's Gem Shop** carries the star garnet, Idaho's "state mineral," in jewelry and various other gift items. ~ 2618 West Idaho Street; 208-342-1151.

Art lovers will want their first stop to be at the **Boise Art Museum Store**, which sells arts, crafts, books and jewelry. ~ 670 South Julia Davis Drive; 208-345-8330; www.boiseartmuseum.org. **Gallery 601** features the nationally acclaimed work of Idaho's Jane Wooster Scott, a modern American folk artist. ~ 211 North 10th Street; 208-336-5899; www.gallery601.com. Other leading fine-art exhibitors include **Brown's Gallery**. ~ 1022 West Main Street; 208-342-6661; www.brownsgallery.com.

Antique shoppers might wander the Hyde Park district situated north of downtown.

Blue Moon Antiques is a girly place with loads of jewelry and decorative Victorian knick-knacks. Closed Sunday and Monday. ~ 1611 North 13th Street; 208-336-5964.

The city's largest bookstores are within sight of one another near Towne Square Mall: **Barnes & Noble** has an espresso bar in the center of the store. ~ 1315 North Milwaukee Street; 208-375-4454. **Borders** often hosts live musical performances. ~ 1123 North Milwaukee Street; 208-322-6668.

For gourmet food lovers, the **Boise Consumer Co-op** is the city's largest natural-food store, gourmet deli and imported wine shop. ~ 888 West Fort Street; 208-342-6652.

Of special interest eight miles west of Boise is the **Orville** ◄ HIDDEN **Jackson Drug Co.**, the nearest thing to an old-time general store in the Boise area. You'll find everything from old medicine bottles, ax handles and kerosene lanterns to Crackerjacks and cow- and pig-shaped cookie cutters. ~ 50 East State Street, Eagle; 208-939-6511.

NIGHTLIFE

Although Boise has an active core of local rock, blues and country bands, it is better known for more sophisticated culture. Tickets for most events can be obtained from **Select-A-Seat** which operates outlets in all Albertson's stores. ~ 208-426-3535; www.idahotickets.com.

The *Idaho Statesman*'s Friday "Scene" section lists five dozen different venues that feature live popular music on a weekly basis. Leading concert sites include the Morrison Center (see below) and the **Bank of America Centre**. ~ 233 South Capitol Boulevard; 208-424-2200, fax 208-424-2222; www.bofacentre.com, e-mail dkling@bofacentre.com.

For alternative rock there's **Neurolux**, which hosts some of the region's most popular bands—including Boise's own Built to Spill—twice a week. ~ 111 North 11th Street; 208-343-0886.

The **Emerald City Club** is a cabaret-style dance establishment that specializes in progressive acts. It's frequented primarily by the local gay community. ~ 415 South 9th Street; 208-342-5446.

Local rock bands perform at such Old Boise bars as **Humpin' Hannah's**. ~ 621 West Main Street; 208-345-7557. **Tom Grainey's Sporting Pub** also features live local bands. Cover. ~ 109 South 6th Street; 208-345-2505.

One of the Rockies' finest blues clubs is the **Blues Bouquet**, which draws touring acts from Chicago to Los Angeles. Cover on Friday and Saturday. ~ 1010 West Main Street; 208-345-6605. The **Boise Blues Society** has information on other events. ~ www.boiseblues.org. On the same street stands the **Cactus Bar**. A bit divey, it's an honest-to-goodness bar with draughts on tap, a jukebox and a pool table in the back. ~ 517 West Main Street; 208-342-9732.

The **TableRock Brewpub/Grill**, between the university and downtown, is an excellent brewpub with a variety of custom beers. ~ 705 Fulton Street; 208-342-0944. There's also **Highland's Hollow Brewhouse**, just off Bogus Basin Road, which also has a wide range of custom brews. ~ 2455 Harrison Hollow; 208-343-6820.

Bronco Stadium is renowned for its blue artificial turf.

The **Ram Restaurant Brewery** is Boise's liveliest sports bar; it has a spacious outdoor patio beside the Greenbelt and a score of TVs in its main bar, restaurant and "Stone House" pool room. ~ 709 East Park Boulevard; 208-345-2929; www.bighornbrewing.com.

The **Bitter Creek Ale House** has the region's largest choice of microbrews by draught or bottle. ~ 246 North 8th Street; 208-345-1813. Across the street, the **Grape Escape** is a gourmet wine bar. ~ 800 West Idaho Street at 8th Street; 208-368-0200.

The **Piper Pub & Grill**, with a Capital Terrace balcony overlooking West Main Street, is Boise's leading singles bar, attracting after-work throngs of 30-something lawyers and legislative aides. ~ 8th and Main streets, Suite 200; 208-343-2444.

Located next to the Basque Museum and Cultural Center, the **Gernika Basque Pub & Eatery** may help quench your thirst for Basque culture. In addition to the company of colorful characters, you'll find traditional wines and eats. Black-and-white photographs depicting early Basque life in Boise adorn the walls. Closed Sunday. ~ 202 South Capitol Boulevard; 208-344-2175.

Coffeehouses are big in Boise. **Flying M Espresso** is open until 11 p.m. on weekends. ~ 500 West Idaho Street; 208-345-4320. There's also **Moxie Java**, in Old Boise, with over ten other shops in the Boise area. ~ 570 West Main Street; 208-343-9033.

Boise's only full-time comedy club is in the 8th Street Market Place: **The Funny Bone** hosts up-and-coming comics working the national circuit. Recent acts have included D.L. Hughley, Gabe Kaplan and Bobcat Goldthwait. ~ 404 South 8th Street, Suite 200; 208-331-2663.

Spectator-sports lovers find plenty to excite them year-round. In summer, the **Boise Hawks** baseball club plays a 76-game, mid-June-to-early-September schedule in the Northwest League as a minor-league affiliate of the Chicago Cubs. Home games are at Memorial Stadium. ~ 5600 Glenwood Street; 208-322-5000, fax 208-322-6846; www.boisehawks.com. In fall and winter, the **Boise State University Broncos** compete in the NCAA Division I Western Athletic Conference; football games are at 30,000-seat Bronco Stadium. ~ 1910 University Drive; 208-426-1286, fax 208-426-1778; www.broncosports.com. Men's and women's basketball games are at the 13,000-seat Pavilion. ~ 1401 Campus Lane; 208-426-4737; www.pavilion.com. The **Idaho Steelheads**, a Western Hockey League franchise, began playing in 1997 at the Bank of America Centre. Their season runs from October through March. ~ 251 South Capitol Boulevard; 208-383-0080, tickets 208-331-8497, fax 208-383-0194.

Horse-racing fans place their bets at **Les Bois Park**, adjacent to the Western Idaho Fairgrounds, between May and mid-August. ~ 5610 Glenwood Street; 208-376-7228.

Players Pub & Grill, near the fairgrounds, is a classic sports bar with satellite feeds to any number of national events. ~ 5504 West Alworth Street, Garden City; 208-376-6563.

Auto-racing enthusiasts have the **Firebird Raceway**, 25 miles northwest of the capital; an April–October season is highlighted by the Nightfire Nationals in August. ~ Route 16, Eagle; 208-938-8986, fax 208-938-8961; www.firebirdonline.com.

SYMPHONY, DANCE, OPERA AND THEATER The **Morrison Center for the Performing Arts** is widely recognized as one of the finest performing-arts halls in the United States, hosting numerous performances every month by musicians, actors, dance troupes and others, from Andrew Lloyd Weber musicals to Riders in the Sky, *STOMP* to Jethro Tull, Lyle Lovett to magician David Copperfield. ~ 2201 Campus Lane, Boise State University; 208-426-1609, fax 208-426-3021; mc.boisestate.edu.

Several resident companies also make use of the Morrison Center. Heading the list is the **Boise Philharmonic**, which performs a concert season from September to May. ~ 516 South 9th Street; 208-344-7849; www.boisephilharmonic.org.

Faculty and students of the **Boise State University Music Department** perform at the Morrison Center as well. ~ 2201 Campus Lane; 208-426-3980.

The city supports the nationally acclaimed **Ballet Idaho**, whose performances (including a Christmas-season *Nutcracker*) extend from September to May. ~ 501 South 8th Street; 208-343-0556.

Opera Idaho, which presents operas by Mozart, Puccini and other classical composers, is also supported by the city. ~ 501 South 8th Street; 208-345-3531.

All of these groups (excluding Boise State University) are based at the **Esther Simplot Performing Arts Academy**, where recitals and rehearsals are sometimes open to the public. ~ 516 South 9th Street; 208-345-9116; www.espaa.org.

The **Boise Master Chorale** performs with the other companies and presents its own series of concerts. ~ 100 West State Street; 208-344-7901.

The **Idaho Shakespeare Festival** features a series of works by the Bard and others from June to September. The theater's outdoor amphitheater, located along the Boise River, is designed to blend into the surrounding habitat. ~ 208-429-9908, 208-336-9221 (box office), fax 208-429-8798; www.idahoshakespeare.org.

Other local troupes perform in regular September-to-June seasons. **Boise Little Theater** tends toward serious theater. ~ 100 East Fort Street; 208-342-5104; www.boiselittletheater.org. **The Stage Coach Theatre** leans toward comedy. ~ Hillcrest Shopping Center, at Overland Road and South Orchard Street; 208-342-2000. The **Knock 'em Dead Dinner Theater** focuses on musicals. ~ 333 South 9th Street; 208-385-0021. **Boise State University Theatre Arts Department** also features a variety of shows. ~ 2201 Campus Lane; 208-426-3980.

In addition to Ballet Idaho, local dance companies include the **Idaho Dance Theatre**. Performances are held at the Special Events Center on campus. ~ P.O. Box 6635, Boise, ID 83707; 208-331-9592.

PARKS   **JULIA DAVIS PARK** 🚲 ⛵ 🚂 🛶 Boise's first city park and the centerpiece of its splendid Greenbelt system lies on the north bank of the Boise River seven blocks south of the State Capitol. Named for a pioneer settler, the wooded, 90-acre park contains the Idaho State Historical Museum and Pioneer Village, the Idaho Black History Museum, the Boise Art Museum, Zoo Boise, The Discovery Center of Idaho and the Boise Tour Train depot. A footbridge over the river connects the park with Boise State University. You may cast a fly for trout in the Boise River. Facilities include picnic tables, restrooms, a rose garden, a bandshell, tennis courts, paddleboat rentals and playgrounds. ~ Located between Capitol Boulevard and Broadway Avenue south of Myrtle Street; 208-384-4240.

ANN MORRISON MEMORIAL PARK 🚲 ⛵ 🛶 The largest Boise city park encompasses 153 acres southwest of downtown on the south bank of the Boise River. Ponds (home to hundreds of geese and ducks) and fountains intersperse the park's broad grassy fields, many used for soccer and other sports. Extensive facilities make this park a busy and popular destination. Morrison Park is the takeout point for floaters who ride the river from Barber Park. You may fish in the river. Facilities include picnic tables, restrooms, athletic fields and a playground. ~ From downtown, take Capitol Boulevard south, then turn west on Royal Boulevard or Ann Morrison Park Drive, both of which continue into the park; 208-384-4240.

KATHRYN ALBERTSON PARK 🚶 An urban wildlife refuge less than one and a half miles from the State Capitol, this park combines creekside woodlands with natural wetlands to create a sanctuary that delights plant and animal lovers alike. Walking paths afford views of such resident creatures as minks and muskrats, kingfishers and great blue herons. Facilities include restrooms. ~ Take 16th Street south from downtown; 16th Street becomes Americana Boulevard; enter opposite the entrance to Ann Morrison Park; 208-384-4240.

VETERANS MEMORIAL STATE PARK This 86-acre park is dedicated to Idahoans who gave their lives in Vietnam, Korea and the World Wars. It combines a broad lawn surrounding the war monuments beside busy State Street, a marshy area that attracts families of mallards and wood ducks, and a former Boise Cascade millpond beside the Boise River. Numerous trails weave past the banks of the river and Boise Cascade Lake, through groves of cottonwoods and 100-year-old cedars. Fishing is excellent for trout, bass and bluegill in Boise Cascade Lake, and for trout in the adjacent Boise River. There are picnic tables, restrooms and a playground. Day-use fee, $4. ~ Take State Street (Route 44) northwest two and a half miles from downtown. Just past 36th Street, turn left on Veterans Memorial Parkway to reach the park entrance, on the left; 208-384-4164.

BARBER PARK This Ada County park on the Boise River at the southeast edge of Boise is especially popular with river floaters during the dog days of summer. Floaters climb into their rafts and inner tubes here for the two-hour, five-and-a-half-mile run to Ann Morrison Park. Shuttle services are offered here and at Morrison Park. Anglers enjoy the year-round fishing for rainbow and brown trout in the Boise River. Facilities include picnic tables, restrooms, raft and inner-tube rentals and a playground. Parking fee for floaters only (summer only), $5. ~ From downtown Boise, take Warm Springs Avenue east for five miles; turn south on Eckert Road and continue one-half mile. The park entrance is on your right, just across the Boise River; 208-343-1328, fax 208-385-9935; www.adaweb.net, e-mail parks@adaweb.net.

LUCKY PEAK STATE PARK Extending 11 miles along the Boise River between the Lucky Peak and Arrowrock dams, Lucky Peak Reservoir is the city's fa-

---

GETTING THEIR KICKS

Ever since Idahoans Paul Revere and the Raiders busted the pop charts in the mid '60s with "Kicks" and "Hungry," Boise has been an active if under-recognized player in the national entertainment scene. Revere (named Revere Dick at birth) and Raiders' lead singer Mark Lindsay still make their homes in Idaho and occasionally emerge from seclusion to perform their repertoire of classic oldies.

vorite getaway for water sports and is an important water resource. Two of the state park's three units are below Lucky Peak Dam. The Discovery Unit, just below the outflow from the dam, is a popular fishing and picnic spot, but swimming here is dangerous and not recommended. There is good fishing for trout, kokanee salmon and smallmouth bass in Lucky Peak Reservoir; all but kokanee below the dam. Sandy Point Beach, at the foot of the towering dam, has an excellent beach and is a great place for children with water-dog tendencies to frolic while their parents watch from a manicured lawn. Spring Shores' 298-slip marina is the largest in the state parks system; this is a base for boating, sailing, waterskiing and board sailing. There is a snack bar at Spring Shores. Some facilities are open from mid-May through October only. Facilities include picnic tables, restrooms, boat rentals, a marina and concessions. Day-use fee, $4. ~ Four miles east of downtown Boise, Warm Springs Avenue joins Route 21. Continue east five miles from here to the Discovery unit; six miles to Sandy Point; 12 miles via Middle Fork Road to Spring Shores; phone/fax 208-334-2432; www.idahoparks.org/parks/luckypeak.html.

Eagle Island State Park is located on the site of a former state-prison honor farm.

EAGLE ISLAND STATE PARK 🏊 ⛵ Area families come in droves on hot summer weekends to the park's 11-acre artificial lake. A special attraction is a waterslide extending down a hillside above a long, sandy beach. Located between two channels of the Boise River, the 545-acre park is mostly undeveloped, making it ideal habitat for deer, raptors and other wildlife. There are about five miles of hiking and biking trails, while fishing for trout in the Boise River is good. Facilities include picnic tables, restrooms and a playground. The park is undergoing changes; call ahead to check status. Day-use fee, $4. ~ Take State Street (Route 44) west 13 miles from downtown Boise; turn south and continue one-half mile on Linden Road, then turn east and proceed one-half mile on Hatchery Road. Or take Chinden Boulevard (Route 20/26) west 12 miles from downtown; at Linden Road, turn north and continue one and a half miles to Hatchery Road, which leads into the park; 208-939-0696, phone/fax 208-939-0704.

Outdoor Adventures

FISHING

The Snake River and its tributaries, including the Boise, are excellent waters for trout fishing. On the Boise River system, Lucky Peak and Arrowrock reservoirs are likely venues for rainbow and brown trout and smallmouth bass.

Bear Creek Fly Shop, a tackleshop, specializes in flyfishing. Closed Sunday. ~ 5622 West State Street; 208-853-8704. **The Idaho Angler** sells all types of flies and equipment. Lessons on flyfishing, fly tying and casting are available as are guided fishing trips. Closed Sunday. ~ 1682 Vista Avenue; 208-389-9957, 800-787-9957; www.idahoangler.com. Also try **Anglers** for flyfishing. Closed Sunday. ~ 7097 Overland Road; 208-323-6768.

RIVER RUNNING

One of America's greatest whitewater rafting rivers, the South Fork of the Payette, is located in the Boise area.

For information on guided trips around Boise and elsewhere in the state, contact the **Idaho Outfitters and Guides Association**. Closed Saturday and Sunday. ~ 711 North 5th Street, Boise; 208-342-1438; www.ioga.org. **Idaho River Sports** is a good place to arrange rentals of rafts, kayaks and essential gear. ~ 1521 North 13th Street; 208-336-4844; www.idahosports.com. **Boise Water Sports** also provides wet suits and other necessary river gear. Closed Sunday. ~ 2404 Orchard Road; 208-342-1378; www.boise watersports.com.

BOATING

The region's most popular destinations for boating and other water sports are Lucky Peak and Arrowrock reservoirs. Lucky Peak has eight boat launch sites and a marina at the Spring Shores unit of Lucky Peak State Park; Arrowrock, just up the Boise River, has an additional boat ramp.

You can rent boats from **Idaho River Sports**. ~ 1521 North 13th Street; 208-336-4844; www.idahosports.com.

Leisurely and informative tours of the Boise River are available from May through September with **Boise River Tours**. ~ 111 Broadway, Suite 133; 208-333-0003; www.boiserivertours.com.

SKIING

The Boise area offers only one ski destination, but it's a good one. **Bogus Basin** may be a "local" area, just 16 road miles north of downtown Boise in Boise National Forest, but it's been called "one of the 12 best-kept secrets in skiing" by no less an authority than *Ski* magazine. From the summit of 7590-foot Shafer Butte there's a vertical drop of 1800 feet to the base of the Pine Creek Chair—not enormous by major resort standards, but sufficient to guarantee a wide range of challenges on its 53 runs, served by chairlifts and one paddle tow. The mountain offers 1600 acres of night skiing. Snow conditions permitting, Bogus keeps its lifts operating from Thanksgiving through Easter. The ski area also has a small terrain park and 32 kilometers of groomed cross-country trails that branch out from the lodge at the foot of the alpine slopes; there's night skiing on 800-foot tube hill runs. ~ 2600 Bogus Basin Road; 208-332-5100, 800-367-4397, fax 208-332-5102; www.bogusbasin.com, e-mail info@bogusbasin.com.
Ski Rentals For downhill and cross-country equipment rentals in the Boise area, check out **Greenwood's Ski Haus**. ~ 2400 Bogus Basin Road; 208-336-4445. **McU Sports** rents snowboards, down-

hill skis and cross-country skis. ~ 2314 Bogus Basin Road; 208-336-2300; www.mcusports.com. **Idaho Mountain Touring and Skier's Edge** specializes in cross-country rentals. ~ 1310 Main Street; 208-336-3854, 877-252-4831; www.idahomountaintouring.com.

GOLF

There are plenty of public 18-hole golf courses in the Boise area to choose from, all of which rent carts and clubs. The **Boise Ranch Golf Course** features eight lakes. ~ 6501 South Cloverdale Road; 208-362-6501; www.golfsouthidaho.com. Tee off at **Quail Hollow Golf Course,** a short, hilly course that boasts target golf. ~ 4520 North 36th Street; 208-344-7807. **Shadow Valley Golf Course** was voted "Best of Treasure Valley" by the area's local newspaper. ~ 15711 Route 55 North; 208-939-6699; www.shadowvalley.com. **Warm Springs Golf Course**'s irrigation system provides plenty of green. ~ 2495 Warm Springs Avenue; 208-343-5661; www.warmspringsgolf.com. In Eagle, try **Eagle Hills Golf Course.** ~ 605 North Edgewood Lane, Eagle; 208-939-0402; www.eaglehillsgolfcourse.com.

There are also four nine-hole golf courses and a quartet of 18-hole private clubs. For more information on Idaho courses, contact the **Idaho Golf Association**. Closed Saturday and Sunday. ~ 4696 Overland Road, Suite 120; 208-342-4442; www.idahogolfassn.org.

TENNIS

About 20 of the city parks in Boise have public tennis courts. Among them is **Ann Morrison Park**. ~ 1000 Americana Boulevard west of Capitol Boulevard. There's also **Julia Davis Park**. ~ Julia Davis Drive east of Capitol Boulevard. **Fort Boise Park** has courts that are lighted for night play. ~ 600 West Garrison Road. Contact **Boise Parks & Recreation Department** for more information. ~ 1104 Royal Boulevard; 208-384-4240, fax 208-384-4127; www.cityofboise.org/parks.

Private tennis clubs in the region include the **Boise Racquet & Swim Club**. Guest memberships and lessons are available. ~ 1116 North Cole Road; 208-376-1052; www.boisetennis.com.

RIDING STABLES

Horses provide an authentic "Western" way to explore the surrounding forests. **Bogus Creek Outfitters** offers summer trail rides by the hour or half-day into Boise National Forest from the Bogus Basin ski area. They also offer wagon-ride dinner shows in summer and winter sleigh rides at the ski area. ~ 7355 South Eagle Road; 208-887-7880, 888-264-8727, fax 208-855-2550; www.boguscreek.com. The **Idaho Equestrian Center** offers English and Western lessons to riders of all abilities. ~ 9400 North Pierce Park Road; 208-853-2065.

City of Trees—and Trails

The Greenbelt now dominates Boise's riverfront and is the pride of every Boisean, but it wasn't always so. For 100 years after Boise's founding, the river was used primarily to flush away the city's raw sewage and the industrial waste of sawmills and slaughterhouses that stood on its banks. But under pressure from citizens, the city began, in 1966, converting its riverfront property into a promenade of parks and parkland. By 1968, the Boise River Greenbelt was born.

There are now almost 20 miles of trail between Sandy Point beneath Lucky Peak Dam at the Greenbelt's east end, and Willow Lane, just past Veterans Park, at its western terminus. Follow Warm Springs Avenue east of Boise and continue approximately seven miles to reach the dam, or follow West State Street to Veterans Park and Willow Lane. On the river's north side the Greenbelt forms an unbroken asphalt path approximately six to eight feet wide that is shared—companionably—by walkers, joggers, bikers, skaters and, sometimes in winter, skiers. Planners also are forging links between the Greenbelt and 70 miles of walking, bicycle and horse trails in the Boise foothills to create a comprehensive, ridge-to-rivers trail system.

It is almost accurate to say that the simplest access to the Greenbelt from anywhere downtown is to head south till you hit the river; and, except for a sometimes incomprehensible layout of one-way streets, this works. Parking is available downtown at Julia Davis and Ann Morrison parks, and at Discovery, Barber, Municipal, Kathryn Albertson and Veterans parks.

Bald eagles now winter in the Boise Greenbelt again, nesting in cottonwood trees that line the river's redeemed shore. Osprey, heron and otters dine on the river's fish population. Wood ducks, teals, pintails, redheads, canvasbacks, coots and Canada geese can be seen in spring and summer, along with great blue herons, kingfishers, killdeer, sandpipers and willets. A few mallards and widgeons reside year-round. On shore are beaver, fox and mule deer. Catchable pan-sized rainbow trout are stocked, and the river supports a resident population of big brown trout, upward of five pounds.

So dense are the riverside brush and trees that the city is all but invisible to anglers who ply the water for trout, and to boaters who float the river in everything from life-jackets and inner tubes to canoes. A shuttle is available where 13th Street dead-ends at the river for the 15 minute drive to the Barber Park put-in. Tubes and small rafts can be rented for the two-hour float back down. All this within city limits.

BIKING

Boise's city grid is laid on the flat floodplain of the Boise River, making it great for bicycling. Besides the Greenbelt, there are many trails outside of town. The **Boise River Greenbelt** is one of the finest urban biking systems you'll find anywhere. The mostly paved network of paths extends over 20 miles through the heart of the city, linking parks from Willow Lane, in the northwest, to Lucky Peak State Park, some ten miles southeast. ~ 1104 Royal Boulevard; 208-384-4240, fax 208-384-4127; www.cityofboise.org/park.

Skinny-tire bicyclists like to ride along the Hill Road bike lane, which follows the base of the foothills north of Boise. For a true workout, climb the pavement to the **Bogus Basin Ski Area**—16 miles one-way, gaining almost a vertical mile; the ride down is hard earned and thrilling.

Ice skate year-round at Idaho Ice World, where Olympic hopefuls glide alongside regular folks. ~ 7072 South Eisenman Road; 208-331-0044.

Popular off-the-pavement trails for Boise-area bikers include the **8th Street Extension** to Hulls Gulch (3 to 6 miles) and Boise Ridge (8 miles), a mile north of Fort Street via North 8th Street.

Additionally, the ski runs at **Bogus Basin** are used on summer weekends by mountain bikers. ~ 2600 Bogus Basin Road; 208-332-5100; www.bogusbasin.com, e-mail info@bogusbasin.com.

There's seemingly endless biking on the trails of **Boise National Forest**. ~ 1249 South Vinnell Way; 208-373-4100.

Bike Rentals   **Idaho Mountain Touring** rents tandems and front-end dual-suspension bikes. ~ 1310 Main Street; 208-336-3854; www.idahomountaintouring.com.

Mountain and road bikes are available from **Bikes to Boards**, located near the Greenbelt. ~ 3525 West State Street; 208-343-0208; www.bikestoboards.com.

HIKING

Greenbelt aside, Boise is a gateway to a wide choice of trails. Following are some of the most popular. All distances listed for hiking trails are one way unless otherwise noted.

Hulls Gulch Interpretive Trail (3.5 miles) is a Bureau of Land Management trail, complete with signs describing natural features, just outside the northern city limits. To reach the upper trailhead, take North 8th Street to the end of the pavement and continue six and a half miles. En route, you'll pass the lower trailhead three and a half miles from the end of the pavement.

Mores Mountain Trail (2-mile loop) is an easy nature hike for kids and families, offering spectacular views from the Treasure Valley to the Sawtooth Range. It begins and ends at the Shafer Butte picnic area, 20 miles from Boise (four miles past the Bogus Basin Recreation Area) on Bogus Basin Road.

Route 84 between Portland, Oregon and Salt Lake City crosses southwestern Idaho diagonally from west to east, providing the major thoroughfare of travel. Route 20, extending east from Mountain Home to Idaho Falls, provides the quickest route to Sun Valley from Boise. Route 21 heads northeast from Boise around the edge of the Sawtooth Mountains, then loops back south into Stanley in the Sawtooth National Recreation Area. Route 55 is the primary northbound route from Boise, following the Payette River through Cascade and McCall to join Route 95 at New Meadows.

Transportation

CAR

AIR

Alaska Airlines, Continental Express, Delta, Northwest, Southwest and United, as well as regional carriers Big Sky Airlines, Frontier Airlines, Horizon and SkyWest, fly into **Boise Airport**, which is located about three and a half miles south of the city.

Airway Taxicab (208-333-0970) and **Boise City Taxi** (208-377-3333) serves Boise Airport.

BUS

Boise's intercity bus depot is located downtown at 1212 West Bannock Street. It is served by **Greyhound Bus Lines** (208-343-3681, 800-231-2222), which makes daily stops in Boise, and by **Boise-Winnemucca/Northwestern Stage Lines** (208-336-3302), a regional coach line that operates daily northbound routes to McCall, Grangeville, Lewiston and Spokane.

CAR RENTALS

Boise has 18 automobile rental agencies. At the airport are **Avis Rent A Car** (800-331-1212), **Budget Rent A Car** (800-527-0700), **Dollar Rent A Car** (800-800-4000), **Enterprise Rent A Car** (800-325-8007), **Hertz Rent A Car** (800-654-3131) and **National Car Rental** (800-227-7368).

Disabled visitors may want to make reservations with **Access Van Rentals**. ~ 6893 Supply Way, Boise; 208-385-7647.

PUBLIC TRANSIT

Boise-area bus service is provided by **Valley Rides**. ~ 208-336-1010. Regular daily service is available at nominal cost on several routes that cover all sections of the city.

TAXIS

At least a half-dozen cab companies operate in the city, including **Boise City Taxi** (208-377-3333) and **Yellow Cab** (208-345-8880).

THREE

Southwestern Idaho

Surrounding Boise is a geographically varied region of desert and river, mountain and canyon, sagebrush and farmland. To the west and northwest, the Treasure Valley extends 50 miles to the Oregon border, where the Boise and Payette rivers empty into the Snake. Their combined waters have created one of Idaho's richest agricultural basins, with broad fields of corn, alfalfa, sugar beets and potatoes, as well as vineyards and fruit orchards. The thriving towns of Nampa and Caldwell are the population centers of the district.

To the north and northeast of Boise, seeming to rise behind the city, is the Boise Front: the tawny foothills of the Rocky Mountains. Cloaked with evergreen forests, this terrain extends unbroken all the way to Canada. In 1862, just 25 miles from modern Boise in what is now known as the Boise Basin, miners struck gold; several ghost towns still stand on the sites of these old mining camps.

Due south of Boise, amid the cliffs and sage-covered hills of the Snake River country, the Snake River Birds of Prey National Conservation Area protects the nesting grounds of the continent's largest concentration of raptors. Farther upstream are the Mountain Home Air Force Base, where the United States has its only air intervention wing; the Bruneau Dunes, America's tallest sand dunes; and Three Island Crossing State Park, which preserves the site of one of the most important river transits of the old Oregon Trail.

The Owyhee Mountains, visible in the distance from Boise, dominate the southern skyline of this region. They carry a mantle of snow during winter, but in summer they are hot and barren, watered by only a few year-round streams.

Treasure Valley

Route 84, the interstate highway, runs westward from the capital through the 50-mile-long Treasure Valley to the Oregon border. Traversing expansive farmland, it skirts the large towns of Nampa and Caldwell between the Boise and Snake rivers. To the north, Route 52 follows the lower Payette River through Emmett and Payette.

Though sometimes passed off as a suburb of Boise, **Nampa** is an **SIGHTS**
important city in its own right: it is Idaho's fourth largest with
50,000 people, including the largest Latino population in the state.
Located 18 miles from Boise, it is the home of the **Canyon County**
Historical Museum housed in a 1902 Oregon Short Line Depot.
The downtown museum has an interesting collection of railroad
memorabilia and other exhibits on the county's past. Closed
Sunday and Monday. ~ 1200 Front Street; 208-467-7611.

A focal point of 21st-century Nampa lies just off the freeway northeast of town. The **Idaho Center** complex includes a
15,000-seat indoor arena that is home to a professional basketball franchise, the Idaho Stampede (box office: 208-388-4667),
and a 9,000-capacity indoor coliseum (with 800 horse stalls)
where the Snake River Stampede is located (box office: 208-466-
8497). When the Idaho Center opened in 1997, visitors began—
you guessed it—stampeding to events, including a kickoff concert by the Moody Blues. Hotels and restaurants are nearby. ~
16200 Can-Ada Road at Garrity Boulevard (Franklin Road);
208-468-1000, fax 208-442-3312; www.idahocenter.com, e-
mail cvos@idahocenter.com.

Five miles southwest of Nampa, a visitors center at **Deer Flat**
National Wildlife Refuge describes some of the 200 species of birds
sighted at the sanctuary's Lake Lowell. Closed weekends. ~
13751 Upper Embankment Road, Nampa; 208-467-9278, fax
208-467-1019. Just east is the **Nampa Hatchery** at Wilson Ponds,
where thousands of trout, from fingerlings to full-size adults, can
be viewed in the outdoor raceways and pond. ~ 3608 South
Powerline Road, Nampa; 208-465-8479. Opposite, on the shores
of **Wilson Ponds**, there are wildlife exhibits in the regional office
of the Idaho Department of Fish & Game. Nature trails offer access to both fishing and birdwatching at the ponds. ~ 3101 South
Powerline Road, Nampa; 208-465-8465, fax 208-465-8467; www.
state.id.us/fishgame.

Before leaving Nampa, be sure to stop by the **Nampa Cham-**
ber of Commerce and pick up a brochure for a "Farm to Market
Tour," a self-guided driving tour of the surrounding farmlands. ~
1305 3rd Street South; 208-466-4641; www.nampa.com. The tour
takes you to ten roadside fruit and vegetable stands and "u-pick"
orchards, and three wineries south and west of town. **Indian Creek**
Winery offers afternoon tours and tastings on weekends and by
appointment. ~ 1000 North McDermott Road, Kuna; 208-922-
4791. Also stop by **Sawtooth Winery** for a tour. ~ 13750 Surrey
Lane, Nampa; 208-467-1200. **Ste. Chapelle Winery**, the largest
in the area, has daily tastings and tours. ~ 19348 Lowell Road,
Caldwell; 208-459-7222, fax 208-453-7831; www.stechapelle.

com. The **Hells Canyon Winery** is open by appointment. ~ 18835 Symms Road, Nampa; 208-454-3300.

The **Warhawk Air Museum** at Nampa Municipal Airport has several World War I and II aircraft on permanent display along with wartime photographs and artifacts. Closed Monday. Admission. ~ 201 Municipal Drive, Nampa; 208-465-6446, fax 208-465-6232; www.warhawkairmuseum.org, e-mail warhawk airmuseum@att.net.

Many of the activities in Nampa's sister city of **Caldwell**, located nine miles up Route 84, are centered around **Albertson College of Idaho**. One of the state's most highly regarded private liberal-arts schools, it was founded as The College of Idaho in 1891 and changed its name upon its centennial to honor alumnus Joe Albertson, the Boise supermarket magnate who bequeathed much of his fortune to the school. Annual enrollment is over 800. ~ 2112 Cleveland Boulevard; 208-459-5011, 800-224-3246, fax 208-459-5175; www.albertson.edu. Albertson's science building, named William Judson Boone Hall for the institution's founder, is the home of the noted **Orma J. Smith Museum of Natural History**, which features research collections from Idaho, the western United States and Baja California. Call ahead to visit or arrange a tour. ~ 2101 Fillmore Street, Caldwell; 208-459-5507.

Located in the same building are the **Glen & Ruth Evans Gem and Mineral Collection**, with more than 50 cases of minerals from around the state and the world; the **Whittenberger Planetarium**, which serves an educational function for local schoolchildren and adults; and the **H. M. Tucker Herbarium**. Access to all of their facilities is by appointment; your chances of getting a tour are better during the academic year.

Other sights in Caldwell include the **Van Slyke Agricultural Museum** in the city's Memorial Park, which features two 1860-era log cabins with period furnishings, two 1950 railroad cars and a wide selection of old farm machinery and tools. Open by appointment only. ~ South Kimball and Irving streets, Caldwell; 208-459-1597.

You may also visit **Our Memories Museum**, a homegrown collection of early-20th-century bric-a-brac exhibited in 22 rooms, modeled after a turn-of-the-20th-century house. Open Friday and Sunday only. ~ 1122 Main Street, Caldwell; 208-459-1413.

A highlight of the city of 25,000 is the **Oregon Trail Centennial Greenway**, a jogging and cycling path that follows the Boise River on the north edge of the city.

The small town of Parma, 14 miles northwest of Caldwell via Route 20/26, is the home of **Old Fort Boise**, a replica of a Hudson's Bay Company adobe trading post built at the mouth of the Boise River, five miles northwest of here, in 1834. The replica

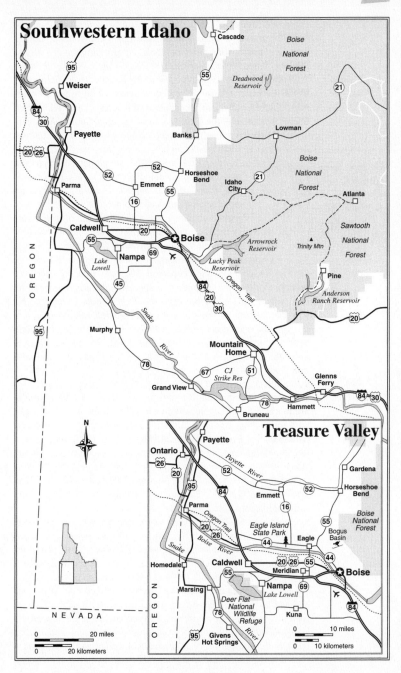

Southwestern Idaho

Cascade

Boise
National
Forest

Weiser

Deadwood
Reservoir

Payette

Banks

Lowman

Parma

Horseshoe
Bend

Emmett

Idaho
City

Boise
National
Forest

Atlanta

Caldwell

Boise

Sawtooth
National
Forest

Nampa

Lake
Lowell

Arrowrock
Reservoir

Trinity Mtn

Lucky Peak
Reservoir

Pine

OREGON

Oregon
Trail

Anderson
Ranch Reservoir

Murphy

Snake

River

Mountain
Home

CJ
Strike Res

Glenns
Ferry

Grand View

Hammett

Bruneau

N

Treasure Valley

Payette

Ontario

Payette River

Gardena

Emmett

Horseshoe
Bend

Parma

Oregon
Trail

Eagle Island
State Park

Boise River

Eagle

Bogus
Basin

Boise
National
Forest

Boise

Snake

Homedale

Caldwell

Meridian

Nampa

Marsing

Deer Flat
National
Wildlife
Refuge

Lake Lowell

Kuna

River

OREGON

Givens
Hot Springs

NEVADA

0   20 miles

0   20 kilometers

0   10 miles

0   10 kilometers

contains a museum and a pioneer cabin; it's open to the public from 1 p.m. to 3 p.m., Friday through Sunday from June to August. Special tours are available by appointment. ~ Route 20/26 at Parma Road, Parma; 208-722-5138.

Emmett sits on the south bank of the Payette River surrounded by hillside fruit orchards, 31 miles northwest of Boise and 29 miles northeast of Caldwell at the junction of Routes 16 and 52. Of particular note here is the **Gem County Historical Society Museum**, open Wednesday through Saturday and by appointment. The five-building complex depicts the area's traditional American Indian culture, its pioneer heritage and the evolution of local industries. ~ 1st and Hawthorne streets, Emmett; 208-365-9530; www.gemcohs.org, e-mail gemcohs@bigskytel.com.

Old Fort Boise was an important Oregon Trail oasis until it washed away during a flood of the Boise River in 1853.

Payette, which is located at the mouth of the Payette River 29 miles downstream from Emmett, boasts a turn-of-the-20th-century downtown with 80 historic buildings. ~ Located 55 miles northwest of Boise via Routes 80 and 95.

The **Payette County Historical Museum** offers displays of vintage clothing and furniture; a special feature is memorabilia of Baseball Hall of Famer Harmon Killebrew, a Payette native who became one of the major leagues' greatest home-run hitters during a 22-year career ending in 1975. Open Wednesday through Saturday and by appointment. ~ 90 South 9th Street, Payette; 208-642-2362, fax 208-642-4883; e-mail payettemuseum@ fmte.com.

LODGING   The area's nicest accommodations are the **Shilo Inn Nampa Suites**. The four-story motor inn has 83 suites, including eight with efficiency kitchens; all have mini-refrigerators and microwaves. Facilities include a 24-hour indoor swimming pool, a whirlpool, a sauna, a steam room and an exercise room. There's also a restaurant, deli and lounge. A complimentary breakfast is included. ~ 1401 Shilo Drive, Nampa; 208-465-3250, 800-222-2244, fax 208-465-5929; www.shiloinns.com, e-mail nampa suites@shiloinns.com. MODERATE TO DELUXE.

In downtown Nampa, the **Desert Inn Motel** has 40 comfortable rooms, some with refrigerators and microwave ovens. All have private baths; a swimming pool is an inviting diversion on hot summer days. ~ 115 9th Avenue South, Nampa; 208-467-1161, fax 208-467-5268; www.sundownerinc.com. BUDGET.

The **La Quinta Inn—Caldwell**, located off Route 84 at the east end of Caldwell, is a standard franchise property with 65 clean, comfortable and modern rooms, all with satellite television. Motel facilities include an indoor swimming pool, a spa, an exercise room and a guest laundry. A generous continental breakfast is included in the room rate, and kitchenettes are available on request.

~ 901 Specht Street, Caldwell; 208-454-2222, 866-454-2300, fax 208-454-9334; www.hotels-west.com, e-mail lq0471gm@la quinta.com. MODERATE.

Just off the 10th Avenue freeway exit is the **Sundowner Motel**. Some of the 66 rooms in the two-story motel have refrigerators and microwaves. Rates include a continental breakfast. ~ 1002 Arthur Street, Caldwell; 208-459-1585, 800-454-9487, fax 208-454-9487; www.sundownerinc.com. BUDGET.

As downtown Nampa becomes more gentrified, a growing number of restaurants are doing bumper business.

DINING

Little Kitchen Grille & Bistro has been a stanchion of downtown Nampa since 1981. Sitting at the entrance to the 1st Street Market, this delightful little café has antique decor and a menu that ranges from salads and sandwiches to all-American blue-plate specials. Breakfast is served anytime. ~ 1224 1st Street South, Nampa; 208-467-9677, fax 208-466-7090; www.littlekitchen diner.com, e-mail littlekitchen@aol.com. BUDGET TO MODERATE.

Nampa's finest Chinese dining is the **Hong Kong Restaurant**. It spreads through several rooms, each one a little different. A buffet-style Mongolian barbecue occupies the restaurant's central room. Cantonese dishes dominate the regular menu, which also features steaks and other American foods. ~ 117 12th Avenue South, Nampa; 208-466-1244, fax 208-463-8355. MODERATE.

In an area with a sizable Latino population you can expect some good Mexican restaurants. One of the best here is **El Charro Café**, a southwest Idaho mainstay since 1954. You can get the standard enchiladas and burritos for lunch and dinner every day, as well as a uniquely south-of-the-border stew: *menudo*. ~ 1701 1st Street North, Nampa; 208-467-5804. BUDGET TO MODERATE.

Caldwell offers a slew of chain restaurants and a mixture of ethnic ones, too. Ethnic here, though, means Chinese or Mexican; otherwise, you'll definitely find your fill of meat and potatoes.

The Golden Palace serves up traditional (Mandarin chicken) and not-so-traditional (sweet-and-sour ribs) Chinese dishes. Though not very authentic, locals still seem to like it. It's a small affair, with colorful fish tanks filling the room. ~ 703 Main Street, Caldwell; 208-459-4303. BUDGET.

If you're really in the mood for meat, meat and more meat, try **Cattlemen's Cafe**. This feedlot restaurant serves up hamburgers, steaks, ribs—almost anything once able to moo. It gets crowded and loud with people eager for some serious grub and gab. Lunch only. Closed Sunday and Monday. ~ 1900 East Chicago Avenue, Caldwell; 208-454-1785. BUDGET.

The Treasure Valley's leading shopping center is **Karcher Mall**. ~ Caldwell Boulevard at Karcher Avenue West, Nampa; 208-

SHOPPING

467-7580, fax 208-467-1989. Department stores include The Bon Marché and Emporium; the mall has a wide choice of clothing stores, bookstores and other shops, such as **Under the Rainbow**, where you'll find unique gifts. ~ 1509 Caldwell Boulevard, Nampa; 208-463-4676. Elsewhere in Nampa, the **Swiss Village Cheese Factory** has a wide selection of meats, cheeses and local wines. ~ 4912 Franklin Road, Nampa; 208-463-6620.

Downtown Nampa is a fine place to shop for antiques. Several dealers at the **Old Towne Antique Mall & Coffee House** sell classic furniture and glassware, jewelry, dolls and vintage clothing, and browsers are never far from an espresso machine. ~ 1212 1st Street South, Nampa; 208-463-4555. **The Yesteryear Shoppe** is stacked to the ceilings with used and rare books, magazines and phonograph records. ~ 1211 1st Street South, Nampa; 208-467-3581; www.yesteryearshoppe.com, e-mail yesteryearshoppe@qwest.net.

NIGHTLIFE   The **Nampa Civic Center** is an important venue for the performing arts, including touring dance troupes and theater companies. ~ 311 3rd Street South, Nampa; 208-465-2252; www.nampa civiccenter.com, e-mail civicntr@ci.nampa.id.us.

The **Langroise Center for the Performing and Fine Arts** boasts a 188-seat music recital hall and a 120-seat theater. ~ Albertson College, Caldwell; 208-459-5836. The **Jewett Auditorium** has another 900 seats for major concerts. ~ Albertson College, Caldwell; 208-459-5836.

The **Hitchin' Post** is a quiet place to have a drink. ~ 1911 1st Street North, Nampa; 208-466-9704.

Orphan Annie's has a singalong piano bar on weekends. ~ 801 Everett Street, Caldwell; 208-455-2660.

HIDDEN ►   Jazz fans wait with bated breath for **Jazz at the Winery**, which is served up on Sunday afternoons from mid-June to September at the Ste. Chapelle Winery southwest of town. ~ 19348 Lowell Road, Caldwell; 208-459-7222, 877-783-2427.

Big-name concerts and other entertainment events are sometimes held at the 15,000-seat **Idaho Center** northeast of Nampa. ~ 16200 Can-Ada Road at Garrity Boulevard (Franklin Road), Nampa; 208-468-1000; www.idahocenter.com. The complex is better known, however, as the home of the **Idaho Stampede**, a professional basketball franchise that made its debut in the Continental Basketball Association in 1997. ~ 208-388-4667; www. idahostampede.com.

At the west end of the Treasure Valley, **Joe's Club** has live country-and-western dance music on weekends. ~ 318 South Main Street, Payette; 208-642-9904.

PARKS   **DEER FLAT NATIONAL WILDLIFE REFUGE** 🚶 🚤 🛥 ⬛ Five miles southwest of Nampa, this 11,430-acre refuge—one of the nation's first—was established in 1909 around seven-and-a-half-mile-long Lake Lowell. Nearly 200 species of resident and migrant waterfowl, shorebirds, upland game birds and raptors have been counted at the refuge, and in late fall, as many as 120,000 ducks make their homes here. Mule deer and coyotes are among resident mammals. The refuge's headquarters also administers 101 Snake River islands between the western border of the Snake River Birds of Prey National Conservation Area, south of Boise, and Farewell Bend, Oregon, west of Weiser. Year-round angling offers largemouth and smallmouth bass, trout, perch, crappie, bluegill, bullhead and channel catfish. There are picnic tables, a visitors center and restrooms. ~ To reach the upper dam, take Route 45 (12th Avenue Road) south one and a half miles from downtown Nampa; then turn west on Lake Lowell Avenue and continue for three and a half miles. The visitors center is located at 13751 Upper Embankment Road; 208-467-9278, fax 208-467-1019; deerflat.fws.gov.

Boise County and Boise Basin

The city of Boise is not in Boise County, nor is much of the Boise River. But miners and loggers in this region laid much of the foundation of southwestern Idaho's social and economic history well over a century ago. The amount of gold dust taken from the Boise Basin, an estimated $250 million, exceeded the take from Yukon mines. The energy and ingenuity of the miners and loggers can still be seen in the county's small towns, rugged hills and creek and river valleys.

At Idaho City's peak population, one-third of the residents were Chinese, 91 percent of them men.

The three principal forks of the Boise River rise on the slope of the Sawtooth Range and rush westward through a series of popular recreational reservoirs, including Anderson Ranch (on the South Fork) and Arrowrock (at the confluence of the three forks). Such small tributaries as Mores and Grimes creeks, which flow south into the Boise at Lucky Peak Reservoir, were a mecca for placer miners during the 19th-century gold rush; their banks harbor a greater concentration of ghost towns and ruins than other parts of the state.

SIGHTS

Excellent highways make the exploration of Boise County an easy daytrip from Boise. Route 55 heading toward McCall joins the Payette River at Horseshoe Bend, 28 miles from Boise. Fourteen miles farther, Route 17 (South Fork Road) heads east up the South Fork of the Payette River 33 miles to Lowman, where it joins Route 21. Travelers here can choose to turn north across the Sawtooth Range to Stanley, 58 miles distant, or return to Boise, 72 miles southwest, via Idaho City. Under normal driving conditions, the full 147-mile loop can easily be covered in four hours without stops. However, construction delays forced by rain-induced landslides may add hours to the drive.

Horseshoe Bend, with 700 people the largest town on the west side of the county, is another Boise Cascade mill town. Its name comes from its position at a huge curve in the Payette River, where the south-flowing stream swings west toward the Snake River.

Tiny **Banks,** situated at the confluence of the North and South forks of the Payette, is important mainly as a whitewater rafting center. Whereas the North Fork, falling steeply from the Long Valley, appeals mainly to expert kayakers, the South Fork, flowing westerly from the summit of the Sawtooths, is one of the most popular rafting rivers in the United States.

During the early mining-boom days of the 1860s and 1870s, homesteads along the South Fork of the Payette grew vegetables for the gold and silver seekers in the mountains—thus, the name "Garden Valley." Natural hot springs warm numerous greenhouses that thrive year-round, providing this valley with a longer growing season than that in most other parts of the state.

Lowman, in the heart of Boise National Forest, is the western gateway to the Sawtooth Range and the hub of a vacation-home community. East from here, Route 21—the **Ponderosa Pine Scenic Route**—climbs to nearly 8000 feet before dropping into the exquisite mountain village of Stanley (see Chapter Eight).

On the western flank of the Sawtooths, just within the Sawtooth National Recreation Area, is the remote outfitting center of **Grandjean,** which is the recreational gateway to the park. Located at the end of six-and-a-half-mile Grandjean Road off Route 21 are the Sawtooth Lodge (208-259-3331; closed from late October to Memorial Day weekend), cabins and a tent and RV campground providing a base for horseback riders and hikers who tackle the craggy peaks overlooking the hamlet. The boundary of the Sawtooth Wilderness is just a mile by trail from the lodge.

Turning south from Lowman on Route 21 brings travelers to **Idaho City,** the center of southern Idaho's biggest mining boom. For a short time in the early 1860s, in fact, Idaho City was the largest community in the Pacific Northwest and Idaho's first territorial capital. Between 1862 and the early 1880s, more than $250 million in gold was recovered by sluicing and placer mining from the hills surrounding Idaho City and other towns of the Boise Basin, including **Centerville, Placerville** and **Pioneerville,** all ten to 17 miles northwest. These three "villes" long ago became ghost towns. All that remain in most of them are pioneer cemeteries and a few abandoned structures. Not so Idaho City. Although the gold ran out and its peak population of some 6200 dwindled to a present-day 500, the town has persisted. See "Walking Tour" for more information.

Another survivor of the gold-mining era is isolated **Atlanta,** on the Middle Fork of the Boise River about 60 miles east of Idaho City. The home of 500 people in the 1870s, it now has about 45 full-time residents and offers facilities for hunters, fishermen, snowmobilers and cross-country skiers.

There are numerous other tiny communities in the Boise Mountains. **Rocky Bar,** 14 miles southwest of Atlanta (via James Creek Road 126) and seven miles north of Featherville, is a ghost town with a trove of mining ruins. **Featherville** and **Pine,** located on the South Fork of the Boise River and reached via Routes 61,

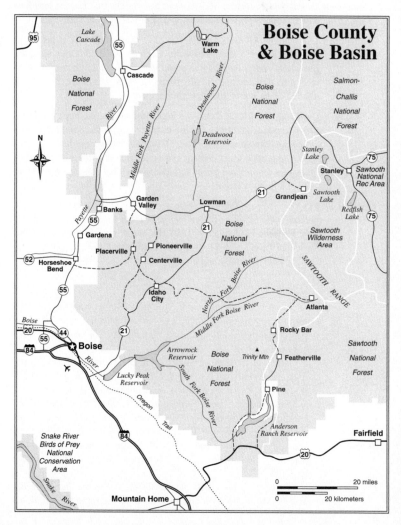

Boise County & Boise Basin

WALKING TOUR
Idaho City

Located 38 miles northeast of the state capital via Route 21 (the Ponderosa Pine Scenic Route), Idaho City remains the seat of Boise County and a shining example of historic preservation. Take time out to stroll down the dusty (all the east–west thoroughfares are unpaved) planked boardwalks that run the length of the town, past the buildings (and hitching posts!) of Idaho's gold-rush era.

IDAHO CITY CHAMBER OF COMMERCE   Start your walk at the Idaho City Chamber of Commerce visitors center, at the entrance to town. The friendly folks here can arm you with maps and information. Also here are displays and a gift shop. ~ Main Street at Route 21; 208-392-6040; www.idahocitychamber.com.

BOISE BASIN MERCANTILE CO.   Back on Main Street, head north towards Commercial Street. On the corner is the Boise Basin Mercantile Co., better known as "The Merc." Once an old grocery store in continuous operation at its present site since 1865, it finally succumbed to a slowing economy and closed in 2002. The original building now houses a deli. ~ 309 Main Street.

HIGH STREET   From The Merc, take a detour east down unpaved Commercial Street to High Street. Overlooking the town from a hillside are **Odd Fellows Hall** (built in 1864, the oldest such lodge west of the Mississippi River) and **St. Joseph's Catholic Church** (Idaho's first Catholic church, established in 1867).

59 and 49 miles northeast of Mountain Home, respectively, have campsites and resort facilities. Several of the Boise National Forest campgrounds, including Elks Flat and Baumgartner, have hot-spring pools.

Pine is at the head of **Anderson Ranch Reservoir Recreational Area**, which surrounds a popular, 17-mile-long fishing and water-skiing lake. There are plenty of boat ramps at Pine; at Fall Creek, halfway down the lake's north shore; and at **Anderson Dam**, which has created this reservoir on the South Fork of the Boise 24 miles above Mountain Home. When built in 1950, 456-foot-tall Anderson Dam was the largest earth-filled dam in the world. ~ 2180 American Legion Boulevard, Mountain Home; 208-587-7961, fax 208-587-9217.

Thirteen miles north of Fall Creek is the trailhead for the **Trinity Mountain Recreation Area**, a scenic region of small al-

DIAMOND LIL'S STEAKHOUSE & SALOON   Return to Main Street and continue north to Wall Street, stopping at Diamond Lil's Steakhouse & Saloon, in the middle of the block. Inside, the Money Bar has a collection of pre-1929 U.S. paper currency laminated to the bar itself. ~ 407 and 409 Main Street; 208-392-4400; www.diamondlils.net.

BOISE BASIN HISTORICAL MUSEUM   Take a left on Wall Street to Montgomery Street. On the corner is the 1867 Boise Basin Historical Museum, built as a post office and used for a while as a Wells Fargo station. The museum recalls 19th-century life in the town through photos and artifacts, and provides guided walking tours (by appointment) of the historic township. Open daily Memorial Day through Labor Day and by appointment. Admission. ~ 503 Montgomery Street, Boise Basin; phone/fax 208-392-4550.

A PEEK AT THE PAST   Surrounding the museum is an array of buildings with peek-in windows. Among them are the adjacent whitewashed **Galbreath House** (1867), the oldest house in Idaho City, and the 1864 **Pest House**, which housed residents with contagious diseases until the 1930s, when it served as a county jail. ~ Montgomery Street. Across from the museum on Wall Street, the **Masonic Temple** was erected in 1865, the oldest lodge of its brotherhood west of the Mississippi. ~ Wall and Montgomery streets. Farther down is the **Idaho Territorial Prison**, Idaho's first territorial penitentiary. ~ Wall Street. From here, you can take Montgomery Street back to the visitors center.

pine lakes surrounding 9451-foot Trinity Mountain. The lakes form small basins, surrounded by large, smooth boulders of granitic rock.

LODGING

Take a **Walk on the Wild Side** when you stay at this remote ranch house turned B&B. Elk and deer graze the inn's five acres of river frontage and guests will find changing activities year-round, from rafting and biking in the summer to skiing and snow shoeing during the winter. The three rooms are appointed with antiques and large beds (two have hot tubs), while the inn combines all the comforts of modern living with the rugged beauty of Idaho's natural wilderness. ~ 68 River Ranch Road, Garden Valley; 208-462-8047; www.wildsidebb.com. moderate to DELUXE.

In Idaho City, the **Idaho City Hotel** offers year-round 19th-century ambience in a two-story country inn. Situated in the heart of the old mining town, the hotel has five quaint rooms with antique furnishings and not-so-antique private bathrooms. ~ 215 Montgomery Street, Idaho City; 208-392-4290, fax 208-392-4505; e-mail idahocityhotel@aol.com. BUDGET.

A One Step Away is a B&B with four cozy rooms decorated with antiques and collectibles; each room has a private bath, TV, microwave, fridge and coffee pot. This hostelry also serves as an antique and collectible store, and is a hub for a train that tours Idaho City's historic district. ~ 112 Cottonwood Street, Idaho City; phone/fax 208-392-4938. MODERATE.

The **Fall Creek Resort,** on Anderson Ranch Reservoir 31 miles from Mountain Home, is a getaway for water-sports enthusiasts and winter snowmobilers. The resort has ten motel units with private baths and a 30-space RV park with hookups. Also at the resort are a marina with boat moorage, a restaurant and lounge, a mini-mart, a hot tub and a workout area. ~ 2147 Fall Creek Road, Fall Creek; 208-653-2242, fax 208-653-2646; www.fall creekresort.net. MODERATE.

DINING

The **Long Branch Saloon,** near the Payette River on the main highway from Boise to McCall, offers breakfast, dinners of hearty steaks and fried chicken, and juicy burgers and other sandwiches at midday, in a ranch-style atmosphere. ~ Route 55, Horseshoe Bend; 208-793-2762. MODERATE TO DELUXE.

Calamity Jayne's is one of the Boise Basin's better dining options. Re-creating the atmosphere of a miners' cookhouse, the small café serves big helpings of steak and eggs in the morning, burgers and deli-style sandwiches (including several vegetarian choices) in the afternoon. They also have a kids menu and a low-carb menu. No dinner. ~ 201 Main Street, Idaho City; 208-392-4453. BUDGET.

AUTHOR FAVORITE

The hefty steaks at **Diamond Lil's Steakhouse & Saloon** are generous to a fault, but it's the original decor that keeps me coming back. Who knew that old-time U.S. currency—plastered all over this restaurant—could be so inventive and strange? A rustic relic of the gold-rush days, Diamond Lil's has a lively bar and a spacious restaurant serving beef, pork and chicken, as well fresh fish in season. Closed Monday and Tuesday from Labor Day to Memorial Day. ~ 407 and 409 Main Street, Idaho City; 208-392-4400; www.diamondlils.net, e-mail hcall@qwest. net. MODERATE TO ULTRA-DELUXE.

A few miles north of Horseshoe Bend, **Cooper's Bean Town** fea- **SHOPPING**
tures the work of master woodcarver Jon Cooper, from chain-
saw art down to finely detailed carvings. This is also a good place ◄ *HIDDEN*
to look for paintings, sculptures and American Indian crafts. ~
Route 55, Gardena; 208-793-2387.

The **Starlight Mountain Theatre** company performs musicals **NIGHTLIFE**
every summer in their outdoor playhouse. On Thursday, Friday
and Saturday nights, they offer dinner and a show, but reservations
are required. Don't forget to bring a sweater because the mountain
air can get nippy. ~ 850 South Middle Fork Road, Garden Valley;
208-462-5523; www.starlightmountaintheatre.com.

There's not a lot happening after dark, but you can find live
rock, Western and the like most weekends at **Harley's Pub**. ~ 305
West Main Street, Idaho City; 208-392-6023.

BOISE NATIONAL FOREST 🚶 🚲 🐎 ✈ 🏠 ⛵ 🚤 � **PARKS**
Rugged mountains, covered with forests of pine, fir and spruce
and sliced by deep river canyons, make up most of this 2.6-million-
acre plot of federal land north and east of Boise. Ranging in elevation from 2600 feet to more than 9800 feet, the national forest
contains numerous 19th-century mining towns, including Idaho
City and Atlanta; and one of Idaho's finest whitewater-rafting
rivers, the South Fork of the Payette. The forest has more than
1300 miles of backcountry trails, more than 250 lakes and reservoirs, and some 7600 miles of rivers and streams. There are designated beaches at some reservoirs and lakes. There's also good
trout fishing, especially in the South and Middle Forks of the Boise
and Payette rivers, and in Anderson Ranch and Arrowrock reservoirs. Facilities include picnic tables, restrooms, boat rentals,
marinas and several resorts. ~ One route to the forest is Route 21
northeast from Boise through Idaho City and Lowman. To reach
Arrowrock Reservoir, take Forest Road 268 (Middle Fork Road)
east off Route 21, east of Boise. To reach Anderson Ranch Reservoir, take Forest Road 134 (Anderson Dam Road) or Route 61
(Louise Creek Road) north off Route 20, northeast of Mountain
Home. To reach Warm Lake, take Forest Road 22 (Warm Lake
Road) east off Route 55 from Cascade. To reach Ten Mile Campground, follow Route 21 ten miles north of Idaho City and you'll
see a sign. To reach Bald Mountain Campground, turn right on
Forest Service Road 304 one mile north of Idaho City. Bear right
at the fork and continue about nine miles to the campground;
208-373-4007, fax 208-373-4111; www.fs.fed.us/r4/boise.

▲ There are 986 RV/tent units in over 70 campgrounds (no
hookups); no charge to $10 per night. Most campgrounds are
open mid-May through September. In addition, 12 rustic cabins—

some summer only, some winter only—accommodate from two to six people for $30 to $45 per night. One good campground that's easily accessible from Idaho City is Ten Mile Campground: There are ten RV/tent sites plus four for tents only; $10 single and $20 double per night). For easy access to hiking trails, try Bald Mountain Campground: There are three tent sites; no charge. Reservations: 877-444-6777; www.reserveusa.com.

Mountain Home and Owyhee County

Mountain Home may seem misnamed. Indeed, the city of 7500 people—many of whom live here because of its proximity to a major air-force base—spreads across a flat tract of high desert, between the Rocky Mountain foothills and the Snake River but not actually a part of either.

For Idaho visitors, Mountain Home is of special interest as a gateway. To the southeast, on the middle Snake River, are unique state parks commemorating a key ford on the Oregon Trail and the tallest sand dunes on the North American continent. To the south and southwest are the vast open spaces of Owyhee County, where raptors outnumber human residents and Idaho's best-preserved 19th-century mining town nestles in a high-mountain dell.

For all their extremes of temperature and topography, the Owyhees are a place of great though subtle beauty: patterns of colored soils, delicate and complementary olive hues of sage, rabbit brush and bitter brush. In spring, meadows and hillsides are blanketed with yellow balsam root, pink-verged primrose and tiny wildflowers of almost every shade.

SIGHTS

Mountain Home, located 48 miles southeast of Boise via Route 84, is of principal importance for its **Mountain Home Air Force Base**, where the United States has its first and only air expeditionary composite wing—which can be deployed anywhere in the world on a moment's notice. Unfortunately, only those accompanied by military personnel are allowed on base. ~ Route 67, Mountain Home; 208-828-6800, fax 208-828-4205.

For history buffs, the **Elmore County Historical Society Museum** displays artifacts of Chinese miners and early American Indian residents, as well as farming tools and memorabilia of turn-of-the-20th-century pioneers. Closed Sunday. ~ 180 South 3rd Street East, Mountain Home; 208-587-2104.

Mountain Home lies near the original route of the Oregon Trail. **Glenns Ferry**, 29 miles east off Route 84, is directly on it. In fact, early pioneers established their main ford of the Snake River here, where three islets broke the river's flow into smaller, more fordable channels. The crossing was a risky but preferable alternative to continuing on a longer, drier route along the edge of the Owyhee Plateau. It wasn't abandoned until a ferry was built two miles upriver in 1869. Each August, that frequently made crossing is re-enacted at **Three Island Crossing State Park**. There's an Oregon Trail interpretive center as well as a campground. ~ West Madison Street, Glenns Ferry; 208-366-2394, fax 208-366-7913; e-mail thr@idpr.id.state.us.

Located at the western extremity of the Magic Valley agricultural district (centered on Twin Falls, 50 miles east), Glenns Ferry boasts a winery, **Carmela Vineyards**. Open daily for tastings and

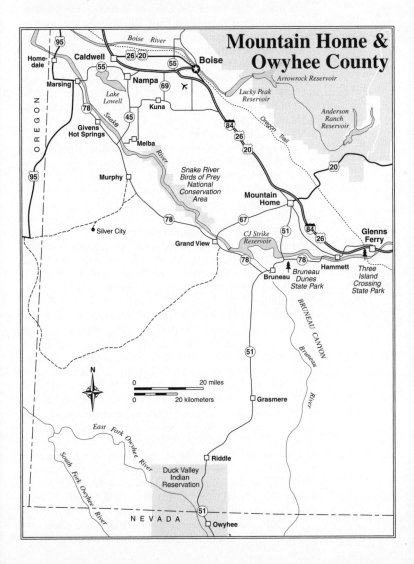

Mountain Home & Owyhee County

tours by appointment. ~ Madison Avenue, Glenns Ferry; 208-366-2313, fax 208-366-2458; e-mail carmelawinery@aol.com.

There's also the **Glenns Ferry Historical Museum**, lodged in a stone schoolhouse that dates from 1909. The museum features artifacts from the Oregon Trail and from the region's more recent ranching history. Open weekends only. ~ 211 West Cleveland Street, Glenns Ferry.

West of Glenns Ferry and south of Mountain Home, on the south side of the Snake River, is one of Idaho's unique scenic attractions: **Bruneau Dunes State Park**. This desert environment includes the largest single-structured sand dunes in North America: 470 feet high and about one square mile at their base. Probably created by the Bonneville Flood of 15,000 years ago, the dunes form at the center of a semicircular natural basin just south of the Snake River; all other dunes on this continent form at the edge of basins. The on-site observatory (fee) is open Friday and Saturday. ~ Route 78, Bruneau; 208-366-7919, fax 208-366-2844; e-mail bru@idpr.state.id.us.

Bruneau Dunes is flanked by the **Snake River Birds of Prey National Conservation Area**, home to the world's largest concentration of nesting eagles (see "An Eagle's-eye View of the Snake" in this chapter).

The village of Bruneau, seven miles southwest of the dunes on Route 51/78, is a gateway to two more scenic attractions. Eighteen miles southeast of the community, an overlook on the Bruneau River gives a dramatic look at the north end of **Bruneau Canyon**, a 60-mile-long gorge whose sheer walls drop between 800 and 1200 feet down to the river's surface. Reach the overlook via Hot Springs and Clover Three Creek roads, both unsurfaced.

Northwest of Bruneau on the Snake and Bruneau rivers is earth-filled, 132-foot-high **C. J. Strike Reservoir**, an 8000-acre, horseshoe-shaped lake surrounded by a wildlife management area; the dam was constructed in 1952. There are nine campgrounds (free) around the shore of the reservoir, five of them with boat ramps for trout and bass anglers. ~ River Road, Grand View; 208-834-2295, fax 208-388-6932.

Bruneau is a good launch pad for exploring **Owyhee County**, Idaho's southernmost county. Though it covers five million acres, it has only about 11,000 residents. Expect to see vast ranchlands, mining ghost towns and plenty of rugged and barren mountain and canyon land. Paved roads and tourist services are few and far between. Good maps—the best can be found at the **Bureau of Land Management**—are a must. Closed weekends. ~ 1387 South Vinnell Way, Boise; 208-373-4039, fax 208-373-3890; www.id.blm.gov.

The high, rolling tablelands—4000 to 5000 feet in elevation—that make up most of this remote area are cut through by the

An Eagle's-eye View of the Snake

South of Boise, the Snake River has scoured a deep trough through the Owyhee Plateau. Basalt cliffs tower hundreds of feet above the river. Prevailing canyon winds create updrafts for the world's largest concentration of nesting eagles, hawks, owls and falcons. In 1993, Congress designated this BLM area the **Snake River Birds of Prey National Conservation Area**. Encompassing 483,000 acres of public land for 81 miles along the Snake River, the preserve is home to more than 800 pairs of raptors.

Canyon crevices and ledges provide ideal shelter for the birds' nests, which they build each spring when they mate and raise their young. From their aeries, the birds soar on warm canyon winds over the surrounding plateau, feeding on ground squirrels, jackrabbits and other rodents.

Fifteen species of raptors call this section of the Snake River their home, including the golden eagle, prairie falcon, northern harrier, turkey vulture and American kestrel. Nine migratory species also make lengthy visits, among them the bald eagle, osprey and peregrine falcon.

The preserve's nearest boundary to Boise is 15 miles southwest of the capital. By road, there are good viewing spots at **Dedication Point** (Swan Falls Road), 23 miles from Boise via Route 84 Exit 44, and at **Celebration Park** (Can-Ada Road), 36 miles from Boise via Route 84 Exit 38. You'll see the greatest number of birds between mid-March and the end of June, especially in late spring.

The best way to view the Birds of Prey Area is by boat or raft down the Snake. Floaters can put in at the Swan Falls Dam and take out ten miles later at Celebration Park after a midway stop to study ancient petroglyphs on 70 boulders at Wees Bar, accessible only by river.

A good introduction to the national conservation area, though administratively unrelated, is the **World Center for Birds of Prey**, six miles south of Boise off Route 84 via South Cole Road. Operated by the conservationist Peregrine Fund, the center is the world's largest and most sophisticated private facility for raptor breeding, research and education. More than 4000 falcons, hawks, eagles and owls of 22 species have been hatched, nurtured and released worldwide by the center since its establishment in 1984. The interpretive center has presentations featuring live birds of prey as well as multimedia exhibits on ecology, conservation and biology. Admission. ~ 5668 West Flying Hawk Lane, Boise; 208-362-8687, fax 208-362-2376; www.peregrinefund.org, e-mail tpf@peregrinefund.org.

Owyhee River and its forks. In places the rivers have carved vertical canyons nearly 1000 feet deep. Bighorn sheep can be seen here, dancing on wafer-thin ledges invisible to our eyes. These sheep are part of a breeding population often transplanted elsewhere in the country where native herds have shrunk or been pressured out of existence.

A good gravel road between Grandview and Jordan Valley, Oregon, loops through this country. Many side roads, available to the adventurous, are poorly marked. Be forewarned that the Owyhee country is so wide and empty that even search-and-rescue teams have become disoriented—that is to say, lost.

From Bruneau, Route 51 branches south across the Great Basin, passing through the **Duck Valley Indian Reservation** on the Nevada border, 71 miles distant, and continuing to Elko, Nevada. The 458-square-mile reservation is home to about 900 Sho-Pai natives, a combined tribe of Western Shoshones and Northern Paiutes.

Northwest of Bruneau, Route 78 follows the Snake River through the county's population belt, such as it is. The county seat of Murphy 47 miles from Bruneau and 45 miles south of Boise, was once the largest livestock-shipping point in the Pacific Northwest. Its excellent **Owyhee County Historical Society and Museum** features a homesteader's cabin with its kitchen still intact, an old schoolhouse and a railroad depot, a reconstructed mining stamp mill with mine equipment, farm machinery and a research library. On the first weekend of June, they hold their annual Outpost Days, a museum fundraiser with barbecue, and vendors. Closed Sunday and Monday. ~ 17085 Bassey Street, Murphy; 208-495-2319; www.owyheecounty.net/museum.

HIDDEN ►   The county's highlight is **Silver City**, Idaho's best-preserved ghost town. The 23-mile dirt Silver City Road turns west off Route 78 about five miles southeast of Murphy; it is normally open from late May to mid-October but is subject to closure because of bad weather. Inquire locally before tackling this route.

AUTHOR FAVORITE

I'll admit to a sort of guilty pleasure at the slightly hokey but genuinely fun historical re-enactment of crossing the Snake River on covered wagons, which takes place each August at **Three Island Crossing State Park**. You'll have to use your imagination the rest of the year, though the 150-year-old wagon ruts still there help identify the pioneers' route across the three gravel bars that broke the river's flow into channels. See pages 79, 84 for more information.

Between 1863, when the first gold was mined here, and 1942, when World War II mining restrictions put the final whammy on a dying community, some $40 million in gold and silver was taken from the Silver City district. Forty wood-frame buildings, in various stages of disrepair, still stand for curious visitors to explore; all buildings are privately owned. Of special note are the 1866 Idaho Hotel and the 1898 Our Lady of Tears Catholic Church. Before entering any, however, contact the folks at the Idaho Hotel (208-583-4104).

Eighteen miles northwest of Murphy is **Givens Hot Springs**, a travelers' rest stop for at least 1200 years. A commercial operation was established here in 1881 by Oregon Trail pioneers. Today, the small resort, located by the Snake River, has an indoor hot-spring swimming pool (swimsuit and towel rentals available), camping and recreational facilities, and a picnic area. Budget-priced rustic cabins dating back to the 1940s can be rented. Fee. ~ Route 78, Marsing; 208-495-2000, fax 208-286-9900; www.givenshotsprings.com, e-mail givenshotsprings@mindspring.com.

The most northwesterly corner of Owyhee County boasts its densest population around the Treasure Valley farming communities of Marsing and Homedale. Highways head back to Boise from here, via Caldwell and Nampa.

LODGING

Mountain Home's finest lodging is the **Best Western Foothills Motor Inn**, located beside the city's main freeway exit. The 76 rooms and suites are clean and comfortable. An outdoor waterfall swimming pool is open May to October, while an indoor hot tub is especially popular with winter travelers. ~ 1080 Route 20, Mountain Home; 208-587-8477, 800-604-8477, fax 208-587-5774; www.bestwestern.com/foothillsmotorinn. MODERATE.

Where the road to Mountain Home Air Force Base meets Route 30 East, you'll find the **Hi Lander Motel**. This two-story motel has 34 rooms with full baths, including four kitchen units. Amenities include a swimming pool. ~ 615 South 3rd Street West, Mountain Home; 208-587-3311. BUDGET.

Visitors to Three Island Crossing State Park can rest their heads at the **Redford Motel**. The 11 rooms of this quaint, privately owned motel have standard facilities and amenities; pets are welcomed. A restaurant and a mini-mart are nearby. ~ 521 West 1st Avenue, Glenns Ferry; 208-366-2421, fax 208-366-7171. BUDGET.

The **Idaho Hotel** is one of the few signs of life in the ghost town of Silver City. Its 18 rooms share baths and have minimal furnishings, but it has a restaurant and lounge on the ground floor. The challenging gravel and rock road to Silver City, 28 miles southwest of Murphy, is normally open from late May to mid-October. ~ Jordan Street, Silver City; 208-583-4104. MODERATE TO ULTRA-DELUXE.

DINING   With air force personnel from all over the nation based in Mountain Home, the town offers all manner of cuisine, from Italian to Korean. But for old-fashioned Southern cooking, the **Top Hat** is a city favorite. The menu delivers everything from catfish to steaks and prawns. Closed Sunday. ~ 145 North 2nd Street East, Mountain Home; 208-587-9223. BUDGET TO MODERATE.

Another outpost of fine dining is the **Sandbar River House**, with a deck overlooking the Snake River 13 miles southwest of Caldwell. Steak and seafood dishes dominate at this casual spot, which offers a special menu for seniors. Reservations recommended. Closed Monday. ~ 18 East Sandbar, Marsing; 208-896-4124. DELUXE.

PARKS   **THREE ISLAND CROSSING STATE PARK** 🏃 🚴 ⛵ One of the principal Snake River crossings on the Oregon Trail is commemorated here. Anglers can fish for trout, catfish and other species in the Snake River. Facilities include picnic tables, restrooms and an interpretive center. Day-use fee, $4. ~ From downtown Glenns Ferry, one mile off Route 84 southeast of Mountain Home, take Commercial Street south about a mile, then Madison Avenue west for about two miles; 208-366-2394, fax 208-366-2060; e-mail thr@idpr.id.state.us.

▲ There are 101 sites, all with electricity and water for RVs; $20 per night. Eight cabins also available; $50 per night.

Owyhee County is named for three natives of the Hawaiian Islands (then sometimes known as "Owyhee") who were lost in this wild region during an 1819 fur-trapping expedition.

BRUNEAU DUNES STATE PARK 🏃 🐎 ⛵ Situated about 20 miles southeast of Mountain Home, this unique park is home to reptiles, raptors and waterfowl. Trails circle the two main dunes and the interconnected ponds at their base. Tubing is popular here and you may fish for bass and bluegill in the park lakes. There are picnic tables, restrooms and a visitors center. Day-use fee, $4. ~ From Route 84 at Mountain Home, take Route 51 south 16 miles, then Route 78 east two miles. From Route 84 at Hammett (20 miles east of Mountain Home), take Route 78 west 18 miles; 208-366-7919, fax 208-366-2844; e-mail bru@idpr.state.id.us.

▲ There are 98 RV/tent sites, 82 of them with RV hookups. Tent sites are $12 per night, RV sites $16.

Outdoor Adventures

FISHING   Trout—rainbow, cutthroat, brook and brown in that order—are caught in southwestern Idaho. Look to any fork or tributary of the Boise River except Mores Creek, which has been poisoned by mine tailings from the early camps in and around Idaho City. Locals will regale you with fish tales of the South Fork Boise, a blue-ribbon wild trout stream just over an hour from downtown, but it can be crowded and the fish are well educated.

Lake Lowell, south of Nampa, is a favorite destination for anglers seeking rainbow trout, smallmouth and largemouth bass, crappie, perch, bluegill and catfish. For information and equipment, visit **Howard's Tackle Shoppe**. ~ 1707 Garrity Boulevard, Nampa; 208-465-0946; www.howardstackleshoppe.com.

Anderson Ranch Reservoir is a good place to find kokanee. C. J. Strike Reservoir near Mountain Home is excellent for trout. The Bruneau and Owyhee rivers boast trophy-size rainbow trout. There are largemouth bass and bluegill in the Bruneau Lakes at Bruneau Dunes State Park. Bring your fishing supplies with you, since there are no places to rent them in this area.

The South Fork of the Payette, one of America's greatest whitewater-rafting rivers, runs through this area. South of the Snake, the infrequently visited Owyhee and Bruneau desert rivers promise steep canyon vistas, thrilling whitewater and excellent wildlife viewing.

RIVER RUNNING

Flatwater sections of the Snake River are ideal for canoeing and birding. The area both up- and downstream of Swan Falls Dam is especially recommended. American Indian petroglyphs can be seen at Wees Bar, about three miles downriver from the dam on the south bank. Please exercise restraint; do not touch or deface these gifts from Idaho's human past so that others may enjoy them, too.

For information on guided trips in southwestern Idaho and elsewhere in the state, contact the **Idaho Outfitters and Guides Association**. ~ 711 North 5th Street, Boise; 208-342-1438; www.ioga.org. **Birds of Prey Expeditions** offers trips through the Snake River and the Birds of Prey National Conservation Area. ~ 4519 North Mountain View Drive, Boise; 208-327-8903; e-mail birdsofprey@cable.net.

Payette River trips, less than an hour's drive north of Boise, draw hundreds of rafters on any given weekend day from May through September. The Payette and its several forks are a virtual finishing school for river-running skills. Beginners develop fundamentals on the main Payette below the confluence of the North and South forks near the town of Banks. Indeed, the North Fork of the Payette immediately above Banks is ranked among the world's finest advanced kayak runs. Intermediates can try the Cabarton run on the upper North Fork, and advanced-intermediates on the lower South Fork with its intimidating Staircase Rapid. Advanced boaters graduate to the remote South Fork Canyon with its string of Class IV rapids and the impressive—and unrunnable—Big Falls, a 40-foot waterfall. The lower North Fork Payette is for experts only, or for those tired of living: most of the run is rated Class V and some Class VI. But be advised that even the main Payette can flip an unwary or unprepared boater. Largest of several outfitters is the **Cascade Raft and Kayak**, with 25 full-time river guides available. April through September. ~ Route 55, Horseshoe Bend; 208-793-2221, 800-292-7238; www.cascaderaft.com. Other outfitters include the **Bear Valley River Company** (May through September). ~ Route 55, Banks; 208-793-2272, 800-235-2327; www.float4fun.com. You may also contact the **Headwaters River Company**(May through September). ~ Route 55, Banks; 208-793-2348, 800-800-7238; www.idaho rivertours.com.

Bruneau Dunes State Park preserves the tallest free-standing sand dunes (470 feet) in North America.

BOATING

One of the region's best-loved destinations for boating and water sports is Anderson Ranch Reservoir, northeast of Mountain Home.

Other popular bodies of water for boating are Lake Lowell, south of Nampa; Black Canyon Reservoir, near Emmett; Dead-wood Reservoir, north of Garden Valley; and C. J. Strike Reservoir, south of Mountain Home.

SKIING

The nearest alpine ski resorts to the Nampa–Caldwell area are **Bogus Basin**, near Boise (Chapter Two) and **Brandage Mountain**, near McCall (Chapter Nine). Mountain Home–area skiers head to **Sun Valley** or **Soldier Mountain** (Chapter Eight).

Popular Park 'n' Ski cross-country areas are **Whoop-Um-Up**, **Gold Fork** and **Banner Ridge**, 18, 20 and 24 miles northeast of Idaho City on Route 21. Banner Ridge has the longest network of trails, 44 kilometers. Call the **Idaho Department of Parks and Recreation** for more information. ~ 208-334-4199, fax 208-334-3741; www.idahoparks.org.

Ski Rentals Downhill equipment, cross-country skis and snow-boards are available at **Gart Sports** in Boise. ~ 1301 North Milwaukee Avenue; 208-378-9590; www.gartsports.com.

GOLF

Though golf is not the main sport in the area, if you'd like to tee off, public links include the 18-hole **Centennial Golf Course**. ~ 2600 Centennial Drive, Nampa; 208-467-3011; www.golfcenten nial.com. Not far away are the 27 holes of **Ridgecrest Golf Club**. ~ 3730 Ridgecrest Drive, Nampa; 208-468-9073; www.ridgecrest golf.com. **Purple Sage Golf Course** is also open to the public with 18 holes. ~ 15192 Purple Sage Road, Caldwell; 208-459-2223. **Scotch Pines Golf Course** also has 18 holes. ~ 10610 Scotch Pines Road, Payette; 208-642-1829. Monday through Friday you may visit the semiprivate **Terrace Lakes Golf Course**. ~ 101 Holiday Drive, Garden Valley; 208-462-3250; www.terracelakes.com. **Silver Sage Golf Course** is popular with servicemen. ~ Airbase Road, Mountain Home; 208-828-6151.

If you want to serve up some fun in Nampa, contact **Nampa Parks & Recreation.** ~ 131 Constitution Way, Nampa; 208-465-2215. In Caldwell, contact **Caldwell Parks & Recreation.** ~ 618 Irving Street, Caldwell; 208-455-3060.

TENNIS

Private tennis clubs in the region include the **River City Racquet Club,** with outdoor and indoor courts. ~ 63 South Midland Boulevard, Nampa; 208-466-2284.

Pack trips are a great way to really explore the wilderness. On the west side of the Sawtooth National Recreation Area, **Sawtooth Wilderness Outfitters** plans two- to ten-day guided pack trips and llama treks anywhere in the Sawtooth Wilderness. ~ P.O. Box 81, Garden Valley, ID 83622; 208-462-3416 in winter, 208-259-3408 in summer; www.sawtoothadventures.com.

PACK TRIPS & LLAMA TREKS

Idaho is a mountain biker's paradise. It's arguable that more roads in Idaho and southwestern Idaho are unpaved than paved. Most any of them can serve as a starting point for mountain biking. The best resource for riders at all levels is *Mountain Biking in Southwest Idaho,* by Stephen Stuebner and Stephen Phipps.

BIKING

The **Oregon Trail**—yes, the pioneer trail—offers a scenic ride across the sage hills southeast of Boise. Begin at the Bonneville Point interpretive area, which can be reached via the Blacks Creek exit on Route 84 about ten miles east of town. Turn left from the off-ramp, traveling underneath the interstate. After about a mile and a half you will see a small, brown Historical Site sign leading you up a gravel road angling off to the left. Bonneville Point is at this road's end; a few moments reading the history of the trail in this area is well spent. The trail itself tracks east and west and lies just north of the structure. It is clearly marked. The truly adventurous can follow its century-old ruts four or five miles to the Boise River where a few detours down jeep trails will connect you with the Boise River Greenbelt.

Leslie Gulch (4 miles), though it is just across the Oregon border, offers a pleasant ride through some of the Owyhee's most spectacular rock formations. The basic ride is some four downhill miles to the Owyhee Reservoir and back again. You will see strangely sculpted and extravagantly colored desert rock. Eagles, red-tailed hawks, turkey vultures and other raptors are frequently sighted and, occasionally, bighorn sheep. Two miles west of Marsing, pick up Route 95 and drive south approximately 25 miles to the Leslie Gulch turnoff. Follow signs.

An adventurous trip in this area, the **Pilot's Peak Lookout Trail** (4.5 miles) offers wide views of the surrounding mountains including the Sawtooth Range. Drive to Mores Creek Summit north of Idaho City on Route 21 and park in the large area on the road's right side. The trail begins across the highway and heads up. When you gain the ridge after about four miles, follow around to the right and continue up another quarter-mile to the fire lookout.

A popular off-the-pavement trail is the **Swan Falls Dam** road through a corner of the Snake River Birds of Prey National Conservation Area, a 45-minute drive from Boise south of Kuna.

Bike Rentals   The closest rental shops are in Boise. However, there are some full-service bike shops that sell and repair bicycles. In Nampa, try **Cafferty's Cyclery**. Closed Sunday. ~ 220 12th Avenue South; 208-466-3647. **Chain Reaction** is a good option in Caldwell. ~ 705 Main Street; 208-459-9197.

HIKING   The area's numerous parks, forests and wilderness areas in Southwestern Idaho offer a wide range of hiking trails. All distances listed for hiking trails are one way unless otherwise noted.

Crooked River Trail (9.5 miles) descends for six and a half miles into the steep and narrow river canyon, then ascends rapidly. This Boise National Forest hike is moderately difficult. The trailhead is on Forest Road 384 (Crooked River Road), just off Route 21 between Idaho City and Lowman; it ends on Forest Road 327 (North Fork Road).

Clear Creek Trail (2 miles) climbs a ridge northeast of Lowman (off Forest Roads 582 and 515) through fir forest and meadows woven with streams. The ascent is gradual, so this is a good one for kids.

Camp Creek Trail (5.7 miles) offers wonderful views across Anderson Ranch Reservoir and the hamlets of Pine and Featherville on the South Fork of the Boise River. This moderately difficult trail, which is open to motorized vehicles, climbs a steep ridge off Lester Creek Road (Forest Road 128) in the Anderson Ranch Reservoir Recreation Area.

Trinity Lakes Trail (3 miles) takes in a dozen or more small alpine lakes nestled at the foot of 9451-foot Trinity Mountain, itself topped by a lookout accessible by four-wheel-drive vehicle. Take Fall Creek Road (Forest Road 129) north from Anderson Dam, off Route 20.

Bruneau Dunes Trail (5-mile loop) in Bruneau Dunes State Park begins and ends at the park visitors center, looping around the ancient 470-foot dunes and the ponds at their base.

South of Kuna in the Birds of Prey Area, there are several hikes that begin near Swan Falls Dam. Park below the dam and follow the roads and trails along the north shore, or drive a mile upriver and park by an old corral. **Swan Falls Dam Hike** (2.5 miles) leads upstream beyond the closed gate leads to lovely, elevated views of the river and to a patch of Nature Conservancy wetland.

Cross the Swan Falls Dam spillway, if it is open, and follow the **Wees Bar Hike** (3 miles) downstream to Wees Bar. Petroglyphs can be seen here, fragile gifts from the area's early residents. Please do not touch or mar these drawings in any way so that others may enjoy them after you. If the spillway is closed, as it sometimes is, Wees Bar is accessible only by water (see "River Running" above).

Transportation

Route 84 crosses southwestern Idaho diagonally from west to east, providing the major thoroughfare of travel. **Route 21** heads northeast from Boise to Idaho City and Lowman. **Route 55** heads north through Horseshoe Bend and Banks. **Route 51** leads south from Mountain Home, and hooks up with **Route 78**, which follows the Snake River northwest to meet up with Route 55 at Marsing.

CAR

Many major airlines fly into **Boise Airport**, the region's closest airport. See Chapter Two for more information. There are private airports in Nampa, Caldwell and Mountain Home.

AIR

Greyhound Bus Lines stops in Nampa and Caldwell, as well as Mountain Home. ~ 800-231-2222; www.greyhound.com. There is a bus terminal in Nampa. ~ 3226 Garrity Boulevard; 208-468-8910. There is also one in Caldwell. ~ 212 South 4th Street; 208-459-2816.

BUS

Several firms have agencies in the Treasure Valley, including **Enterprise Rent A Car**. ~ 407 Caldwell Boulevard, Nampa; 800-325-8007.

CAR RENTALS

Treasure Valley Transit operates a limited hourly route Monday through Friday in Nampa and Caldwell. They also offer door-to-door service in both towns; call ahead to schedule. ~ 3515-A Garrity Boulevard, Nampa; 208-465-6411.

PUBLIC TRANSIT

In the Treasure Valley, call **Stop-N-Go Taxi Service**. ~ 208-466-4999 in Nampa, 208-459-4999 in Caldwell.

TAXIS

FOUR

Twin Falls and South Central Idaho

 South Central Idaho is often called the "Middle Snake," and here is where the great river is at its best. Midway between Pocatello and Boise, slowed by a series of dams, it patiently irrigates the state's famous fields of potatoes and forage crops before sprinting northwesterly toward the Oregon border and Hells Canyon.

En route, like a master illusionist, the river manifests its own magic. Here you'll find a broad waterfall, higher than Niagara, and sheer canyon walls from which burst thousands of underground springs. And the Snake is nature's history book. There are fossil remains of the Hagerman horse, a zebralike Pliocene ancestor of the modern steed, and wagon ruts from the mid-19th-century Oregon Trail, which traced the banks of the river for hundreds of miles.

The vast Snake River Plain owes its fertility to prehistoric Lakes Idaho and Bonneville, both of them enormous inland seas. Lake Idaho, geologists say, covered this region between 2.5 and 8 million years ago; it left behind rich silt deposits and a meandering Snake River. Lake Bonneville, which stretched across western Utah and neighboring states beginning about 1.5 million years ago, burst its walls south of modern Pocatello toward the end of the Pleistocene era (about 15,000 years ago) and created a flood of biblical scale. Discharging waters like a faster-flowing Amazon (at 15 million cubic feet per second), the Bonneville Flood—estimated to have been 300 feet deep in places—swept across the riverbed of old Lake Idaho, scouring the Snake River Canyon and Hells Canyon nearly to their present depths and eventually finding its way down the Columbia River Gorge to the Pacific Ocean.

Volcanic soils make the Snake River Plain fertile. North of the river, about 15 million years ago, fiery lava began seeping through cracks in the earth's crust; when it cooled, it left the many oddly shaped rock formations evident today. There was intense volcanic activity as recently as 2000 years ago northeast of Rupert. Today, these porous lava beds act as a deep aquifer that captures the entire flow of the Lost River drainage from Idaho's central mountains. The streams disappear near the nuclear chimneys of the Idaho National Engineering Laboratory and reemerge 100 miles distant (and, according to geologists, up to 1000 years later) in the Snake's Hagerman Valley.

The area's first permanent inhabitants arrived here perhaps 16,000 years ago. They survived on the territory's abundant game, including the now-extinct mastodon and saber-toothed tigers. To the west, near Hagerman, archaeologists have turned up a trove of skeletons of a small, zebralike Pliocene horse extinct for three million years and found nowhere else.

At the close of the 19th century the federal government backed large irrigation schemes throughout the West. Near Twin Falls, that effort resulted in the construction of Milner Dam. In effect, the region was open for business. To prepare the land for plowing, farmers hitched horse teams to the ends of long railroad irons and dragged them across the sage desert, tearing out all vegetation in their path. Milner Dam opened almost a quarter-million acres that today grow alfalfa, feed and malt barleys, garden bean seed, sugar beets and, as the state license plate proclaims, Idaho's famous potatoes.

Twin Falls Area

Twin Falls—"Twin" to locals—is poised a stone's throw from the Snake River Canyon's south rim. Now a city of 30,000, it was founded in 1904 and named for a waterfall split by a large rock outcrop about six miles east of town. Ironically, the great Shoshone Falls are both larger and closer to the community; one wonders if city founders pondered the proximity of two spectacular "twin" falls in choosing a name.

While Twin has a distinctly rural flavor, its cultural evolution revolves around the College of Southern Idaho. The two-year institution offers museums, a planetarium, a fine auditorium and a library. Downtown Twin Falls has a homey charm that would make small-town residents from anywhere in the country feel immediately at ease.

Twin is situated near the empty northeast corner of Nevada, which has been measured as having the nation's cleanest air. It gives Twin and the surrounding Magic Valley crystal-clear and starry nights. The moon, when full, simply jumps out of the sky.

SIGHTS

Most folks approach the town from the north off Route 84, via Route 93 across the 1500-foot-long **Perrine Bridge**. The world's highest bridge when it opened in 1927, it was replaced in 1976 but still offers a breathtaking view from 486 feet above the Snake River Canyon.

At the south end of the bridge is the **Buzz Langdon Visitors Center**. Pedestrian walkways and overlooks afford bird's-eye scrutiny of the lush canyon floor, including golf courses and the site of a ramp from which daredevil Evel Knievel attempted to jump the canyon on a rocket-powered motorcycle in 1974. (He failed but parachuted to safety.) Closed mid-October to mid-March. ~ Route

93 North; 208-733-3974, 800-255-8946, fax 208-733-9216; e-mail info@twinfallschamber.com.

Downtown Twin Falls nestles on the north side of Rock Creek, about three miles south of the Snake River Canyon. The town

HIDDEN ► has two interesting small museums. The **Herrett Center for Arts and Science**, located at the College of Southern Idaho, exhibits more than 18,000 artifacts ranging from American Indian and pre-Columbian Maya to modern Hopi. It also features rotating art and anthropology displays. The art gallery features six yearly exhibits of contemporary art by local and regional artists. Attached to the museum is the **Faulkner Planetarium**, which opened in 1995 as one of the largest planetariums in the Pacific Northwest. Summer matinee and evening shows, presented on a 50-foot screen, focus on such recent phenomena as the Hale-Bopp comet and the Hubbell Telescope. Closed Sunday and Monday. Admission to planetarium. ~ 315 Falls Avenue, Twin Falls; 208-732-6655, fax 208-736-4712; www.csi.edu/herrett, e-mail herrett@csi.edu.

The **Twin Falls County Historical Museum**, in a 1914 pioneer school five miles west of downtown, displays some of the state's oldest farm equipment such as a horse-powered sagegrubber. Closed Sunday through Tuesday. ~ Route 30 West, Twin Falls; 208-736-4675.

The city took its name from the impressive but often over-looked **Twin Falls** on the Snake River about six miles east of the Perrine Bridge. There's an **overlook** a mile north of Falls Avenue East. The falls are about 70 feet high and 50 feet across during most of the year; in winter and spring they're usually bigger. ~ 3500 East Road, Kimberly; 208-423-4223.

The Twin Falls might be due more acclaim were they not so near **Shoshone Falls**, among the most impressive cataracts in the western United States. Plummeting 212 feet—52 feet more than famed Niagara Falls—Shoshone Falls pour massive amounts of Snake River water over a 1000-foot-wide, horseshoe-shaped basalt rock face in spring. At other times, when irrigation canals have diverted the river's flow, visitors may see only a trickle of water passing the powerhouse at the head of the falls. But the lava-walled canyon scene remains spectacular. Admission. ~ 3300 East Road, Twin Falls; 208-736-2265, fax 208-736-1548; www.tfid.org.

For a taste of Idaho's pioneer past, drive 14 miles southeast from Twin Falls, via the community of Hansen and Rock Creek Road, to the **Stricker Ranch**. During the stagecoach days between 1865 (the end of the Civil War) and 1883 (the completion of the Oregon Short Line Railroad), the Rock Creek Stage Station was the only sign of Western settlement between Fort Hall (near modern Pocatello) and Fort Boise. A general store next to the stage station was bought by rancher Herman Stricker in 1876. By the

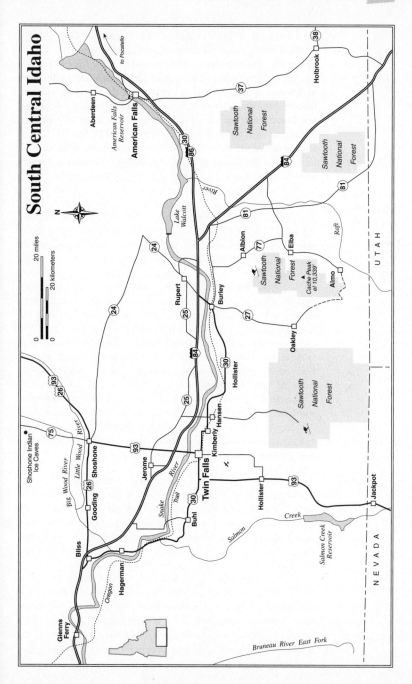

South Central Idaho

N

20 miles

0

20 kilometers

0

to Pocatello

Aberdeen

American Falls Reservoir

American Falls

Holbrook

38

37

86

30

Sawtooth National Forest

84

Sawtooth National Forest

81

River

Lake Walcott

24

81

Albion

77

Elba

Raft

Rupert

Burley

Sawtooth National Forest

Cache Peak
el 10,339'

Almo

UTAH

25

27

24

84

Oakley

Hollister

30

25

Sawtooth National Forest

Kimberly

Hansen

93

26

Shoshone Indian
Ice Caves

75

Little Wood River

Big Wood River

Shoshone

93

Jerome

Twin Falls

Hollister

93

26

Gooding

Snake River

Oregon Trail

Buhl

30

Salmon

Creek

Jackpot

Bliss

Hagerman

Salmon Creek
Reservoir

NEVADA

Glenns
Ferry

Bruneau River East Fork

turn of the 20th century, Stricker had built a ranch house, a saloon and dance hall, a 40-horse stable and numerous outbuildings. Vestiges of the ranch are open for self-guided tours daily; volunteer hosts open the home; call for details. ~ 208-423-4000.

A short drive north of Twin Falls, across the Snake, is the town of Jerome, an agricultural center and the home of the **Jerome County Historical Museum.** This log building houses exhibits on the Minidoka Relocation Center, where thousands of Japanese-American citizens were interned during World War II. Closed Sunday and Monday. ~ 220 North Lincoln Street, Jerome; 208-324-5641. The actual site of the **Minidoka Relocation Center,** known to most as the "Hunt Camp," is 20 miles east of Jerome on Route 25, on the edge of the uninhabitable lava lands. A memorial, an overlook and historical exhibits mark the site.

Continuing north from Jerome on Route 93 toward Sun Valley, it's 15 miles to **Shoshone,** an old railroad town whose influence suffered a blow when Amtrak ceased its Portland-to-Salt Lake route in 1997. (Shoshone was the depot for both Twin Falls and Sun Valley.)

Shoshone has several intriguing cave systems that beckon spelunkers. Most important are the **Shoshone Indian Ice Caves,** where American Indians once found relief from desert heat. Forty-minute guided tours descend into the longest of the caves, a lava tube 1000 feet long with a floor of ice that ranges up to 30 feet deep. Air currents, never warmer than 33°F, have formed fantastic shapes. Located 17 miles north of Shoshone, the cave is closed October through April. Admission. ~ Route 75 North; 208-886-2058.

Route 93 leads to the Nevada border at **Jackpot,** 47 miles south of Twin Falls. Jackpot provides Idaho with its nearest taste of Las Vegas. Four casinos seduce with roulette, craps tables, blackjack, keno and other games of chance as well as the ubiquitous "one-armed bandits," or slot machines.

LODGING   Twin Falls is big on chain properties and franchises, but for a smaller, well-kept motel, check out the **Monterey Motor Inn.** Located on westbound Route 30/93, this single-story motel has 28 rooms—cozy except for a couple of two-bedroom units—with standard amenities plus a hot tub and coin laundry. All rooms have refrigerators and microwaves. ~ 433 Addison Avenue West, Twin Falls; 208-733-5151, fax 208-734-5091. BUDGET.

Up the price ladder is the **Red Lion Hotel Canyon Springs** at the north end of the city. Two stories and 112 rooms face a central swimming pool and exercise room. All of the warmly decorated, carpeted rooms have king- or queen-size beds and spacious baths. Children under 17 stay free with a parent. Facilities include a restaurant, a lounge and an espresso shop. ~ 1357 Blue Lakes

Boulevard North, Twin Falls; 208-734-5000, 800-733-5466, fax 208-733-3813; www.redlion.com. MODERATE TO DELUXE.

Near the lava beds and ice caves of the Snake River Plain, you can sojourn in century-old luxury at the **Governor's Mansion Bed and Breakfast** in the rail town of Shoshone. Indeed, an early Idaho governor did once make his home here. Today his estate is a five-room B&B that (surprise!) even accepts pets. Half of the individually decorated rooms share a bath. A full breakfast is served each morning. ~ 315 South Greenwood Street, Shoshone; 208-886-2858. BUDGET.

Since 1927, Twin Falls' **Depot Grill** has been dishing up three meals a day from the railroad station. The passenger depot is gone now, but the restaurant lives on, open 24 hours daily (except Sunday) to keep hungry farm boys fed. This is all-American food, and lots of it. ~ 545 Shoshone Street South, Twin Falls; 208-733-0710, fax 208-736-6727; sorans.com, e-mail steve@sorans.com. BUDGET TO MODERATE.

DINING

The small yellow house just south of the railroad tracks would not attract much attention were it not an outstanding Mexican restaurant. **La Casita** features all-homemade cuisine in a simple atmosphere. ~ 111 South Park Avenue West, Twin Falls; 208-734-7974. BUDGET.

◀ HIDDEN

Just a couple of doors down is the **Metropolis B@kery C@fé**, a hip, cyber-savvy coffee house that serves excellent pastries and inventive lunches. The lunch menu changes daily but features such delights as spicy Thai chicken soup, couscous salad with sun-dried tomatoes, and pizza primavera. Lunch only. Closed Sunday. ~ 125 Main Street, Twin Falls; 208-734-4457; www.magiclink.com/web/metchef. BUDGET TO MODERATE.

AUTHOR FAVORITE

I usually don't sing the praises of resort accommodations, but I make an exception for **Cactus Petes**, which offers pure indulgence in the good life—plus gambling (it's just a quick hop over the Nevada–Idaho state line). This full-service resort, less than an hour's drive from Twin Falls, features 419 handsome rooms (12 of them jacuzzi suites) in a ten-story tower. Besides the casino, there are a cocktail showroom, four other restaurants and three bars, a swimming pool, a golf course and tennis courts. ~ Route 93, Jackpot, NV; 775-755-2321, 800-821-1103, fax 775-755-2725; www.ameristarcasinos.com. DELUXE TO ULTRA-DELUXE.

Step into a cozy and relaxing Mediterranean garden–inspired eatery at the **Garden Café and Bakery**. The menu changes seasonally, but lunch always offers staples like sandwiches, pastas and salads, while dinner has lots of fresh fish, shrimp and scallops. Everything is homemade, including their sinful cheesecakes. The flavors change daily and the café's featured well over a 100 varieties since its opening. Closed Sunday. ~ 2221 Addison Avenue East, Twin Falls; 208-735-0722. BUDGET TO MODERATE.

SHOPPING   South central Idaho's largest shopping center is the **Magic Valley Mall**, at the intersection of Blue Lakes Boulevard just south of the Perrine Bridge. Its 60 stores include Barnes and Noble (208-733-1361), Bath & Body Works and the Sunglass Hut. ~ 1485 Pole Line Road East, Twin Falls; 208-733-3000.

The **Black Sheep Gallery** carries handmade crafts fashioned by 40 artisans, from clothing to furniture. Closed Sunday. ~ 830 Blue Lakes Boulevard North, Twin Falls; 208-733-9971.

NIGHTLIFE   To find out what's happening in the cultural realm in Twin Falls, contact the **Magic Valley Arts Council**. The association represents the Magic Valley Symphony, which presents four seasonal concerts a year. ~ 132 Main Avenue South, Twin Falls; 208-734-2787.

Several community theater groups perform regularly, most frequently at Twin Falls' finest stage, the **College of Southern Idaho Fine Arts Auditorium**. ~ 315 Falls Avenue West, Twin Falls; 208-733-9554.

Country-and-western is the preferred genre for live music in Twin Falls. **Honker's Place** has weekend bands. ~ 121 4th Avenue South; 208-733-4613. For a good pint of beer, look no further than **O' Dunken's**, which boasts 21 handcrafted Northwest microbrews on tap. ~ 102 Main Avenue North; 208-733-8114.

For most folks in the Twin Falls area, a big night out means making the 47-mile drive to Jackpot, Nevada. The town's four casinos are all in a quarter-mile stretch of Route 93. **Cactus Petes Resort Casino** is the largest, with 30,000 square feet of gaming tables, slot machines and other devices designed to separate gamblers from their nest eggs. The showroom here brings in a wide range of entertainers for shows that have included Chubby Checker, the Charlie Daniels Band, Air Supply and the Sons of the Pioneers. There's also a cabaret lounge. During the summer, the casino's amphitheater hosts a summer outdoor concert series with performers like LeAnn Rimes. ~ 208-736-1626. There's lower-key live entertainment and dancing at **The Horseshu Hotel Casino**. ~ 775-755-7777. There's also cozy but sometimes lucrative gaming at **Barton's Club 93**. ~ 775-755-2341. Also visit **The Four Jacks Casino**. ~ 775-755-2491.

Leaps of Faith

Shoshone Falls, often called the "Niagara of the West," pours torrents of Snake River water over the horseshoe-shaped basalt rock face each spring when snows melt in the mountains. During the rest of the year, irrigation canals divert much of the river's flow and there may only be a thin stream of water flowing through the spectacular 1000-foot-wide canyon. Its height, 212 feet (52 feet higher than Niagara), has lured three men to intentionally take the plunge—and all three survived.

Harry Wilson, the first daredevil, made the leap in 1905 and walked away with a cut knee. "A painful, though not a serious wound," reported the Twin Falls *Daily News*. "Harry Wilson ... created a sensation by jumping over the falls and landing in the whirlpool below. He swam to a rock and calmly awaited the arrival of his clothing, which had been removed before making the leap. Mr. Wilson said he performed the feat simply to show he had the nerve."

Al Faussett, unlike Mr. Wilson, made a profession of waterfall descents. He first earned acclaim for plummeting 104 vertical feet along a 275-foot tumbling falls while huddled inside a canoe. Three years and four waterfalls later, Faussett sat at the brink of Shoshone Falls, chosen over Niagara for its location in the West and for its additional height. He had built a 12-foot, football-shaped canoe, reinforced with fir ribs and covered with orange canvas. He stuffed the body of his craft with inflated inner tubes, building a kind of rubber bumper around him, and, with his head showing through a slit in the canvas, he fared only slightly worse than Mr. Wilson, suffering a broken hand. "I am certain that the nose of the boat hit a rock, from the feeling I had ... upon landing and the resultant bounce," he told the press, who were present in force.

Tom Rauckhorst happened into Twin Falls the day before Evel Knievel's attempted motorcycle leap of the Snake River Canyon. That show, and its throng of reporters, was three miles downriver just east of the Perrine Bridge. Rauckhorst, without fanfare, simply declared to bystanders his intention to dive into the pool below the falls and did so. He resurfaced and then scrambled up to the fall's southern edge, where a witness drove him to the hospital. Three crushed vertebrae was the doctor's diagnosis.

Evel Knievel, for his part, had not left the launch ramp before the parachute opened on his rocket-motorcycle. Knievel was already traveling at 350 miles per hour. That speed helped propel him upward more than 1000 feet before floating under his main chute down to the river, a drop of almost 1500 feet. He fared worst of all, suffering facial cuts and bruises to his stunt-battered body and to his ego.

PARKS   **SHOSHONE FALLS/DIERKES LAKE PARK** 🏃 🚣 🛶 🚤 ⛵ This city park offers two recreation areas in one: a 300-acre plot with picnic grounds beside a scenic overlook of the "Niagara of the West," and a 190-acre area surrounding the small reservoir on a bench above the river. There is a designated beach at Dierkes Lake for swimming. You may fish there or in the Snake below the falls. Facilities include picnic tables, restrooms, a playground and concession. Day-use fee (summer only), $3. ~ From Blue Lakes Boulevard (Route 93) in Twin Falls, take Falls Avenue east three miles to 3300 East Road; then turn north and continue for two miles; 208-736-2265, fax 208-736-1548; www.tfid.org.

SAWTOOTH NATIONAL FOREST 🏃 🎿 ⛵ Comprising a total of five parcels from northern Utah to the summits of the Sawtooth Range, this 2.1-million-acre national forest includes a district south of Twin Falls and Burley. Set on over 600,000 acres, the Minidoka District, managed by the Minidoka Ranger District, boasts pine-covered mountains, 870 miles of streams and more than 200 miles worth of multiple-use trails. There is good trout fishing in the streams. Facilities include picnic tables, restrooms and two alpine ski areas. ~ The South Hills unit is located on G3, south of Hansen; 208-737-3200, fax 208-737-3236; www.fs.fed.us/r4/sawtooth.

Shoshone Falls are at their fullest in the early spring, before irrigation water is diverted.

🔺 There are 19 campgrounds with 272 RV/tent sites (no hookups); $3 to $12 per night. Most sites are open from June to October only.

Hagerman Valley Area

Probably the most interesting daytrip in the Twin Falls area is a loop that takes drivers west and north on Route 30 through the lush Hagerman Valley. This region offers more intriguing attractions within close proximity than probably anywhere else in the state. Within an hour drive from Twin Falls the visitor can discover ancient fossils at Hagerman Fossil Beds National Monument, cascading water falls along the Thousand Springs Scenic Route, dramatic geologic formations at Malad Gorge State Park and dozens of commercial trout farms. Keep an eye aloft for eagles soaring the updrafts of the Snake River breaks.

SIGHTS   **Buhl,** 17 miles west of Twin Falls, is surrounded by picturesque barns and rich farmland. Southwest of the community is one of Idaho's geological oddities: **Balanced Rock,** a 40-foot, mushroom-shaped boulder perched upon a pedestal only a few feet in diameter. Geologists say it's been that way since prehistoric times. ~ Take Castleford Road south four miles from Buhl, then Orchard Drive nine miles west.

West of Buhl, Route 30 curves north to return to the Snake River and the 68-mile **Thousand Springs Scenic Route**. From the roadway along the river's southwest bank, you can look to the black cliffs on the opposite canyon wall and see dozens of apparently sourceless waterfalls cascading from what seems sheer rock. (There once may have been several hundred of these springs, but most have been diverted for irrigation or fish farming.) The spectacular springs are thought to be the outflow from the Snake River Plain Aquifer, which drains a basin that extends from Yellowstone National Park in the east to the Oregon state line. One of the largest and most accessible of the Thousand Springs can be seen at **Niagara Springs State Park**; see "Hagerman Valley Area Parks" below. Admission. ~ Niagara Springs Road, Wendell; phone/fax 208-837-4505; e-mail mal@idpr.state.id.us.

Route 30 continues north past several commercial hot springs and enters an agricultural area carpeted with grassy pastures and melon fields. For a soak, visit **Banbury Hot Springs**. Closed Labor Day to mid-May. ~ Banbury Road, one and a half miles east off Route 30; 208-543-4098; www.banburyhotsprings.com. There's also **Miracle Hot Springs**. Closed Sunday. ~ Route 30; 208-543-6002; www.mhsprings.com. This is the Hagerman Valley, where pioneers along the Oregon Trail traded with the native peoples for fresh trout.

Today a much more distant history attracts visitors to the **Hagerman Fossil Beds National Monument**. In the late 1920s and early 1930s, a Smithsonian Institution expedition unearthed 20 complete skeletons of *Equus simplicidens,* a zebralike Pliocene horse more than three million years old, above the west bank of the Snake River. More than 150 individual horse fossils have been excavated since, as well as fossils of mastodons, saber-tooth cats and smaller mammals, birds and fish. The Hagerman Fossil Beds are the richest known deposit of terrestrial fossils from the Pliocene epoch, when this region was marshy and semitropical. ~ A **visitors center** is located in downtown Hagerman. There are also self-guided driving tours. Open daily from Memorial Day through Labor Day, and Thursday through Monday in winter. ~ 221 North State Street (visitors center); 208-837-4793, fax 208-837-4857; www.nps.gov/hafo; to reach the national monument grounds, turn west on Route 30 just south of the Snake River bridge, south of Hagerman (be aware that roads can be hazardous or impassable in winter and early spring). There's an overlook above the Upper Salmon Falls Reservoir, two miles from the junction. Guided tours are offered in the summer. Collection and removal of fossils are prohibited.

You can see a full-cast replica of the original Hagerman horse and view a mural of how this area looked in Pliocene times at the

Hagerman Valley Historical Museum. Open Wednesday through Sunday from mid-March through October. ~ State and Main streets, Hagerman; 208-837-6288; e-mail bwunderle@id.freei.net.

Three miles north off Route 30 is **Malad Gorge State Park**, another example of the dramatic hand of nature in southern Idaho. Here, where the Big Wood River tumbles over a 60-foot waterfall into the Devil's Washbowl, a steel footbridge spans the 250-foot-deep gorge, offering striking glimpses of million-year-old geology. ~ 1074 East 2350 Road South, Hagerman; phone/fax 208-837-4505; e-mail mal@idpr.state.id.us.

HIDDEN ▶ Not far from Malad Gorge State Park is **Earl M. Hardy Box Canyon Preserve**, a pristine and little-touristed example of the local ecosystem. The gorge features numerous springs that spout from canyon walls and a 20-foot waterfall that crashes into the river below. Along the way knowledgeable rangers fill you in on the geology, wildlife and history of the area. Self-guided tours last between one and two hours. ~ 3500 South 1500 East, Hagerman; 208-837-4505; e-mail mal@idpr.state.id.us.

Before Route 30 climbs out of the Hagerman Valley at Bliss, where it rejoins Route 84, take a left-hand turn down the River Road. On your left near a hilltop, you might spy **Teater's Knoll**, a 1952 Frank Lloyd Wright home designed as a residence and studio for artist Archie Teater. The secluded house is not open for visits, but it's easily seen from the riverside deck at **Snake River Pottery**, Idaho's oldest ceramics studio. ~ River Road, Bliss; 208-837-6527.

LODGING There's not much to choose from in Buhl, but the **Oregon Trail Motel** offers 17 standard rooms. ~ 510 South Broadway, Buhl; 208-543-8814. MODERATE. Otherwise, just up the street stands the **Siesta Motel.** All twelve rooms have a mini-fridge and microwave, while four contain full kitchenettes. ~ 629 South Broadway, Buhl; 208-543-6427. BUDGET.

HIDDEN ▶ There are two good places to hang your hat along the Thousand Springs Scenic Route. My favorite is the **Billingsley Creek Lodge and Retreat**, a mile north of Hagerman, where Billingsley Creek runs under the road. The creek tumbles past this freshly updated eight-room resort and is the source of its appeal. It is, in fact, one of the Thousand Springs, appearing about eight miles above the lodge, clear and cold—58°F year-round—and supporting fat rainbow trout. The rooms are small and neat, paneled in real old-time knotty pine, and with individual wooden decks opening onto the lawn and creek; some rooms have kitchens. Three cottages are available, one right on the water with a hot tub on its screened porch. A private hot tub with its own waterfall is available to guests. ~ 17940 Route 30, Hagerman; 208-837-4822, fax 208-837-6467; www.billingsleycreeklodge.com. MODERATE TO DELUXE.

With 16 clean, comfortable rooms, the **Hagerman Valley Inn** is not a big place, but it's redone and it's near the Snake River Grill at the south end of town. ~ State Street and Hagerman Avenue, Hagerman; 208-837-6196; www.northrim.net/hvimotel. BUDGET.

One of the region's few lodgings is the **Gooding Hotel Bed & Breakfast**. This historic downtown hotel has ten private rooms, one with a private bathroom. The hotel dates from 1906, 20 years before the town was founded. Guests share washrooms, showers, a kitchen and a TV room. A full breakfast is served to those who want it. ~ 112 Main Street, Gooding; 208-934-4374, 888-260-6656, fax 208-934-8950. BUDGET TO MODERATE.

DINING

It's no surprise that the **Snake River Grill**, located in the heart of the nation's premier fish-farming region, serves up in Idaho rainbow trout. Steaks and shrimp are popular dinner choices, and they offer a large selection of wine by the glass. Breakfast and lunch are also served; no dinner on Monday. ~ State Street and Hagerman Avenue, Hagerman; 208-837-6227; www.snakeriver-grill.com. BUDGET TO DELUXE.

Larry & Mary's Cafe is the place to go for hearty home cooking. You'll find omelettes, French toast, biscuits and gravy, and

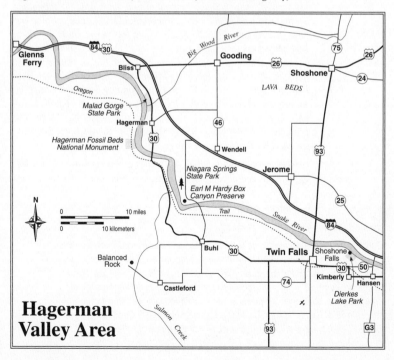

Hagerman Valley Area

ham and eggs on the breakfast menu; burgers and sandwiches are featured at lunch. Dinner entrées include steak, chicken and chicken-fried steak, but on Friday and Saturday nights, prime rib specials reign. ~ 141 North State Street, Hagerman; 208-837-6475. BUDGET TO MODERATE.

SHOPPING Art lovers won't want to miss **Snake River Pottery**, Idaho's oldest ceramics studio, which exhibits wheel-turned earthenware and other works of art. ~ River Road, Bliss; 208-837-6527.

NIGHTLIFE Bars are just not done up like **Wilson's Club** anymore—red and burgundy Naugahyde-covered stools, shuffleboard, pool table, Willie Nelson in the juke, pot-bellied stove for winter warmth. Two antique display cases hold a buried treasure of old watches, rocks, bottles, jars, light bulbs, sewing machines, almost everything a Huck Finn with summer's time on his hands might bring home and save. And the walls are hung with moose, antelope and deer trophies. ~ 200 North State Street, Hagerman; no phone.

PARKS **NIAGARA SPRINGS STATE PARK** 🧍 💧 One of the largest and most visible of the Thousand Springs that gush from a lava aquifer through the walls of the Snake River Canyon is Niagara Springs, dubbed a "national natural landmark." Their icy blue waters pour down a cliffside at 250 cubic feet per second. This 179-acre park also contains Crystal Springs. There is year-round fishing in Crystal Springs Lake. There are picnic tables, restrooms and hiking trails. Day-use fee, $4. ~ From Wendell, take Route 46 (Rex Leland Highway) south five miles to Niagara Springs Road, continuing another three and a half miles to the park. The final descent is narrow and steep, not recommended in a large RV or with a trailer; phone/fax 208-837-4505; e-mail mal@idpr.state.id.us.
▲ There is primitive camping.

HAGERMAN FOSSIL BEDS NATIONAL MONUMENT 🧍 🚲 🐎 💧 Still in the development stage, this area preserves the richest

---

TREASURE TROVE OF TROUT

Buhl is home to the world's largest commercial trout farm: **Clear Springs Foods**. Self-guided tours of aquaculture operations are offered from a visitors center. Don't miss the display of live white sturgeon. Clear Springs is in the heart of a 30-mile stretch, between Twin Falls and Hagerman, from which come more than 70 percent of all commercially raised trout in the United States. ~ 1585 Clear Lake Grade, Buhl; 208-543-4316, fax 208-543-5608; www.clearsprings.com, e-mail csf@clearsprings.com.

known deposit of Pliocene epoch fossils, mainly mammals from over three million years ago. The best way to visit the monument, located along the bluffs on the west side of the Snake River facing Hagerman, is on a self-guided driving tour. There is fishing in the Snake River adjacent to the national monument. Facilities include a visitors center, overlooks, interpretive exhibits and organized tours. Open daily from Memorial Day through Labor Day, and Thursday through Monday in winter. ~ The visitors center is in downtown Hagerman at 221 North State Street. To reach the national monument grounds, turn west on Route 30 just south of the Snake River bridge, south of Hagerman (in winter and early spring, roads may be dangerous or impassable). There's an overlook above Upper Salmon Falls Reservoir, two miles from the junction; 208-837-4793, fax 208-837-4857; www.nps.gov/hafo.

MALAD GORGE STATE PARK 🏃 ⤵ Some geologists believe that a torrent from an ancient glacier created this 250-foot-deep, two-and-a-half-mile-long gorge, one of Idaho's most dramatic sights. The Big Wood River, cascading through a needle-thin chasm, ends at a 60-foot waterfall that churns into the Devil's Washbowl, where the Malad River begins its two-and-a-half-mile run to the Snake (giving the Malad perhaps undue claim to being one of the world's shortest rivers). A steel footbridge overlooks the gorge above the falls. The 651-acre park includes two miles of trails. There is a great trout stream for fishing, but it's difficult to get to, unless you come upstream by boat from the Snake River. You can also try taking Idaho Power access roads, located near the Route 30 bridge over the Malad River, about six miles from Hagerman. There are picnic tables, a playground and restrooms. Day-use fee, $4.~ From Route 84, take Exit 147 at Tuttle. From Hagerman, go north two miles on Route 30, then east and north three miles on Justice Grade to Exit 147 near the park entrance; phone/fax 208-837-4505; e-mail mal@idpr.state.id.us.

Minidoka and Cassia counties, known to most Idahoans simply as "Mini-Cassia," make up a well-irrigated farming and ranching region that flanks the Snake River. It's an area most Idaho visitors miss . . . which is a shame, because there's a lot to see once you get off the interstate. There's the historic quarry town of Oakley, the monolithic magnificence of the City of Rocks, and the serenity of the Minidoka National Wildlife Refuge.

▼▼▼▼▼▼▼▼▼▼▼▼
Mini-Cassia Area

The region's hub is **Burley**, located on the south shore of Milner Reservoir 40 miles east of Twin Falls. Burley is best known as a power-boating center: The reservoir, 20 miles long and a few hundred yards wide, hosts the Idaho Regatta every June. The town's

SIGHTS

HIDDEN ► **Cassia County Historical Museum** describes Burley's 19th-century role as the focus of five pioneer byways, including the Oregon, Mormon and California trails. Closed November through March. ~ East Main Street and Highland Avenue, Burley; 208-678-7172.

Oakley, which has Idaho's highest concentration of late-19th-century buildings, most of them intricate stone and wood structures, is 20 miles south of Burley in the Goose Creek Mountains. The entire town of 660—laid out by Mormon leaders in 1882—is listed on the National Register of Historic Places.

The granite pillars of **City of Rocks National Reserve** marked the crossroads of the California Trail and Kelton Stage Road for pioneer travelers. Their inscriptions can still be seen scrawled in axle grease on the rock columns towering 60 stories above the desert sage. Take a gravel road 18 miles southeast from Oakley, or reach City of Rocks via Route 77 southeast from Burley. A visitors center is open daily during the summer, and Monday through Friday in winter; winter snowstorms may close the park's gravel roads. Call for road conditions. ~ City of Rocks Road, Almo; 208-824-5519, fax 208-824-5563.

North of the City of Rocks and southeast of Burley is the little town of **Albion**, whose past is far more impressive than its present. The ranching center, founded in the 1870s, was once the seat of Cassia County and the home of Southern Idaho College of Education. The school closed in 1951, and an attempted religious institution (Magic Christian College, 1957–1967) also failed. But the 40-acre campus, its structures solidly built of locally quarried stone, still dominates this tiny town.

Rupert, eight miles from Burley on the north side of the Snake, boomed as an agricultural center after the completion in 1906 of the nearby **Minidoka Dam**, the Pacific Northwest's first hydroelectric power house. Today, Rupert has perhaps the most traditional town square in Idaho, with downtown businesses facing the lively plaza and its bandstand.

The dam holds back **Lake Walcott**, a reservoir popular among boaters, waterskiers and anglers. Along with 11 miles of the Snake River to its east, the lake is encompassed by the 25,000-acre **Minidoka National Wildlife Refuge**, described in "Parks" below.

LODGING   A great place for families, and for the less adventurous, is the **Best Western Burley Inn & Convention Center**. Sitting on the north bank of the Snake River at Route 84 Exit 208, this 126-room complex has a swimming pool, a playground, a volleyball net and a coin laundry; what's more, children 18 and under stay free with parents. Blowdryers, coffeemakers and dataports are among the room amenities. Facilities include a fine-dining restaurant and a cocktail lounge. ~ 800 North Overland Avenue, Burley; 208-678-3501, 800-599-1849, fax 208-678-9532; www.bestwestern.com, e-mail bisales@pmt.org. MODERATE.

Next door is the 139-room **Budget Motel,** which is probably a slightly better though less convenient deal. All the facilities of the neighboring Best Western are available to guests here, since both are run by the same management. Rooms in the new wing are priced higher but are also, well . . . newer. ~ 900 North Overland Avenue, Burley; 208-678-2200, 800-635-4952, fax 208-677-2576. BUDGET.

In rural Cassia County, the **Mountain Manor Bed and Breakfast** takes the cake for best lodging in the area. The B&B is located in the ranching town of Albion, en route to the Pomerelle Ski Area and City of Rocks National Reserve. There are three bedrooms; one has a private bath, while the other two share. All have TVs. Continental breakfast is served each morning. ~ 249 West North Street, Albion; 208-673-6642. BUDGET.

DINING

Price's Cafe is a four-generation favorite (it's been around since 1932) that offers breakfasts, lunches, steaks and seafood dinners, as well as homemade pies for dessert. Closed Sunday. ~ 2444 Overland Avenue, Burley; 208-678-5149, fax 208-678-4273. BUDGET TO MODERATE.

Shon Hing has found a cadre of local followers. Like Chinese restaurants everywhere, the decor is spare, but the owners have dressed the tables with blue linen, covered with glass, accompa-

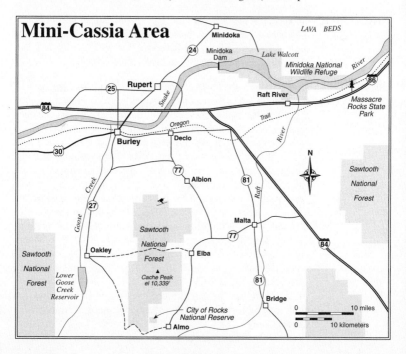

nied by red cushioned chairs. Against the white walls, the effect is crisp and comfortable. The Mandarin and Cantonese menu holds no surprises: chow mein, sweet-and-sour pork and fried rice are the mainstays. ~ 109 East Main Street, Burley; 208-678-4950. BUDGET.

Charlie's Cafe draws legions of locals for breakfast, lunch and dinner with its Mexican and American fare. *Huevos rancheros* are popular morning eats. Closed Sunday. ~ 615 East Main Street, Burley; 208-678-0112. BUDGET TO MODERATE.

Don't let the mall location put you off: **Le's Chopsticks**, the only Vietnamese restaurant in the area, serves up tasty Southeast Asian cuisine. ~ 2126 Overland Avenue, Burley; 208-678-2003. BUDGET.

SHOPPING   Overland Avenue, which seems more like Main Street, houses several antique stores and boutiques. The most appealing, and best stocked, is **The Golden Goose**. The place overflows with collectibles displayed on antique chairs, desks and dressers, and half a dozen antique oak hutches hold baskets, porcelain wash bowls and pitchers, china dolls, wreaths and even Christmas ornaments. Along the walls are beautiful old wooden bars, hauled from a drugstore in nearby Oakley, that alone are worth a stop to see. ~ 1229 Overland Avenue, Burley; 208-678-9122.

NIGHTLIFE   For cocktails, beer and bar food, try **Nelsons Cafe & Pilots Lounge**. ~ 125 West Main Street, Burley; 208-678-7171.

For karaoke, hit up the **Riverside Bar** on Thursday and Saturday nights. ~ 197 Route 30, Burley; 208-678-9120.

PARKS   **SAWTOOTH NATIONAL FOREST** 🏃 🏕 ⚓ 🚤 🚣 The three southeastern units of this national forest cover over 250,000 acres and offer alpine lakes, miles of streams, pine forests and open meadows. The land in these units, managed by the Burley/Twin Falls Ranger District, was mined for silver and lead in the 1800s and gold was discovered in the 1950s. Now, fishing, hunting, hiking and cross-country skiing are popular pastimes in these parts. Swimming is possible in the alpine lakes, but very cold year-round. There is good trout fishing in the many streams and lakes. Facilities include picnic tables, restrooms and two alpine ski areas. ~ The Albion Mountains are south of Albion via Route 77 and Howell Canyon or Cottrel Road. The Black Pine Mountains are between Routes 81 and 84 southeast of Malta. The division that's farthest east is on Yale Road, accessible from Exit 18 off Route 84; 208-678-0430, fax 208-677-4878.

▲ There are 16 campgrounds with 171 RV/tent sites (no hookups); $3 to $12 per night. Most sites are open from June to October only.

CITY OF ROCKS NATIONAL RESERVE 🚶 🚵 🐎 ⛺ Estab-   ◄ *HIDDEN*
lished in 1988, the Reserve encompasses 14,107 acres of land
renowned for its scenic, geologic, and historic significance. Some
of the granitic rock formations—shaped by weathering forces to
form the fantastic shapes you see today—overlook the desert
landscape by 500 feet or more. Rock climbers from around the
world visit this park to scale lofty granite columns. California/
Oregon Trail wagon ruts and pioneer graffiti written with axle
grease can still be seen. There are picnic tables, restrooms, and a
visitors center. ~ From Burley, take Route 81 east nine miles to
Declo, Route 77 south 20 miles via Albion to Connor, the Elba-
Almo Highway southwest 16 miles to Almo, and City of Rocks
Road west two miles to the reserve. Or take Route 27 south 20
miles from Burley to Oakley, the gravel Birch Creek Road southeast 14 miles, then Emery Canyon Road east four miles; 208-
824-5519, fax 208-824-5563; www.nps.gov/ciro.

▲ There are 75 primitive sites (no hookups); $7 per night.
Firewood cannot be collected on the reserve; it's best to bring
your own.

MINIDOKA NATIONAL WILDLIFE REFUGE 🏖 🚣 ⛴ 🛶
Famous for the 100,000-plus ducks and geese that cluster here
each fall, this refuge is home to over 230 species of resident and
migratory birds, including swans, herons and egrets. Created in
1909, the refuge encompasses 11-mile-long Lake Walcott and
another 11 miles of the Snake River east of it. Most of the reservoir is closed to boats to protect the birds and their habitat.
There's a fall–winter hunting season along the lake's southern
shore and around Tule Island in the Snake. You may fish for trout
and bass in Lake Walcott and the Snake River. Facilities include
picnic tables, restrooms and interpretive exhibits. ~ From Rupert,
take Route 24 northeast six miles, then Minidoka Dam Road east
five miles; 208-436-3589, fax 208-436-1570.

◆◆

TRIAL IN ERROR

The Mini-Cassia region's cultural highlight takes place in Albion each July
when a community theater group reenacts **"The Trial of Diamondfield
Jack"** on the campus of the old Southern Idaho College of Education.
Jackson Davis was a security man who in 1897 was sentenced in Albion
to hang for the murder of two sheepherders during a range war.
Although the true perpetrators confessed to the crime (and were
acquitted) a year and a half later, Davis was not released from impris-
onment until 1902 after one of the most remarkable trials in Idaho
history.

▲ There are 22 sites (all with hookups) at Lake Walcott State Park (208-436-1258), and two cabins and tent sites; call park for rates.

▼▼▼▼▼▼▼▼▼▼▼▼▼▼
Outdoor Adventures

It's no accident that fishing the middle Snake River and surrounding waters is so rewarding: More than two million rainbow and steelhead trout, as well as catfish, are produced each year in hatcheries and "fish farms" along this stretch of the river. Between Hagerman and Twin Falls, the five Oster Lakes feature bass and bluegill fishing that begins in March, two months earlier than the general season (which runs from Memorial Day through November). Salmon Falls Reservoir, 39 miles southwest of Twin Falls, offers rainbow and brown trout, kokanee salmon and trophy-size walleye, bass and perch. For local advice, contact **Blue Lakes Sporting Goods**. ~ 1236 Blue Lakes Boulevard North, Twin Falls; 208-733-6446, fax 208-733-1688; www.bluelakesport.com.

FISHING

BOATING

This region of Idaho offers several lakes and reservoirs; unfortunately, you'll have to bring your boat since no place in the area rents. A popular lake is **Salmon Creek Reservoir**, south of Twin Falls. **Milner Reservoir** at Burley hosts the Idaho Regatta each June; one of only six nationally sanctioned speedboat races, it attracts nearly 100 boats of all kinds, from hydroplanes to flatbottoms. Located near Rupert, **Lake Walcott** draws many private boaters.

RIVER RUNNING

The Snake River can be docile for long stretches, but it can also be deceivingly dangerous. The "Hagerman Run," a six-and-a-half-mile stretch past Malad Gorge from the Lower Salmon Dam to the Bliss Bridge, draws raves from beginning rafters with experienced guides. An outfitter to try is **High Adventure River Tours**. ~ 1211 East 2350 South, Hagerman; 800-286-4123. **Idaho Guide Service** also operates on this stretch. ~ 563 Trotter Avenue, Twin Falls; 208-734-4998; www.idahoguideservice.com. Another popular river is the Raft, east of Burley.

SKIING

South central Idaho lacks the glamour of Sun Valley when it comes to skiing. But it does have two small, family-oriented alpine destinations, neither with overnight accommodations:

Magic Mountain Ski Area, 38 miles southeast of Twin Falls via Route 84 Exit 182. Located in Sawtooth National Forest, the area has one chair, one poma lift, one rope tow and 20 runs on a 800-foot vertical. ~ Route G3, Kimberly; 208-423-6221, 800-255-8946, fax 208-423-5817.

Pomerelle Ski Area is 32 miles southeast of Burley via Route 84 Exit 216. On the eastern slope of 9265-foot Mount Harrison in the Albion Mountains, the resort has two chairlifts, a rope tow and 24 runs on a 1000-foot vertical. Night skiing is available Tuesday through Saturday. ~ Howell Canyon Road, Albion; 208-673-5599, fax 208-673-6265; www.pomerelle-mtn.com, e-mail info@pomerelle-mtn.com.

Ski Rentals   Aside from the resort facilities themselves, there are several places to rent skiing and snowboarding equipment, one of which is **Pinetree Sports**. Closed Sunday. ~ 2165 Overland Avenue, Burley; 208-678-5869; www.pinetreesports.com.

GOLF

The area's temperate climate is conducive to playing golf much of the year. Twin Falls' beautiful **Canyon Springs Golf Course** is located beneath the Perrine Bridge in the Snake River Canyon. ~ Canyon Springs Road; 208-734-7609. Other courses include the **Twin Falls Municipal Golf Course**. ~ Grandview Drive, Twin Falls; 208-733-3326; www.tfid.org. You also can try the **Jerome Country Club**. ~ Golf Course Road, Jerome; 208-324-5281.

There's also the **Jackpot Golf Club**. ~ Route 93, Jackpot, NV; 775-755-2260. Tee off at **Clear Lake Country Club**, which has the friendliest staff around. ~ 403 Clear Lake Lane, Buhl; 208-543-4849. Or visit **Burley Municipal Golf Course**. ~ Route 81, Burley; 208-878-9807. All of these are 18-hole courses.

There are three nine-hole courses in the region. Try **Candleridge Golf Course**. ~ 2097 Candleridge Road, Twin Falls; 208-733-6577. Tee off at **Gooding Golf Course**. ~ Route 26, Gooding; 208-934-9977. Or visit **Ponderosa Golf Course**. ~ Route 75 at Route 84, Burley; 208-679-5730.

TENNIS

Twin Falls is *the* place in south central Idaho if you feel like playing a little tennis. Twenty-seven public courts, including six at **Twin Falls High School** are what you'll find. ~ Locust Street and Stadium Boulevard. Contact the **City of Twin Falls Parks & Recreation Department**. ~ 208-736-2265, fax 208-736-1548; www.hici.org.

AUTHOR FAVORITE

Scrambling around on the boulders in the **City of Rocks National Reserve** gives me a real appreciation for the pioneers, a number of whom found the time to scrawl their names on these massive rocks as they passed by. Many of the granitic rock formations are over 2.5 billion years old, some of the oldest rocks in North America. See page 107 for more information.

RIDING STABLES

Equestrian trails around Twin Falls provide another viewpoint altogether. **Pioneer Mountain Outfitters** has stables and offers half- and full-day trail excursions. Wagon rides and customized pack trips are also available. ~ 3267 East 3225 North, Twin Falls; 208-774-3737 or 208-734-3679; www.pioneermountain.com.

BIKING

The **Snake River Rim Recreation Trail** offers cyclists several miles of relatively easy riding above the Snake River Canyon, beginning from the northeast corner of the Perrine Bridge at Twin Falls. The route is mainly dirt or gravel, with occasional soft sand.

South from Twin Falls, the **Third Fork–Harrington Fork Trail Complex** (25 miles) offers challenging scenic riding through grassy meadows, stands of aspen and, at higher elevations, pine forests.

Other popular biking destinations are south of Burley in the Mount Harrison/Lake Cleveland area of Sawtooth National Forest and in the City of Rocks National Reserve, as well as in some of the Bureau of Land Management–administered lava lands of the Snake River Plain near Shoshone.

Bike Rentals **Pinetree Sports** rents mountain and children's bikes; helmets are included in the rental. They also do repairs. ~ 2165 Overland Avenue, Burley; 208-678-5869; www.pinetree sports.com. In Twin Falls, the **College of Southern Idaho** provides rentals through its Outdoor Program department. ~ 315 Falls Avenue, Twin Falls; 208-733-9554 ext. 2697.

HIKING

In addition to the state parks in the area, there are numerous hiking trails in Sawtooth National Forest. All distances listed for hiking trails are one way unless otherwise noted.

Malad Gorge Trail (2 miles), in Malad Gorge State Park, crosses a steel footbridge over the 250-foot chasm, then follows the canyon rim for additional overlooks of the river and the 60-foot waterfall that tumbles into the Devil's Washbowl.

Independence Lakes Trail (3.1 miles) ascends a saddle of 10,339-foot Cache Peak, in Sawtooth National Forest north of the City of Rocks National Reserve, to a lovely group of trout-rich alpine ponds at the 9000-foot level of the mountain. The trailhead is off Cottley Road, west of Elba and southeast of Burley via Route 77.

▼▼▼▼▼▼▼▼▼▼

Transportation

CAR

Eastbound **Route 84** from Portland and Boise continues in a southeasterly direction and skirts Twin Falls and Burley before turning southeast into Utah. **Route 93**, extending north from Jackpot, Nevada, goes through Twin Falls and Shoshone, where it intersects with **Route 26**, before veering off to the northeast. The highway continues north to Sun Valley as **Route 75**. On the south side of the Snake River canyon,

Route 30 branches off Route 84 at Bliss and passes through Ha-german, Twin Falls and Burley before rejoining the interstate near Rupert.

The **Joslin Field Magic Valley Regional Airport,** ten miles south of downtown Twin Falls, is served by SkyWest from Salt Lake City. **AIR**

Greyhound Bus Lines (800-231-2222; www.greyhound.com) fol-low the interstate corridor from Boise to Salt Lake City or West Yellowstone, Montana. There's a depot in Twin Falls. ~ 1390 Blue Lakes Boulevard North; 208-733-3002. Other stops are made (from west to east) in Bliss, Hagerman, Buhl, Burley and Rupert. **BUS**

Gamblers can hop aboard the **Cactus Petes Connection,** which travels to Jackpot, Nevada, from the Boise area and Mountain Home. ~ 800-700-3833.

Avis Rent A Car (800-331-1212), **Budget Rent A Car** (800-527-0700), **Hertz Rent A Car** (800-654-3131) and **National Car Rental** (800-328-4567) have outlets at the Twin Falls airport. **CAR RENTALS**

Trans IV Buses offers service in Twin Falls (call 24-hours in ad-vance to schedule). ~ 496 Madrona Street; 208-736-2133. **PUBLIC TRANSIT**

Every city has its taxis. In south central Idaho, try **Magic Valley Taxi.** ~ Twin Falls; 208-733-9101. **TAXIS**

FIVE

Pocatello and Southeastern Idaho

Tucked away in the mountainous southeastern corner of Idaho, Pocatello is the state's second-largest city and home to Idaho State University. Southeastern Idahoans are predominantly Mormon, having settled in the region as Brigham Young's growing community at Salt Lake expanded.

Joining them were pioneers originally bound for the Willamette Valley of Oregon who first had to cross southern Idaho. Their introduction to the state occurred here in its southeastern corner. After crossing the high grasslands of Wyoming, the travelers climbed past Bear Lake, descending along the Portneuf River to Fort Hall, where they rested their stock and replenished supplies.

They wouldn't have known that their path down into the Snake River Plain traced, in part, the path of the Bonneville Flood some 15,000 years earlier. Lake Bonneville was a vast inland sea stretching across western Utah and parts of eastern Nevada equal in size to the five Great Lakes combined. Geologists speculate that the basin simply overflowed during the wet climate of the last ice age, and erosion breached a soft earthen barrier at Red Rock Pass, north of Preston.

That natural act let loose a flood of biblical scale. Discharging waters like a raging Amazon swollen to three times its size, the Bonneville Flood poured into the Snake River. The Snake at that time meandered through the rich silt deposits of old Lake Idaho, which covered this region between two and eight million years ago. The floodwaters scoured the Snake River Canyon across all of southern Idaho to a depth of about 600 feet—overflowing the brim in places—and carved Hells Canyon nearly to its present depth. The flooding continued unabated for several months.

Though the Upper Snake was bypassed by Lewis and Clark during their 1803–1806 expedition, fur trappers and other explorers became well acquainted with the region in the decades that followed. The trappers held regular trading rendezvous here, near Fort Hall, at the mineral baths of Lava Hot Springs and at the southern end of Bear Lake. And not unlike a modern-day trade show, the gatherings featured a potent share of revelry and merrymaking.

The Fort Hall trading post, formally established near modern Pocatello in 1834 to compete with the Hudson's Bay Company, became an oasis in the 1840s and 1850s for travelers who used the Oregon Trail and other pioneer paths to reach the promised lands of the Pacific Northwest and California. Many later returned in the 1860s to settle Idaho, first to mine gold and silver, later to reap the bounty of rich evergreen forests and farm the richly fertile river valleys.

Snake River Valley elevations near Pocatello are about 4500 feet. Winters are windy and long, and spring comes late. Like almost everywhere else in Idaho, outdoor activities in this corner of the state abound—hiking, river running, skiing, rock climbing, fishing, hunting. . . the list goes on. And this is perhaps the main attraction of Pocatello for residents: access to the outdoors with the cultural amenities of a medium-sized university town located in an out-of-the-way corner of the state.

Pocatello Area

Pocatello is a transportation hub in the heart of a rich agricultural and phosphate-mining region. Located on the Portneuf River ten miles upstream from American Falls Reservoir, a water-sports mecca on the Snake River, the city of 46,000 is close to the Fort Hall Indian Reservation, the geological wonders of Massacre Rocks State Park and the Great Rift National Landmark, and the expansive potato fields near Blackfoot.

Main Street in Pocatello is laid out along the Portneuf River, To walk down Main is to travel back in time to a 1950s Idaho. Few chain stores are in evidence. The shops—most have brick facades—sell jewelry, music, books and hardware and are almost all independently owned, which lends the town a flavor of another era.

SIGHTS

Named for a Shoshone chief who granted the Union Pacific a right-of-way through the Fort Hall reservation, Pocatello in the early 20th century was America's largest rail center west of the Mississippi River. The **Oregon Short Line Depot**, a three-story station dedicated in 1915 by former U.S. president William Howard Taft, is in the heart of its 12-square-block **Downtown Historic District**. ~ Union Pacific Avenue at Bonneville Street.

The district includes five churches on the National Register of Historic Places and such other unusual buildings as the 1916 **Yellowstone Hotel**, behind whose wine-colored bricks and terracotta trim early train passengers overnighted. Today the hotel is closed but restoration is planned. ~ 230 West Bonneville Street.

The 1902 **Stanrod Mansion** is regarded as the finest Victorian building in Idaho. ~ 648 North Garfield Avenue.

Stop by the **Greater Pocatello Convention and Visitors Bureau** for walking-tour maps and other information. Closed Saturday and Sunday in winter. ~ 343 West Center Street; 208-233-7333, 877-922-7659, fax 208-233-1527; www.pocatelloidaho.com.

East of downtown is **Idaho State University** (ISU). Covering about six city blocks, the wooded campus is home to 13,600 students. The university specializes in health studies and features the only pharmaceutical program in the state. ~ 741 South 7th Avenue; 208-282-0211, fax 208-282-4231; www.isu.edu, e-mail info @isu.edu. On campus, the **Idaho Museum of Natural History** has fine exhibits on fossil and archaeological prehistory, including the "Dinosaur Times" exhibit, showcasing fossils of the giants that once roamed the state.. There are also displays on threatened and endangered animal and plant species, a children's discovery area and a gift shop. Closed weekends. ~ Hutchinson Quadrangle; 208-282-3168, fax 208-282-5893; www.isu.edu/departments/museum.

Pocatello's "don't-miss" attraction is **Ross Park**. Within this urban oasis are a re-created 19th-century Pocatello townsite; a Union Pacific display; a rose garden and bandstand; and recreational facilities including an aquatic center (swimming pool and water slide) with all the traditional amenities of a city park such as picnic tables, ball fields and volleyball courts. You'll also find the **Pocatello Zoo** (208-234-6196, fax 208-234-6265), specializing in creatures native to the northern Rocky Mountains. Closed in winter. Admission. ~ The park is located on the south side of the city at 2900 South 2nd Avenue; 208-234-6232.

HIDDEN ► Ross Park also hosts the **Bannock County Historical Museum**, an outstanding, well-presented small museum with exhibits spanning pre-European to modern times. It features collections of local Indian and railroad artifacts. Of unusual interest is the muralized Donor Wall, an illustrated county history. The museum is open daily in summer, closed Sunday and Monday the rest of the year; open half-days from Labor Day to Memorial Day. Admission. ~ Ross Park; 208-233-0434.

The nearby **Fort Hall Replica** is a full-scale historic reconstruction of the Portneuf River trading post that served Oregon Trail travelers from 1843 to 1865. Created from original Hudson's Bay Company plans, it includes a guardhouse, blacksmith shop, tack shop, living quarters and museum with pioneer, military and American Indian artifacts. Closed October through March. Admission. ~ Ross Park; 208-234-6233.

NORTH OF POCATELLO The original site of Fort Hall is 20 miles north of Ross Park on the **Fort Hall Indian Reservation**, headquarters of the Shoshone-Bannock tribes. A small obelisk marks the site beside Oregon Trail ruts on Sheepskin Road about six miles west of Route 91 at Spring Creek.~ Route 91, Fort Hall; 208-237-9791, fax 208-237-4318.

The 820-square-mile reservation, created in 1869, is home to 3000 Shoshone-Bannocks. Once separate tribes with similar semi-nomadic cultures but different languages, Shoshones and Ban-

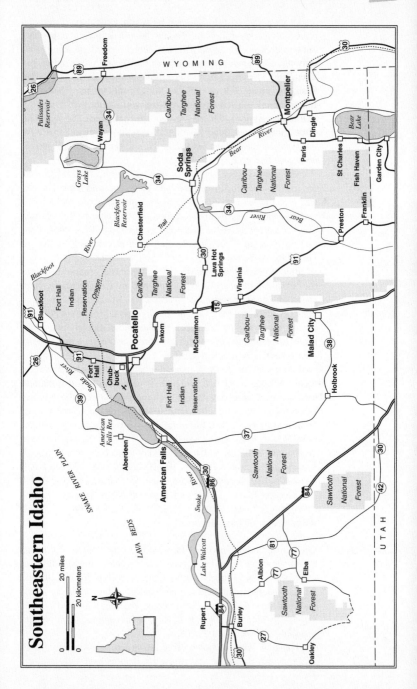

Southeastern Idaho

nocks were forced into alliance by white settlement. Intermarriage predictably followed. Today the tribes have a phosphate mine and extensive Snake River fishing rights; their tribal festival and rodeo each August is one of the West's major native celebrations. The small but interesting **Shoshone-Bannock Tribal Museum** is west of Route 15 Exit 80, 11 miles north of Pocatello. The museum features early black-and-white photos of Fort Hall and interpretations. Closed October through April. A bingo hall, restaurant, grocery store and retail store are nearby. Admission. ~ Gay Mine Road, Fort Hall; 208-237-9791, fax 208-237-4318; www.sho-ban.com.

The drive to Fort Hall is a good beginning for a 125-mile daytrip loop around American Falls Reservoir and back to Pocatello. Continue up Route 15 to Blackfoot. Cross the Snake River and take secondary Route 39 through potato country to the town of American Falls. After a side trip to Massacre Rocks State Park (see "American Falls Area" later in this chapter), return to Pocatello via Route 86.

Blackfoot, halfway between Pocatello and Idaho Falls, is in the heart of the state's leading potato region. Eastern Idaho's high elevation, its light and moist volcanic soil, its hot days and cool nights are ideal for the russet Burbank potato. More than 300,000 acres are devoted to this tuber, whose yellow flowers and viney leaves are especially evident in late spring and early summer. Digging takes place in autumn.

Idaho's Potato Expo is located in a 1912 Union Pacific train depot. Museum exhibits and videos place the Idaho potato in international context with entertaining displays on the potato's history, growth, production, nutritional value, economic importance and more. Packed full of fascinating tidbits and spud memorabilia, this place is well worth a visit. There's a farm machinery display and a gift shop. Closed Sunday from November through March, and closed weekends from May through October. Admission. ~ 130 Northwest Main Street, Blackfoot; 208-785-2517. The **Greater Blackfoot Area Chamber of Commerce** also has an office here. Closed Sunday. ~ 208-785-0510, fax 208-785-7974; www.blackfootchamber.org.

LODGING

The **Econo Lodge University Hotel** suits wallet watchers. Located across the street from the Idaho State University campus, the two-story motel has 54 nicely appointed guest rooms. You'll also find a fitness room and an adjacent coffee shop. Continental breakfast is included. ~ 835 South 5th Avenue, Pocatello; 208-233-0451, 800-377-0451, fax 208-478-1618; www.econolodge.com, e-mail econoldg@ida.net. MODERATE.

The **Best Western CottonTree Inn** is a three-story hotel with 149 spacious rooms just off Route 15. Rooms have standard fur-

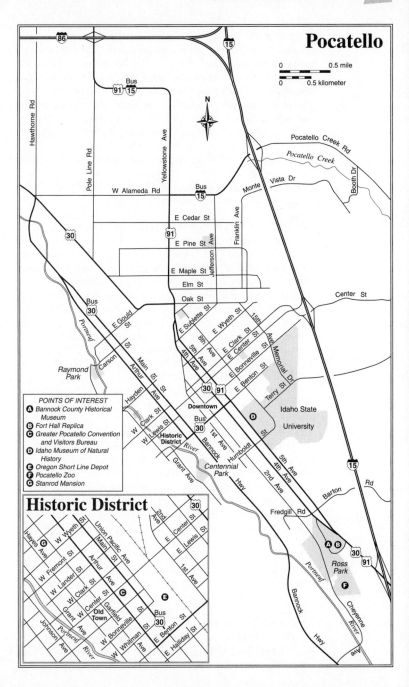

Pocatello

POINTS OF INTEREST
A Bannock County Historical Museum
B Fort Hall Replica
C Greater Pocatello Convention and Visitors Bureau
D Idaho Museum of Natural History
E Oregon Short Line Depot
F Pocatello Zoo
G Stanrod Mansion

Historic District

nishings and about 40 rooms have kitchenettes, though no utensils are provided; there are no elevators. The hotel includes a
lounge, a coin laundry, an indoor pool and a hot tub. A continental breakfast is included. ~ 1415 Bench Road, Pocatello;
208-237-7650, 800-662-6886, fax 208-238-1355; www.cotton-
tree.net, e-mail sales@cottontree.net. MODERATE TO DELUXE.

Of similar high standard to the CottonTree is the nearby
Pocatello Red Lion Hotel. This property is especially attractive
to business travelers, who will find generous conference facilities
and high-speed wireless internet in all 150 guest rooms. The
hotel has an indoor swimming pool and spa and workout facilities. as well as a full-service restaurant and lounge. ~ 1555 Pocatello Creek Road, Pocatello; 208-233-2200, 800-527-5202, fax
208-234-4524; www.redlion.com. MODERATE.

DINING   **Eduardo's Mexican Restaurant** is as friendly a place as you'll find
anywhere. Even the host greets you as a long-lost "amigo." The
decor is casual and the fare traditional—generous portions of burritos, enchiladas, chimichangas and the like. ~ 612 Yellowstone
Avenue, Pocatello; 208-233-9440. BUDGET TO MODERATE.

The Continental Bistro is a pleasant addition to Pocatello's
historic district: contemporary American cuisine and European
service in a spacious room that features light jazz music for atmosphere. There's outdoor dining in the summer and as weather
permits. A popular and upbeat lounge adjoins. Closed Sunday. ~
140 South Main Street, Pocatello; 208-233-4433, fax 208-233-
4082. MODERATE TO ULTRA-DELUXE.

Remo's is a great place to take the family or to have a pleasant
meal in garden surroundings on the outdoor patio in summer.
Specializing in steaks, prime rib and fresh fish, Remo's is also noted
for its outstanding Italian cuisine, including ravioli and fettuccine,
chicken cacciatore and veal piccata. The wine list is the most extensive in southeastern Idaho. ~ 160 West Cedar Street, Pocatello;
208-233-1710, fax 208-233-1438. MODERATE TO ULTRA-DELUXE.

If you've had your fill of meat and potatoes, try **Food for
Thought**. Offering "healthier" alternatives, this places dishes up
a mean Cobb salad (the owners tout it as being "world famous")
and delivers an array of fresh home made soups, salads and sandwiches. It's an eclectic little place. Lunch only. Closed weekends.
~ 504 East Center Street, Pocatello; 208-233-7267. BUDGET.

Another good spot for salad is **Buddy's Italian Restaurant**. The
interior leaves a bit to be desired, but you can always order your
meal to go. They also serve traditional fare like calzones, pizza and
pasta. Closed Sunday. ~ 626 East Lewis Street, Pocatello; 208-233-
1172. BUDGET TO MODERATE.

The world's potato capital isn't the place you would expect to
find Chinese food, but the **Hong Kong Restaurant** may fill your
needs. They serve hefty portions of egg foo yung, chop suey and

chow mein, and for a taste of American, they offer cheeseburgers. ~ 156 North Broadway, Blackfoot; 208-785-7102. BUDGET.

SHOPPING

Southeastern Idaho's regional shopping center is the **Pine Ridge Mall**, just south of Route 86 on the north end of Pocatello. ~ 4155 Yellowstone Avenue, Chubbuck; 208-237-7160. Among its 65 shops is **Idaho Unlimited**, which features a fine selection of Idaho-made gift items, foods and wines. ~ 208-237-0749; www.idahounlimited.com.

Art lovers in Pocatello can check out the **Cinnamon Tree Art and Frame.** ~ Westwood Mall, 1800 Garrett Way; 208-232-6371. There's also the **Pocatello Art Center.** ~ 444 North Main Street; 208-232-0970; www.pocatellaartctr.org. Also visit the **Tara-James Gallery**. ~ 200 South Main Street; 208-232-2925. The **East Side Antique Mall** has a fine selection of furniture, primitives, glassware and much more. ~ 128 North 2nd Avenue; 208-232-0236.

Two bookstores of note in Pocatello include **Walrus & Carpenter Books.** ~ 251 North Main Street; 208-233-0821. The other is the gay-friendly **Pegasus Book Store**, featuring magazines and used books. ~ 246 West Center Street; 208-232-6493.

NIGHTLIFE

Cultural life in Pocatello revolves around Idaho State University (ISU). ~ 741 South 7th Avenue; 208-282-0211; www.isu.edu. The ISU **Department of Music**, which includes a university band, choir and children's chorus, has regular student and faculty performances primarily at Goranson Hall, during the spring and fall. ~ 208-282-3636. The **Idaho State Civic Symphony** has an October-to-May schedule. ~ 208-234-1587. **Theatre ISU** offers six plays—two each in the fall, winter and spring—at Frazier Hall. ~ 208-282-3595.

Concerts by country-and-western and pop performers are normally scheduled at ISU's **Holt Arena**, at the north end of the campus. The 12,000-seat arena, America's first indoor college football stadium when it was built around 1970, still hosts NCAA Big Sky Conference athletics as well as other major shows, community events and exhibits, including the Dodge National Circuit Finals Rodeo in mid-March each year. ~ Memorial Drive, Pocatello; 208-282-2831, fax 208-282-4089.

AUTHOR FAVORITE

I'm too much of a city slicker to try my luck on the mechanical bull, but I will happily join in the line dancing at **The Green Triangle**, Idaho's largest country-and-western bar. The club has music nightly. ~ 4010 West Yellowstone Avenue, Chubbuck; 208-237-0354.

The pride and joy of Pocatello's arts community was the 1938 art deco–style Chief Theatre, which burned to the ground several years ago. Immediately after its demise, Pocatello's civic leaders began planning its reconstruction as a convention center and symphony hall. At press time, these plans were on hold indefinitely and all that remains of the theater is an empty lot.

The First National Bar occasionally presents bands in an old bank building in Pocatello's historic district. ~ 232 West Center Street; 208-233-1516. The college crowd gathers at the **Center Street Clubhouse.** ~ 542 East Center Street; 208-232-9654.

Bobby Joe's Five Mile Inn has live country-and-western music and dancing Friday and Saturday. ~ 4828 Yellowstone Avenue, Chubbuck; 208-237-9950.

Horse-racing fans head to **Pocatello Downs** in May for parimutuel racing. Horse and greyhound races are simulcast year-round. Closed Monday and Tuesday. ~ 10560 North Fairgrounds Road; 208-238-1721, fax 208-238-1991.

In Fort Hall, year-round gamblers can visit **Shoshone-Bannock High Stakes Bingo.** ~ Take Route 15 to Exit 80 and turn left to Simplot Road; 208-237-8774.

PARKS

CARIBOU–TARGHEE NATIONAL FOREST 🏃🏇🎿🏠🎣
Covering thousands of forested acres, the Pocatello district of Caribou–Targhee National Forest offers a myriad of recreation possibilities close to town. In addition to downhill and Nordic ski areas, the forest offers hiking and horseback riding, and cross-country skiing trails crisscross the area. There are rainbow and brook trout in Pebble Creek near Big Springs Campground. Facilities include picnic areas, restrooms and Pebble Creek ski area. ~ Major access points off Route 15 south of Pocatello are from Exits 63 west, 58 east, 22 west, 17 and 13 east. The park headquarters are located at 499 North 2400 East, St. Anthony. To reach Scout Mountain Campground, follow South Bannock Highway out of Pocatello (it will turn into Mink Creek Road) for about ten miles and take a left on Scout Mountain Road; 208-236-7500.

▲ There are 48 RV/tent sites (no hookups); $8 per night. Only ten miles out of Pocatello is Scout Mountain Campground: There are 33 RV/tent sites; $8 per night.

▼▼▼▼▼▼▼▼▼▼▼▼▼
American Falls Area

When a Bureau of Reclamation dam created American Falls Reservoir in 1927, it obliterated a 50-foot Snake River waterfall that had been known to Oregon Trail pioneers and myriad other travelers. But the reservoir itself, largest on the Snake, gave birth to an 86-mile network of irrigation canals that helped turn lava desert into fertile farmland and make Idaho the leading potato-producing state in America.

Today the town of **American Falls**, a potato processing and ship-ping center that was moved to its present site when the reservoir was created, is a good departure point for exploring this recon-stituted terrain. ~ Located on Route 86, 26 miles southwest of Pocatello.

Free tours are offered weekday afternoons at **American Falls Dam** by the Idaho Power Company. The current dam, built in 1976 at a cost of $46 million, is 86 feet high and 2900 feet long. ~ Route 39, American Falls; 208-226-2434, fax 208-236-7823. There are several day-use parks along the shore of **American Falls Reservoir**, the largest reservoir on the Snake with 935 square miles of water surface when full.

Eleven miles downstream (west) from American Falls, **Mas-sacre Rocks State Park** is where the Oregon Trail passed through a break in the high rock walls lining the Snake River. A visitors center (closed Labor Day to Memorial Day) has displays and in-terpretive programs on Shoshone and pioneer history, geology and the area's prolific plant and animal life. The grisly name stems from an 1862 Shoshone attack on a pioneer wagon train.

American Falls Area

Great Rift National Landmark

Aberdeen

39

LAVA BEDS

American Falls Res

Oregon Trail

86

30

N

American Falls Dam

American Falls

Willow Bay Recreation Area

0   10 miles

0   10 kilometers

River

Fort Hall

Indian

Reservation

Bannock

Minidoka National Wildlife Refuge

Snake

Trail

30

86

37

Oregon

Raft River

Massacre Rocks State Park

Rockland

Creek

The day after the massacre, another wagon train joined with the original group and the settlers decided to band together and seek vengeance on their attackers. A total of 30 emigrants fought the Indians, but the fight went badly for the settlers and the Shoshone pursued them back to the settlers' camp, killing three and wounding more in the process. When the dust had cleared, ten settlers died as a result of the skirmishes. Admission. ~ 3592 North Park Lane, American Falls; 208-548-2672; e-mail mas@idpr.state.id.us.

Look for the Indian's head carving at Register Rock made in 1866 by J. J. Hansen, then seven years old. He came back in 1913 as a 54-year-old sculptor and dated the rock again.

Three miles downstream from the park is 20-foot-high **Register Rock**, where pioneers carved their names or scrawled them in axle grease. In the upper loop of the park's campground, the rocky **Devils Garden** represents one of nature's volcanic oddities. As the lava was solidifying, air bubbles formed, creating little rounded spires about three inches high and four inches in diameter that cover the black rock.

North from American Falls, you can take Route 39 eastward, around the back side of the reservoir and through the potato-farming communities of Aberdeen, Springfield, Pingree and Rockford to Blackfoot.

A side trip leads to the captivating volcanic terrain of the **Great Rift National Landmark**, the longest exposed rift in North America. The lava fields look fresh, as if they were from a recent lava flow, but in fact they are about 2000 years old. The rift is the deepest in the world. The Great Rift, on Bureau of Land Management public lands, extends north to Craters of the Moon National Monument. To reach it, leave Route 39 seven miles south of Aberdeen or five miles north of American Falls, taking North Pleasant Valley Road west. After 11 miles, follow signs north on Winter Road for four miles, then west again another 13 miles on a gravel BLM road.

Within the national landmark is the **King's Bowl**, a dramatic crater—150 feet deep and 100 feet across—formed by a violent explosion about 2100 years ago.

LODGING   A low brick structure removed a bit from the street, the **American Motel** is certainly a very good choice. The rooms feature country-style decor, are well-maintained and include kitchenettes. ~ 2814 Pocatello Avenue, American Falls; 208-226-7271, fax 208-226-2263; e-mail fpowell163@aol.com. BUDGET.

The **Hillview Motel** earns its name from its site on a bluff above town overlooking American Falls Reservoir. The rooms are basic hotel fare, but they're large and all of them peer down on the lake, though the upper rooms have the better view. Even the swimming pool enjoys the expansive view. ~ 2799 Lakeview

Drive, American Falls; phone/fax 208-226-5151, 800-538-8112.
BUDGET.

When American Falls-ians go out for dinner they tend toward
the **China City Restaurant**, a white, wood-frame building a block
from the city park. The ambience is sunny and sort of Chinese
with a Western rough-hewn feel. The menu is Cantonese but includes two curries; their bacon fried rice is unique. They also serve
an American menu of beef, veal and chicken that includes sandwiches and fries. ~ 220 Harrison Street, American Falls; 208-226-
7038. BUDGET.

DINING

The locals gather for lunch at the bowling alley—there's only
one. The entrance brings you immediately to the **Melody Cafe**
counter and a row of booths; the nonsmoking section is a large,
bright room past the counter. No surprises on the menu; the
Melody serves a standard fare of sandwiches, hamburgers and
chicken fingers. Oh, and there are eight alleys for bowlers at **The
Melody Lanes**. ~ 152 Harrison Street, American Falls; 208-226-
2815, fax 208-226-1098; e-mail rmc518@aol.com. BUDGET.

Your safest bet here is the **Silver Horseshoe Bar**. Located downtown, this friendly place is decorated with wooden tiles seared
with the brands of most Idaho ranches—hundreds and hundreds.
A pool table greets you as you enter, but there is also a foosball
table and dartboard to help while away your time; there are tables filling the back. ~ 572 Fort Hall Avenue, American Falls;
208-226-9600. The more adventurous might quaff a draft at the
Sagebrush Inn, a clamorous and friendly cinder-block roadhouse
on the outskirts of town. ~ 2810 Pocatello Avenue, American
Falls; 208-226-9636.

NIGHTLIFE

WILLOW BAY RECREATION AREA The
largest park on American Falls Reservoir, Willow Bay is popular
for its fishing access and its sandy beach. There's also a lakeview
café that operates during the summer. American Falls Reservoir
has an outstanding rainbow trout fishery and numerous other
species. There are picnic tables, restrooms, a playground and concessions. ~ From the town of American Falls, take Marina Road
north two miles across Route 39; 208-226-2688; e-mail llarayc@
aol.com.

PARKS

▲ There are 26 RV/tent sites (with hookups), plus an undeveloped overflow area; $11 to $16 per night. Closed November through March; reservations recommended.

MASSACRE ROCKS STATE PARK This scenic
1000-acre park on the Snake River was well-known to mid-19th-
century travelers on the Oregon Trail. Look for wagon ruts and

for migrants' names scrawled on 20-foot-high Register Rock, three miles downstream from the visitors center. Unusual geology (it was gouged by the prehistoric Bonneville Flood), a prolific natural history (300 species of desert plants, more than 200 kinds of birds), hiking, water sports and an interpretive program attract many visitors. Fishing is good for trout and smallmouth bass in the Snake River. There are picnic areas, restrooms and a visitors center. Day-use fee, $4. ~ From American Falls, take Route 86 west 11 miles to well-marked Exit 28; 208-548-2672, fax 208-548-2671; www.idahoparks.org/parks/massacre.html, e-mail mas@idpr.state.id.us.

▲ There are 48 RV/tent sites (most with hookups); $16.72 to $31.80 per night. There are also two rustic cabins with electricity that sleep up to six; $41.10 per night.

▼▼▼▼▼▼▼▼▼▼▼▼▼▼▼

Bear River Country

History takes a front seat in southeasternmost Idaho's Bear River country, from the ruts of the Oregon Trail to the earliest white settlement in the state. The varied region also contains Lava Hot Springs, Idaho's leading hot-springs resort; the phosphate-mining center of Soda Springs, with the world's largest captive geyser; and Minnetonka Cave, its ice-crystal walls preserving prehistoric marine fossils, overlooking turquoise-blue Bear Lake.

The Bear River provides a common theme. The only major stream in Idaho that is *not* a tributary (directly or indirectly) of the Snake or Columbia river, it rises in Utah's Uinta Mountains and—after a meandering, 350-mile course through parts of Wyoming and Idaho—flows into the Great Salt Lake. In Idaho, the slow-flowing Bear passes through or near the region's three major towns, Montpelier, Soda Springs and Preston. Below Montpelier, it is joined by the waters flowing from huge Bear Lake, adding to its importance as an irrigation resource.

The first permanent non–American Indian communities in Idaho were founded in the Bear River country in the 1860s by settlers of the Mormon faith. Drifting north from their Salt Lake City base, the Mormons sought respect for their doctrines, particularly polygamy but also economic and social tenets. Today they are the largest religious group in Idaho, about 400,000 strong; in southeastern Idaho, a non-Mormon is the exception.

Plan two days to explore the Bear River country, on a loop drive beginning to the southeast of Pocatello off Route 15. From McCammon, take Route 30 east through Lava Hot Springs and Soda Springs to Montpelier. Follow Route 89 south past Bear Lake to Logan, Utah; then return through Idaho via Franklin and Preston to Route 15 and Pocatello. The full circuit, minus almost-obligatory detours, is 245 miles.

Before Oregon Trail pioneers arrived, Bannock and Shoshone tribes had declared **Lava Hot Springs** to be a truce zone. Hydrogeologists say the mineral pools, at the base of lava cliffs along the Portneuf River, have remained at 102 to 110°F for 50 million years. Today the hot springs are promoted as **Idaho's World Famous Hot Springs & Olympic Swimming Complex**. There are two swimming pools and four mineral-rich but sulfur-free soaking pools, two of them with whirlpools (open year-round). The Sunken Gardens bloom on the lava walls near the pools. The Olympic Swimming Complex is closed October to mid-May. Admission. ~ 430 East Main Street, Lava Hot Springs; 208-776-5221, 800-423-8597, fax 208-776-5273; www.lavahotsprings.org, e-mail mlowe@lhs.state.id.us.

The small resort community of 450 people has a wide range of lodgings (some with private soaking tubs) and restaurants, as well as the **South Bannock County Historical Center**. An exhibit on the ◀ *HIDDEN* evolution of transportation in the region highlights the museum, which also has displays on American Indian and pioneer history. ~ 110 East Main Street, Lava Hot Springs; phone/fax 208-776-5254.

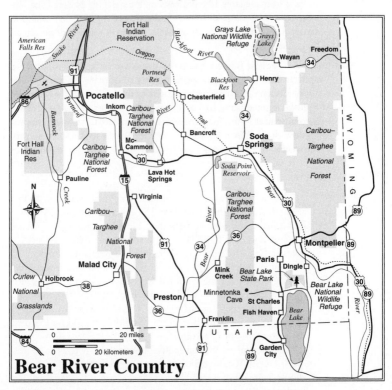

Bear River Country

Bear Lake—Caribou Scenic Byway

South of Grays Lake, Route 34 becomes the breathtaking Bear Lake—Caribou Scenic Byway. At Soda Springs (page 126), the drive continues southeast along Route 30 to Montpelier, where it proceeds southwest towards the Utah border.

MONTPELIER   The first Idaho settlement on the Oregon Trail, Montpelier was initially settled by Mormons who lived on very good terms with Bannock and Shoshone tribes. Today, Montpelier is the hub of the Bear Lake area.

PARIS   As it approaches Bear Lake, Route 89 enters the charming farming village of Paris, Idaho's second-oldest settlement (1863). Paris is best known for its **Paris Idaho Stake Tabernacle**. The Mormon house of worship was built in 1889 in Gothic style from red sandstone, sledded to Paris from a quarry 18 miles away on the east side of Bear Lake. The interior woodwork is all handcrafted and held together by handmade square nails. Guided tours are available. Closed in winter. ~ Main Street, Paris; 208-945-3333.

BEAR LAKE   Follow Route 89 south to the village of St. Charles, where it reaches Bear Lake. Unique for its brilliant aquamarine color caused by a high concentration of limestone particles, this lake—seven miles across and twenty miles long, half of it across the border in Utah—contains several species of fish found nowhere else on earth. The annual spawning runs of the Bonneville cisco, a swift, sardinelike whitefish, begin with the winter frost; ice fishermen dip nets and buckets for them. **Bear**

A side trip leads to **Chesterfield**, a 19th-century village that seems frozen in time. Established in 1879 by a dozen Mormon families and laid out in a perfect 35-block grid, it quickly reached a population of 400 (80 percent of whom were related to founder Chester Call). Relegated to virtual ghost-town status by war, depression and the opening of better farming lands, the entire community is now on the National Register of Historic Places. Remaining are 23 buildings, all but two of them pre-1910, preserved by the Chesterfield Foundation. ~ Drive seven miles east from Lava Hot Springs, then turn north 15 miles on 1300 East Road via the community of Bancroft.

The phosphate-mining center of **Soda Springs** is 27 miles east on Route 30. What is claimed as the world's only "captive geyser" shoots a stream of water 150 feet into the air at **Geyser Park**. Unleashed in 1937 when a drill crew inadvertently struck an under-

Lake State Park has two units, both of them offering excellent swimming. A sandbar divides Bear Lake from marshy Mud Lake and the **Bear Lake National Wildlife Refuge**, to its north. ~ 325 Webster Street, Montpelier; 208-847-1757, fax 208-847-1319.

ST. CHARLES St. Charles was the birthplace of Gutzon Borglum (1867–1941), sculptor of Mount Rushmore. A monument on the church grounds, beside Route 93 in the heart of town, commemorates his life. The Utah state border is eight miles south; the **Bear Lake Convention and Visitors Bureau** has its headquarters just two miles north of the border. Closed weekends. ~ Fish Haven; 208-945-3333, 800-448-2327, fax 208-945-2072.

GARDEN CITY The Utah end of the lake, focused around the berry-growing center of Garden City, has more resort and marina facilities than the Idaho side. It was here, along the lake's southwestern shore, that legendary fur trappers like Jim Bridger, Donald Mackenzie and Jedediah Smith attended American Indian trade rendezvous during the summers of 1827 and 1828.

MINNETONKA CAVE West of Bear Lake, gravel roads climb creek canyons to the 9000-foot heights of the Wasatch Range and Caribou–Targhee National Forest. Of particular interest is Minnetonka Cave. The half-mile-long limestone cavern is noted for its stalagmites and stalactites, ice-crystal walls, banded travertine rock and fossils of prehistoric plants and marine mammals. Guided tours through its nine chilly chambers are offered from mid-June to Labor Day. Expect a workout: You'll climb or descend 448 steps at 7700-foot elevation. Admission. ~ Forest Road 412, St. Charles; 208-847-0375..

ground chamber of carbon dioxide at a depth of 315 feet, the geyser has been capped and now erupts by timer: every hour on the hour. ~ 39 West 1st Street South, Soda Springs; 208-547-2600, fax 208-547-2601; www.sodaspringsid.com, e-mail soda coc@sodachamber.com.

Outside of town on Route 34, amazing travertine rock formations and caves make up the **Formation Springs Preserve**. The travertine, or calcium carbonate, is formed as spring water saturated with calcium bubbles up out of the ground and mixes with the oxygen in the air. Over the years, layers of travertine build up to create pools, formations and caves. ~ 208-788-8988, fax 208-788-9040; www.nature.org.

Two designated scenic byways meet at Soda Springs. Route 34, the **Pioneer Historic Byway**, runs 49 miles south to Preston (discussed later in this tour) and 47 miles northeast to the village of Freedom in Wyoming's Star Valley. En route it skirts the **Grays Lake National Wildlife Refuge** in a mountain valley at 6400 feet. ~ 74 Grays Lake Road, Wayan; 208-574-2755, fax 208-574-2756; e-mail dick_sjostrom@fws.gov.

Southeast of Soda Springs, the **Bear Lake–Caribou Scenic Byway** follows Route 30 to Montpelier, then Route 89 down the western shore of Bear Lake and into Utah. See "Bear Lake–Caribou Scenic Byway" on page 126 for information on this picturesque drive.

From Bear Lake you can return north up Route 89 to its junction with secondary Route 36, four miles north of Paris, and continue west to Franklin, a 65-mile drive from Fish Haven. Or you can continue west on Route 89 from Garden City, surmounting scenic Sunrise Summit and descending the Logan Canyon to bustling Logan, Utah. Just past the Utah State University campus, turn north on Route 91 and cross the border to Franklin, 66 miles from Fish Haven.

Franklin is one and a quarter miles north of the Utah border. When founded in 1860 as the first white settlement in what is now Idaho, it was believed to be south of the 42nd parallel and thus in Brigham Young's Utah. An 1872 survey gave townspeople a big surprise. The National Register of Historic Places today lists two places in town. The **Lorenzo Hatch Home** was built in 1870 in Greek revival style; the interior is under renovation until 2006, but it's worth driving by for a look at the outside. ~ 127 East Main Street; 208-334-2844. The **Pioneer Relic Hall**, a small early settlers' museum residing in a two-story stone store built in 1895, features black-and-white photos of pioneers, an original Yellowstone stagecoach and a replica of the old pioneer fort. Open Tuesday through Saturday from May through September. ~ East Main Street and 1st Street East; 208-334-2844.

Northwest of Franklin, Route 91 proceeds through **Preston**—a farming town whose 3800 people make it the largest community in Bear River country—to **Red Rock Pass**. It was here that

AUTHOR FAVORITE

After a long day of highway driving, I like knowing that I can plunge into a mineral pool just as soon as I arrive at **Lava Hot Springs Inn**: The private hot mineral pools at this European-style inn are open daily to guests. Built as a hospital on the banks of the Portneuf River in the 1920s, the inn has 28 rooms with an art deco–era decor. Twelve jacuzzi suites have private baths; other rooms share facilities. A full gourmet breakfast is served to all guests. Gay-friendly. ~ 94 Portneuf Avenue, Lava Hot Springs; phone 208-776-5830, 800-527-5830, fax 208-776-5521; www.lavahotsprings inn.com, e-mail lavahotspringsinn@msn.com. MODERATE TO DELUXE.

Lake Bonneville burst its banks some 15,000 years ago (22 miles from modern Preston) and began the catastrophic Bonneville Flood. The highway joins Route 15 at Virginia, 33 miles from Preston and 35 miles south of Pocatello.

LODGING

Hot mineral pools are an amenity at the **Riverside Inn & Hot Spring**. This historic three-story bed-and-breakfast hotel beside the Portneuf River has 16 rooms; some low-cost rooms share bathrooms while others have private facilities. A continental breakfast is included. ~ 255 East Portneuf Avenue, Lava Hot Springs; 208-776-5504, 800-733-5504, fax 208-776-5504; www.riversideinn hotspring.com, e-mail riversideinn901@cs.com. DELUXE.

Oregon Trail wagon ruts can still be seen at the **Bar H Bar Ranch**, eight miles southeast of Soda Springs off Route 30. The historic, 9000-acre working ranch in the foothills of the Bear River Range runs 2000 head of beef cattle; guests are invited to assist in branding and calving, repairing fences and other day-to-day chores. A maximum of six guests stay in four private rooms in a rustic bunkhouse with lodge-style furnishings and eat three hearty meals a day with their hosts. In summer there's horseback riding, fishing and hiking; in winter, cross-country skiing and snowmobiling. ~ 1501 Eight Mile Creek Road, Soda Springs; 208-547-3082, 800-743-9505, fax 208-547-0203; e-mail barhbar@ aol.com. MODERATE.

Bear Lake Bed & Breakfast overlooks the shimmering aquamarine lake from a hillside just off Route 89, two miles north of the Utah border. Five of the seven bedrooms in the log home are rented to guests; there's a recreation room with TV and an outdoor hot tub; a full breakfast is served. A deluxe room has a fireplace, queen-size bed and private bath; others share bathrooms. ~ 500 Loveland Lane, Fish Haven; 208-945-2688; www.bearlake bedandbreakfast.com. MODERATE.

DINING

Ye Ole Chuck Wagon serves up typical Western fare—sirloin, hamburgers, chicken-fried steak. They also have an extensive seafood menu, including salmon, halibut and shrimp. ~ 211 East Main Street, Lava Hot Springs; 208-776-5141. BUDGET TO MODERATE.

The outlaw gang that once robbed a bank in Montpelier lives on at **Butch Cassidy's Restaurant and Saloon**. Steak, prime rib and seafood are the evening bill of fare at this popular dining spot, which serves three meals daily. ~ 230 North 4th Street, Montpelier; 208-847-3501, fax 208-847-3503; e-mail butchcassidy@ ohgolly.com. MODERATE TO DELUXE.

SHOPPING

Dedicated shoppers will want to tour Main Street in Lava Hot Springs. Most of the usual tourist bric-a-brac is available here— moccasins, T-shirts and turquoise jewelry. Look attentively for the true "finds." **Dempsey Creek Trading Company** sells the best collection of silver rings, necklaces and earrings. ~ 89 East Main Street, Lava Hot Springs; 208-776-5665, fax 208-776-5662; e-mail dempseycr1@aol.com.

At **Lava Lil's**, you can stock up on old-time photos, unique Western furniture, housewares and souvenirs. If you forgot your bathing suit, they sell them here, too. ~ 222 East Main Street, Lava Hot Springs; 208-776-5239, fax 208-776-5399.

The **Purple Moon Crystal Company** has jewelry, crystals, incense and items with a magical or mystical theme, though what relation that bears to the local hot pools remains, um . . . a mystery. ~ 50 East Main Street, Lava Hot Springs; 208-776-5475; www.purplemooncrystal.com.

NIGHTLIFE   The **Blue Moon Bar and Grill** presents live music Friday and Saturday in otherwise quiet Lava Hot Springs. If a band is not booked, look for karaoke on Wednesday and Sunday, plus bingo Wednesday, Friday and Sunday. There is ample table seating and a small dancefloor on the music side of this nondescript but popular club, and for entertainment besides music, you'll find pool, darts and video games. ~ 89 South 1st Street East, Lava Hot Springs; 208-776-5077.

PARKS   **CARIBOU–TARGHEE NATIONAL FOREST** 🚶 🏇 🏠 ⛵ 🛥️ 🛶 The tall tales of Canadian miner Jesse "Cariboo Jack" Fairchild, who in 1870 discovered gold on the slopes of 9600-foot Caribou Mountain, gave this region its name. The million-acre forest has seven parcels in Idaho and bits in Wyoming and Utah; the largest part extends from Palisades Reservoir south to Montpelier, and there's an additional section (a portion of Cache National Forest) south of Soda Springs that reaches to the Utah border. Timbered and sage-covered slopes are ripe for exploring—by foot, on horseback, on cross-country skis or snowmobiles. Swimming is possible in mountain lakes. There's rainbow, brook, brown and cutthroat trout, bluegill and bass for fishing. Facilities here include picnic areas and restrooms. ~ From Soda Springs, take Route 34 north or Eight Mile Canyon Road 425 south; from Montpelier, take Route 36 west or Crow Creek Road 111 north; from Bear Lake, take Paris Canyon Road 421, Bloomington Canyon Road 409 or St. Charles Creek Road 412 west. To reach Eight Mile Campground, follow the Forest Service signs on the south end of town to Eight Mile Road, which turns into Forest Service Road 325. There are signs for the campground; 208-847-0375, fax 208-847-3426; www.fs.fed.us/r4/caribou.

▲ There are 140 RV/tent sites (no hookups), plus 182 sites for tents only; $8 per night. Three guard stations are available for rental in the Soda Springs Ranger District for $30 per night;

reservations, 208-547-4356, fax 208-547-2235; www.fs.fed.us/ r4/caribou. Only eight miles out of Soda Springs is Eight Mile Campground, with seven small RV/tent sites; no charge.

GRAYS LAKE NATIONAL WILDLIFE REFUGE 🏃 🏕 The world's largest nesting population of greater sandhill cranes (about 200 pairs) makes its home at this 32,000-acre lake, which is actually an expansive marsh filled with bulrushes and cat- tails. A couple of hundred other species of birds, mainly waterfowl, have been seen here, while moose, elk, mule deer and smaller mammals are com- mon. A visitors center is open April to mid-November. There are restrooms and a visitors center (April to mid-November). ~ From Route 34 near Wayan, 35 miles northeast of Soda Springs, take Grays Lake Road three miles north to the visitors center; 208-574-2755, fax 208-574-2756.

> Butch Cassidy and his Wild Bunch got away with $7000 when they robbed the Montpelier bank in 1896.

BEAR LAKE STATE PARK 🏃 ⛵ 🎣 🚣 🚤 Spanning the border of Idaho and Utah, Bear Lake is noted for its remarkable turquoise color caused by suspended limestone particles. Known in the 1820s as the site of an annual mountain men's rendezvous, the lake contains several species of fish found nowhere else. The 52-acre state park consists of two parcels: one-and-a-half-mile-long East Beach, site of a campground, and two-mile-long North Beach, whose white sands are a swimmer's delight. Fishing is excellent for cutthroat and native lake trout, as well as other species; ice fishing for the unique Bonneville cisco in winter. Water sports and winter snowmobiling are popular activities. There are picnic tables and restrooms. Day-use fee, $4. ~ From St. Charles, 18 miles south of Montpelier on Route 89, take North Beach Road five miles east to North Beach, then Eastside Lake Road another eight miles east and south to East Beach; 208-847-1045, fax 208-847-1056; www.idahoparks.org/parks/index.html, e-mail bea@ idpr.state.id.us.

▲ There are 48 RV/tent sites at East Beach (20 with hookups); $13 per night for RVs, $9 for tents. Closed November through April.

BEAR LAKE NATIONAL WILDLIFE REFUGE 🚤 🚣 Encompassing Mud Lake and the Dingle Swamp immediately north of Bear Lake, this boggy 20,000-acre preserve is home to a large Canada geese population, as well as large numbers of ducks (mallard, canvasback, pintail, redhead and teal), herons, egrets, white pelicans and white-faced ibis. Boating is only allowed from September 20 to January 20 (though there is a canoe trail open July through September). There is limited fishing in season, consisting mainly of carp. Facilities include restrooms. ~ From Montpelier, take Route 89 west for four miles, turn left at the refuge sign and follow the gravel road for four miles until you reach the refuge entrance; 208-847-1757, fax 208-847-1319.

CURLEW NATIONAL GRASSLAND Caribou–Targhee National Forest administers the three parcels of this 47,000-acre grassland along Rock Creek and Deep Creek west of Malad City. Open to homestead settlement in the 1920s and 1930s, this land was severely eroded by farming and laid to waste; the abandoned land was purchased by the government and is now a federal sustained-yield management area open for grazing, fall game-bird hunting and year-round recreation, mainly at three-mile-long Stone Reservoir located south of Holbrook. Swimming is allowed at the beach at Stone Reservoir, also noted for crappie fishing; trout have also been stocked. There are picnic tables and restrooms. ~ From Malad City, 58 miles south of Pocatello on Route 15, take Route 38 west 23 miles to Holbrook. The Stone Reservoir parcel of the grassland is immediately south, the two Rock Creek parcels just to the north; 208-766-5900, fax 208-766-5914.

▲ There are 18 RV/tent sites (no hookups) at two campgrounds (Curlew Twin Springs); $8 per night at Curlew Campground, free at Twin Springs.

Outdoor Adventures

FISHING

While not the most famous fishing region of eastern Idaho (that title belongs to Henry's Fork), this area provides ample fishing opportunities. Anglers pursue rainbow trout in American Falls Reservoir, cutthroat trout in Blackfoot Reservoir. For fishing gear and advice on local conditions, contact **All-Seasons Angler**. ~ 509 East Oak Street, Pocatello; 208-232-3042.

Idaho's most unique fishery is at Bear Lake, which has four species of fish found nowhere else on earth. The winter run of the swift, sardinelike Bonneville cisco thrills ice fishermen. Bear Lake also draws anglers with its five species of trout, including huge mackinaw, and the Bear Lake and Bonneville whitefish.

Guides include **Bear Lake Outfitters**. ~ 2123 South Bear Lake Boulevard, Garden City, UT; 435-946-2855.

WATER SPORTS

Reservoirs and lakes dot Southeastern Idaho, providing boaters, sailboarders and waterskiers ample opportunity to try their sport. Bear Lake is one of the most popular bodies of water among board sailors and waterskiers. The **marina** at Bear Lake is in Garden City, Utah, but with the northern half of the lake in Idaho, this is widely used by Idaho boaters. Rentals are available here as well as at the **Bear Lake Marina Concession**. ~ 1865 North Bear Lake Boulevard; 435-946-3343.

American Falls Reservoir is another popular place among board sailors and waterskiers. The waters are also busy with boating enthusiasts.

Mountain Man Rendezvous

Trappers were the first Europeans in Idaho. They were hardy men, often loners who could tolerate and even thrive in the rugged conditions found in the Rocky Mountains and desert interior. A year or two might pass between encounters with "civilization," which might be no more than a shanty town erected at the edge of the vast prairie below the mountains.

But a mountain man can get to feeling lonely, too, even for his own kind. The stoutest must have looked forward tremendously to swapping stories, trading for equipment, tools and drink, and testing their frontier skills against those of fellow trappers. Such meetings came rarely and probably first occurred on the fringes of traditional American Indian gatherings that celebrated growing and harvest seasons. The mineral baths on the Portneuf River were such a neutral ground for neighboring tribes.

Mountain men trapped this area. They found game and beaver plentiful around Blue Lake and the Blue Spring Hills south of what is now Pocatello. Jim Bridger led trapping and trading expeditions to Bear Lake and the Bear Lake Valley as early as 1826. And consecutive rendezvous took place at the southern end of the lake in 1827 and 1828, attended by Bridger and Jedediah Smith. As trading in furs expanded, rendezvous were planned by larger companies, a sort of frontiersmen's trade show and convention. Pierre's Hole, in what is now the Teton Valley on the western slope of the Teton Range, was the site of an annual rendezvous organized by the Rocky Mountain Fur Company.

Today history buffs stage annual re-enactments of these rendezvous. Buckskin clothing is painstakingly re-created, as are skinning knives and "hawks," small tomahawks used for throwing. These and refurbished and replica flintlock rifles and pistols are carefully thrown and fired at targets in friendly competition. Trading booths are erected near lodges and tepees where buckskins and all the frontiersmen regalia can be purchased by visitors.

All are welcome to participate in events. All you need is an interest in history and a sense of adventure—and maybe a little cash for mementos. Southeastern Idaho boasts one rendezvous: the **Mountain Man Rendezvous** (Bear Lake State Park; 435-946-3343; e-mail nrdpr.brsp@state.ut.us), located near the site of Bridger's rendezvous at the south end of Bear Lake in northern Utah, gathers in mid-September.

RIVER RUNNING   Idaho is strewn with rivers waiting to be explored. Rafters and kayakers in southeastern Idaho can try the Snake, through American Falls; the Blackfoot, east of Blackfoot and the Bear, through Montpelier and Soda Springs. To enjoy the whitewater here, you'll have to bring your own gear, as rentals are not available except through Idaho State University's **Wilderness Equipment Rental Center**. They rent canoes, kayaks, rafts and camping equipment. Closed Sunday in winter, weekends in summer. ~ Pond Student Union, 8th and Humbolt streets, Pocatello; 208-282-2945, fax 208-282-4600.

SKIING   Skiers may not be able to fly down many mountains in southeastern Idaho—there's only one downhill-ski resort—but cross-country skiers will find more options.

Located 19 miles southeast of Pocatello, **Pebble Creek** is situated on the west side of 9271-foot Mount Bonneville in Caribou–Targhee National Forest. This resort boasts a 2200-foot vertical drop and 52 runs served by three chairlifts. There's a terrain and rail park. Rentals and instruction are available at the mountain. Closed mid-April to mid-December, depending on snow conditions. ~ 3340 East Green Canyon Road via Route 15 Exit 58, Inkom; 208-775-4452, 877-524-7669, fax 208-775-4453; www.pebble creekskiarea.com, e-mail info@pebblecreekskiarea.com.

The first toy ever to be marketed on American TV was Mr. Potato Head.

Cross-country Park 'n' Ski areas in southeastern Idaho include **Mink Creek** (24 kilometers, intermediate), on the Bannock Highway 15 miles south of Pocatello in Caribou–Targhee National Forest. Contact the Idaho Department of Parks and Recreation for more information. ~ 208-334-4199, fax 208-334-3741; www.idahoparks.org.

If you're into backcountry skiing, consider the series of primitive yurts in the Portneuf Range administered by the **Wilderness Equipment Rental Center** at Idaho State University. Closed Sunday in winter. ~ Pond Student Union, 8th and Humbolt streets, Pocatello; 208-282-2945, fax 208-282-4600.

Ski Rentals   Aside from the resort facilities themselves, there are many places to rent skiing and snowboarding equipment. In the Pocatello area, try **Scotts Ski & Sports** for skis and snowboards. ~ 224 North Main Street, Pocatello; 208-232-1449. **Barry's Ski & Sports** also rents equipment. ~ 1800 Garrett Way; 208-232-8996. Or you can rent from **Gart Brothers**. ~ 625 Yellowstone Street; 208-232-2981; www.gartsports.com. The **Wilderness Equipment Rental Center** at Idaho State University rents skis, snowboards and snowshoes, as well as ice-climbing gear. Closed Sunday in winter. ~ Pond Student Union, 8th and Humbolt streets, Pocatello; 208-282-2945, fax 208-282-4600.

If you're feeling the need to tee off, head to one of the area's golf courses. In Pocatello, try **Highland Golf Course.** ~ 201 Von Elm Lane; 208-237-9922. **Riverside Golf Course** has 18 holes. ~ 3500 Bannock Highway; 208-232-9515. The 18-hole course at the **Juniper Hills Country Club** is open to the public on Monday mornings. ~ 6600 Bannock Highway; 208-233-0241. There's a good municipal 18-hole course in Blackfoot—**Blackfoot Golf Course.** ~ 3115 Teeples Drive; 208-785-9960. There are also nine-hole courses in Aberdeen, American Falls, Soda Springs and Montpelier.

GOLF

Tennis must be a hot sport in Pocatello. Idaho State University has six outdoor and four indoor courts, and there are 25 more courts in the city and suburbs; contact the **Pocatello Parks and Recreation Department** for locations. ~ 208-234-6232.

TENNIS

Bicycling is a great way to experience the region's nature up close. Massacre Rocks State Park (west of American Falls) and the trails of Caribou–Targhee National Forest are popular destinations for bikers.
Bike Rentals Scott's Bike Shop rents bikes and can point you in the right direction. ~ 224 North Main Street, Pocatello; 208-232-4964. **Gateway Performance Outfitters** specializes in mountain bikes. ~ 404 South Arthur Street, Pocatello; 208-232-3711.

BIKING

The following trails are just a sample of some of the hikes available in the region's parks. All distances listed for hiking trails are one way unless otherwise noted.

The **West Fork of Mink Creek Trail** (6.6 miles) follows an old jeep road up a stream in Caribou–Targhee National Forest, only 13 miles south of downtown Pocatello. The creek contains numerous beaver ponds; you'll have to watch closely to spot the rodents themselves. The trailhead is one mile south of the ranger station on Bannock Highway.

Petticoat Peak Trail (2 miles) climbs to the summit of the 8000-foot-plus Fish Creek Range, just four miles northeast of Lava Hot Springs. The hike, very steep in places and not recommended for children, is worthwhile for the marvelous views from the summit.

HIKING

An interstate freeway system of three separate routes is the primary connecting network through southeastern Idaho, linking the region with Boise and Portland (Oregon) to the west, Salt Lake City (Utah) to the south and Butte (Montana) to the north.

Southbound **Route 15** from Butte climbs over the Continental Divide to Idaho Falls and Pocatello, proceeding south into Utah, where it is joined by Route 84. The highway continues to Salt

Transportation

CAR

Lake City, Las Vegas (Nevada) and southern California. **Routes 84** and **15** are linked between Burley and Pocatello by **Route 86**, which follows the Snake River through American Falls. **Route 30** branches off Route 15 to the east to link up Soda Springs and Montpelier before heading into Wyoming. **Route 89** veers south from Montpelier to Paris and then wraps around Bear Lake.

AIR

SkyWest and Horizon serve **Pocatello Regional Airport,** six miles west of Pocatello at Exit 56 on Route 86 West. Most visitors fly to either Boise or Salt Lake City, then drive. ~ 208-234-6154.

BUS

Greyhound Bus Lines (800-231-2222; www.greyhound.com) follow the corridor from Boise to Salt Lake City or West Yellowstone, Montana. There's a depot in Pocatello. ~ 215 West Bonneville Street; 208-232-5365. It also stops in Blackfoot at 1245 Parkway Drive.

CAR RENTALS

Avis Rent A Car (800-331-1212), **Budget Rent A Car** (800-527-0700) and **Hertz Rent A Car** (800-654-3131) have outlets at Pocatello airport. **U-Save Auto Rental** (800-272-8728) and **Enterprise Rent A Car** (800-325-8007) have downtown locations.

PUBLIC TRANSIT

Pocatello Regional Transit has extensive routes through the city. Fares are nominal. No service on Sunday. ~ 215 West Bonneville Street; 208-234-2287.

TAXIS

Pocatello's central dispatching office for cabs has the unmistakable name of **Taxi Dispatching.** ~ 208-232-1115.

SIX

Idaho Falls and Eastern Idaho

Eastern Idaho shares a border with Montana and Wyoming and, at its upper corner, claims a thin strip of Yellowstone National Park. The Snake River Basin is higher here than in western Idaho, and elevations begin at just under 5000 feet and climb to Teton and Yellowstone parks. On a clear day, and there are many, the thrusting high peaks of the Grand Tetons are visible across the plain to the east, and it is possible to see the intervening agricultural land rising gradually to meet them at their base.

The eastern Idaho climate is cooler, the winters longer and wetter than Twin Falls or Boise. The soils are every bit as fertile and here is the potato-growing capital of Idaho. The fields are ubiquitous, but a good place to view them is along Swan Valley east of Idaho Falls. The Snake River drains this valley beneath the controlled flow of Palisades Dam. Besides irrigating the valley's rich volcanic soils, the South Fork of the Snake, as it is known, supports a prized trout fishery.

This main branch of the river rises in the southern portion of Yellowstone Park and makes its way past the eastern front of the Teton Range before entering Idaho. The Henry's Fork of the Snake River, named for Major Andrew Henry who explored this valley in 1810, drains the northern area of the region. It rises in Idaho, near the Montana border, from one of the 40 largest springs in the nation, which produces 120 million gallons a day—enough water to supply a city of one million people. Big Spring flows at a steady temperature of 52°F, the mean average local temperature, and it feeds schools of overfed and eager trout. Unfortunately for anglers, fishing for the brutes is not allowed. Downstream, however, the Henry's Fork draws anglers from around the world.

Route 20 follows this broad, pastoral stream for most of its meanderings to the confluence with the South Fork above Idaho Falls, and Route 15 tracks the Snake River from the confluence southward to Pocatello. Most of the region's population lives along this corridor, and Idaho Falls is the largest city. This city is of interest to travelers mostly as the commercial center and jumping-off point for excursions to the national parks and backcountry nearby. Established in 1865, Idaho Falls had previously been known as Eagle Rock because of a large boulder in mid-river where eagles nested. The Eagle Rock Ferry, nearby, was then the only means of crossing the Snake. The site is upriver of the present-day "falls" downtown, which are a manmade spillway above a small rocky cascade.

Settlements and services on Route 20 become increasingly rural and resort-flavored in proximity to Yellowstone. Driving north on Route 15 takes travelers into Montana over the Continental Divide at Monida Pass, elevation 6823 feet. This windswept highway, which veers away from the evergreen Yellowstone country and through the tawny grasslands of the western Centennial Mountains, can be closed during winter storms.

▼▼▼▼▼▼▼▼▼▼▼▼
Idaho Falls Area

Idaho Falls, the state's major eastern gateway, marks a place of transition from the Snake River Plain to the Rocky Mountain wilderness. Part of the fertile region that made Idaho potatoes world famous, this very pretty, verdant city of 48,000 is within a two-hour drive of Yellowstone and Grand Teton national parks. Above Idaho Falls, the Snake flows out of the high Tetons, their crests visible for miles around. The Idaho Falls area lures outdoors lovers with its rich wildlife and scenic beauty.

SIGHTS

Idaho Falls dates back to 1865. Built at the site of an early bridge across a narrow stretch of the Snake, the village name was changed from Eagle Rock to Idaho Falls in 1891 to attract settlers. Oddly, there were no falls until 1911, when a power diversion weir created a 20-foot drop which validated the name. The falls can be viewed from the bridge where Broadway crosses the Snake River between downtown Idaho Falls and Route 15. They mark the southern end of the city's **Snake River Greenbelt,** one of 39 parks administered by Idaho Falls City Parks. Extending along both sides of the river for two and a half miles north to the Route 20 bridge, it includes a biking path and the Rotary International Peace Park, whose granite lanterns were a gift from Idaho Falls' sister city in Japan.

The **Greater Idaho Falls Chamber of Commerce** shares a visitors center with the Bureau of Land Management and U.S. Forest Service on the west side of the Greenbelt. Closed weekends.~ 630 West Broadway, Idaho Falls; 208-523-1010, fax 208-523-2255; www.idahofallschamber.com, e-mail ifcofc@ida.net.

A city architectural landmark, the impressive bright, white **Idaho Falls Temple** of the Church of Jesus Christ of Latter-day Saints (Mormons), bounds the Greenbelt to the east. ~ 1000 Memorial Drive, Idaho Falls; 208-523-4504.

The 75-acre **Russell Freeman Park** is connected to the Greenbelt along the Snake; reached via Fremont Avenue north of Route 20, it contains the **Idaho State Vietnam Veterans Memorial,** an inverted steel V accompanied by the names of all Idaho fatalities and MIAs from the Southeast Asian war. It was dedicated in 1990. ~ Science Center Drive, Idaho Falls; 208-529-1478, fax 208-529-1179.

With 80 acres south of downtown, **Tautphaus Park** is the city's largest. Once in the park, you might want to stop by the **Idaho Falls Tautphaus Park Zoo** (admission), with 300 animals of more than 85 species, including several large cats and an African penguin exhibit. Open weekends only from April through October. Closed November through March. ~ Rollandet Avenue at 25th

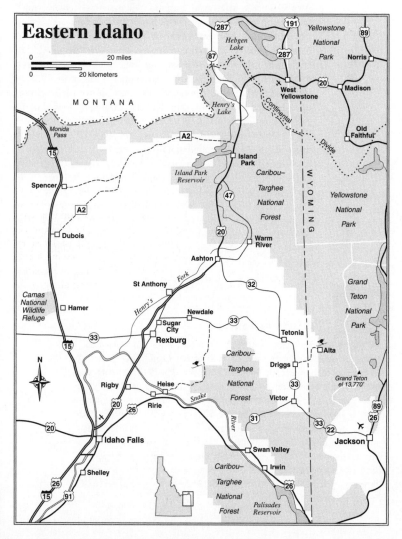

Eastern Idaho

Street, Idaho Falls;208-528-5552,fax208-528-6256; www.idaho fallszoo.org, e-mail ifzoo@ci.idaho-falls.id.us.

To learn more about Idaho Falls' history, stop at the **Museum of Idaho,** located in the 1916 Carnegie building. Its permanent exhibits range from natural history, early agriculture and mining to the atomic era. Admission. ~ 200 North Eastern Avenue, Idaho Falls; 208-522-1400, 800-325-7328; fax 208-524-5060; www. museumofidaho.org; e-mail nickgailey@onewest.net.

Gallery crawlers can start their exploration at the Idaho Falls Arts Council's **Miles and Virginia Willard Arts Center,** which houses two galleries featuring exhibits of local and regional artists. Closed Sunday. Also part of the Willard Arts Center is the 1919 **Colonial Theater,** which began life as a vaudeville theater with incredible acoustics (a whisper from the stage can be heard at the top of the balcony). Renamed the Paramount Theater in 1929, it began screening movies in addition to hosting live performances until it closed in the 1980s. This 970-seat theater, re-opened in the 1990s, now offers a variety of events. Closed Sunday. ~ 450 A Street, Idaho Falls; 208-522-0471, fax 208-522-0413; www.idaho fallsarts.org, e-mail ifac@idahofallsarts.org.

Clotheshorses will enjoy viewing the evolution of 20th-century styles (in addition to theatrical garb) at the **Idaho Falls Opera.** Call for hours. ~ 1753 West Broadway, Idaho Falls; 208-522-0875.

North of Idaho Falls, Route 15 makes a virtual beeline for the Montana border, 77 miles north, and the 6823-foot Monida Pass on the Continental Divide. Other than scenic beauty, there's not a whole lot to see along this route. **Camas National Wildlife Refuge** is immediately to the west of the interstate, 30 miles north of Idaho Falls; gravel roads through the refuge are open daily. See "Idaho

sights

AUTHOR FAVORITE

I immediately forget about Idaho's gold-rush past when I begin digging for my own hidden treasure at **Spencer Opal Mines,** the only commercial opal mine in North America. Discovered in 1948 by hunters, it is noted for its plentiful star opals, red, green, pink, yellow or blue in color. Rock hounds can obtain a permit and directions to the open-pit mine at the mine headquarters in tiny Spencer, 60 miles north of Idaho Falls; the mine is seven miles east on a south-facing hillside at 7000 feet. Washing water is available at the mine, where equipment can be rented or bought. The mine is only open to public digging on select days; call ahead. The headquarters boasts a mini-mine open seven days a week. Admission. ~ Idmon Road, Spencer; 208-374-5476, fax 208-374-5107; www.spenceropalmine.com.

Falls Area Parks" below. ~ Refuge Road, Hamer; 208-662-5423, fax 208-662-5525.

Route 20 from Idaho Falls more or less follows the stream to its source. Before crossing the main Snake, Route 20 passes through **Rigby**, a childhood home of Philo Taylor Farnsworth III. Farnsworth lived in Idaho from age 12 to 16. His science classes and fascination with electronics inspired him to daydream as he plowed the fields after school. He was just 14 (in 1920) when he conceived the idea of a dissector that could reduce pictures to their basic electrons, transmit them to a receiver and reassemble them into a visual image. By the time he was 22, Farnsworth had created the first cathode-ray tube and the first electronic television. Memorabilia about Farnsworth are displayed at the **Jefferson County Historical Society Farnsworth TV and Pioneer Museum**. Closed Sunday and Monday. Admission. ~ 118 West 1st Street South, Rigby; 208-745-8423.

One of eastern Idaho's better lodging bargains is the **Littletree Inn**. Located near the Pinecrest golf course off Route 26 on the northeast side of Idaho Falls, it's a hit with business travelers. Its 73 nicely kept rooms include some cooking units with refrigerators and microwave ovens. Facilities include a swimming pool, hot tub, fitness center, coin laundry and a lounge (open Thursday only). ~ 888 North Holmes Avenue, Idaho Falls; 208-523-5993, 800-521-5993, fax 208-523-7104. www.littletreeinn.com, e-mail iflit tletree@msn.com. BUDGET TO MODERATE.

LODGING

Motel West is one of those privately run motels you wish every city had. A step above the standard "ma and pa" label with 80 guest rooms, it retains the friendly feel of a smaller lodging. Each pleasant, comfortable room has nice wood decor. There's an indoor pool, a hot tub, a coin laundry and an adjacent café. The motel is on the west side of town, on Route 20 toward Arco. ~ 1540 West Broadway, Idaho Falls; 208-522-1112, 800-582-1063, fax 208-524-1144. MODERATE.

Many major hotel chains are represented in Idaho Falls, including Holiday Inn, Quality Inn, Shilo Inn, Comfort Inn and Super 8, all on the west side of the Snake just off Route 15.

If you want to escape cookie-cutter accommodations, travel 15 miles north of Idaho Falls to Rigby. The **BlackSmith Inn** features five cozy guest rooms, individually decorated with Western-themed wall murals and colorful quilts; all have private baths as well as TVs and VCRs. Rounding out the amenities are a video library and a hot tub. A hearty full breakfast is included in the rates. Reservations recommended. ~ 227 North 3900 East, Rigby; 208-745-6208, 888-745-6208, fax 208-745-0602; www. blacksmithinn.com, e-mail theinn@blacksmithinn.com. MODERATE TO DELUXE.

DINING

HIDDEN ▶

If you enjoy great "greasy spoons," you can't go wrong at the **North Highway Cafe**. Huge portions of chicken, seafood and hickory-smoked beef are served up for lunch and dinner, often to real Idaho cowboys from the state's largest stockyard across the street. Breakfast starts at 5 a.m. ~ 460 Northgate Mile, Idaho Falls; 208-522-6212. BUDGET TO MODERATE.

Of course, the hawg in **Hawg Smoke Cafe** has little to do with a porcine-flavored menu, but is a sly reference to the owner's liking for Harley-Davidson motorcycles—he built one from the ground up. But this is not a biker restaurant; the owner-chef is a refugee from Sun Valley kitchens who offers an eclectic new menu daily with an emphasis on fresh fish, beef tenderloin, and a spicy curry that hints at a Mexican mole. Inside, the dining tables are set about a casual room that is intended to imitate your own home— family photos cover the walls, along with some bike memorabilia. Meals by reservation only. No credit cards. ~ 4330 North Yellowstone Highway, Idaho Falls; 208-523-4804. DELUXE.

Mama Inez, behind an unimposing storefront in the downtown historic district, offers authentic Mexican food. Closed Sunday. ~ 344 Park Avenue, Idaho Falls; 208-525-8968. BUDGET TO MODERATE.

Jaker's Steak and Fish House is a classy dining spot with a family emphasis. You'll find a wide variety of choices on the menu including seafood, beef, chicken, salads, pasta and desserts. No lunch on weekends. ~ 851 Lindsay Boulevard, Idaho Falls; 208-524-5240, fax 208-524-1937; www.jakers.com. DELUXE TO ULTRA-DELUXE.

SHOPPING

There are over 60 shops at the **Grand Teton Mall**, eastern Idaho's largest shopping center. Among them is an excellent regional gift shop, **Made in Idaho**. ~ 2300 East 17th Street, Idaho Falls; 208-525-8300.

NIGHTLIFE

The **Idaho Falls Symphony Orchestra and Chorale** offers an annual five-concert series with guest artists of international repute. ~ 498 A Street; 208-529-1080. The **Idaho Falls Opera Theater** hosts a New York production once a year and offers other works with professional and amateur singers. ~ 1753 West Broadway; 208-522-0875. Both companies perform at the **Idaho Falls Civic Auditorium**. ~ 501 South Holmes Avenue; 208-529-1396.

Committed to promoting arts education and presenting quality cultural events in Eastern Idaho, the **Idaho Falls Arts Council** coordinates a wide choice of activities, including year-round art classes for children. The council also sponsors free summer concerts on the Snake River Greenbelt on Tuesdays at 7 p.m. Closed Sunday. ~ 498 A Street, Idaho Falls; 208-522-0471; www.idaho fallsarts.org, e-mail ifac@idahofallsarts.org.

The historic **Colonial Theater** presents musicals, dramas and concerts. ~ 450 A Street, Idaho Falls; 208-522-0471.

Karaoke comes to **The Outlaw Bar** Friday and Saturday nights; otherwise, there are pool tables, dart boards and tasty margaritas. ~ 300 South Yellowstone Highway, Idaho Falls; 208-552-6363.

TAUTPHAUS PARK Idaho Falls' largest city park with 80 acres south of downtown, this has a little of everything, including an excellent small zoo (closed November through March), a miniature golf course, an ice skating rink, tennis courts, softball fields and a small amusement park. Facilities include picnic tables, restrooms, playground and sports facilities. ~ From downtown Idaho Falls, take 17th East Street to South Boulevard and turn south to the park; 208-528-5552, fax 208-528-6256; www.idahofallszoo.org, e-mail ifzoo@ci.idaho-falls.id.us.

PARKS

CAMAS NATIONAL WILDLIFE REFUGE A variety of waterfowl are attracted to this marshy 10,578-acre refuge on the northern fringe of the porous Snake River Plain. Camas Creek meanders through the preserve, bounded on the east by Route 15. Besides geese, swans, herons, cranes and other waterfowl, many of which nest here from spring to fall, look for ospreys and eagles, deer and antelope, beaver and smaller mammals. Gravel roads extend through the refuge. ~ From Idaho Falls, take Route 15 north 30 miles to Hamer Exit 150, and proceed north another three miles on a frontage road. Turn west on Refuge Road to the refuge, two miles farther; 208-662-5423, fax 208-662-5525.

> The 1981 movie *Continental Divide*, starring John Belushi and Blair Brown, prominently features the Teton Valley's majestic scenery..

There are two routes from Idaho Falls to Jackson, Wyoming, and Grand Teton National Park, both via the upper Snake River.

Swan and Teton Valleys

Route 26 runs southeasterly through the lovely Swan Valley and along the shore of Palisades Reservoir to Jackson. Route 31 branches northeasterly at Swan Valley and offers a slower but spectacular detour through the isolated Teton Valley. It also provides a back door to Wyoming's Grand Targhee resort area on the Teton Range's west slope.

The road to the Swan Valley passes near **Heise Hot Springs**, a popular weekend getaway for eastern Idahoans located 23 miles northeast of Idaho Falls on the bank of the Snake River. The resort's hand-hewn, three-story log hotel was built in 1898; today it has two commercial pools and a golf course. Closed November and weekends during the winter. Admission. ~ 5116 East Heise Road, Ririe; 208-538-7312, fax 208-538-6039; e-mail heise@srv.net.

SIGHTS

Above Heise, Route 26 follows the Snake 35 miles to the Palisades Dam, a stretch considered one of Idaho's most pristine wildlife habitats. The gently rippling river is known for huge trout and birds, including bald eagles and great blue herons.

Palisades Dam is at the northwest end of 17-mile-long **Palisades Reservoir**, which extends to the Wyoming border at Alpine. The Bureau of Reclamation dam was the largest earth dam yet built when it was completed in 1959 at a cost of $76 million. Visitors can drive across, but the power station and other facilities remain closed to the public. ~ Route 26, Irwin; 208-483-2025, fax 208-483-4635. Surrounding the reservoir and the Snake River is the 2.8-million-acre **Caribou–Targhee National Forest**. It's described in "Parks" below.

The village of Swan Valley, 11 miles west of the dam, has limited tourist facilities; it is more a junction than a town, the point from which Route 31 (also the 69-mile Teton Scenic Byway) traverses 6764-foot Pine Creek Pass in the Big Hole Range to the **Teton Valley**. The 13,000-foot crest of the Teton Range stands sentinel over a valley that has adopted its name. Thirty miles long and 15 miles wide, the valley was known as Pierre's Hole when it hosted mountain men's gatherings in the 1830s. Local residents who revel in the rustic re-enact the rendezvous in August.

Most of the year, cattle ranching and hay farming sustain the economy of Driggs, the valley's main town; Victor, six miles to its south; and Tetonia, eight miles north. Some younger residents have brought ecotourism to the region with businesses geared to outdoor recreation, guest ranches, bed-and-breakfast inns and small restaurants.

This trend has largely followed the development of the **Grand Targhee Ski & Summer Resort**, which opened in 1969. The Wyoming resort—which can be reached only through Driggs, 12 miles away—has lodges, condominiums, restaurants and some of the finest powder skiing in the Rockies during its mid-November-to-mid-April ski season. ~ Ski Hill Road, Alta, WY; 307-353-2300, 800-827-4433, fax 307-353-8619; www.grandtarghee.com, e-mail info@grandtarghee.com.

At Tetonia, Route 33 turns sharply west to Rexburg. Travelers to Jackson return to Victor and take the highway southeast across 8429-foot **Teton Pass**. This spectacular route, pioneered in 1811 and opened as a Forest Service road in 1913, is steep and winding—not for the faint-hearted—but is paved and well maintained. Its views on either side of the Teton Range are worth the drive.

LODGING   A small, family-friendly inn, **The Pines Motel Guest Haus** features seven rooms in a lovingly remodeled early-20th-century log cabin. Some rooms have queen-sized beds, and all guests have access to an oversized outdoor jacuzzi. An optional country breakfast is not included in the rate. Pets are welcome, and the huge tree-covered lawn makes for an ideal play area. ~ 105 South Main Street, Driggs; 208-354-2774, 800-354-2778; e-mail thepines@ tetonvalley.net. MODERATE.

A hideaway for lovers of luxury is the 4000-acre **Teton Ridge Ranch**. It has five suites with private whirlpools, steam showers and wood-burning stoves. There are fireplaces in the living and dining rooms and library, a bar, and a game room with a TV and stereo; guest computers are also available. Winter and summer wilderness programs are offered. Rates include all meals. Open January through March and from June through October, with a three-night minimum stay in midsummer. ~ 200 Valley View Road, Tetonia; 208-456-2650, fax 208-456-2218; www.tetonridge.com, e-mail info@tetonridge.com. ULTRA-DELUXE.

Grand Targhee Ski & Summer Resort has rooms in three alpine lodges at situated 8000 feet. All have Southwestern decor with handcrafted lodgepole furnishings and private baths. The Targhee Lodge has motel-style rooms; the Teewinot Lodge has hotel-style rooms; the condo-style Sioux Lodge features bunk beds, kiva fireplaces and kitchenettes. All are an easy walk from restaurants, lounges, shops and sports facilities. Closed mid-April to early June and mid-September to mid-November. ~ Ski Hill Road, Alta, WY; 307-353-2300, 800-827-4433, fax 307-353-8148; www.grandtarghee.com, e-mail info@grandtarghee.com. ULTRA-DELUXE.

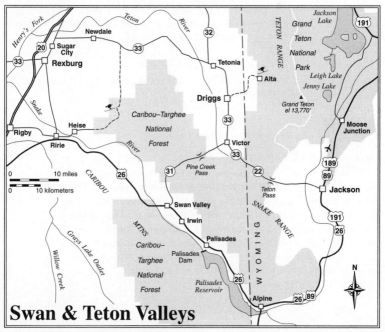

Swan & Teton Valleys

DINING   O'Rourke's Sports Bar & Grille touts its pizzas, but it's also a fine place to look for steaks, deep-fried seafood and luncheon sandwiches. You'll find it right in the heart of Driggs. Closed Sunday. ~ 42 East Little Avenue, Driggs; 208-354-8115. MODERATE.

Known for its variety of microbrews, the **Royal Wolf** is a casual, nonsmoking bar/restaurant that has a billiard table in its back room. The eclectic dinner menu includes *chimichangas,* chicken, and pasta. In the summer, the deck out back makes for a pleasant dining experience. Dinner only. ~ 63 Depot Street, Driggs; 208-354-8365. MODERATE TO DELUXE.

Targhee Steak House is a favorite of skiers and summer sports enthusiasts. Located in the Rendezvous Base Lodge, it offers wholesome breakfasts, energizing lunches and gourmet Continental cuisine for dinner. There's a children's menu; box lunches can be prepared for daytrippers. Closed April to mid-June and mid-September to mid-November. ~ Grand Targhee Resort, Ski Hill Road, Alta, WY; 307-353-2300, 800-827-4433, fax 307-353-8619; www.grandtarghee.com, e-mail info@grandtarghee.com. MODERATE TO DELUXE.

NIGHTLIFE   Ask any local about nightlife in the Swan and Teton Valleys and you'll likely draw a belly laugh. Videos, they say, or the **Spud Drive-In Theatre**. It's easy to spot on the highway about two miles south of the Grand Targhee turnoff; look for the ten-foot-long potato on the bed of a red truck permanently parked at the entrance. And hope that the movie is one you haven't seen. ~ 231 Route 33, Driggs; 208-354-2727; www.spuddrivein.com.

Check out the **Royal Wolf**, whose ten draft microbrews change weekly. Wine is also available at this friendly bar/restaurant, where a pool table beckons in the back room. ~ 63 Depot Street, Driggs; 208-354-8365.

AUTHOR FAVORITE

My stomach's growls seem to reverberate through the Teton Valley whenever I'm near **The Old Dewey House Restaurant**. This intimate restaurant, housed in a historic stone building, serves a wide range of imaginative dishes such as grilled salmon in sweet red-chile butter, blue-corn chicken with mozzarella, charbroiled sesame pork steaks and rack of lamb. Vegetarians will find pasta and stir-fry dishes to choose from. An extensive wine list rounds out the experience. Reservations are strongly recommended. Closed Tuesday. ~ 37 South Main Street, Victor; 208-787-2092; www.odh.com. DELUXE.

CARIBOU–TARGHEE NATIONAL FOREST 🏃 🎿 ⛵ 🚣 🚤 ⚓   **PARKS**

The Palisades division of the forest covers 390,000 acres. Within this region Palisades Reservoir offers fishing and boating. In winter Kelly Canyon Ski Area sports miles of downhill ski trails. During the rest of the year visitors can traverse the 570 miles of hiking trails or enjoy the beaches at Palisades Reservoir. Excellent fishing for rainbow, brook, brown and cutthroat trout, kokanee salmon and mountain whitefish is available at Palisades Reservoir and other streams. Facilities include picnic tables and restrooms. ~ Route 26 (Idaho Falls to Jackson, Wyoming) passes through large segments of the forest, and there is access from numerous other roads. To reach Falls Campground, take Route 26 east to the Snake River. Take a right immediately before the Snake River and follow the signs to the campground. To reach Bear Creek Campground, take Route 26 east to Palisades Dam. Turn right to cross over the dam and follow the signs to the campground; 208-523-1412, fax 208-523-1418.

▲ There are 160 RV/tent sites (no hookups) $7 to $20 per night. Reservations are available at some campgrounds (877-444-6777; www.reserveusa.com). For good fishing, check out Falls Campground, which has 27 RV/tent sites; $8 per night. Bear Creek Campground is primitive; no fee.

Palisades Reservoir 🏃 ⛵ 🎣 🍴 🚣 🚤 ⚓ Created in 1959 by the damming of the Snake River, this reservoir, located within the Caribou–Targhee National Forest, is a popular destination for anglers and other water-sports lovers. A Bureau of Reclamation recreational site at the dam outflow attracts many day visitors. Interpretive tours of the facility can be arranged through the Bureau of Reclamation (208-483-2392). Fishing is excellent for rainbow, brown and cutthroat trout. There's a boat ramp at Blowout Campground. Facilities include picnic tables and restrooms. ~ Take Route 26 east 54 miles from Idaho Falls, 11 miles from the Route 31 junction at Swan Valley; 208-523-1412, fax 208-523-1418.

▲ There are 41 RV/tent sites (no hookups) at lakeside Calamity Campground; $10 to $20 per night. Blowout, Riverside, McCoy Creek and Alpine campgrounds are within walking distance of the reservoir.

Henry's Fork

About 20 miles north of Idaho Falls, the northwest-flowing Snake makes a 120-degree turn south and begins a long, arcing run through southern Idaho's heavily irrigated lava plain. Just before the dogleg, it is joined by Henry's Fork, perhaps the single finest trout stream in the United States. The river rises on the Continental Divide near West Yellowstone, Montana, and flows about 100 miles southwest to the main Snake.

SIGHTS   Fast-growing **Rexburg**, about 30 miles northeast of Idaho Falls, is the home of **Brigham Young University—Idaho**, formerly Ricks College, a Mormon church–operated junior college. It's now a four-year institution with nearly 11,000 students. Founded in 1888, the pleasant campus occupies about eight city blocks. ~ South Center Street and West 4th Street South, Rexburg; 208-496-2011, fax 208-496-1884; www.byui.edu.

The whimsical **Porter Park Carousel** dates from the early 20th century. Fully restored to its initial glory, the carousel serenades its riders with a traditional band organ. Admission. ~ 250 West 2nd South, Rexburg; 208-359-3020.

Rexburg's architectural highlight is the twin-towered building that now houses the **Upper Snake River Valley Historical Society** and **Teton Flood Museum**. Built in 1911 as a Mormon tabernacle, the gray stone Italianate-style church was sold to the city in 1978. Most visitors are particularly interested in its exhibits about the June 5, 1976, Teton Dam collapse, which caused one of the worst floods in American history. Closed Saturday in winter; closed Sunday year-round. Admission. ~ 51 North Center Street, Rexburg; 208-359-3063.

The dam was 17 miles up the Teton River from Rexburg. An observation post today overlooks the **Teton Dam Site**, a mile north of Route 33 between Sugar City and Tetonia. The ill-conceived Bureau of Reclamation project was approaching completion, its reservoir nearly filled, when it collapsed at midday, sending 80 billion gallons of water downstream at 15 miles per hour. Flood waters were contained three days later by American Falls Reservoir. Remarkably, only six people drowned, but 25,000 were driven from their homes, 18,000 head of stock were lost and $800 million damage was suffered by the residents of eastern Idaho. Closed Sunday. ~ Teton Dam Road, Newdale; 208-356-5700, 888-463-6880, fax 208-356-5799; www.rexcc.com, e-mail info@rexcc.com.

Yellowstone Bear World is a wild animal park that offers visitors a drive-through look at black bears and grizzlies, as well as elk, reindeer, bison and a resident wolf pack. Baby bear cubs frolic in the cub yard and hundreds of ducks, geese and swans inhabit the park's natural waterways. Closed mid-October to mid-May. Admission. ~ 6010 South 4300 West, Rexburg; 208-359-9688, fax 208-356-9732; www.yellowstonebearworld.com, e-mail info@yellowstonebearworld.com.

St. Anthony, 12 miles northeast of Rexburg, is gateway to the **St. Anthony Sand Dunes**, eight miles northwest. The band of dunes, 35 miles long and up to five miles wide, has individual peaks as high as 1300 feet, taller than those of Death Valley. ~ Red Road, St. Anthony; 800-634-3246.

Ashton, 14 miles from St. Anthony, marks the north end of the 69-mile **Teton Scenic Byway,** which begins as Route 31 near Swan Valley, and the south end of **Mesa Falls Scenic Byway.** (See "Scenic Drive" for details.)

One of Idaho's most popular state parks, **Harriman State Park** was a working ranch from the early 20th century until 1977. The grounds still boast several of the log cabins that housed the working hands. Daily tours of the 27 original buildings are of-

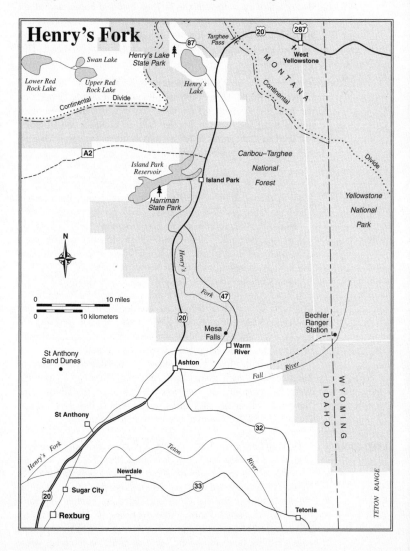

Henry's Fork

Swan Lake

Henry's Lake State Park

Targhee Pass

West Yellowstone

Lower Red Rock Lake

Upper Red Rock Lake

Henry's Lake

MONTANA

Continental Divide

A2

Island Park Reservoir

Island Park

Caribou–Targhee National Forest

Continental Divide

Yellowstone National Park

Harriman State Park

N

Henry's

0   10 miles

0   10 kilometers

Fork

Mesa Falls

Warm River

Bechler Ranger Station

St Anthony Sand Dunes

Ashton

Fall River

St Anthony

Teton River

WYOMING

IDAHO

Newdale

Sugar City

Rexburg

Henry's Fork

Tetonia

TETON RANGE

SCENIC DRIVE

Mesa Falls Scenic Byway

Travelers can take an hour-long detour from Ashton onto Route 47, the Mesa Falls Scenic Byway, which cuts through the Targhee National Forest and offers moose, deer and elk sightings, as well as spectacular views of the Teton Mountain Range. This 28-mile circuit skirts two undisturbed waterfalls on Henry's Fork and accesses the remote southwest corner of Yellowstone National Park. *Note:* This route is closed in winter.

YELLOWSTONE ROUTE   The Yellowstone route begins six miles east of the byway off Route 47 (as Marysville Road) and extends 19 miles to **Cave Falls** on Wyoming's Falls River. You can hike the three miles roundtrip along Fall River to Bechler Falls, or backpack the **Bechler River Trail** to Old Faithful in Yellowstone National Park (see Chapter Seven), a hike of approximately four days.

fered in the summer. ~ 3489 Green Canyon Road, Island Park; 208-558-7368, fax 208-558-7045; e-mail har@idpr.state.id.us.

Island Park Reservoir, created by a dam on Henry's Fork six miles from the park, fills the crater of an old caldera. The resort community of Island Park is on Route 20 at its eastern end, and five boat launches provide access for water sports.

Henry's Lake, 19 miles north of Island Park, occupies a mountain bowl four miles long, three miles wide and 6470 feet above sea level. Several trout-fishing resorts dot its shores. You'll also find **Henry's Lake State Park**, which is well-known among anglers. The lake is home to some big trout; brook, rainbow and cutthroat-rainbow hybrids all range from five to eight pounds.

It's five miles from Henry's Lake to the 7072-foot summit of **Targhee Pass**, which crosses the Continental Divide into Montana. West Yellowstone, at the western entrance to Yellowstone National Park, is 12 miles farther east. ~ Goose Bay Road, Island Park; 208-558-7532; e-mail hen@idpr.state.id.us.

LODGING   **C-J's Motel** has ten modest rooms, a picnic area and an outdoor jacuzzi. ~ 357 West 4th South, Rexburg; 208-356-5477. BUDGET.

Settle along the shores of Island Park at **Lakeside Lodge & Resort**. Eight standard hotel rooms are housed in the main building while six cabins, each with one bedroom, kitchen and family room, are scattered throughout the property. The place is airy and comfortable, great for an idyllic retreat. During the summer, rent a fishing boat and spend the afternoon on the lake, while

UPPER AND LOWER MESA FALLS   More spectacular are the Upper and Lower Mesa Falls, located about 15 miles northeast of Ashton just off the drive. From an overlook at Targhee National Forest's Grandview campground you can see Lower Mesa Falls thunder 65 feet through a narrow gorge. Upriver three-fourths of a mile, Upper Mesa Falls drop 114 feet to a frothy pool. Boardwalk trails lead from a paved parking area, past a historic forest lodge, to viewing platforms.

ISLAND PARK CALDERA   The falls mark the edge of the Island Park Caldera, 18 by 23 miles in diameter, first identified by geologists in 1939 and now regarded as the world's largest crater. This collapsed prehistoric volcano, with a 1200-foot scarp on its south and west sides, is now covered with dense pine forest and extensive meadows. Mesa Falls Scenic Byway rejoins Route 20 just north of the entrance to Harriman State Park, 18 miles from Ashton

snowmobile rentals and ice fishing are fun winter options. There's an on-site restaurant. ~ 3857 Lakeside Lane, Island Park; 208-558-7147, fax 208-558-0176. MODERATE TO ULTRA-DELUXE.

Sawtelle Mountain Resort is geared to fishing and snowmobiling, among other recreational opportunities, with rentals nearby and direct access to 600 miles of trails. Lodging is in 36 motel rooms, all with private baths. There are laundry facilities, an indoor swimming pool and hot tubs (one outdoors); a continental breakfast is included. ~ Route 20 and Sawtelle Mountain Road, Island Park; 208-558-9366, 866-558-9366, fax 208-558-9769. BUDGET TO MODERATE.

Me 'n Stan's Restaurant is a family-style place just a block from the Porter Park carousel. Steak and seafood highlight the menu, and a big salad bar is a big hit with many. Special menus are available for kids and seniors. Breakfast, lunch and dinner. ~ 167 West Main Street, Rexburg; 208-356-7330, fax 208-359-1722. MODERATE TO DELUXE.

DINING

With locations in Rexburg and Ashton, **Big Jud's Country Diner** captures many locals along with the drive-by crowd. You'll get lunch and dinner at both locations. Closed Sunday. ~ 411 West 7800 South, Rexburg; 208-359-2833. Also 1370 North Route 20, Ashton; 208-652-7806. BUDGET.

Up on Henry's Fork, the **A-Bar Motel & Supper Club**, near the north edge of Harriman State Park by the Last Chance Lodge, serves hearty ranch-style portions of chili, Texas burgers, steaks and the like from 10 a.m. until 11:30 p.m. daily. It's right on the riverbank. ~ 3433 Route 20, Island Park; 208-558-7358, 800-286-7358, fax 208-558-7790; e-mail abar@fremontnet.com. BUDGET TO DELUXE.

PARKS

ST. ANTHONY SAND DUNES Administered by the Bureau of Land Management, this recreation site provides access for dune buggy and other off-road vehicle drivers to 150 square miles of shifting sand. The white-quartz dunes, some of them a quarter-mile tall, have been deposited by alluvial action and blown by prevailing winds to the northeastern end of the Snake River Plain over millions of years. There are toilets and off-road vehicle rentals nearby. ~ From St. Anthony, on Route 20 northeast of Idaho Falls, take North Parker Road west five miles, then Red Road north three miles; 800-634-3246.

HARRIMAN STATE PARK Established as a private Union Pacific Railroad retreat by the wealthy Harriman family in 1902, this 4330-acre park—Idaho's second largest—became a state park in 1977. The visitors center becomes a warming hut for cross-country skiers in winter. A 11,000-acre wildlife refuge surrounds the park, which lies along nine miles of Henry's Fork. Elk, moose, deer, beaver, muskrats, otters, trumpeter swans, sandhill cranes, great blue heron, eagles, ospreys and a great many more wild creatures are often seen. There's great trout fishery in Henry's Fork. Facilities include picnic tables, restrooms and a visitors center. Day-use fee, $4. ~ From Idaho Falls, take Route 20 northeast 65 miles to Green Canyon Road; turn west one mile to the park entrance; 208-558-7368, fax 208-558-7045; e-mail har@idpr.state.id.us.

CARIBOU–TARGHEE NATIONAL FOREST Island Park Reservoir, Henry's Lake and Upper and Lower Mesa Falls are among the highlights of this segment of the forest, which extends from the Tetons west to the Lemhi Range, and which follows the Continental Divide from Montana to the edge of Yellowstone and Grand Teton national parks in Wyoming, and south to the Utah border. The gen-

JOHNNY SACK CABIN

Near Island Park, the **Johnny Sack Cabin** is open to the public during the summer. Built in 1934 by a German immigrant, the interior of the cabin features intricate handmade woodwork fashioned out of lodgepole pine. Open to visitors July 4 through Labor Day. ~ Located off Route 20 on Lower Big Springs Road.

tle **Big Springs Water Trail** (put-in point at Route 84) was the first National Water Scenic Trail established by the U.S. Forest Service. Fishing is excellent at Henry's Fork of the Snake River and at the Island Park area. Other streams are also good. Game fish include rainbow, brook, brown and cutthroat trout, kokanee salmon and mountain whitefish. Facilities include picnic tables and restrooms. There is a day-use fee of $3 at Upper Mesa Falls from late May to mid-October. ~ Route 20 (Ashton to West Yellowstone, Montana) passes through large segments of the forest, and there is access from numerous other roads. Buffalo Campground is located 77 miles north of Idaho Falls, in the town of Island Park, on the east side of the road one-quarter mile north of the Island Park Ranger station; 208-558-7301, fax 208-558-7812.

▲ There are nine campgrounds in this area: 400 RV/tent sites; $10 to $15 per night. Reservations are available at some campgrounds; call 800-280-2267. Three cabins—near Island Park, accommodating two to ten people—are available year-round for $25 to $45 per night; call 208-652-7442 for information and reservations. If you're looking for hiking, biking or boating, try Buffalo Campground: There are 126 RV/tent sites; $10 to $15 per night.

HENRY'S LAKE STATE PARK 🏃 🚲 ⛵ 🚤 ⬦ A quiet mountain oasis just 15 miles from Yellowstone National Park's west entrance, sheltered on three sides by the Continental Divide just south of the Montana border, Henry's Lake fills an alpine valley of about 12 square miles. The 585-acre park, on the southeast shore near its outlet to Henry's Fork, is ideal for fishing enthusiasts. Cutthroat and brook trout and cutthroat-rainbow hybrids are available here. Facilities include picnic tables and restrooms. Day-use fee, $4. ~ From Idaho Falls, take Route 20 northeast 87 miles to the Henry's Lake State Park entrance signs; turn west two miles to the park entrance; 208-558-7532; e-mail hen@idpr.state.id.us.

▲ There are 45 RV/tent sites (25 with hookups); $20 per night for RVs, $16 for tents. Open Memorial Day weekend through Labor Day (though sometimes open later).

Outdoor Adventures

FISHING

The main Snake (sometimes called the South Fork), upstream from its confluence with Henry's Fork, and Palisades Reservoir teem with giant trout. Coho salmon are found in Ririe Reservoir. The **Teton Valley Lodge** has a large staff of professional guides. ~ 379 Adams Road, Driggs; 208-354-2386 (summer), 208-354-8124 (winter), 800-455-1182.

Henry's Fork of the Snake boasts native cutthroat trout that may weigh over ten pounds. There are coho salmon in Island Park

Reservoir, rainbow and hybrid cutthroat trout in Henry's Lake. **Henry's Fork Anglers**, south of Island Park Reservoir, provides specialized guide service from Memorial Day weekend to the end of November. ~ Route 20, Last Chance, Island Park; 208-558-7525; www.henrysforkanglers.com.

An outstanding flyfishing supply shop in Idaho Falls is **Jimmy's All Seasons Angler**. Closed Sunday in winter. ~ 275 A Street; 208-524-7160.

BOATING

Snake River reservoirs are popular places for boating. Island Park Reservoir and Henry's Lake, both north of Idaho Falls, and Palisades Reservoir, on the Wyoming border southeast of Swan Valley, draw many private boaters. A good place to get away from the crowds and still find a little fishing is Ririe Lake, east of Idaho Falls, and Mud Lake, off Route 33 and west of Route 15. Unfortunately, this is a BYOB (bring your own boat) area; there are no marinas that offer boat rentals.

RIVER RUNNING

Henry's Fork is *the* river to run in this neck of the woods. **Canyon Whitewater Supply** has rentals. Closed Sunday from April through October; call for winter hours. ~ 450 South Yellowstone Highway, Idaho Falls; 208-522-3932.

SKIING

There is no better way to appreciate a winter's day than on a pair of skis, so head over to **Kelly Canyon**. Twenty-five miles northeast of Idaho Falls via Route 26, Kelly Canyon overlooks the Snake River's south fork in Caribou–Targhee National Forest, and has five chairlifts and 26 runs with a 1000-foot vertical drop. Instruction and rentals are available. ~ Kelly Canyon Road, Heise; 208-538-6261, fax 208-538-7130l; www.skikelly.com.

Swan and Teton valleys boast the other leading ski runs. **Grand Targhee** is nestled on the west slope of the Tetons. Although technically in Wyoming, it can be reached only via Driggs, 12 miles west. Each winter, Targhee is blessed with more than 500 inches of snow, more than 40 feet, making it a favorite of powder skiers. One of its two mountains, 9800-foot Peaked Mountain, is perpetually ungroomed: Skiers are ferried there by Sno-Cat in groups of ten, accompanied by two guides. Fred's Mountain, only slightly smaller at 10,000 feet, has three chairlifts, one rope tow and 46 runs. Both mountains have 2000 acres of skiable terrain; the vertical drop is 2822 feet. This is a destination resort with lodging and dining as well as a full ski school and rental shop. ~ Ski Hill Road, Alta, WY; 307-353-2300, 800-827-4433, fax 307-353-8619; www.grandtarghee.com, e-mail info@grandtarghee.com.

Cross-country Park 'n' Ski areas in eastern Idaho include **Fall River Ridge** (11 kilometers, beginner and intermediate), on Cave

Flyfishing Heaven

The prospect of laying a hand-tied lure on a placid stretch of river and reeling in a giant trout has a romance shared by few outdoor recreations. And few places are better suited to flyfishing than southeastern Idaho.

Author Ernest Hemingway made Silver Creek, southeast of Sun Valley, famous as his favorite fishing hole. Henry's Fork of the Snake River, northeast of Idaho Falls, is considered to be among the best trout streams on earth. Many other streams, from the Big Wood River to the Big Lost River, the Salmon River to Salmon Falls Creek, are equally enticing.

The roots of flyfishing date back at least 2000 years to the Roman Empire. But flyfishing as it's known today did not become possible until about a century ago, when the horsehair line was reinvented. The modern flycasting line—typically nylon with a plastic covering, tapered to a monofilament leader—provides the weight for casting the virtually weightless fly; it can float atop the water or sink below the surface. A flexible fiberglass or graphite rod, usually about eight feet long, is whipped in an often individualized motion that sends the line and lure to a precise location in the water.

Artificial flies may be made from silk, fur or feathers, but they usually represent a natural food source for the fish: aquatic or terrestrial insects, freshwater shrimp or snails, for instance. Most commonly imitated are mayflies, caddis flies and midges, all of which begin their lives in the water as nymphs before emerging as winged insects. Females return to the water to lay eggs.

It is the angler's challenge to simulate the insect's natural behavior and outwit the fish—either by "wet-fly" fishing with the lure underwater, or "dry-fly" fishing on the surface of the water. Dry-fly anglers try to cast a slack line, allowing their lure to remain naturally on the surface as long as possible before it is caught in the current.

Lodges throughout southeastern Idaho provide flyfishing guides and instruction. For visitors with money to burn and a powerful passion to catch trophy-size cutthroat, rainbow and German brown trout, it's hard to top **The Lodge at Palisades Creek**. From June to October, experienced guides take visitors out fishing on the upper Snake. ~ Irwin; 208-483-2222; www.tlapc.com.

Hemingway's Silver Creek fishing hole is now owned and monitored by the preservationist Nature Conservancy as the **Silver Creek Preserve**. The water temperature of the spring-fed stream stays between 40° and 50° year-round; its rainbow and brown trout are big and smart. A strict catch-and-release policy applies, enabling the fish to get older, bigger and smarter. ~ Picabo; 208-788-2203, phone/fax 208-788-7910.

Falls Road ten miles east of Ashton, and **Brimstone/Buffalo River** (4 kilometers, beginner), on Route 20, a quarter-mile north of the Island Park Ranger Station, all in Caribou–Targhee National Forest. Call the Idaho Department of Parks and Recreation for more information. ~ 208-334-4199, fax 208-334-3741; www. idahoparks.org.

Ski Rentals   Aside from the resort facilities themselves, there are places to rent skiing and snowboarding equipment. **Gart Sports** rents downhill skis, snowboards and snowshoes. ~ 1592 East 17th Street, Idaho Falls; 208-524-2525; www.gartsports.com. **Peaked Sports** can also outfit you. ~ 70 East Little Avenue, Driggs; 208-354-2354.

ICE SKATING

For indoor ice-skating aficionados, Idaho Falls offers **Tautphaus Park**, which has a rink and rentals. Open November through March. ~ Rollandet Avenue at 25th Street; 208-529-1470.

GOLF

The area's level terrain lends itself well to golf. Idaho Falls has **Pinecrest Golf Course**. ~ 701 East Elva Street; 208-529-1485. You may also tee off at the **Sage Lakes Golf Course**. ~ 100 East 65th Street North; 208-528-5535. There's also **Sand Creek Golf Course**. ~ 5200 25th Road East; 208-529-1115. **Rexburg Municipal Golf Course** is a 9-hole course. ~ South Airport Road, Rexburg; 208-359-3037. Or try the 18-hole **Teton Lakes Golf Course**. ~ 1014 North Hibbard Highway, Rexburg; 208-359-3036. Courses are also available in nearby towns.

TENNIS

If you feel like lobbing a ball around, Idaho Falls has several courts. The best place to find them is **Tautphaus Park**. ~ Rollandet Avenue and 25th Street. Contact the Idaho Falls Parks and Recreation Division for more information. ~ 208-529-1480.

RIDING STABLES & PACK TRIPS

When you're tired of walking, a horse may be the way to go. **Bustle Creek Outfitters**, just inside the Wyoming border via Driggs, Idaho, offers one-hour trips from Grand Targhee and full-day expeditions into the nearby Jedediah Smith Wilderness. Closed in May and October. ~ Grand Targhee Resort, Alta, WY; 307-353-2300, fax 307-353-8619; www.grandtarghee.com.

A fun way to explore the mountains is with a pack horse on an extended overnight journey. **Dry Ridge Outfitters** arranges backcountry pack trips into the Caribou–Targhee National Wilderness and the Jedediah Smith Wilderness in the Teton Mountain Range. ~ P.O. Box 863, Driggs, ID 83422; 208-354-2284.

BIKING

Bike riding is the love of many locals in this region of Idaho. Popular biking areas include Idaho Falls' own five-mile Snake River Greenbelt and Mount Taylor, south of Idaho Falls.

Caribou–Targhee National Forest near Swan Valley and Driggs has numerous single-track trails. **Big Hole Mountain Sports** offers free downhill runs, for those at the appropriate experience level, on the west side of the Tetons near Grand Targhee Resort. ~ 65 South Main Street, Driggs; 208-354-2209.

The Mesa Falls and Island Park areas north of Ashton, as well as Harriman State Park, feature fine trails for bicycling. **Bike Rentals** Rentals and repairs are offered by **Bill's Bike Shop**. Closed Sunday. ~ 805 Holmes South Avenue, Idaho Falls; 208-522-3341. **Big Hole Mountain Sports** has a wide selection of rentals. ~ 65 South Main Street, Driggs; 208-354-2209. A full-service bike shop, **Peaked Sports** is also in the area. ~ 70 East Little Avenue, Driggs; 208-354-2354.

HIKING

The Idaho Falls area offers several parks where you can stretch your legs. All distances listed are one way unless otherwise noted.

Darby Canyon Trail (2.7 miles) climbs into Wyoming's Jedediah Smith Wilderness, on the west slope of the Tetons, to the Wind and Ice Cave on 10,966-foot Mount Bannon. The climb begins in woods and passes through alpine meadows accented by waterfalls. The trailhead is at the east end of eight-mile Darby Canyon Road, off Route 33 between Driggs and Victor.

The **Coffee Pot Rapids Trail** (2.5 miles) follows Henry's Fork of the Snake River downstream from placid waters to boiling rapids. The easy walk begins at the Upper Coffeepot campground in Targhee National Forest, six miles north of Island Park.

The best way to hike the **Sawtell Peak–Rock Creek Basin Trail** (3 miles) is from the top down. Get a drop-off where steep, winding, 11-mile Forest Road 024 (off Route 20) ends at the Federal Aviation Administration radar installation atop 9866-foot Sawtell Peak. The view from here extends across three states and the entire Island Park Caldera. Then descend to the Rock Creek Basin near Henry's Lake State Park.

AUTHOR FAVORITE

Upper Palisades Lake Trail (7 miles) is closed to all motorized vehicles, which makes it a pleasant overnight camping excursion for backpackers. Three miles above the mile-long lake, located at about 7200-foot elevation, is an impressive waterfall. The trailhead is at the Palisades Creek campground, just south of Irwin

▼ ▼ ▼ ▼ ▼ ▼ ▼ ▼ ▼ ▼ ▼

Transportation

CAR

Southbound **Route 15** from Butte climbs over the Continental Divide to Idaho Falls and Pocatello, proceeding south into Utah. **Route 20** climbs northeast from Idaho Falls on its way to Yellowstone National Park. **Route 26** travels southeast from Idaho Falls along the Snake River. After it crosses the Wyoming state line, it veers north to Jackson and changes into **Route 191/189.**

AIR

Located on the northwest side of the city, **Idaho Falls Regional Airport** is served by Horizon (from Boise) and SkyWest (from Salt Lake City and Butte). Local buses and taxis provide ground transportation. ~ 208-529-1221.

BUS

Greyhound Bus Lines (800-231-2222; www.greyhound.com) follow the interstate corridor from Boise to Salt Lake City or West Yellowstone, Montana. There is a major depot in Idaho Falls. ~ 850 Denver Street; 208-522-0912.

C.A.R.T. ("Community and Rural Transportation") serves eastern Idaho from Idaho Falls. No weekend service. ~ 850 Denver Street; 208-522-2278. Other main depots are in Driggs and Rexburg.

CAR RENTALS

Avis Rent A Car (800-331-1212), **Budget Rent A Car** (800-527-0700), **Hertz Rent A Car** (800-654-3131) and **National Car Rental** (800-328-4567) have outlets at the Idaho Falls airport. **U-Save Auto Rental** (800-272-8728) has a downtown location.

PUBLIC TRANSIT

Idaho Falls' **C.A.R.T. Transit** has extensive routes that serve the city. No weekend service. ~ 850 Denver Street; 208-522-2278.

TAXIS

To get a cab in Idaho Falls, contact **Easy-Way Taxi.** ~ 208-525-8344.

SEVEN

Yellowstone National Park

Recipe for a great trip: Start with the world's oldest and best-known national park, Yellowstone. Mix in the dramatic scenery of hot springs, geysers and river gorges. Stir in generous portions of history and culture, from the Crow and Shoshone Indians to President Teddy Roosevelt. Liberally season with fishing, hiking, skiing, rafting, horseback riding and other outdoor activities. Garnish with some of the richest wildlife on the continent and . . . voila! You have Yellowstone National Park. Come prepared with an appetite for adventure.

The glories of this corner of the earth weren't lost on the Shoshone and Crow Indians who inhabited the valleys surrounding the park. The plateau that is now Yellowstone National Park was too high and cold to be a suitable year-round home for the tribes, but they would come in summer to hunt and to quarry obsidian, which was valued for its sharp edges used to make arrowheads and other projectile weapons. Historians believe that a tribe numbering only 100 to 200 souls, the Sheepeaters, named after their fondness for bighorn sheep, may have lived in the park year-round, but there is no conclusive evidence to prove this.

In 1807 the intrepid John Colter, who had gone to the Pacific with Lewis and Clark but soloed his return, was apparently the first white man to see this corner of Wyoming and the thermal phenomena of the Yellowstone basin. And it wasn't long before mountain men and fur trappers penetrated the region in search of beaver and other pelts that were earning top dollar on the East Coast.

After 1845, the demand for furs diminished, the trappers moved out, and northwestern Wyoming briefly settled back into splendid isolation. The remoteness of the Grand Teton country south of Yellowstone meant that the area surrounding the national park was relatively untouched until the end of the century, and even today its population remains sparse.

The community of West Yellowstone, which serves as the park's only western entrance, offers visitors all the services and facilities they could want as they enter or exit the park. Surrounded by forests on all sides, this pretty little town that didn't pave its streets until 1988 retains its Old West flavor with its main street and its turn-of-the-20th-century buildings.

From Old Faithful Geyser to the Grand Canyon of the Yellowstone, to the bison herds of the Hayden Valley and the elk that bed down in the Mammoth Hot Springs, Yellowstone National Park deserves days of exploration.

▼▼▼▼▼▼▼▼▼▼▼▼▼
West Yellowstone

Just east of the Idaho border, and just outside the western Montana entrance to Yellowstone National Park, is West Yellowstone, a small town that serves a year-round coterie of tourists and outdoor-sports lovers. With about 900 full-time residents, it is the park's primary "suburb," as it were. Founded in 1909 as a Union Pacific railroad terminus where Yellowstone visitors could transfer to stagecoaches for their tour of the national park, West Yellowstone gradually grew into the tourism-focused community it is today. This entrance is open to vehicle traffic from mid-April to early November only. The road reopens for snowmobile traffic from mid-December to mid-March.

SIGHTS

To introduce you to the park, the **Yellowstone IMAX Theatre** presents *Yellowstone* on its six-story screen with digital stereo surround sound, as well as three to five other films, which change from year to year. The films are shown hourly from June through September; times vary the rest of the year. Admission. ~ 101 South Canyon Street; 406-646-4100, fax 406-646-4101.

Next door to the theater, on the south side, is the **Grizzly & Wolf Discovery Center**, where visitors can observe the natural behavior of grizzly bears in an outdoor viewing area constructed with minimal barriers. Several bears reside here; they have been orphaned or taken in as a habitual "problem" bear. The center also has a pack of gray wolves in a naturalistic habitat, museum displays and a gift shop. Admission. ~ Canyon Street; 406-646-7001, 800-257-2570, fax 406-646-7004, www.grizzlydiscovery ctr.org, e-mail info@grizzlydiscoveryctr.com.

The **West Yellowstone Chamber of Commerce**, open year-round, is one of the most comprehensive you'll find. Besides pro-

◆◆

SHAKIN' ALL OVER

The great earthquake of August 17, 1959, had its epicenter just northeast of Hebgen Lake. The tremor dropped Hebgen's north shore 19 feet and caused a landslide that blocked the Madison River canyon, forging adjacent Quake Lake. Twenty-eight campers died. The **Madison Canyon Earthquake Area and Visitor Center**, at the west end of Quake Lake, overlooks the area of the slide caused by the earthquake. Closed September to Memorial Day. Admission. ~ Route 287; 406-823-6961, fax 406-823-6990; www.fs.fed.us/r1/gallatin.

viding basic information on the town and the national park, forest rangers advise on nearby camping when "Full" signs cover the campground board at Yellowstone's west entrance. Reduced hours in the fall and winter. ~ 30 Yellowstone Avenue; 406-646-7701, fax 406-646-9691; www.westyellowstonechamber.com, e-mail wycc@wyellowstone.com.

North of West Yellowstone, two miles up Route 287, is the **West Yellowstone Interagency Fire Center**, where summer visitors take a facility tour, including a closer look at smokejumping techniques. Closed October through May. ~ Route 287 at the Yellowstone Airport; 406-646-7691, fax 406-646-9598; www.fs. fed.us/r1/gallatin.

One of the most popular places to send campers is **Hebgen Lake**, less than five miles northwest of the town. Numerous recreation areas and campgrounds speckle the south and west shores of the 15-mile-long lake. Hebgen is especially popular among boaters, fishermen and wildlife watchers, who keep their eyes peeled for moose and trumpeter swans.

Doing Yellowstone on the cheap? The **Madison Hotel Youth Hostel** is a good place to start. The hotel can accommodate as many as two dozen backpackers in nonsmoking dormitories and hotel and motel rooms. Shared facilities include toilets and showers, a TV lounge and a coffee bar. There's no kitchen, unfortunately. Closed from mid-October to the end of May. ~ 139 Yellowstone Avenue; 406-646-7745, 800-838-7745, fax 406-646-9766; www. wyellowstone.com/madisonhotel. BUDGET TO MODERATE.

LODGING

West Yellowstone's best bet is the **Travelers Lodge**. This two-story motor hotel has 44 rooms of varying sizes. All have TVs and some have refrigerators. Facilities include a whirlpool, a heated pool and a coin laundry. Continental breakfast included. Closed November and first two weeks in April. ~ 225 Yellowstone Avenue; 406-646-9561, 800-831-5741, fax 406-646-4478; www.travelersyellowstone.com, e-mail travelers@montana.com. MODERATE.

The **Stage Coach Inn** is one of the nicest motels around. A shingle-roofed lodging with a rock facade and a balcony that surrounds its large, knotty pine–paneled lobby and stone fireplace, it looks as if it came straight out of a storybook. The 87 guest rooms are cozy but nicely decorated. The inn has an upscale dining room, a casino-lounge, a spa and sauna, and a guest laundry. ~ 209 Madison Avenue; 406-646-7381, 800-842-2882, fax 406-646-9575; www.yellowstoneinn.com, e-mail sci@yellowstoneinn. com. MODERATE TO DELUXE.

Sleepy Hollow Lodge serves as the home away from home for countless anglers and vacationing families. Thirteen log cabins are appointed with handmade furniture, refrigerators and coffeemakers;

some have kitchens. In addition to a continental breakfast, Sleepy Hollow offers a fly-tying bench. Closed in winter. ~ 124 Electric Street; 406-646-7707; www.sleepyhollowlodge.com, e-mail sleepyhollow@wyellowstone.com. MODERATE.

Just outside the entrance to Yellowstone, **The Hibernation Station** is within walking distance to all the local sights. Its individually decorated log cabins are far from rustic—most of them boast jacuzzi tubs, fireplaces and kitchenettes. Several family-sized cabins that sleep up to six people are also available. Snowmobile rentals available in winter. ~ 212 Gray Wolf Avenue; 406-646-4200, 800-580-3557, fax 406-646-7060; www.hibernationstation.com, e-mail reserve@hibernationstation.com. DELUXE TO ULTRA-DELUXE.

Right down the street, the **Yellowstone Lodge** offers a more standard hotel experience. Its rooms and suites are spacious and bright; several have microwaves and refrigerators. Amenities include an indoor pool, a jacuzzi and a guest laundry. A deluxe continental breakfast is included in the rate. ~ 251 South Electric Street; 406-646-0020, 877-239-9298, fax 406-646-0110; www.yellowstonelodge.com, e-mail ylodge@yellowstonelodge.com. DELUXE.

DINING

Regional game dishes—including elk and buffalo—are available at the **Rustler's Roost**, in the Best Western Pine Motel. Rainbow trout, chicken and prime rib are also on the menu at this family establishment, which offers a soup-and-salad bar and a children's menu as well. Three meals a day during summer. ~ 234 Firehole Avenue; 406-646-7622, fax 406-646-9443. MODERATE TO DELUXE.

The **Three Bear Restaurant**, located in a motor lodge of the same name, serves breakfast and dinner every day from mid-May to mid-October and from mid-December to mid-March. The non-smoking, family-style restaurant touts its salad bar, prime rib and homemade pastries. The Grizzly Lounge is attached. ~ 217 Yellowstone Avenue; 406-646-7811, fax 406-646-4567; www.threebearlodge.com. DELUXE TO ULTRA-DELUXE.

Seafood and pastas dominate the menu at **Bullwinkle's Saloon & Eatery**. You'll find fresh Idaho trout, Black Angus sirloin, and vegetable primavera here, as well as unusual burger choices such as buffalo and portobello mushroom. Closed April and November. ~ 19 Madison Avenue; 406-646-7974, fax 406-646-7924; www.wyellowstone.com/bullwinkles. e-mail bullwinkles@wyellowstone.com. MODERATE TO ULTRA-DELUXE.

HIDDEN ▶

Alice's Restaurant is seven and a half miles west of the park entrance on Route 20, but many folks find it worth the drive for its old-time gas station atmosphere and menu of standards like ribeye steak and trout dinners. The restaurant is located at the foot of the Continental Divide just east of the Idaho border. Breakfast, lunch and dinner in winter; breakfast and dinner in summer. Closed in spring and fall. ~ 1545 Targhee Pass Highway; 406-646-7296. MODERATE.

Check out **Eagle's Store** for Western wear, outdoor equipment and American Indian crafts. Closed April and November. ~ 3 Canyon Street; 406-646-9300. Also try the **Madison Gift Shop** for a large selection of souvenirs. Closed October 10 through Memorial Day. ~ 139 Yellowstone Avenue; 406-646-7745. **Oak N Pine** is renowned for its custom lodge-style furniture and handmade quilts. Closed mid-October through December. ~ 120 Canyon Street;

SHOPPING

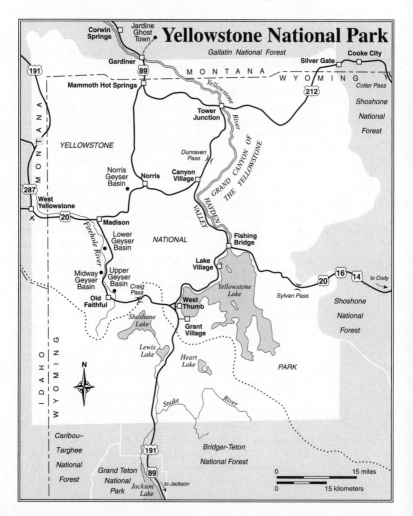

208-558-9511. **The Cradleboard Gift Shop** carries jewelry, pottery and American Indian rugs. ~ 104-D Canyon Street; 406-646-9577; www.cradleboard.com.

NIGHTLIFE Theater is growing in popularity in the gateway communities. The **Playmill Theatre** has presented a summer season of melodrama and musical comedy since 1964. ~ 29 Madison Avenue; 406-646-7757; www.playmill.com.

For pure imbibing, travel nine miles north of West Yellowstone on Route 191 (just past the Route 287 junction) to **Eino's Tavern,** which has a grill alongside Hebgen Lake, big-screen TV and even fuel for snowmobilers. Closed for two weeks after Thanksgiving. ~ 8955 Gallatin Road; 406-646-9344.

▼▼▼▼▼▼▼▼▼▼▼▼▼▼▼▼▼
Yellowstone National Park

The world's first national park remains first on nearly every visitor's list of Most Remarkable Places.

Nowhere else on earth is there as large and varied a collection of hydrothermal features—erupting geysers, bubbling mud caldrons, hissing fumaroles, gurgling mineral springs. The park is estimated to contain 10,000 thermal features, including more than 200 active geysers. Sites like Old Faithful Geyser and Mammoth Hot Springs have become part of the American lexicon, if not the American identity.

No other place in the contiguous 48 states has as great a concentration of mammals as does Yellowstone, or as extensive an interactive ecosystem. The park is home to an amazing five dozen species of mammals, including eight hoofed animals (bighorn sheep, pronghorn antelope, mountain goat, bison, elk, moose, mule deer, white-tailed deer) and two bears (black and grizzly).

Then there's the magnificent Grand Canyon of the Yellowstone, with its spectacular waterfalls; 136-square-mile Yellowstone Lake, the largest lake in North America at so high an elevation; rugged mountains reaching above 10,000 feet in all directions. It's no wonder city folk didn't believe the first stories they heard coming out of the West.

The park's 2.2 million acres were set aside by Congress as a national park on March 1, 1872. But convincing Washington had not been easy.

The heart of Yellowstone was once a giant volcanic caldera, 28 miles wide, 47 miles long and thousands of feet deep. Some geologists think the explosion that created this crater 600,000 years ago may have been 2000 times greater than Mount St. Helens' in 1980. Three ice ages sculpted the modern landscape, but they couldn't quiet the earth beneath. Nomadic tribes, who lived and hunted in the area for thousands of years thereafter, apparently avoided the most active geothermal areas, as did the

Lewis and Clark expedition of 1804. Ever respectful of native superstition, William Clark noted that Indians who visited the region had "frequently heard a loud noise like thunder, which makes the earth tremble. . . .They conceive it possessed of spirits, who were adverse that men should be near them."

John Colter, a wayward member of the Lewis and Clark party, spent the winter of 1807 trapping and wandering throughout the area; he apparently was the first white man to observe the natural wonders of Yellowstone. But no one back East believed him. It didn't help when Jim Bridger, a mountain man as famous for his tall tales as for his knowledge of wilderness survival, claimed that "a fellow can catch a fish in an icy river, pull it into a boiling pool, and cook his fish without ever taking it off the hook."

> The Norris Geyser Basin is pervaded by the perpetual, pungent smell of hydrogen sulfide.

Finally, in 1870, a group of respected Montana citizens set out to explore the area and put an end to rumor. Astonished by its discoveries (including Old Faithful), this Washburn-Langford-Doane party convinced Dr. Ferdinand Hayden, U.S. Geological Survey director, to investigate. In June 1871, Hayden took a survey party of 34 men, including painter Thomas Moran and photographer William Henry Jackson, to northwestern Wyoming. Their visuals and Hayden's 500-page report helped convince Congress to set aside this remarkable wilderness the following year. By the early 20th century, when rail access to the north entrance became possible, tourists were flooding in.

With 3472 square miles of terrain, Yellowstone measures 54 miles east to west and 63 miles north to south, making it bigger than the state of Delaware. Its elevation ranges from 11,358 feet, atop Eagle Peak in the Absarokas, to 5314 feet, at the north entrance. The park has 370 miles of paved roads and more than 1200 miles of marked backcountry trails. In summer, when tourists descend tourists visit, its population is greater than that of St. Louis or Cleveland. Its rainfall varies from 80 inches a year, in the southwestern Falls River Basin, to 10 inches at Mammoth Hot Springs. Snow can fall in any month of the year.

Generally speaking, the park is open only from May through October, and many of its lodges and campgrounds have shorter seasons than that. But a second, winter season—running from mid-December to mid-March—attracts snowmobilers and cross-country skiers to the Old Faithful and Mammoth Hot Springs areas. Ironically, although 96 percent of the park is in Wyoming, only two of its entrances are in that state. Three entrances, including West Yellowstone, are in Montana, which contains only 3 percent of the park. Idaho has the other 1 percent.

The following touring itinerary assumes that you're heading west from Idaho and entering the park from the West Yellowstone en-

SIGHTS

WALKING TOUR
The Norris Geyser Basin

In a walk of less than two miles beginning just a few hundred yards west of the road junction, you can take in dozens of geysers, hot springs, mud pools and silica terraces in "one of the most extreme environments on earth," as it's called by some park publications.

NORRIS GEYSER BASIN MUSEUM   Start your visit at the rustic Norris Geyser Basin Museum, where displays interpret hydrothermal geology. Then set out on the one-and-a-half-mile loop trail through patchily forested Back Basin (to the south) or the half-mile loop around the more open Porcelain Basin (to the north). ~ 307-344-2812.

DARK CAVERN GEYSER   From an overlook northeast of the Norris museum you can get a good panorama of **Porcelain Basin**, which appears as a steaming sheet of whitish rock. Silica and clay are responsible for the milky color characteristic of this area's various springs and geysers; some are rimmed with orange, indicating the presence of iron compounds. This is a very dynamic basin whose features come and go every few years. The Dark Cavern Geyser, which erupts several times an hour to heights of 15 to 20 feet, is among the more constant.

trance. From the Madison junction, the route proceeds clockwise around the park circuit for 141 miles and returns to Madison (which sits at nine o'clock). The agenda can be easily picked up from any other gateway. This entrance is only open to vehicle traffic from mid-April to early November. The road then reopens for snowmobile traffic from mid-December to mid-March.

MADISON AREA–WEST ENTRANCE   You will enter the park on **West Entrance Road**, which closely parallels the Madison River and is excellent for wildlife viewing. Allow yourself plenty of time to travel on the busy Yellowstone National Park roads; there's lots of traffic, junctions and turnouts. Keep in mind that road construction is on-going and routes may be closed. Yellowstone's official website (www.nps.gov/yell) has up-to-date information posted.

Keep an eye open for rare trumpeter swans at Seven Mile Bridge (their unmistakable, blaring cry when in flight can be heard from two miles away) and for elk and mule deer in the meadows. It's about seven miles to Madison, one of the park's smaller junctions. It does not offer overnight lodging (aside from camping),

EMERALD SPRING   The first thing you'll encounter along the **Back Basin** is the highly acidic Emerald Spring, which has a pH of 4.5—nearly that of tomato juice. Its water, however, is crystal clear and green in color when bright sunlight filters through to its sulfur-coated floor, 27 feet deep. This is an extremely hot pool, normally about 194°, just 5° below the boiling point at this elevation.

STEAMBOAT GEYSER   Next is Back Basin's Steamboat Geyser, the world's tallest active geyser—when it is, indeed, active. Its eruptions, though spectacular, are *highly* unpredictable. After its 1969 eruption, Steamboat lay dormant for nine years. In May 2000 the geyser erupted again, ending another long period of dormancy. When the geyser does blast, it sends a shower of water 300 feet into the air for as long as 40 minutes. It was last active in October 2003..

ECHINUS GEYSER   Echinus Geyser is far more dependable than Steamboat Geyser, though the rate and duration of its eruptions have slowed in recent years. Its explosions come only a few times a day, and they last only up to four minutes. Still, the water rises skyward 40 to 60 feet. Small crowds gather on benches around its cone much as they do (on a larger scale!) around Old Faithful. Echinus is also the largest acid-water geyser known, with a pH level between 3.3 and 3.6—almost as high as vinegar. Acid-water geysers are extremely rare; most of those known to exist on earth are in the Norris Geyser Basin.

stores or service stations, but it has a campground, a ranger station, an amphitheater, an information station and a bookstore (seasonal hours). ~ 307-344-7381.

To begin your tour, turn left at Madison onto the park's Grand Loop Road. About four and a half miles ahead, and right beside the highway, is **Gibbon Falls**, a veil-like 84-foot drop over a rock face. Grand Loop Road continues to ascend through the minor Monument and Gibbon geyser basins to Norris, 14 miles northeast of Madison.

NORRIS AREA   For many visitors, Yellowstone's most intriguing thermal area is not the Upper Geyser Basin around Old Faithful but the **Norris Geyser Basin**. Thermal activity seems to be on the increase here. After a moderate earthquake struck the area in March 1994, long-dormant geysers surged back to life, and geologists monitored dramatic increases in ground temperature in certain parts of the basin. See the "Walking Tour" for more information.   ◄ *HIDDEN*

From Norris junction, the **Norris Canyon Road** proceeds 12 miles east to Canyon Village, effectively dividing the Grand Loop

Road into two smaller loops. En route, about three miles east of Norris, it passes the pretty **Virginia Cascades**, where the Gibbon River slides through a narrow canyon and drops 60 feet. Most of the route is densely forested.

Less than a mile north of the junction off of Norris Canyon Road, at the entrance to the Norris campground, is the **Museum of the National Park Ranger**. Housed in a restored log cabin built in 1908 as a U.S. Army outpost, the museum contains exhibits explaining how park protection began as a domestic military function and evolved into the highly specialized occupation it is today. ~ 307-344-7353.

The Grand Loop Road north from Norris to Mammoth Hot Springs, a distance of 21 miles, passes several interesting geothermal features. Vents in the slopes of **Roaring Mountain**, five miles from Norris, hiss and steam at the side of the road. A glossy black volcanic glass from which ancient American Indians made utensils and tools forms 200-foot-high **Obsidian Cliff**, nine miles from Norris. **Sheepeater Cliff**, 14 miles from Norris, is composed of pentagonal and heptagonal columns of basalt, another volcanic byproduct.

This region of low-lying streams and small lakes is a favorite of moose, who feed on willow shrubs and underwater plants, and who often wander through the **Indian Creek campground**, located just to the southwest of Sheepeater Cliff.

MAMMOTH HOT SPRINGS AREA   The Grand Loop Road begins its descent to Mammoth Hot Springs and the north entrance at **Golden Gate Canyon**, so named for the yellow lichen that paints its otherwise-barren rock walls.

Where Glen Creek tumbles out of Swan Lake Flat, **Rustic Falls** drop 47 feet into the canyon. To the east, one-way **Bunsen Peak Road** winds around the base of Bunsen Peak, following the rim of the Gardiner River's 800-foot **Sheepeater Canyon**. Trails leave this road for the summit of 8564-foot Bunsen Peak and the foot of pretty **Osprey Falls**, deep in Sheepeater Canyon.

The **Mammoth Hot Springs**, truly one of the park's highlights, are a spectacular series of steaming travertine terraces in a steady

ELK MAGNET

One of the most surprising aspects of Mammoth Hot Springs is their apparent allure to elk. Dozens of the magnificent antlered creatures bed down in the terraces, seemingly oblivious to tourists who pass within a few feet. Keep in mind, however, that these are dangerous animals—it is illegal to approach within 25 yards of an elk.

state of metamorphosis. Super-heated ground water rises to the surface as carbonic acid, dissolving great quantities of natural limestone. As it seeps through cracks in the earth, it deposits the limestone, which solidifies again as travertine (calcium carbonate). This white mineral provides a habitat for colorful bacterial algae (cyanobacteria), whose varying pastel hues reflect the temperature of the water they inhabit: White bacteria live in the hottest water, followed, in descending order, by yellow, orange, brown and, in the coolest, green.

The result of this thermal dynamism on the lower slopes of Terrace Mountain is a lopsided wedding cake of a hillside. About 500 gallons of water flow from the springs per minute; by some estimates, two tons of dissolved limestone are deposited each day. But the springs and terraces are constantly changing, new ones emerging while others become dormant.

Visitors coming from the south will get their first glimpse of Mammoth Hot Springs from the one-and-a-half-mile Upper Terrace Loop Drive, a narrow, one-way route that turns left off the Grand Loop Road about a mile and a half south of Mammoth village. The thermal landscape here is highly varied: Some terraces have been inactive for five centuries, others (such as the pure white **Angel Terrace**) have come back to life after decades of dormancy, and still others (such as **New Highland Spring**) have erupted from verdant forest in relatively recent times—even as park rangers and frequent visitors watched.

Probably the best place to view the entire Mammoth area is from the **Lower Terrace Overlook** off the Upper Terrace Loop Drive. Boardwalk trails lead a half mile downhill through the main terrace region to the village beyond. Features like **Minerva Spring** and **Jupiter Spring** go through cycles of activity and dormancy lasting years at a time. **Opal Terrace**, at the foot of the hill, deposits as much as a foot of travertine per year in its most active periods. **Liberty Cap**, a cone formed by a long-extinct hot spring, marks the north end of the Mammoth Hot Springs; it is 37 feet high and 20 feet in diameter at its base.

Mammoth was the first settlement in Yellowstone. Park headquarters are lodged in the gray stone buildings of the former **Fort Yellowstone**, a cavalry post during the three decades the park was administered by the U.S. Army, from 1886 to 1917. ~ 307-344-7381. Also in the historic fort is the **Horace M. Albright Visitors Center**, whose exhibits explain the Army's role during those early years. There are also excellent wildlife displays and theater programs explaining the evolution of the national park. ~ 307-344-2263.

Other village facilities, open year-round, include a hotel, restaurants, a general store and other shops, a gas station with repair and towing services, a medical clinic, a post office, a campground and an amphitheater for evening programs. There's even a corral for trail riders. For park visitors planning to complete a circuit of the Grand Loop Road in two days, this is a good halfway point for food and lodging on the tour from Grant Village.

The **North Entrance Road,** which connects Mammoth Hot Springs with Gardiner, Montana, five miles to the north, is the only route into the park that is open year-round. (The Northeast Entrance Road is open beyond the park boundary to Cooke City, Montana, but the Beartooth Highway beyond that point is closed from mid-October through May.)

The North Entrance Road passes through 600-foot-deep **Gardiner Canyon** and swings by the steaming, subterranean outlet where the **Boiling River** flows into the Gardiner River. At the north entrance, the route passes beneath the 30-foot stone **Roosevelt Arch,** dedicated in 1903 by President Theodore Roosevelt and inscribed, "For the Benefit and Enjoyment of the People."

East of Mammoth Hot Springs, the Grand Loop Road continues 18 miles to Tower Junction. En route, about four miles from Mammoth, it passes **Undine Falls,** which drop 60 feet between perpendicular cliff walls on Lava Creek.

TOWER JUNCTION–ROOSEVELT AREA The saddle between Mammoth and Tower Junction is known as the **Blacktail Deer Plateau.** Nature lovers may spot the mule deer from which it gets its name on **Blacktail Plateau Drive,** a one-way, six-and-a-half-mile eastbound dirt road that leaves the main road about ten miles east of Mammoth (eight miles west of Tower Junction) to traverse forests of fir, spruce, pine and aspen, and hills covered with sagebrush and wildflowers.

If you stay on the Grand Loop Road, about three and a half miles before Tower Junction—just north of Elk Creek (yes, there are lots of those creatures here, too)—you'll pass **Garnet Hill.** The rocks here are Precambrian granite gneiss estimated to be roughly 2.7 billion years old, formed before the first primitive lifeforms even began to appear on the planet. Imperfect garnets can be found in this ancient formation.

A short side road a little over a mile west of Tower Junction leads to a **petrified tree,** enclosed by a tall iron fence to prevent the vandalism that consumed its former neighbors. Petrified trees—like this upright 20-foot redwood stump—were fossilized 50 million years ago after falling volcanic ash covered them. They can be found in isolated locations throughout northern Yellowstone, especially nearby **Specimen Ridge,** where between nine and twelve separate petrified forests—one on top of another—have been identified.

HIDDEN ►

Tower Junction takes its name from the unusual basalt pinnacles that rise above the Yellowstone River canyon just south of here. They include **Overhanging Cliff,** a columnar formation that actually hangs over the road, and **The Needle**, a 260-foot spire of volcanic breccia.

Tower Fall is about two miles south of the junction off the Grand Loop Road; it plummets 132 feet from the palisades into **The Narrows**, at 500 feet the deepest part of this section of the canyon, and its most confined. A trail that leads to the foot of the waterfall reveals more steam vents and hot springs, including **Calcite Springs**, where the geothermal waters deposit calcite, gypsum and sulfur.

At Tower Junction itself are a ranger station, a service station, horse corrals and the **Roosevelt Lodge**, a rustic 1920s log building (with cabins and a restaurant) named for Teddy Roosevelt. The environmentalist president favored this area's rolling hills for camping around the turn of the 20th century.

There are really two junctions at Tower Junction: that of the Grand Loop Road with the **Northeast Entrance Road**, and that of the **Lamar River** with the Yellowstone River. The Northeast Entrance Road follows the Lamar Valley upstream for the first half of its 29-mile run to the park's Northeast Entrance, closely paralleling an old American Indian route, the Bannock Trail. Bison and elk winter in the broad, open meadows of this glacial valley. The **Lamar Buffalo Ranch**, ten miles east of Tower Junction, was used as a breeding preserve for bison for a half century after its establishment in 1907, during which time it helped Yellowstone's once-rare bison population increase from 25 to a modern estimate of over 3000. It's now home to the **Yellowstone Association Institute**, a nonprofit field school offering field courses on the park's wildlife, geology, flora and history. Some courses earn university credit. ~ 307-344-2294, fax 307-344-2485; www.yellowassociation.org, e-mail registrar@yellowstoneassociation.org.

> The fastest mammal found in Yellowstone is the pronghorn antelope, which can reach speeds of up to 60 miles per hour.

There are two park campgrounds along this route. **Slough Creek campground**, Yellowstone's smallest with 29 sites, is about eight miles northeast of Tower Junction at the end of three-mile Slough Creek Road. The trout fishing is said to be excellent in this area. **Pebble Creek campground**, with 36 sites, is about 18 miles east of Tower Junction at the mouth of Pebble Creek Canyon.

The Northeast Entrance Road turns away from the Lamar River about three miles past Buffalo Ranch and follows **Soda Butte Creek** for the next 20 miles. **Soda Butte** itself, on the south side of the highway about five miles from Buffalo Ranch, is a long-dead travertine terrace not unlike those of Mammoth Hot Springs. The route climbs through the Absaroka Range, cutting a path between 10,928-foot **Abiathar Peak** and 10,404-foot **Barronette Peak**, en route to the Northeast Entrance, just across the Montana state line.

South of Tower Junction, the Grand Loop Road passes Tower Fall, then begins a 12-mile ascent into the Washburn Range, a stretch that is Yellowstone's highest road. The area southeast of the highway, between Antelope Creek and the rim of the Yellowstone canyon, is a refuge for grizzly bears. Any human travel (even by foot) is prohibited in the area. Note: As of 2004, the road from Chittlendend to Canyon will be closed until 2005.

Trails from 8859-foot **Dunraven Pass** lead through groves of gnarled whitebark pine and subalpine fir to the fire lookout atop 10,243-foot **Mount Washburn**, a summer range for bighorn sheep. There are magnificent views from here across the Yellowstone caldera to the Red Mountains, 35 miles away, and on clear days to the Teton Range, 100 miles to the southwest.

Yellowstone's population of flying insects is kept in check by the violetgreen swallows who make their home in the canyon's cliffs.

CANYON AREA From Dunraven Pass the Grand Loop Road makes a five-mile descent through dense stands of lodgepole pine to **Canyon Village**. Note: Until 2005, the roadway from Canyon to Fishing bridge will undergo major construction. Expect delays.

Visitors will find two lodges here, as well as dining facilities and a lounge, a campground and an amphitheater, riding stables and a general store, service station, post office and ranger station. Exhibits at the **Canyon Visitors Center** describe the creation of the Yellowstone River canyon by lava, glaciers and floods as well as other aspects of park geology. You'll also find a history of the bison. ~ 307-242-2550.

While the **Grand Canyon of the Yellowstone** extends 24 miles to The Narrows, just past Tower Fall at its northern end, the truly "grand" part is its first couple of miles, which include the Upper and Lower Yellowstone Falls. For your first view of the falls (you'll want more than one), take the two-and-a-half-mile, one-way North Rim Drive east and south from Canyon Village.

Your first stop is **Inspiration Point**, where you can park and descend several dozen steps to a lookout. To the southwest (about 1.4 miles) is the **Lower Falls**, at 308 feet Yellowstone's highest waterfall. (Around the corner to the south, out of view from this point, are the 109-foot **Upper Falls**.) The canyon is about 1000 feet deep at this point (it ranges from 800 to 1200), while the distance from here to the South Rim is about 1500 feet. Farther downriver are places where it widens out to about 4000 feet.

The vivid hues of the canyon walls—yellow, orange, brown, red and even blue—are proof of ancient hydrothermal action on rhyolite, a fine-grained volcanic rock heavy in silica, and its mineral oxides. Though the cliffs still exude steam and seem forbidding, they make a fine home for ospreys, which scan for fish from their huge summer nests built on rock porches high above the Yellowstone River.

Southwest of Inspiration Point, nearer Lower Falls, there are additional viewing points off North Rim Drive at **Grandview Point, Lookout Point** and **Red Rock Point.** A parking area just before the drive rejoins the Grand Loop Road signals a three-quarter-mile paved trail that switchbacks 600 feet downhill to the lip of the Lower Falls.

Less than a half mile south, after Grand Loop Road crosses Cascade Creek (whose own **Crystal Falls** empty into the Yellowstone just below this point), look for a turnout to the Upper Falls. The trail to the brink of these falls is almost a stairway, and it's only a couple of hundred yards in either direction.

Just over a half mile from the Upper Falls turnout, and about 2.3 miles south of Canyon Village, cross the Chittenden Bridge to Artist Point Road, which branches northeast along the canyon's South Rim. It ends .8 mile beyond at **Artist Point,** directly opposite Grandview Point but with a strikingly different perspective on the canyon. En route, you'll pass a parking area for a network of trails that head out for closer views of both waterfalls and the canyon. Among them is **Uncle Tom's Trail,** named not for a Harriet Beecher Stowe character but for Tom Richardson, who built the first trail into the canyon in 1898.

The contrast between the reckless river that rushes through the Yellowstone canyon and the tranquil stream that meanders through the **Hayden Valley** is quite striking. Yet only about three miles separate these two opposite faces of the Yellowstone River. Whereas the canyon is hostile to most wildlife, the lush, six-mile valley between Alum and Trout creeks is a natural sanctuary.

Bison, moose, elk, bear and other large animals wander the former lakebed, whose rolling hills, meadows and marshlands are a veritable garden of tasty grasses and shrubs. The trumpeter swans, sandhill cranes, great blue herons, white pelicans and other stately waterfowl abound in the marshes. Fishing is prohibited in the valley—for the peace of the animals and the safety of anglers.

Numerous roadside parking areas have been created to accommodate wildlife viewing. Nevertheless, traffic jams are common. Park officials continually warn visitors to view large animals only from a distance, even if they're in their cars. The ferocity of grizzly bears is well documented, but bison, though they may seem docile, can be unpredictable and temperamental as well.

An intense thermal area beyond Elk Antler Creek marks the south end of the Hayden Valley, about 11 miles from Canyon Village. The varied features here are arguably the park's most foul smelling. The stench of hydrogen sulfide gas emanates from the constantly churning caldron of murky **Mud Volcano.** Rising volcanic gases continually bubble to the surface of **Black Dragon's Caldron,** which erupted in 1948 with such frenzy that it flung pitch-black mud dozens of feet around; Sour Lake, whose acid water has killed nearby trees; Dragon's Mouth, whose bursts of steam roar and echo within its cavern; and Sulphur Caldron, its water yellow with sulfur.

YELLOWSTONE LAKE AREA   Spawning cutthroat trout leap up the cascades at **LeHardy Rapids** on the Yellowstone River in June and July, making their final approach to nearby Yellowstone Lake. **Lake Junction** is just three miles south from this point.

The first of three communities situated along the lake's northwest shore is **Fishing Bridge**, whose facilities (just east of Lake Junction) include a full-service garage, a general store, a an RV park, a ranger station and a park for hard-sided recreational vehicles. A camping restriction was imposed because of the area's popularity among park bears.

Despite its name, the bridge—which spans the Yellowstone River at its outlet from Yellowstone Lake—was closed to fishing in 1973. Visitors now use it primarily for watching the summer spawning spectacular of native cutthroat trout returning to the lake to lay their eggs. Pelicans, gulls and even bears are a part of the show. Exhibits at the **Fishing Bridge Visitors Center** focus on the geology and bird and fish life of the Yellowstone Lake area. ~ 307-242-2450.

If you want to head out the park's **East Entrance Road** toward Cody, Wyoming, 77 miles from Lake Junction, take a left at Fishing Bridge. It's 26 miles from there, through the dense evergreen forests surrounding 8530-foot Sylvan Pass in the Absaroka Range, to the East Entrance station.

For its first nine miles, the East Entrance Road traces the north shore of Yellowstone Lake. Moose often browse in the fens and sedge meadows of the **Pelican Creek Flats**, one to three miles east of Fishing Bridge. Although there's no immediate cause for alarm, the earth in this area is rising by as much as an inch per year—a warning of future volcanic activity, perhaps along the line of what exists in the Norris Geyser Basin today.

It wasn't long ago, in geological terms, that hydrothermal explosions created the craters now filled by **Mary Bay** and adjacent **Indian Pond**. The bottom sediment in Mary Bay is still very warm, and a fault line that runs along Yellowstone Lake's north-

AUTHOR FAVORITE

Few spectacles I've witnessed are half as entrancing as the sandhill cranes in their courtship dance, so if I'm within 100 miles I make sure to visit **Hayden Valley**. If the cranes aren't strutting their stuff, it's near certain I'll be able to watch some of the many other creatures often spotted here. See page 173 for more information.

eastern shore continues to feed hot springs, among them **Beach Springs** (at Mary Bay), **Steamboat Springs** (at Steamboat Point) and **Butte Springs** (at the foot of Lake Butte). There are picnic areas at each of these thermal locations, which are five, six and seven miles, respectively, from Fishing Bridge.

A short spur road climbs 600 feet to the **Lake Butte Overlook** for one last panoramic glimpse of Yellowstone Lake. Then it's back to the East Entrance Road and up the west side of the Absaroka Range. Look out for marmots and pikas on the rocky slopes at higher elevations. Beyond **Sylvan Pass**, 20 miles from Fishing Bridge, the highway descends nearly 1600 feet in seven miles to the park's east entrance.

To continue the tour, take the turnoff from the Grand Loop Road less than two miles south of Lake Junction to **Lake Village**. Lake Village is the home of the park's oldest lodging, the **Lake Yellowstone Hotel**, which opened to visitors in 1891. Though renovated, it has kept its historic flavor and is still going strong. Lake Village also has cabins, restaurants, stores, a ranger station and a hospital.

Another two miles south is **Bridge Bay**, the lake's primary abode for tent campers and, with 429 sites, the park's largest campground. Besides a ranger station, amphitheater and store, Bridge Bay boasts a marina. You will need permits both to fish and to operate your boat; obtain them at ranger stations. You can swim without a permit, but be cautious: The average lake surface temperature, even in mid-August, is about 60°.

As you follow the lakeshore south and west from Bridge Bay to West Thumb, a distance of about 17 miles, passing a half-dozen picnic sites en route, you'll get a feeling for the breadth of this huge mountain lake: It covers 136 square miles and has an average depth of 139 feet, though at its deepest point it's 390 feet. Of five islands in the lake, three—Stevenson, Dot and Frank—are easily visible from this lakeshore drive.

GRANT VILLAGE–WEST THUMB AREA West Thumb is at the south junction of the Grand Loop Road. To continue the loop, you should take the westbound fork, which crosses the Continental Divide twice more—the first time at 8391 feet elevation—en route to Old Faithful.

If you turn left, you'll head south en route to the park's Southern Entrance. You'll soon pass the **West Thumb Geyser Basin**, noted for the vivid colors of its springs. A walkway winds past features like the Thumb Paint Pots, the intensity and hue of whose colors seem to change seasonally with the light; Abyss Pool, with a deep, cobalt blue crater of remarkably clear water; Fishing Cone, a spring whose volcano-like mound is surrounded by lake water; and Lakeshore Geyser, which spouts up to 60 feet high when it's not submerged by Yellowstone Lake.

Grant Village lies two miles farther south, on Yellowstone Lake's **West Thumb,** a bay so named because early surveyors thought the lake was shaped like a hand. (In my opinion, it's shaped more like a tired backpacker, and this bay is his or her head.) Measuring 20 miles from north to south, 14 miles from east to west, and with 110 miles of shoreline, this is the highest (7733 feet) large lake in the Western Hemisphere outside of South America's High Andes.

A couple of miles south of West Thumb, turn off a mile east to **Grant Village,** on the shore of **Yellowstone Lake.** The southern-most of numerous park communities you'll pass through on this park circuit, Grant Village was named for Ulysses S. Grant, who as president signed the bill that created Yellowstone National Park in 1872. It has motel-style lodge buildings, restaurants, camp-grounds, boat ramps, several shops, a service station, a post office and other facilities.

Much of southern Yellowstone bears the scars of the dramatic 1988 forest fires that ravaged about 36 percent (783,000 acres) of the park's vegetation and that took 25,000 firefighters about three months and $120 million to quell. But exhibits at the **Grant Village Visitors Center** (307-242-2650; www.travelyellowstone.com), beside the lakeshore amphitheater, explain fire's role not only as a destruc- tive force but also as a creative one—clearing areas for the growth of new vegetation, which in turn nurtures a greater diversity of wildlife. Naturalists say major fires such as these occur once or twice a century when nature is allowed to take its course.

> The namesake of Lewis Lake is explorer Meri- wether Lewis although he never set foot within 100 miles of it.

Twenty-two miles south, you'll find yourself on the east shore of **Lewis Lake,** a pretty three-mile-long, two-mile-wide favorite of anglers. The lake lies just within the ancient Yellowstone caldera.

En route to the South Entrance ranger station, the road leaves the by-now slowly meandering Snake River and traces the steep-sided canyon rim of the tributary **Lewis River,** its black lava walls 600 feet high. Look for turnouts for **Lewis Falls,** a 37-foot drop, and **Moose Falls,** a split waterfall that enters the Lewis from Crawfish Creek. Just before exiting the park, the road leaves the Lewis River and meets up with the slowly mean- dering Snake River.

OLD FAITHFUL AREA   In a saddle between the crossings of the Divide, you can turn off at Shoshone Point for a view down Delacy Creek to Shoshone Lake, the park's second-largest body of water, three miles south. This is moose country. In the far distance, on clear days, you can see the towering spires of the Grand Tetons.

At Craig Pass, straddling the Divide, is tiny, spring-fed **Isa Lake,** whose waters drain west (via the Lewis, Snake and Colum- bia rivers) to the Pacific Ocean and east (via the Firehole, Madison, Missouri and Mississippi rivers) to the Gulf of Mexico and the Atlantic Ocean. Brilliant water lilies cover the lake's surface in midsummer.

About 15 miles from West Thumb is a wooden platform from which you can view the **Keppler Cascades**. This series of falls and rapids near the headwaters of the Firehole River plunges more than 100 feet between nearly vertical canyon walls.

It's only another two miles to the cloverleaf junction for **Old Faithful Geyser**, Yellowstone's best-known sight and the world's most famous geyser. While not the largest, the highest or the most regular geyser in the park, Old Faithful has demonstrated remarkably consistent behavior since its 1870 discovery. It erupts 19 to 21 times per day at intervals averaging about 76 minutes, varying by 45 to 100 minutes on either side. Eruptions, lasting from 90 seconds to five minutes, eject between 4000 and 8000 gallons of boiling water to heights of up to 180 feet.

The **Old Faithful Visitors Center**, next to the Old Faithful Inn by the west parking area, can tell you when to expect the next discharge. Normally, the shorter and smaller the last eruption, the less time you'll have to wait before for next one.

The park community of Old Faithful is one of Yellowstone's largest villages, with three overnight lodges; several restaurants, cafeterias and snack bars; a number of stores and shops; a full-service garage; a 24-hour medical clinic; a post office and other community facilities.

It's also the focal point of Yellowstone's spectacular **Upper Geyser Basin**, which contains the world's single largest concentration of geysers. Weaving from the visitors center through the basin, on either side of the aptly named **Firehole River**, are about four miles of boardwalks and paved, wheelchair-accessible trails as well as many more miles of dirt paths. The geysers of Upper Geyser Basin are a motley group whose very unpredictability makes Old Faithful's consistency seem all the more remarkable.

◄ HIDDEN

Directly opposite Old Faithful, overlooking the northeast bank of the river, is the Geyser Hill Group. It includes the **Anemone Geyser**, which bubbles explosively every 15 minutes; the **Plume Geyser**, which has erupted to 25 feet high every 20 minutes since 1942, when it first became active; the **Beehive Geyser**, which shoots water 150 feet or higher at irregular intervals of one to ten days; the four **Lion Geysers**, connected underground, which gush two or three times a day; and the **Giantess Geyser**, which erupts violently once or twice an hour, during a half- to two-day period, two to six times a year, and returns to dormancy in between.

Downstream is the **Castle Geyser**, possibly the oldest in the park. Its ancient cone is 120 feet around. Castle's twice-daily explosions rise to 90 feet, last about 20 minutes and are followed by another 30 to 40 minutes of furious steaming. Nearby **Grand**

Geyser, the world's tallest predictable geyser, erupts like a fountain up to 200 feet high every seven to fifteen hours.

Farther down the trail, keep your eyes out for the **Giant Geyser,** one of Yellowstone's largest (up to 250 feet), which, after long spells of dormancy, has recently been erupting every three to ten days. Also look for the **Grotto Geyser,** whose weirdly shaped cone has absorbed the tree trunks that once surrounded it, and the **Riverside Geyser,** whose 75-foot column of water arches over the Firehole River for 20 minutes every seven hours or so.

Upper Geyser Basin also includes several attractive springs and pools, the best known of which is **Morning Glory Pool,** reached by a one-and-a-half-mile stroll from the visitors center. Labeled in 1880 for its likeness to its namesake flower, the hot spring began to cloud because of vandalism (mainly trash thrown in the pool). The vivid colors of these pools—yellow, orange, brown and green—are due to the presence of photosynthetic algae on the submerged earth. There are several more geyser basins along the Grand Loop Road as it proceeds north from Old Faithful toward the Madison junction.

Black Sand Basin, on Iron Creek just a mile south of Old Faithful village, is so named for its obsidian sand. It includes the **Emerald Pool,** whose deep-green center is bordered by orange and brown, and **Cliff Geyser,** a wildly unpredictable feature whose frequent eruptions vary in length from minutes to hours.

Biscuit Basin, another 1.7 miles north, got its name from a now-defunct feature of **Sapphire Pool.** Prior to the earthquake of 1959, this pool was a small geyser surrounded by biscuitlike mounds of geyserite, the hardened deposits of mineral water ejected by the geyser. Immediately after the quake, Sapphire Geyser staged a series of huge and violent eruptions, scattering the biscuits far across the basin. It hasn't erupted since. But nearby **Jewel Geyser,** surrounded by gemlike balls of geyserite set in colorful bacteria, erupts four or five times an hour.

The principal features of **Midway Geyser Basin,** about three miles north of Biscuit Basin, are **Excelsior Geyser** and **Grand Prismatic Spring.** Excelsior Geyser erupted in 1888 (to a height of 300 feet) and again in 1985 (nonstop for two days, to a height of 55 feet. If you missed it then, don't hold your breath). At all other times, it's like a pot of scalding water that continually boils over—at a rate of five million gallons *per day.* When the air cools at sunset, the geyser's steam fills the entire basin. Grand Prismatic Spring is Yellowstone's largest hot spring at 370 feet in diameter; it has azure blue water at its center, colorful algae around its edges.

Two miles past Midway, a turnoff down the three-mile, one-way **Firehole Lake Drive** marks the beginning of **Lower Geyser Basin.** This basin covers more ground than some of the others but its geysers are not as striking, with the exception of the **Great**

Fountain Geyser, whose hour-long eruptions reach heights of 100 to 230 feet; intervals between eruptions vary from seven to 15 hours. Where the drive rejoins the Grand Loop Road you'll see the **Fountain Paint Pots**, a multicolored collection of gurgling mud pools that vary in size, color and intensity.

Proceed to a turnoff for one-way **Firehole Canyon Drive**, about a half mile from Madison, and then backtrack. The two-mile route penetrates the 800-foot, black lava walls of the canyon, reaching its climax where the 40-foot **Firehole Falls** tumble and churn into the **Firehole Cascades**. Above the falls is a big swimming hole; the miles of geothermal activity upstream raise the river's temperature about 30° higher than normally would be expected at this elevation and latitude.

You are now at Madison, where this tour began, and you can turn left to continue back 14 miles on West Entrance Road to West Yellowstone.

LODGING

Yellowstone National Park probably offers more accommodations and more hotels of historic value than any other national park. In all, Yellowstone boasts nine properties with 1043 hotel rooms and 1159 cabin units. *Note:* All accommodations must be booked through **Xanterra Parks & Resorts**. ~ Yellowstone National Park, WY 82190; 307-344-7311, fax 307-344-7456; www.xanterra.com.

One of two park accommodations open in both winter and summer is the **Mammoth Hot Springs Hotel**, built in 1937, which incorporates a wing of an earlier inn from 1911 (during the heyday of Fort Yellowstone). Its 223 rooms and cabin units come either with (deluxe) or without (moderate) private baths; four ultra-deluxe-priced, suite-style cabins have private hot tubs. Facilities include a dining room, a fast-food outlet, a lounge and a gift shop.

AUTHOR FAVORITE

Yellowstone boasts a few grand old lodges—I'm partial to **Lake Yellowstone Hotel & Cabins**. The grande dame of Yellowstone hostelries, it first opened in 1891 and is listed on the National Register of Historic Places. The 296-room hotel has been fully renovated and again boasts its long-sequestered 1920s wicker furniture. The Sun Room, which has great lake views (especially at sunrise!), has evening cocktail service and frequent piano or chamber-music performances. Other facilities include a lakeside dining room, a deli and a gift shop. Guests choose between ultra-deluxe hotel rooms, less-expensive annex rooms or cabins with private baths. Closed early October to mid-May. ~ Lake Village; 307-344-7311. MODERATE TO ULTRA-DELUXE.

A decorative highlight is a huge United States map made of 15 woods from nine different countries. Closed early March to mid-May and November to mid-December. ~ Mammoth Hot Springs; 307-344-7311. BUDGET TO ULTRA-DELUXE.

The rustic **Roosevelt Lodge and Cabins**, so named because of its proximity to President Teddy Roosevelt's favorite camping areas, has the feel of an earlier era. Its cabins are of simple frame construction; some have electric heat and private baths, but most have wood-burning stoves and share a bathhouse. In the main lodge are two stone fireplaces, a family-style restaurant, a lounge and a gift shop. Closed early September to mid-June. ~ Tower Junction; 307-344-7311. BUDGET TO MODERATE.

Not far from the Grand Canyon of the Yellowstone is the 609-room **Canyon Lodge & Cabins**. The two multi-story lodges have hotel-style rooms with private baths; cabins are single-story four or six-plex units, all with private toilets and showers, while more modest, single motel-style cabins are also available. In the main lodge are a dining room, cafeteria, snack shop, lounge and gift shop. Closed late August to early June. ~ Canyon Village; 307-344-7311. MODERATE TO DELUXE.

Old Faithful Inn was built of pine logs from the surrounding forests and volcanic rock from a nearby quarry.

Relax in rocking chairs on the lodge porch of the **Lake Lodge Cabins** to take in a sweeping view of Yellowstone Lake to the east. The Lake Lodge has 186 cabins—some cozy, some spacious, all with private baths. In the classic log lodge are a big fireplace, a cafeteria, a lobby bar and a gift shop. There's also a guest laundry. Closed late-September to mid-June. ~ Lake Village; 307-344-7311. BUDGET TO MODERATE.

Grant Village features 299 standard rooms, all with private bathrooms and showers. Facilities include a dining room and a separate restaurant, a lounge, a gift shop and a guest laundry. Closed late September to late May. ~ West Thumb; 307-344-7311. MODERATE TO DELUXE.

The massive yet rustic **Old Faithful Inn** was acclaimed a National Historic Landmark in 1987. This 325-room hotel is said to be one of the largest log structures in the world. The gables on its steeply pitched roof were a trademark of architect Robert Reamer. In the enormous lobby are a stone fireplace and a clock handcrafted from copper, wood and wrought iron. The inn has ultra-deluxe-priced suites, and rooms with private baths, along with moderately priced rooms with shared toilets and showers down the hall. There's also a restaurant and deli. Closed mid-October through April. ~ Old Faithful; 307-344-7311. MODERATE TO ULTRA-DELUXE.

From the **Old Faithful Lodge Cabins**, just a couple of hundred yards south of the famous geyser, it seems as if you can reach out and touch the park landmark. The 97 rustic cabins include "pioneer" and "frontier" units, with private toilets and showers, and budget units that share a common bathhouse. Closed mid-September to mid-May. ~ Old Faithful; 307-344-7311. BUDGET TO MODERATE.

Winter activities in this thermal basin center around the **Old Faithful Snow Lodge & Cabins.** Most cabins have private baths; the lodge has rooms with private baths. Closed mid-March to mid-May and early October to mid-December. ~ Old Faithful; 307-344-7311, 307-545-4810 ext. 4998. MODERATE TO DELUXE.

Most restaurants within Yellowstone National Park are in the hotels and lodges themselves. Reservations are accepted at some hotel dining rooms and the Old West Dinner Cookout.

DINING

Patrons of the **Mammoth Hotel Dining Room** can enjoy three American-style meals a day amid the steaming travertine terraces for which the area is named. Closed mid-October to mid-May. ~ Mammoth Hot Springs; 307-344-7311. MODERATE. In the same lodge, **The Terrace Grill** dishes up fast food and snacks. BUDGET.

For a taste of how things used to be, look no further than the **Old West Dinner Cookout.** Adventurous diners mount horses or clamber aboard a wagon and ride a short distance to Yancey's Hole, where they are served a hearty chuck-wagon dinner of steak, corn, baked beans, corn muffins, cole slaw and more. Available mid-June to early September. ~ Roosevelt Lodge, Tower Junction; 307-344-7311. DELUXE.

The **Canyon Lodge Dining Room** offers steak-and-seafood dinners nightly in a forested setting located just a half mile from the north rim of the Grand Canyon of the Yellowstone. Their cafeteria does three meals daily and the deli offers up sandwiches. Closed early June to early September. ~ Canyon Village; 307-344-7311. DELUXE.

Yellowstone's top-end culinary experience is at the **Lake Yellowstone Hotel Dining Room.** Prime rib, steak, seafood, chicken and vegetarian meals, as well as daily specials, are served in a classic lakeside setting of etched glass and wicker furniture. Breakfast and lunch are also available. Closed mid-October to late May. ~ Lake Yellowstone Hotel, Lake Village; 307-242-3899. DELUXE.

The Lakehouse serves up pizzas, pastas and steak entrées along with a sterling view across Yellowstone Lake. Breakfasts buffets are served as well. No lunch. ~ Grant Village, West Thumb; 307-344-7311. MODERATE.

The **Old Faithful Dining Room** offers a gourmet menu of prime rib, steak, seafood and poultry beneath the log beams and braces of this immense lodge. Etched glass panels are replicas of carved-wood murals. Three meals a day are served. Reservations required for dinner. Closed mid-October to early May. MODER-

ATE. The hotel's **Pony Express** serves a take-out lunch and dinner menu. ~ Old Faithful Inn, Old Faithful; 307-344-7311. BUDGET.

Fast food and other light fare are the specialties of the **Geyser Grill**. Closed early November to mid-April. ~ Old Faithful Snow Lodge, Old Faithful. BUDGET.

SHOPPING

Nine of Yellowstone's lodging facilities have gift shops for your souvenir needs. In addition, there's **Yellowstone General**. Headquartered in Bozeman and West Yellowstone, Montana, this company operates all general stores, photography shops and tackle shops within the park. That means prices don't differ from one location to another. They're open year-round at Mammoth Hot Springs (307-344-7702) and seasonally at Tower Fall (307-344-7786), Canyon Village (307-242-7377), Fishing Bridge (307-242-7200), Lake Village (307-242-7563), Bridge Bay (307-242-7326), Grant Village (307-242-7390) and Old Faithful (307-545-7282, 307-545-7237 or 307-545-7255).

NIGHTLIFE

Clearly, no one comes to Yellowstone for its nightlife, which is mostly limited to lounging around a lodge fireplace or swapping stories around a campfire. For more social interaction, there are comfortable lounges with full bar service at Grant Village, Old Faithful Inn, Mammoth Hot Springs Hotel, Roosevelt Lodge, Canyon Lodge, Lake Yellowstone Hotel and Lake Lodge.

PARKS

YELLOWSTONE NATIONAL PARK 🚶 🚲 🏇 🎣 🚤 🛶 🚣
Superlatives rule in Yellowstone's 2.2 million acres: the largest and most varied hydrothermal region on earth, the largest lake in North America at an incredibly high elevation (7700 feet), the greatest diversity of wildlife in the Lower 48—the list goes on. Within the park are 9 overnight lodges, 24 restaurants and snack shops, 11 general stores and numerous other shops, 49 picnic areas, restrooms, 5 visitors centers, 2 museums, 11 amphitheaters, a marina, and 1200 miles of hiking and horse trails with 97 trailheads. Swimming is prohibited in thermal features and discouraged in Yellowstone and other lakes because of the risk of hypothermia from the cold waters. Park fishing permits ($20 for seven days) can be obtained at ranger stations, visitors centers, general stores and most angler shops in neighboring communities; the fishing season is generally from late May through October. Anglers must release all native sport fish; refer to park fishing regulations for further information. Permits are required for boating and float tubes. Motorized boating permits can be obtained at the South Entrance, Lewis Lake campground, Grant Village Ranger Station, Bridge Bay Marina and the Lake Ranger Station. Non-motorized boating permits are more widely available and can be found at the same locations for motorized. Cut-

Beware the Bear

O f all the great mammals of the Rocky Mountains, none is as feared or as respected as the grizzly bear. Once numbering at about 50,000 in the lower 48 states, ranging from the Mississippi River west to the Pacific Ocean, this great bear was reduced by white settlement to fewer than 1000 on 2 percent of its former range. Today, most grizzlies—protected as a threatened species under the federal Endangered Species Act—inhabit the national parks and wilderness areas running down the spine of the Rockies from the Canadian border through Yellowstone National Park. In the park alone, biologists estimate there are between 200 and 250 resident grizzlies.

Ursus arctos horribilis is the second largest omnivore (that is, meat and plant eater) in North America, superseded only by the polar bear. Males can weigh more than 1000 pounds, females 600. Though nocturnal, an adult can be aggressive if intruders disturb it . . . or its cubs.

The grizzly is easily distinguished from the more docile American black bear (*Ursus americanus*) by its broad head; a well-defined shoulder muscle, which helps it dig for rodents, insects and roots; and its frequently silver-tipped, or "grizzled," fur coat. Grizzlies don't climb trees as well as black bears, but they can outrun horses in a sprint.

Only occasionally do backcountry visitors see grizzlies today. Even in Yellowstone Park, once renowned for its begging roadside bears, they have been removed to the wilderness. Wildlife watchers who want to observe grizzlies should look during the dawn and dusk hours around the fringes of woodlands and meadows, near water . . . from a distance.

To avoid grizzly encounters, travel in numbers, make plenty of noise (by talking, singing or even wearing bells) and avoid hiking at night. Clean cooking gear immediately after use, and store food in airtight containers away from your campsite. Don't bury your garbage; pack it out.

If confronted by a grizzly while hiking, do *not* turn your back and run. Move slowly away, avoiding eye contact. If the grizzly charges, stand your ground: Bears often feign a charge or run past you. As a last resort, curl into a ball and play dead, covering your neck and head with your hands and arms. If a grizzly invades your camp, find a tree or boulder to climb as high as you can. If you are attacked, fight back with any weapon, including your fists. Playing dead will *not* work here.

Grizzlies kill humans only infrequently; more often the bears die at the hands of man. But like the wise scout, it's best to be prepared.

throat trout, Arctic grayling and mountain whitefish are native to Yellowstone waters. There are brown trout in the Madison and Firehole rivers (flyfishing only), mackinaw (lake trout) in Lewis, Yellowstone and Shoshone lakes, and Arctic grayling in Wolf and Grebe lakes, between Norris and Canyon Village. Entrance fee: $20 weekly vehicle pass (includes Grand Teton National Park). ~ From Idaho you'll enter via West Yellowstone, Route 20 from Idaho Falls, Route 191 from Bozeman and Route 287 from Ennis. Other entrances include: South (via Route 89/191 from Jackson and Route 287 from Dubois); North (via Gardiner, Route 89 from Livingston); Northeast (via Cooke City, Route 212 from Red Lodge and Billings); and East (Route 14/16/20 from Cody); 307-344-7381, fax 307-344-2005; www.nps.gov/yell.

▲ There are 2203 units (1863 for tents/RVs, 340 for RVs only) at 12 campgrounds (hookups at Fishing Bridge only), plus 300 backcountry tent sites. Numbers of sites, open dates and fees are listed below. National Park Service campgrounds: *Lewis Lake* (85, mid-June to early November, $12); *Norris* (116, mid-May to late September, $14); *Indian Creek* (75, early June to mid-September, $12); *Mammoth* (85, year-round, $14); *Tower Fall* (32, mid-May to late September, $12); *Slough Creek* (29, late-May to October 31, $12); *Pebble Creek* (36, early June to late September, $12). Xanterra Parks & Resorts campgrounds: *Grant Village* (425, mid-June to early October, $17); *Madison* (280, early May to late October, $17); *Canyon* (271, early June to early September, $17); *Bridge Bay* (429, late-May to mid-September, $17; reservations for stays from early June to Labor Day through Xanterra Parks & Resorts [P.O. Box 165, Yellowstone National Park, WY 82190; 307-344-7311]); *Fishing Bridge* (340, RVs only, full hookups, mid-May to mid-September, $31). Funding restrictions may force the National Park Service to temporarily close down some of these campgrounds or raise their fees significantly.

▼▼▼▼▼▼▼▼▼▼▼▼▼▼

Outdoor Adventures

FISHING

Within the boundaries of Yellowstone National Park, anglers regardless of residency must buy a seven- or ten-day park license, which can be purchased at any of the park's visitors centers; call the park's switchboard for more information. ~ 307-344-7381.

Yellowstone Lake is renowned for its cutthroat trout, as is the upper portion of the Yellowstone River between Fishing Bridge and the Hayden Valley. Rainbow and brook trout and grayling are native to waters on the west side of the Continental Divide, including Shoshone and Lewis lakes, and Hebgen Lake, outside the park near West Yellowstone, Montana.

Outfitters in West Yellowstone include **Bud Lilly's Trout Shop**, a full-blown fly shop that offers guide services and organizes trips;

www.budlillys.com. ~ 39 Madison Avenue, West Yellowstone, MT; 406-646-7801. Or try **Jacklin's Outfitters for the World of Fly Fishing** for trout guides. ~ 105 Yellowstone Avenue, West Yellowstone, MT; 406-646-7336; www.jacklinsflyshop.com.

Within the park, you can buy or rent complete fishing gear at marinas on Yellowstone Lake; guides are generally available at the marinas as well. **Bridge Bay Marina** rents rods and reels. ~ Bridge Bay Marina; 307-242-3876. Or try **Grant Village** for your supplies. ~ West Thumb; 307-242-3400. Tackle is also available at **Yellowstone General Stores** located throughout the park. ~ Mammoth Hot Springs; 307-344-7702.

BOATING

Marinas in Yellowstone National Park (on Yellowstone Lake) offer full boat-rental services and guided lake trips. Ranger stations provide boat-operating permits on request. Excursion boats that can carry up to 40 passengers leave the **Bridge Bay Marina** several times daily on lake cruises; there are also twilight trips and individual motorboat rentals. Closed October through May. ~ Bridge Bay; 307-344-7381.

SKIING

Yellowstone National Park has hundreds of miles of marked cross-country ski trails, including groomed tracks near Old Faithful and the Grand Canyon of the Yellowstone. Trail maps are available at all visitors centers; very detailed ski maps are available at the Horace M. Albright Visitors Center in Mammoth Hot Springs.

Just outside the park boundaries, **The Rendezvous Ski Trails** offer 30 kilometers of groomed trails, from November through March. The U.S. national cross-country and biathlon (skiing and shooting) teams train here each year. ~ West Yellowstone; 406-646-7701; www.west yellowstonechamber.com.

> Yellowstone National Park's name derives from the yellow rock cliffs of the Yellowstone River, which originates in the park.

Yellowstone Expeditions leads cross-country skiing tours through Yellowstone from their yurt camp. ~ P.O. Box 865, West Yellowstone, MT 59758; 406-646-9333, 800-728-9333; www. yellowstoneexpeditions.com.

Ski Rentals **Bud Lilly's Trout and Ski Shop** rents cross-country skis and snowshoes rentals. ~ 39 Madison Street; 406-646-7801; www.budlillys.com. Try **Yellowstone Alpen Guides** for cross-country rentals only. ~ 555 Yellowstone Avenue; 406-646-9591. For ski, pole and boot rentals call **Freeheel & Wheel**. ~ 40 Yellowstone Avenue, West Yellowstone; 406-646-7744.

ICE SKATING

If you're looking to ward off the winter's chill, **Mammoth Hot Springs Hotel** has an outdoor rink with skate rentals where you can work up a sweat. ~ Mammoth Hot Springs; 307-344-5400.

RIDING STABLES   Three stables in Yellowstone National Park offer park visitors ample opportunities for one- and two-hour guided rides in off-the-road wilderness. Some outfitters offer riding lessons; more commonly, novice riders will be matched with gentler horses.

One-hour guided trail rides depart from corrals at **Mammoth Hot Springs**. ~ 307-344-5400. **Roosevelt Lodge** also offers trail rides regularly. Roosevelt visitors can also ride to Yancey's Hole for an Old West dinner cookout or hop aboard a horse-drawn stagecoach for half-hour rambles around the Tower Junction area. ~ 307-344-5273. Also try **Canyon Village**. ~ 307-344-7901. Schedules vary; the summer riding season is longest at lower-lying Mammoth than at the other two sites.

BIKING   Mountain bikes have become a common sight in recent years, joining touring bikes on and off the roads of northwestern Wyoming. Many of the routes here are narrow and dangerous, so helmets and rear-view mirrors, small tool kits, first-aid kits and emergency survival kits are essential accessories.

Bike Rentals   A good full-service bicycle shop is **Yellowstone Bicycles**. ~ 132 Madison Avenue, West Yellowstone, MT; 406-646-7815. The full-service **Freeheel & Wheel** rents mountain, tour and kid's bikes that come with helmets. ~ 40 Yellowstone Avenue, West Yellowstone; 406-646-7744.

HIKING   Yellowstone contains more than 1200 miles of marked hiking trails and 97 trailheads. Trails include the boardwalks and handicapped-accessible trails at **Upper Geyser Basin** (Old Faithful), **Norris Geyser Basin** and **Mammoth Hot Springs**, among others. All distances listed for hiking trails are one way unless otherwise noted.

For youngsters, the **Fountain Paint Pot Nature Trail** (.5 mile) in the Lower Geyser Basin and the **Children's Fire Trail** (.5 mile) east of Mammoth Hot Springs have several interpretive stations to help teach about thermal activity and forest fires, respectively.

BIKE SAFETY

Bicycling through Yellowstone can be an exhilarating experience but it is not without peril. There are no bicycle lanes along park roads, and because roads are narrow and winding, high-visibility clothing, helmets and rear-view mirrors are recommended. Keep an eye out for campers and RVs passing you from behind; their projecting mirrors pose a particular safety threat. Though a few bike paths do exist around park communities, bicycles are not permitted on boardwalks or backcountry trails.

Backcountry permits are required for all overnight hikes in Yellowstone Park. They can be obtained at no charge from ranger stations and visitors centers within 48 hours before you start your hike. Or you can write to the park to reserve permits in advance for a $15 fee. ~ Backcountry Office, P.O. Box 168, Yellowstone National Park, WY 82190; 307-344-2160. Topographic maps are sold at Hamilton Stores.

Avalanche Peak Trail (2.5 miles) is a strenuous ascent to a 10,566-foot summit, one mile west of Sylvan Pass on the East Entrance Road. Look for the unsigned trailhead opposite the Eleanor Lake picnic area. The trail transits several eco-zones before achieving the peak, which provides spectacular views across Yellowstone Lake to the Tetons and beyond.

Mount Washburn Trail (3 miles) leads to another panoramic point, but the climb isn't as steep as Avalanche Peak. Bighorn sheep are often seen on top. There are trailheads on the Grand Loop Road (north of Canyon Village) at the Dunraven Pass picnic area and the Chittenden Road parking area.

Seven Mile Hole Trail (5.5 miles) offers an impressive way to see the Grand Canyon of the Yellowstone . . . close up. Beginning on the Inspiration Point spur road a mile east of Canyon Village, it clings to the rim of the gorge for the first mile and a half, then swings into the pine forest and drops rapidly for three miles to the canyon floor near Sulphur Creek. Perhaps needless to say, the return climb is harder than the descent.

The moderate **Bechler River Trail** (32 miles) traverses the park's rarely visited southwest corner. It begins at Old Faithful, crosses the Continental Divide three times and then descends steep-sided Bechler Canyon, passing dazzling waterfalls and hot springs. The trail crosses Bechler Meadows, a low-lying haven for moose, black bear and trumpeter swans, and ends at Bechler River Ranger Station, off Cave Falls Road 25 miles east of Ashton, Idaho.

Transportation

CAR

Route 20 winds northeast from Idaho Falls, veers across the Montana border, and reaches Yellowstone National Park at the town of West Yellowstone. To enter the park at Mammoth Hot Springs, take **Route 15** north to Butte, or **Route 20/191** north to Bozeman, Montana, head east on **Route 90** until Livingston, and south on **Route 89** to the park entrance.

AIR

The region's primary airport is in Jackson, Wyoming. West Yellowstone is served by commuter airlines in summer.

Jackson Hole Airport has regular daily nonstop arrivals from and departures to Denver and Salt Lake City, with connecting flights from many other cities. It is served by American Airlines, SkyWest Airlines, United and United Express. Regional charters and scenic flights are available at the aviation center adjacent to the airport. ~ 307-733-7695.

The **West Yellowstone Airport** in West Yellowstone, at the west entrance to Yellowstone National Park, is served by regular SkyWest commuter flights and by charters. The airport closes from mid-October to mid-May.

Limousines and taxis take visitors to and from the airports. In Jackson, call **Buckboard Cab**. ~ 307-733-1112. In West Yellowstone, call **The 4 by 4 Stage**. ~ 406-388-6404, 800-517-8243.

BUS

Greyhound Bus Lines serves West Yellowstone, Montana (between Idaho Falls, Idaho, and Bozeman, Montana), in summer. ~ 800-231-2222; www.greyhound.com.

Gray Line (800-443-6133) offers seasonal charter service and guided tours through Yellowstone Park. There's an office in Jackson Hole. ~ 1680 Martin Lane, Jackson; 307-733-4325.

CAR RENTALS

In West Yellowstone, you'll find **Avis Rent A Car** at the Yellowstone Airport. ~ 800-331-1212. **Big Sky** rents vehicles in town. ~ 415 Yellowstone Avenue; 406-646-9564. **Budget Rent A Car** also has an office here. ~ 131 Dunraven Street; 800-527-0700.

PUBLIC TRANSIT

Guided all-day motorcoach tours of Yellowstone National Park are offered from various park lodgings by **Xanterra Parks & Resorts**. ~ 307-344-7311; www.xanterra.com.

During the winter season, from mid-December to mid-March, when no vehicular traffic is allowed in Yellowstone Park, heated ten-passenger snowcoaches (track vans) run from the west entrance as well as from Mammoth Hot Springs. Coaches operated by **Xanterra Parks & Resorts** depart from the south entrance for Old Faithful every afternoon, returning every morning. Similar trips connect Old Faithful and Canyon Village with West Yellowstone and Mammoth Hot Springs. ~ Mammoth Hot Springs; 307-344-7311. Other snowcoaches are run by **Yellowstone Alpen Guides**. ~ 555 Yellowstone Avenue, West Yellowstone; 406-646-9591.

EIGHT

Sun Valley and Central Idaho

Imagine interstate Routes 84, 86 and 15 as the outline of a shallow bowl across Idaho's broad base, with Boise and Idaho Falls at either end; then central Idaho is what's held in that bowl.

There is a nearly impassable granitic plug at Idaho's center, called by geologists the Idaho batholith and by most everyone else just damned beautiful country. Most of it is empty, because early settlers found it too rough. Recreationists find its summits and valleys perfect for, well . . . just about everything under the sun. So it's not surprising that Sun Valley became the nation's first destination resort.

Central Idaho is a land of mountains, and the mountains have been cut and shaped by water. Some of Idaho's most spectacular scenery can be found here: the craggy peaks of the Sawtooths, the White Clouds and the Pioneers; the broad and gentle Stanley Basin; and the other-worldly volcanic landscape of Craters of the Moon. Elevations range almost 9000 feet, from the town of Salmon at 4004 feet to Idaho's highest mountain, Borah Peak, at 12,662 feet.

Moose, elk, deer, mountain lion, mountain goats, bighorn sheep, wolverine, wolves, black bear and even grizzly bear make their homes in these hills. In between the mountains are clear rivers that provide habitat for rainbow, cutthroat and Dolly Varden trout, for chinook, sockeye and kokanee salmon, and for otter, mink, beaver, heron, kingfisher, osprey and eagles. Taken together with the Frank Church–River of No Return and the Selway-Bitterroot wildernesses, this region contains much of the wildlands remaining in the lower 48 states.

They invite exploration, whether on foot, skis, horseback, bicycle, in boats or even aircraft, and reward those souls adventurous enough with a glimpse of the real and permanent wild residents of the interior, and with a perspective on our place in the scheme of things large and small. The late Idaho senator Frank Church politicked long and hard in favor of wilderness, and this explains in part the importance of wilderness here. The nation's largest wilderness area outside Alaska, Idaho's River of No Return Wilderness, was named for him. During the floor fight in the U.S. Senate for the Wilderness Act of 1964, Church said, "I never knew a man who felt self-important in the morning after spending a night in the open on an Idaho mountainside, under a star-studded summer sky. Save some time in your life for the out of doors."

Three distinct mountain ranges surround Sun Valley and Ketchum. They are the Boulders, the Pioneers and the Smokies. The narrow Big Wood River valley and Route 75, which follows its course, separates the Pioneers from the Smokies south of Ketchum and separates the Smokies from the Boulders to the north of town. Trail Creek Road, leading east from Ketchum's only traffic light and past Sun Valley, divides the Pioneers and the Boulders.

The Sawtooth National Recreation Area, north of Ketchum, encompasses the Sawtooth Range, the White Clouds, parts of the Boulders and—north of Galena Summit, which at almost 9000 feet divides the Big Wood drainage from the headwaters of the Salmon River—the Stanley Basin. This is often called the "Heart of Idaho" and is all that many travelers see of wild Idaho. There is much more, and much of it is close by.

Farther north are the Salmon River Mountains and to the west the Frank Church–River of No Return Wilderness, locally known simply as the "Frank Church." The Lost River and Lemhi ranges, the Hawley Mountains and the Donkey Hills are to the east, draining the Lemhi, Pahsimeroi, Big Lost and Little Lost rivers. This is steep country and less visited, so while exploring here you might have an entire basin to yourself.

Settlement came late to this part of Idaho, about 1880. Trappers had come earlier, and the explorers Lewis and Clark passed across Idaho in 1804 near the town of Salmon. Not until gold and silver were discovered were town sites established and homesteads built. The Yankee Fork basin is Idaho's best example of the terrible damage mining can do. A drive through the valley reveals 20- and 30-foot piles of barren rubble and rock that fill the mile-wide valley for almost ten miles, tailings piles from a dredge mine that tore up the streambed as it moved along. Gold fever continues to draw prospectors today.

Travelers gravitate toward Sun Valley, which is really a small but posh bedroom, condominium and resort community up the road from Ketchum. Most of the pleasures—a plethora of good restaurants and Idaho's best boutique shopping (one might even call it glitzy)—ascribed to a Sun Valley vacation are actually found in undersung Ketchum. And as refreshing as it is to discover this oasis of restaurateurs and Western dry goods, travelers prospecting for a more authentic Idaho experience won't tarry. Up the road are Stanley, which hasn't yet seen an advantage to paving its streets; then the cowboy and mining towns of Challis and Salmon, which is also the last-stop supply center for float trips down the Salmon River. But more than any town, it is the land that makes Idaho special; allow some time, as Frank Church advised, to see and experience it.

Here in Idaho's high country, nighttime temperatures can be cool, even in summer, and be warned that snow can come at any time of year, but expect summer highs in the 80s and 90s. Winters are cold and longish. Salmon is half again as high above sea level as Boise, and Ketchum is over twice as high at 5920 feet. Roads, except during the worst winter storms, are kept passable, although Galena Pass above Ketchum and Lost Trail Pass above Salmon may take longer to reopen.

Text continued on page 194.

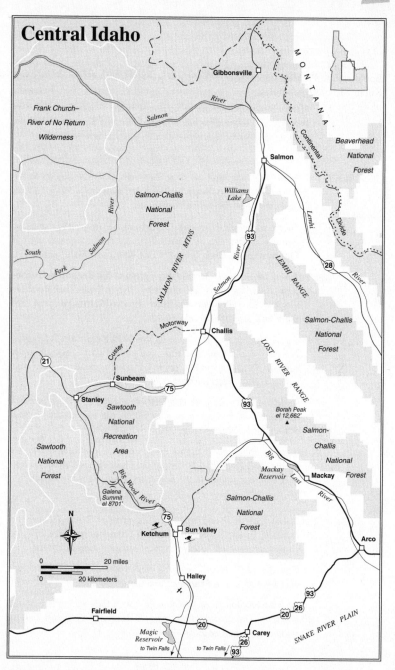

Central Idaho

Summer in the Sawtooth, Salmon and Snake Reg

Idaho's mountains are home to some of the West's most startling sites, justly renowned for wilderness adventures. Summer is the best time to reach remote areas and catch everything when it's open.

DAY 1
- From Twin Falls, head north to Ketchum. On your way up Route 75, stop at the **Shoshone Indian Ice Caves** (page 94) for a look inside naturally refrigerated lava tubes.

- Spend some time soaking in **Ketchum**'s (page 196) updated Western atmosphere with a stroll around downtown and lunch at **The Sawtooth Club** (page 199) or **Ketchum Grill** (page 199).

- Make a pilgrimage to Hemingway's grave at the **Ketchum Cemetery** (page 196), then take the brief drive to Trail Creek Road for a look at Sun Valley's **Ernest Hemingway Memorial** (page 196) and a walk along the creek.

- If you're feeling energetic, hike up the **Bald Mountain Trail** (page 226) or rent a bike and tour the network of creekside trails between Ketchum and Sun Valley. Otherwise, spend the afternoon poking around Ketchum's art galleries and cafés.

- Settle in to **The Cafe at the Brewery** (page 201) in Hailey for a tasty pub meal and microbrew, or sample the international cuisine of Ketchum's **Globus** (page 200).

- If you're up for some drama, take in one of the **New Theatre's Company**'s (page 202) performances. Music fans will also find plenty of summer sounds in the Sun Valley area's many nightspots.

DAY 2
- Get an early start and drive 41 miles north on Route 75, over the dramatic Galena Summit, to **Redfish Lake Lodge** (page 207) for a breakfast that will satisfy the most insistent flapjack craving.

- Give the meal a chance to settle while you look at mining and logging artifacts at the **Stanley Museum** (page 205).

- Pack a picnic lunch (or have the Sawtooth Cafe pack one for you) and spend the afternoon canoeing on **Redfish Lake** (page 220) or walking into the Sawtooth Wilderness.

• Overnight at the **Redfish Lake Lodge** (page 206), or pitch a tent in one of the nearby campgrounds.

DAY 3 • Follow Route 75 as it bends eastward along the Salmon River. Take in the beauty of the area.

• Rattle your bones on the gravel Custer Motorway (actually, it's well-graded as far as Custer), pausing at the ghost town of Bonanza and at the **Yankee Fork Gold Dredge** (page 209), a monstrous relic of relatively recent mining. Take an hour or two to wander through the well-preserved ruins of **Custer** and visit the Custer Museum (pages 209).

• Backtrack to Route 75 or, if you have a four-wheel-drive vehicle, continue along the (now truly bone-rattling) dirt road to **Challis** (page 210). Have lunch at **Antonio's** (page 212) and then amble around the working Western town.

• Head south on Route 93, past Mount Borah, noticing how the terrain changes from craggy peaks to lava beds as you enter the Snake River Plain.

• From Arco, if your curiosity gets the better of you, take a detour 11 miles east to **Experimental Breeder Reactor No. 1** (page 216), the world's first atomic power station.

• Spend the rest of the afternoon (at least two hours) at the eerily beautiful **Craters of the Moon National Monument** (page 219).

• From here, it's about an hour to Twin Falls or back to Ketchum.

IF YOU HAVE MORE TIME

If you have extra time, continue north from Challis for deeper forays into the wilderness or book a guided whitewater trip (see "Outdoor Adventures") on the Salmon River.

Sun Valley Area

A logical base for any exploration of the central Idaho Rockies is the famed summer-winter resort of Sun Valley, which was established in the Wood River Valley in 1936. Together with its adjacent communities of Ketchum and Hailey, both of them newly gentrified mining towns, Sun Valley is a great starting point to discover outlying areas. Of course, you might never want to leave this magical spot.

SIGHTS

The story of **Sun Valley** began after the 1932 Winter Olympic Games in Lake Placid, New York. The Games made an enormous impression upon avid skier W. Averell Harriman, the future New York governor and international diplomat who was then chief executive of Union Pacific Railroad. Harriman beseeched Austrian Count Felix Schaffgotsch to search the West to find a site for a winter resort "of the same character as the Swiss and Austrian Alps." Schaffgotsch's exploration ended at the old mining and ranching center of Ketchum.

Within weeks, an ecstatic Harriman had purchased a 4000-acre ranch in the name of the Union Pacific and had begun building a handsome lodge. Then he enlisted marketing genius Steve Hannagan, who coined the name *Sun Valley*, encouraged the haute-couture orientation of the complex and flew in a bevy of Hollywood stars to promote its official opening in 1936. Clark Gable, Errol Flynn and Claudette Colbert were among the film notables who came for the debut. You can see many of the luminaries' black-and-white photos today on the "Wall of Fame" in the **Sun Valley Lodge**.

With luxury accommodations, fine dining and entertainment in place, Harriman set about creating the world's finest ski area. He instructed Union Pacific engineers to construct a chairlift (modeled after a maritime banana-boat hoist); when unveiled on Dollar Mountain, it became the prototype for what is now standard issue at all alpine resorts. Today, Sun Valley has 20 lifts on its two ski mountains. Thirteen are on Bald Mountain ("Baldy"), one of North America's largest ski mountains with a vertical drop of 3400 feet from its 9150-foot summit.

Union Pacific sold Sun Valley in 1964, but the resort has continued to expand, improve and modernize under its current owner, Little America. Today, **Sun Valley Resort** is like a European village with two elegant 1930s lodges (both fully renovated), hundreds of condominiums, multiple sports facilities, upscale restaurants and shops.

Sun Valley's 18-hole golf course and 18 tennis courts make it one of America's leading sports resorts. There's also swimming, hiking, horseback riding, bicycling and year-round skating, plus world-class trout fishing in nearby streams. On summer weekend

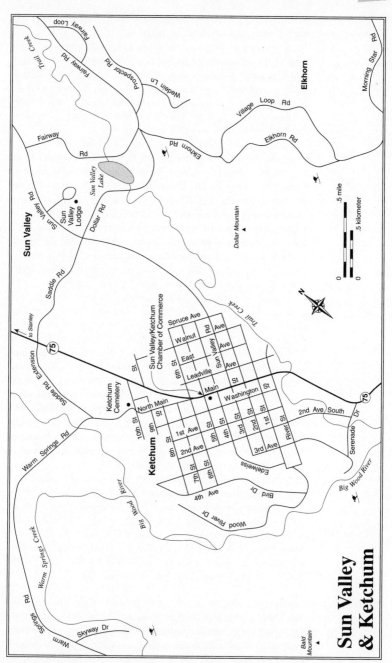

Sun Valley & Ketchum

evenings, the Sun Valley Lodge hosts world-class ice shows featuring many former Olympic medalists.

If the furs-and-pearls crowd are attracted to the venerable Sun Valley village, the slightly less affluent congregate in gentrified **Ketchum**, two miles west of Sun Valley village. Founded as a silver- and lead-mining camp around 1880, Ketchum evolved into the largest sheep-shipping center in the western United States in the early 20th century. That boom was in decline when along came Mr. Harriman and new prosperity.

Whereas Sun Valley has an alpine feel, downtown Ketchum is strictly Western. Restaurants, bars, galleries and specialty shops are housed in late-19th-century brick buildings along Main Street (Route 75), while the ski lifts of Baldy rise to the west of town, just across the Big Wood River. All this shopping and restauranteuring brings Ketchum and Sun Valley as close as Idaho gets to supporting a true tourist mecca, and it is pretty close—the town has been called California's little piece of Idaho. But the setting and the scenery California can't duplicate; nestled in a narrow rolling valley against the steep wall of the Smokies and where Trail Creek joins the Big Wood River, they are superb.

Hailey, 12 miles south of Ketchum, was the richest town in Idaho in the 1880s and the first to have a telephone exchange and electric lighting. It was the birthplace of poet Ezra Pound (1885–1972), one of the most important and controversial figures in 20th-century literature. Local history is recounted at the **Blaine County Museum** with an original pioneer living room, a mine tunnel replica and an old-fashioned schoolroom, as well as an extensive political button collection. Modern history, on the other hand, is being rewritten by resident movie star Bruce Willis *(Die Hard, The Sixth Sense)*, who has bought up a half-dozen downtown buildings, including the Hailey theater and newspaper, with plans for a retail and entertainment complex. Admission. ~ North Main Street, Hailey; 208-788-4185.

Perhaps the Wood River Valley's most famous resident ever was Nobel Prize–winning author Ernest Hemingway (1899–1961). An ardent fly-fisherman, "Papa" Hemingway spent the last years of his globetrotting life in Ketchum. He is buried among four pine trees in the heart of **Ketchum Cemetery**. ~ 1026 North Main Street; 208-726-9201. The **Ernest Hemingway Memorial**—a bust and an epitaph—stands beside Trail Creek, a mile northeast of the Sun Valley Lodge via Trail Creek Road.

HIDDEN ►

LODGING   Heading the slate of luxury accommodations are the venerable **Sun Valley Lodge** and **The Sun Valley Inn**. The stately and historic four-story lodge, which opened in 1936, has 148 rooms; the two-story chalet-style inn, a year younger, has 106. Both have handsome, spacious rooms and suites with views of golf courses, ski runs and/or an outdoor ice skating rink. More than 100 apartment and condominium units with full kitchens are also available. Village facilities include 12 restaurants, four lounges and a plethora of posh shops. There are outdoor heated pools at each hotel, saunas, hot tubs, fitness rooms, a bowling alley and movie theater, trap and skeet shooting, golf courses and tennis courts. In winter, besides alpine skiing, there's a Nordic center and sleigh rides. ~ 1 Sun Valley Road, Sun Valley; 208-622-4111, 800-786-8259, fax 208-622-3700; www.sunvalley.com, e-mail ski@sun valley.com. MODERATE TO ULTRA-DELUXE.

A short walk from the River Run day lodge on Bald Mountain is the Bavarian-style **Best Western Tyrolean Lodge**, offering 56 standard rooms and suites; some suites have in-room hot tubs. Hotel amenities include an outdoor heated pool and hot tub, a sauna, an exercise room, a game room and laundry facilities. Complimentary continental breakfast included. ~ 260 Cottonwood Street, Ketchum; 208-726-5336, 800-528-1234, fax 208-726-2081; www.bestwestern.com/tyrolean, e-mail tyrolean@cox-inter net.com. DELUXE TO ULTRA-DELUXE.

Also close to the River Run lodge is the **Lift Tower Lodge**, which prides itself as a haven for budget-conscious skiers. In fact, a 1939 lift tower, with four chairs attached, is a landmark of the motel. Its 14 guest rooms feature private baths and refrigerators. An outdoor jacuzzi offers a view of the mountain, and continental breakfast is included in the rate. ~ 703 South Main Street, Ketchum; 208-726-5163, 800-462-8646, fax 208-726-0945; e-mail ltowel@mindspring.com. MODERATE.

The **Best Western Kentwood Lodge** is located in the heart of downtown. Lodge-style architecture, furnishings and decor are the hallmark of the 57 spacious rooms here. All have full baths, cable TV, phones, microwaves and refrigerators. There are also honeymoon and family suites. Facilities include a heated indoor swimming pool, hot tub, fitness room and a restaurant on the premises. ~ 180 South Main Street, Ketchum; 208-726-4114, 800-805-1001, fax 208-726-2417; www.bestwestern.com/kent woodlodge. ULTRA-DELUXE.

SHOP AROUND

Because Sun Valley is a major resort, the average price of lodging in the area is higher than anywhere else in the northern Rockies. The best times to seek bargains are the spring and fall "shoulder seasons," between the skiers and the golfers, or even in the early (pre-Christmas) or late (April) ski seasons. Winter peak-season rates are the highest.

The **Knob Hill Inn** is more than a B&B, and in many ways, more than a hotel. It's an intimate European-style inn with 26 luxurious rooms and suites, each with a marble bath and separate shower, a wet bar, and a balcony that opens to the mountains. Many rooms have fireplaces. Facilities include an indoor-outdoor swimming pool and a fitness room; complimentary breakfast is served in the Konditorei. Closed early April to mid-May and the first half of November. ~ 960 North Main Street, Ketchum; 208-726-8010, 800-526-8010, fax 208-726-2712; www.knobhill inn.com, e-mail khi@knobhillinn.com. ULTRA-DELUXE.

A few blocks away, the spacious **Tamarack Lodge** has sunny rooms with open-beam ceilings, balconies and mountain views. Amenities include fireplaces (in some rooms), and microwaves and refrigerators in all of them. An indoor pool and an outdoor jacuzzi are available year-round. ~ 291 Walnut Avenue, Ketchum; 208-726-3344, 800-521-5379, fax 208-726-3347; www.tamaracksun valley.com, e-mail reservations@tamaracksunvalley.com. DELUXE TO ULTRA-DELUXE.

If a 12-mile commute isn't a problem, look in Hailey for the best lodging rates in the Sun Valley area. The two-story **Airport Inn**, a block off Route 75 at 4th Cedar Street, has 29 plain but clean and comfortable rooms. Some kitchen units and fireplace suites are available. Amenities include an outdoor hot tub, a coin laundry and internet access. ~ 820 4th Avenue South, Hailey; 208-788-2477, fax 208-788-3195; www.taylorhotelgroup.com, e-mail bookings@taylorgroup.com. MODERATE.

Housed in a blue 1893 Victorian trimmed in white, **Povey Pensione** has three tastefully appointed rooms with private baths; request the attic room for a special treat. The sitting room is a fine place to curl up with a book and a steamy cup of tea. No children under 12 allowed. Full breakfast is served in the dining room. ~ 128 West Bullion Street, Hailey; 208-788-4682, 800-370-4682; www.poveypensione.com, e-mail info@poveypensione.com. MODERATE TO DELUXE.

The **Wood River Inn**'s 56 air-conditioned rooms and suites may lack decorative flair but they do come with frills: microwaves, refrigerators, coffeemakers and dataports. In addition, some suites feature fireplaces, hot tubs and full kitchens. A heated indoor pool, a jacuzzi and laundry facilities round out the amenities. Continental breakfast is included. ~ 603 North Main Street, Hailey; 208-578-0600, 877-542-0600, fax 208-578-0700; www.woodriverinn.com, e-mail reservations@woodriverinn.com. MODERATE TO ULTRA-DELUXE.

DINING

Every European-style ski resort must have its **Konditorei**. Breakfast pastries, open-faced lunch sandwiches and light dinners, as well as ice-cream specialties, are served in an Austrian-coffeehouse atmosphere. ~ Sun Valley Village Mall, Sun Valley; 208-622-2235. BUDGET TO MODERATE.

The top-of-the-line choice is the **Lodge Dining Room** at the historic Sun Valley Lodge. Elegant French and Continental cuisine is served by tuxedoed waiters beneath crystal chandeliers. Orchestral combos play music nightly for dancing at the foot of a marble staircase. Reservations are preferred for dinner but are not accepted for the outstanding Sunday buffet brunch. ~ 1 Sun Valley Road, Sun Valley; 208-622-2150, fax 208-622-2030; www.sunvalley.com, e-mail svcexec@sunvalley.com. DELUXE TO ULTRA-DELUXE.

In Ketchum, **The Kneadery** is worth a visit just to see the life-size animal carvings ("The Ketchum Zoo") and lovely flower arrangements on its deck. But do plan to eat here. The pleasant, casual restaurant serves omelettes for breakfast and healthy soups and salads at lunch. ~ 260 Leadville Avenue North, Ketchum; 208-726-9462. BUDGET TO MODERATE.

Local diners love **The Sawtooth Club**. The creative cuisine, much of it prepared on a mesquite grill, varies from the expected (steaks, fresh seafood) to the serendipitous (chicken Senegalese in an apple brandy curry, Cajun shellfish pasta). A big stone fireplace anchors the ground-floor lounge, and patio dining is available in the summer. ~ 231 North Main Street, Ketchum; 208-726-5233, fax 208-726-8923. MODERATE TO ULTRA-DELUXE.

The **Ketchum Grill** takes a similarly creative approach to cooking but with a more distinctively Idaho approach, including a nightly selection of game and fish dishes. There are also interesting pizzas and pastas. Locals enjoy the casual, rustic atmosphere and an excellent wine selection. Dinner only. ~ 520 East Avenue North, Ketchum; 208-726-4660, fax 208-788-9803; www.ketchumgrill.com, e-mail twochefs@sunvalley.net. MODERATE TO DELUXE.

AUTHOR FAVORITE

In winter, there's no more charming evening out than to take a horse-drawn sleigh to the **Trail Creek Cabin**. Book three days in advance for the trip to this rustic cabin in the woods. A roaring fire, hearty homemade soup and squaw bread with honey butter greet guests; a robust Western-style dinner—complete with accordion music—follows. Open mainly by reservation. Closed Sunday and Monday. ~ Trail Creek Road, Sun Valley; 208-622-2135, fax 208-622-2236. DELUXE TO ULTRA-DELUXE.

"Eclectic" describes **Globus**, which brings a cosmopolitan flavor to Ketchum. Cuisine is international, from vegetarian curries and Asian noodle dishes to western meats and seafoods, and features nightly sushi specials. Dinner only. ~ 6th Avenue East and Main Street, Ketchum; 208-726-1301, fax 208-726-1712; www.globusrestaurant.com. DELUXE.

Local game, exotic fowl and fresh seafood are central to the cuisine at **Gean's Restaurant**, a cozy eatery located in a quaint old house. Entrées include pheasant marsala, seared ahi, and Thai shrimp. Dinners may be ordered à la carte or prix fixe. A pretty outdoor patio awaits summer diners. Dinner only. ~ Located in Trail Creek Village, 180 West 6th Street, Ketchum; 208-726-8911. DELUXE.

Sushi on Second is a hip, casual Japanese restaurant serving contemporary and traditional dishes to a lively crowd. You can sample fresh sashimi and sushi at the bar or retire to a private tatami-mat room for a full meal. A kid's menu is available. Dinner only. ~ Main Street and 2nd Avenue, Ketchum; 208-726-5181, fax 208-726-6266; e-mail sushionsecond@aol.com. MODERATE TO DELUXE.

Desperate for familiar food? The **Pioneer Saloon** is the place for steaks, prime rib and nightly fish specials. One of Ketchum's oldest businesses (and looking like it), the Pioneer also boasts shrimp teriyaki, pork chops and a classic cheeseburger. ~ 308 North Main Street, Ketchum; 208-726-3139, fax 208-726-9764. DELUXE TO ULTRA-DELUXE.

There are several Mexican restaurants in the valley, but you won't find better prices than at **Desperado's**. The menu features traditional tacos and enchiladas; south-of-the-border plates like *carnitas* and *chiles rellenos*; and in-house creations as well. ~ 211 4th Avenue East, Ketchum; 208-726-3068, fax 208-725-7895. BUDGET TO MODERATE.

Whether you're eating in or packing a lunch to go, casual **Esta** provides tasty sandwiches like corned beef reubens, as well as dishes such as Greek salads and fajitas. Young ones will appreciate the kid's play area filled with toys and other amusements. No dinner. ~ 180 Main Street, Ketchum; 208-726-1668. MODERATE.

A longtime Hailey standby is the **Red Elephant Saloon**, which keeps its grill open 'til midnight nightly. Those who aren't too busy playing foosball chow down on steaks, seafood, pasta—or perhaps just hamburgers or buffalo wings. ~ 107 South Main Street, Hailey; 208-788-6047, fax 208-788-4173; www.redelephant.hailey.com. MODERATE TO DELUXE.

Innovative "pub grub" is the claim of **The Cafe at the Brewery** in the Sun Valley Brewing Co. building. Sure, you'll get the standard steaks, but how about homemade chicken pot pie? Roasted-vegetable quesadillas? The soups, pizzas and homemade desserts are excellent, as are the draft brews. ~ 202 North Main Street, Hailey; 208-788-0805, fax 208-788-6319; e-mail gordosvbrew@ juno.com. MODERATE TO DELUXE.

Sun Valley and Ketchum have become important centers for art collectors. There are at least two dozen fine-art galleries in Ketchum and a couple more in Sun Valley Village.

SHOPPING

You might want to start at the **Sun Valley Center for the Arts and Humanities** for a sampling of contemporary regional artists. The Sun Valley Center organizes a wine auction as well as an arts-and-crafts festival held at the Sun Valley Resort. ~ 191 5th Street East, Ketchum; 208-726-9491; www.sunvalleycenter.org.

Idahoans are represented in many other major galleries in Ketchum, including the **Friesen Gallery**. ~ 320 1st Avenue North; 208-726-4174. There's also the **Kneeland Gallery**. ~ 271 1st Avenue North; 208-726-5512; www.kneelandgallery.com. Check out the **American West Gallery** for American folk art, rustic antique furnishings and cowboy collectibles. ~ 520 4th Street East; 208-726-1333. **The Roland Art Glass Gallery** offers modern Northwest art glass creations. ~ Sun Valley Road at East Avenue; 208-726-2333.

Galleries aside, a good place to browse and buy in the Sun Valley area include **North Main Street** in downtown Ketchum. You'll find boutiques, gift shops and a variety of other unusual shops here.

At **Sun Valley Village Mall**, near the lodges, don't miss the **Sun Valley Gift Shop** (208-622-2206), offering a full range of souvenirs. Also stop in at **Towne & Parke** (208-622-3522), a custom jeweler. **The Kitzbühel Collection** (208-622-2227) features fine imported European fashions. ~ 1 Sun Valley Road.

Giacobbi Square, the area's largest indoor mall, is home to **Chicken Lipps** (208-726-3199), which focuses on children's clothes, toys and souvenirs. ~ 4th Avenue East and Leadville Avenue North, Ketchum.

The **Board Bin** outfits snowboarders in the know with speciality gear and streetwear. Within the store is **Girl Street**, which carries hip and funky clothing and accessories. ~ 180 4th Street, Ketchum; 208-726-1222; www.boardbin.com.

The Toy Store has a unique array of games, puzzles, dolls and stuffed animals. ~ 102 Washington Avenue Plaza, Ketchum; 208-726-5966; www.toystoresunvally.com.

There are some excellent bookshops to check out in this area. **Chapter One** combines shelf space with a juice bar. ~ 160 North Main Street, Ketchum; 208-726-5425; www.chapteronebookstore.com. Looking for an obscure Hemingway title? You may very well find it at **Iconoclast Books**, which features a special collection of Papa's books. They also carry a wide variety of new and used titles. ~ 211 North Main Street, Ketchum; 208-726-1564. At the resort village is **Ex Libris**. ~ Sun Valley Village Mall, Sun Valley; 208-622-8174.

NIGHTLIFE   Like any major resort, Sun Valley has a lively evening scene. And it's far from restricted to bar activities.

The weekly **Sun Valley Ice Shows** fill the 600-seat Sun Valley Lodge Terrace to capacity from mid-June to mid-September. The world's best skaters—like Scott Hamilton, Brian Boitano, Oksana Baiul, Katarina Witt, Nancy Kerrigan and Kristi Yamaguchi—perform under starry skies each Saturday night. Terrace seating includes a buffet dinner; book well in advance. ~ 208-622-2135, fax 208-622-6130; e-mail ski@sunvalley.com.

The clearinghouse for Wood River Valley culture is the **Sun Valley Center for the Arts and Humanities**, which sponsors a series of year-round events that include the Sun Valley Music Festival in July and the Northern Rockies Folk Festival in August. ~ 191 5th Street East, Ketchum; 208-726-9491; www.sunvalleycenter.org.

The 80-member **Sun Valley Summer Symphony** performs a series of 12 free outdoor concerts in a large tent at the Sun Valley Lodge Esplanade from the first through the third weekend of August. ~ 208-622-5607.

The **New Theatre Company** offers summer and winter stage seasons at the nexStage Theatre, featuring contemporary drama and comedy. ~ 120 South Main Street, Ketchum; 208-726-2271. A second thespian group, the **Laughing Stock Theatre Company**, offers one production each in fall, winter and spring. ~ 208-726-3576.

The **Footlight Dance Centre** offers workshops and recitals at Wood River High School. ~ 1050 Fox Acres Road, Hailey; 208-788-3481.

For live music, the **Duchin Bar** at the Sun Valley Lodge has light jazz trios performing traditional dance music nightly during the peak summer and winter seasons. ~ 1 Sun Valley Road, Sun Valley; 208-622-2145.

Enjoy smoke-free surroundings at **The Galleria Wine & Espresso Bar**. ~ 4th Avenue North and Leadville Avenue North, Ketchum; 208-726-1707.

If your ear is more attuned to rock, blues, funk and reggae, there's plenty to suit you in Ketchum. **Whiskey Jacques** has live music and dancing Tuesday through Sunday. Cover. ~ 251 North Main Street, Ketchum; 208-726-5297; whiskeyjacques.com, e-mail whiskeyjacques@yahoo.com.

For country-and-western, drive 17 miles south to Bellevue, where the **Silver Dollar Saloon** has country-and-western as well

as rock and jazz bands on Friday nights. Cover on Fridays. ~ 101
South Main Street, Bellevue; 208-788-2900.

A handful of venues without live music are dear to après-ski
lovers. Stop by **Lefty's Bar & Grill** for a game of pool. ~ 213 6th
Street East, Ketchum; 208-726-2744. The **Roos-**
evelt Tavern has a full bar but also serves dinner,
and kids are made welcome with a special children's
menu. ~ 280 Main Street, Ketchum; 208-726-0051.
The Casino is another option. ~ 220 North Main
Street, Ketchum; 208-726-9901.

> Whiskey Jacques in
> Ketchum was rumored
> to be a favorite bar of
> Ernest Hemingway's.

Also try the **Boiler Room**, in the Sun Valley Village.
~ 1 Sun Valley Road, Sun Valley; 208-622-2225; e-mail
ski@sunvalley.com.

Beer drinkers appreciate the **Sun Valley Brewing Co.**, which offers handcrafted ales and beers, and tours by appointment. ~ 202
North Main Street, Hailey; 208-788-5777.

The Old West atmosphere makes the **Hailey Hotel Bar** a favorite local hangout. ~ 201 South Main Street, Hailey; 208-788-
3140.

SAWTOOTH NATIONAL FOREST 🏃 🚵 🛶 ⛏ The Ketchum
district of this national forest is one of the most popular and used
of all four parcels. Encompassing over 320,000 acres, the Ketchum
district boasts numerous streams and 30 high mountain lakes.
Visitors enjoy the scenic drives over the Dollar Hide and Trail
Creek summits, and miles of hiking and biking trails. Facilities are
limited to one alpine ski area. ~ This unit of the national forest is
north (via Route 75) and west (via Forest Road 227) of Ketchum;
208-622-5371, fax 208-622-3923; www.fs.fed.us/r4/sawtooth.

PARKS

▲ Boundary Campground has 9 sites (water only); $10 per
night. Closed October through May.

Stanley and the Sawtooths

A mecca for outdoor enthusiasts in
this part of Idaho, the Sawtooth National Recreation Area (SNRA) is cen-
tered on the tiny outfitting community of Stanley. It encompasses
more than 1180 square miles and boasts the highest peaks of
Idaho's central Rockies—including the striking Sawtooth, White
Cloud and Boulder ranges.

With more than 300 alpine lakes and the headwaters of the
Salmon, Big Wood, Boise and South Fork Payette rivers, it's no
wonder sports lovers secret themselves to their favorite spots.
Hunting, fishing, boating, sailing, rafting, backpacking, horseback riding and myriad other outdoor pursuits, including cross-
country skiing and snowmobiling in winter, are all here. Within
the SNRA are nearly 500 campsites, several secluded guest ranches
and a handful of motels, cabin complexes and small resort lodges.

SIGHTS

The recreation area begins just eight miles north of Ketchum via Route 75. As you're heading north, be sure to swing by the Forest Service's **Ketchum Ranger District Office**. ~ 206 Sun Valley Road, Ketchum; 208-622-5371. Or stop by the SNRA **Visitor Center** to pick up maps, information and a free **audiocassette or CD** that describes the 61-mile drive to Stanley. You return the loaned items at the Redfish Lake or Stanley ranger stations. ~ Route 75 North, Ketchum; 208-726-5013, 800-260-5970, fax 208-727-5029.

Before leaving Ketchum, you may want to pay a visit to the **Wolf Education and Research Center**. This controversial facility maintains a captive pack of the endangered gray wolf. Ranchers and others have fought the release of the animals, the first wave of which occurred in January 1995 in the Frank Church–River of No Return Wilderness. Fourteen wolves were freed without any immediate damage to livestock, although they were suspects in two subsequent killings. ~ 206 Spruce Street, Ketchum; 208-924-6960, fax 208-924-6954.

Thirty miles from Ketchum, the drive takes you over the 8701-foot **Galena Summit**, from which the Big Wood River begins. The Summit offers an impressive view of the Sawtooth and White Cloud ranges and the headwaters of the Salmon River between them.

As Route 75 switchbacks down to the Sawtooth Valley at about 7000 feet elevation, it skirts a series of opaline mountain lakes to its west. Largest of them are **Alturas Lake** (Forest Road 205), 24 miles south of Stanley (41 miles north of Ketchum), and **Redfish Lake** (Forest Road 214), seven miles south of Stanley. Alturas Lake is popular with swimmers, sailors and anglers trolling for rainbow trout and kokanee salmon. The nearby **Sawtooth Fish Hatchery**, the highest-elevation hatchery in the nation, offers a daily tour (1:30 p.m. tour) in summer. Chinook salmon are raised here each year as part of a conservation-recovery program. ~ Route 75, Stanley; 208-774-3684, fax 208-774-3413; email sfh@ruralnetwork.net.

Redfish Lake is the crown jewel of the SNRA. Three hundred feet deep, nestled at the foot of two craggy 10,000-foot mountains and skirted by sandy beaches, it's a major recreation center: swimming, boating, waterskiing, fishing, hiking and horseback riding are among the popular pursuits. The **Redfish Lake Lodge** sports a general store and offers lake tours from its marina. Closed late September to Memorial Day. ~ Redfish Lake Road (Route 75), Stanley; 208-774-3536, fax 208-774-3546, phone/fax 208-644-9096 (winter); www.redfishlake.com.

In the heart of the SNRA is the village of **Stanley**, where Route 21 from Boise (135 miles southwest) joins Route 75 from Ketchum and Salmon. An all-seasons outfitting center with an Old West facade and a permanent population of fewer than 100, Stanley still has the same dirt roads (including the main Ace of Diamonds Street) and log cabins it must have had in the 1890s, when it was settled. The **Stanley Museum,** in the 1934 Valley Creek Ranger Station a half-mile north of the Route 21 junction, tells the story of Sawtooth Valley logging and mining in photographs and artifacts; it's open daily from Memorial Day to Labor Day. ~ Route 75, Stanley; 208-774-3517.

Outdoor endeavors begin and end in Stanley: fishing and whitewater trips on the Salmon River and the remote Middle Fork Salmon; hiking, horse packing and mountaineering trips into the Sawtooth Wilderness; winter snowmobile and cross-country ski expeditions and many others. The village's lodgings, restaurants and gift shops belie its population. For more information on the

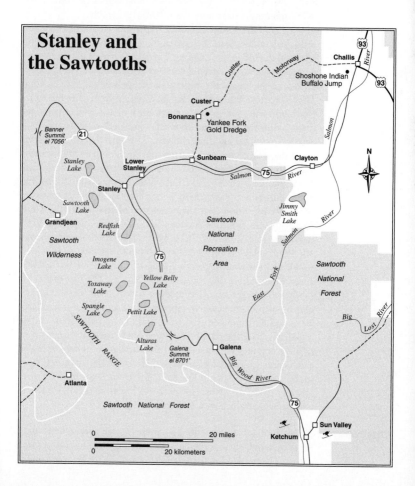

Stanley and the Sawtooths

town, contact the **Stanley Chamber of Commerce.** ~ Route 21 at Route 75, Stanley; 208-774-3411.

LODGING   A number of rustic motels and log-cabin motel resorts line Route 21 through Stanley and Route 75 through Lower Stanley, and all offer good accommodations, many are excellent.

Located at the junction of Routes 21 and 75, the **Mountain Village Resort** has 61 rooms and suites with coffeemakers, phones and satellite TV. Suites are also outfitted with microwaves and refrigerators; a kitchenette is available. If your muscles are in need of a good soak, be sure to reserve time for the lodge's natural hot springs. Other amenities include a guest laundry, a store and a restaurant. Pets accepted. ~ Stanley; 208-774-3661, 800-843-5475, fax 208-774-3761; www.mountainvillage.com, e-mail info@mountainvillage.com. MODERATE TO DELUXE.

HIDDEN ►   **Redfish Lake Lodge** sits at the outflow of Redfish Lake, home of Idaho's endangered sockeye salmon, the red fish that give the lake and the lodge their names. The lake is one of the most spectacular in Idaho, and even if you stay elsewhere, stop at the lodge to soak in the mountain scenery, sit on the beach or rent a canoe. The ten rooms in the old log lodge, whose lawn reaches out to the beach and lake, share a bath down the hall as well as the lodge's rustic ambience. Scattered about the timbered grounds are single and duplex cabins and suites housing 25 rooms that can each sleep up to six. The rooms are spartan and rustic, but each has a sink and a four-poster bed. The cabins are more modern, with standard, hotel-like features. The Lake Cabin, near the lakeshore, has three bedrooms and a two-story rock fireplace. Campgrounds are also available. Closed late September to Memorial Day. ~ Route 75, five miles south of Stanley; 208-774-3536, 208-644-9096 (winter), fax 208-644-9616; www.redfishlake.com, e-mail info@redfishlake.com. MODERATE TO ULTRA-DELUXE.

Open year-round, **Jerry's Motel** is situated on the Salmon River about a mile downstream from Stanley. The two-story, log cabin–style motel has nine modern rooms, each with a knotty pine built-in kitchenette equipped with stove, refrigerator, microwave and coffeemaker. And each room has a back door leading to a deck above the river and looking out across a green meadow to the rising mountains. Fifteen rustic moderate-to-deluxe-priced cabins are also available, eight of them riverside. Take two steps to the river and cast your line for Idaho trout. ~ Route 75, Lower Stanley; 208-774-3566, 800-972-4627, fax 208-774-3518; e-mail janet@ruralnetwork.net. MODERATE.

DINING   About 20 miles south of Stanley, Smiley Creek enters the Salmon River high in its basin where it's still small enough to almost jump across. The **Smiley Creek Lodge** sits near their confluence, a rambling log cabin with views across green meadows to Sawtooth peaks. The restaurant stretches down one side with a long counter and booths, all very rustic. This is a down-home operation serving a simple menu: eggs and omelettes for breakfast, burgers and chicken sandwiches for lunch, steak, chicken and fish for dinner. ~ Route 75, Sawtooth City; 208-774-3547, fax 208-774-2280; e-mail smileyck@ruralnetwork.net. MODERATE TO DELUXE.

The seasonal restaurant at **Redfish Lake Lodge**, situated in an atmospheric log cabin with plate-glass windows overlooking the lake, serves perhaps the most varied menu around Stanley. Vegetarian and spicy chorizo omelettes, egg burrito, fruit and yogurt, fruit smoothies and granola are offered for breakfast along with eggs and pancakes. Five salads are on the lunch menu, including spinach and smoked trout, Cobb salad and a mixture of tomato, cucumber, feta, pine nuts and fresh basil over romaine lettuce in a balsamic vinaigrette. A nice break from roadhouse fare. King salmon, Idaho trout and lamb chops head the dinner entrées. And they serve a selection of wines. Closed late September to Memorial Day. ~ Route 75, five miles south of Stanley; 208-774-3536, 208-644-9096 (winter), fax 208-774-3546; www.redfishlake.com. MODERATE TO DELUXE.

◄ **HIDDEN**

> Stanley is the only town in Idaho where three scenic byways meet: the Sawtooth, the Salmon River, and the Ponderosa.

The **Mountain Village Resort** dominates the junction of Routes 21 and 75 in Stanley. The resort is the obvious choice for almost everything a traveler in Stanley needs. The restaurant is friendly, the food is good and the all-wood post-and-beam interior creates a comfortable atmosphere. Notable on the dinner menu is prime rib. You'll find the standard array of burgers and sandwiches for lunch. You won't find a lot of local color here, but give it all time to season. ~ Stanley; 208-774-3317, 800-843-5475, fax 208-774-3761; www.mountainvillage.com, e-mail info@mountainvillage.com. DELUXE.

If you're in the wilds of the Sawtooth National Recreation Area, you can re-enter the wilds of civilization at the **Rod & Gun Club Saloon**, which draws an eclectic cross-section of mankind for live music and dancing two or three nights a week, year-round. ~ Ace of Diamonds Street, Stanley; phone/fax 208-774-9920.

NIGHTLIFE

SAWTOOTH NATIONAL RECREATION AREA (SNRA) AND WILDERNESS 🚶 🚤 🚣 Spread across three-quarters of a million acres and three national forests—the Sawtooth, Salmon-Challis and Boise—the SNRA is a year-round playground for mountain recreation lovers. No vehicular travel is permitted on the trails of the Sawtooth Wilderness, which borders the Boise National Forest on its west and includes the craggy and dramatic

PARKS

summit of the Sawtooth Range. There are beaches at Redfish, Stanley Pettit and Alturas lakes. Outstanding angling opportunities are available in the Salmon, Big Wood, Boise and South Fork of the Payette rivers, as well as in major lakes. Facilities include picnic tables, restrooms, a marina (at Redfish Lake) and four visitors centers. ~ The town of Stanley is located within the national recreation area. Best access to the wilderness is from Redfish Lake, seven miles south of Stanley, or from Grandjean, 44 miles west of Stanley. To reach Stanley Lake Campground, go eight miles north of Stanley on Route 21 and turn left on Forest Service Road 455. Follow the signs to the campground. To reach Smokey Bear Campground, go nine miles south of Obsidian, turn west on Alturas Lake Road and continue for two miles; 208-727-5000, fax 208-727-5029.

▲ There are 492 RV/tent sites (no hookups) at 33 developed campgrounds; $8 to $24 per night. Ten campgrounds are available by reservation (877-444-6777; www.reserveusa.com). Most sites are open from June to October only. Right on Stanley Lake, convenient for fishing and boating, is Stanley Lake Campground with 16 RV/tent sites; $11 to $22 per night. On Alturas Lake, Smokey Bear Campground is small and scenic and has 14 RV/tent sites; $8.50 per night.

FRANK CHURCH–RIVER OF NO RETURN WILDERNESS AREA
The Frank Church–River of No Return Wilderness Area covers much of the surrounding area. See the "McCall Area Parks" in Chapter Nine for more information.

▼▼▼▼▼▼▼▼▼▼▼▼▼
The Upper Salmon Between its source in the high Sawtooth and its mid-river outfitting center at the town of Salmon —the largest community in this part of Idaho— the Salmon River courses northeastward about 150 miles through the Sawtooth National Recreation Area and the Salmon-Challis National Forest. It curves sharply west at North Fork, 20 miles north of Salmon, and proceeds about 250 miles more, dividing Idaho neatly in two. Then the Salmon joins the Snake River just south of the Washington–Oregon border. Nicknamed "The River of No Return" because no boat was able to travel upriver until jet boats were developed after World War II, the Salmon drains 14,000 square miles of central Idaho.

SIGHTS A century ago, the Yankee Fork of the Salmon River was a popular stream among placer gold miners. Today, the **Land of the Yankee Fork Historic Area**, established for Idaho's centennial of statehood in 1990, preserves many artifacts from its rich past. Comprising numerous pioneer routes within Challis National Forest, this historic area—officially a part of the state parks system—is best explored via the **Custer Motorway**, a 36-mile gravel mountain road from Sunbeam to Challis. (A high clearance vehicle is recommended for this route.)

The twin ghost towns of **Bonanza** and **Custer** are north of Sunbeam eight and ten miles, respectively, at the foot of Bachelor Mountain. Bonanza had a peak population of 600 in 1881 but had all but disappeared three decades later after the demise of the last large mine. There's not much to see today but a 1934 guard station and the Boot Hill and Bonanza cemeteries, one-half mile west.

A quarter-mile past Bonanza at the mouth of Jordan Creek is the **Yankee Fork Gold Dredge**. Until 1949, long after mining had ceased in Bonanza and Custer, the Snake River Mining Company operated this unwieldy-looking dredge that dug gravel from the Yankee Fork river bank, separated the gold out and spewed washed tailings behind. Modern environmentalism never would have permitted it. Measuring 112 feet long, 54 feet wide, 64 feet high and weighing 988 tons, the diesel-powered dredge recovered more than $1 million in gold and silver. It has been restored as a museum and is open for guided tours from Memorial Day through Labor Day. Admission. ~ Custer Motorway, Custer; 208-879-5244.

Custer still has a few buildings that survive from the 1880s and 1890s, including the **Custer Museum** in a one-room schoolhouse. Mining equipment, kitchenware, clothing, gambling tables and old weapons are on display in summer. You can pan for gold or walk a self-guided trail past the General Custer stamp mill, which processed $12 million in gold between 1881 and 1904. The general store and tiny cemetery are also worth visits. Open Memorial Day through Labor Day. ~ Custer Motorway, Custer; 208-838-3300, fax 208-838-3329.

Beyond Custer, the Custer Motorway passes a handful of campgrounds and the ruins of old mining sites en route to Challis. High-clearance vehicles are recommended, four-wheel drives preferred, as this stretch of road is minimally maintained. You may prefer to retrace your tread marks to Sunbeam and con-

◆◆◆

"RIVER OF NO RETURN" NO MORE

Explorers Meriwether Lewis and William Clark nicknamed the Salmon the "River of No Return" in 1805. (In fact, the birthplace of their famed Shoshone guide, Sacajawea, was just up the Lemhi River from Salmon.) During its early fur-trapping history, the swiftly flowing Salmon was just that, allowing intrepid boatmen passage downstream but prohibiting return trips by water. Today, with jet boats, small airplanes and helicopters, outfitters can float travelers downstream and return them to civilization almost at the snap of their fingers.

tinue east and north on Route 75 from there. En route, you'll pass Clayton, 33 miles from Stanley, still a center of modern silver and lead mining.

The **Land of the Yankee Fork Historic Area Interpretive Center** (closed Saturday and Sunday from November through March) is located at the junction of Routes 93 and 75 just south of the town of Challis. The visitors center has audiovisual programs, historical exhibits and general information on the Yankee Fork area. A 60-foot cliff that rises near the building was a **Shoshone Indian Buffalo Jump** used from the 13th to 19th centuries to slaughter bison by herding them off the precipice; the archaeological site is on the National Register of Historic Places. ~ Route 75 South, Challis; 208-879-5244, fax 208-879-5243; e-mail lan@idpr.state.id.us.

The first commercial trip down the remote Middle Fork of the Salmon River was made in 1936 in boats of plywood and Masonite.

Challis, 55 miles from Stanley, was founded in 1878 as a supply center for the Yankee Fork and Clayton mining districts, each of them an arduous day's journey away. Now with a population of 1100, it still supports area miners, but it has thrived as a cattle-ranching town and the Custer County seat. This working town has only a few services off the highway targeted specifically at tourists, but many of its historic downtown buildings, marked only by small chiseled wooden signs, are as authentic as any in Idaho. Follow the sign pointing from the highway to the city center and continue several blocks to the area around Bux Bar and the Challis Messenger.

Route 93 follows the banks of the main Salmon River for 60 miles from Challis to Salmon. There's a lot of beautiful mountain and river scenery along this stretch, but not a lot else. There are summer home communities at Cabin Creek and Rye Grass Creek, and a national forest campground at Williams Lake.

Although its economy is traditionally based on timber and cattle ranching, **Salmon** (population 3000) is regarded far and wide as the "whitewater capital of the world." The Lemhi River joins the Salmon River here, and the number of rafting, fishing and horse-packing outfitters based in the town are prominent reminders that you're at the edge of the wilderness.

The **Salmon-Challis National Forest** surrounds the town on all sides. There's the rugged Lemhi Range to the south, the timbered Salmon River Mountains to the west and the historic Bitterroot Range to the northeast, marking the Montana border. Farther west, about 25 miles as the eagle flies, is the **Frank Church–River of No Return Wilderness,** the largest single designated wilderness area in the lower 48 states. Recreational opportunities abound here, but none beckon quite the way the river does.

A trip down the main Salmon River or its remote Middle Fork is not for the timorous. Deer, elk, black bear, mountain goats and now wolves are among the hundreds of species of animals that thrive in these rugged mountains and grassy pine meadows. If you look closely in the deep river gorges, you'll see ancient American Indian bivouacs with cave paintings and petroglyphs estimated to be as old as 8000 years.

North of Salmon 25 miles, Route 93 crosses the **Lost Trail Pass** into Montana, up the Bitterroot Valley to Missoula.

You can complete a broad loop back to Sun Valley via Arco by turning southeasterly on Route 28 up the Lemhi River from Salmon. The route parallels the Continental Divide for 106 miles to Route 22, then follows that highway another 46 miles along the edge of the Idaho National Engineering & Environmental Laboratory (INEEL) without passing through a single community of more than 75 people along the way.

LODGING

The **Suncrest Motel** is a group of three long and tidy buildings arranged in a "U" and located on the highway south of town. Neatly painted a light steel gray with white trim, the buildings surround a shaded grassy area with several picnic tables. The rooms are equally neat and bright. All have been updated and equipped with small refrigerators, and there are three kitchenettes. The rooms are rented months in advance during the hunting season. People like it here, and it's easy to see why: it's clean and comfortable. ~ 705 South Challis Street, Salmon; 208-756-2294, fax 208-756-2299. BUDGET TO MODERATE.

North of town on Route 93 are Salmon's two largest motels. Both motels are modern and well kept with space enough in the rooms for a desk and a small table. The **Stagecoach Inn Motel** sits directly by the river and is slightly more expensive; its downstairs rooms open onto a patio and lawn that extends to the riverbank; upstairs rooms each have a small balcony. ~ 201 Route 93 North, Salmon; 208-756-2919. MODERATE.

The **Wagons West Motel** backs against a small canal that draws water from the river, and some of the rooms have kitchenettes. Access to the river is via a wooden footbridge. ~ 503 Route 93 North, Salmon; 208-756-4281, 800-756-4281; www.wagonswest motel.com. BUDGET.

Nestled in the foothills of the Salmon Mountains, the 1894 **Greyhouse Inn Bed & Breakfast** has four inviting bedrooms boasting Victorian decor and antique furniture. Two of the rooms share a bathroom with clawfoot tub and porcelain shower. There's also a log cabin with two cozy wilderness-themed guest rooms, each with private bath. For more privacy, you may prefer staying in the separate carriage house. A full breakfast is included. ~ 1115 Route 93 South, Salmon; 208-756-3968, 800-348-8097; www.greyhouse inn.com, e-mail greyhouse@greyhouseinn.com. MODERATE TO DELUXE.

HIDDEN ▶   The **Broken Arrow Resort** is an out-of-the-way place north
of Salmon, nearing the Montana border, in the whistle-stop town
of Gibbonsville. Six of the ten units are cabins that are spread
out on a broad lawn shaded by poplars and surrounded by pine
trees. The cabins share bathrooms and showers located in a central building (except Cabin Five, which has its own half-bath).
Each cabin—they all might qualify for the National Register of
Historic Places—is furnished with rustic period beds, dressers,
bookcases (stocked) and tables. There is a half-acre pond, and
the North Fork of the Salmon River runs just behind the property. Campsites and a small, 12-unit RV park are also available.
During hunting season, call ahead; this place often books a year
in advance. ~ Route 93, Gibbonsville; 208-865-2241; www.the-
brokenarrowresort.com. BUDGET.

DINING   When hunger strikes as you drive through Challis, you'd be wise
to take yourself to **Antonio's**, an uptown pizza-and-pasta joint.
There's a soup-and-salad bar, or order an Italian sausage hoagie
and wash it down with a glass of Chianti. ~ 5th and Main streets,
Challis; 208-879-2210. MODERATE.

The best meal in Salmon, almost everyone agrees, can be had
at **The Shady Nook**, housed in a white cottage surrounded by a
white picket fence. Its four dining rooms, finished with lots of
wood, range from airy to intimate, and the Western-themed paintings decorating the walls—wildlife and scenery—are for sale. That's
not true for the menagerie of elk, antelope, deer, bear, pheasant
and fish trophies displayed in the main dining room. Prime rib is
a specialty, as are Alaskan king crab and a seafood platter of cod,
shrimp and crab. The seafood entrées are extensive, including
salmon and fresh Idaho trout. Dinner only. Closed a few nights
in winter; call ahead. ~ Route 93 North, Salmon; 208-756-4182.
MODERATE TO ULTRA-DELUXE.

If you want to be like everybody else in Salmon, or anyway
with everybody else, eat breakfast at the **Salmon River Inn**. It's
the kind of place where the waitress calls you "babe" and
"sweetheart." There might be room at the curved counter up
front or at one of the six booths, but if not look in back where
there are plenty of tables. Eggs Benedict, huevos rancheros, and
chiles rellenos omelettes add variety to the standard breakfast
menu. They also make a light-as-air baking-powder biscuits,
blueberry pancakes and a specialty—layers of meat, hash browns
and scrambled eggs topped with cheese—called a Polish breakfast. For lunch, there's a basic menu of burgers, and for dinner,
you'll find steaks and seafood. ~ 606 Main Street, Salmon; 208-
756-3521. BUDGET TO DELUXE.

Rose Marie Ramey—part Spanish, French and Aztec, she
HIDDEN ▶   says—has charge of the **Broken Arrow Cafe**, a Mexican eatery

that is an unlikely find way out here. The restaurant is located in the log-cabin main lodge of the Broken Arrow Resort. The place doesn't feel decorated, it just feels like home, which it is for the Rameys. A few casually mismatched tables make up the dining area, and the counter seats about nine. The colorful eight-page menu features a wide selection of burritos, fajitas, *rellenos*, enchiladas, smoked prime rib, black angus and more. And if the restaurant should be closed, Rose Marie may invite you to share a meal with her family. ~ Route 93, Gibbonsville; 208-865-2241. BUDGET TO DELUXE.

The Salmon River twists nearly 400 miles through central Idaho, making it the longest river contained in any single state outside Alaska.

SHOPPING

More than 100 local and regional artists display their work at the **Ponderosa Gallery**, you'll also find rustic furnishings made from materials like rawhide, wrought iron, and copper, as well as home and body products and locally produced foods. ~ 415 Main Street, Salmon; 208-756-8610; www.ponderosagallery.com.

PARKS

LAND OF THE YANKEE FORK HISTORIC AREA 🎣🚶 A tribute to Idaho's mining heritage created for the state's 1990 centennial, this district, along the Yankee Fork of the Salmon River, preserves the ghost towns of Bonanza and Custer and the Yankee Fork Gold Dredge, among other historical sites. You can fish for trout in the Yankee Fork. Facilities include picnic tables, restrooms and a visitors center. ~ From Challis, take Garden Creek Road west into the Custer Motorway. From Sunbeam (13 miles east of Stanley and 42 miles southwest of Challis on Route 75), take the Custer Motorway (Yankee Fork Road) north eight miles to Bonanza and ten miles to Custer; then continue to Challis; 208-879-5244, fax 208-879-5243; e-mail lan@idpr.state.id.us.

▲ There are 47 RV/tent sites (no hookups) at six campgrounds; most are $5 per night.

SALMON-CHALLIS NATIONAL FOREST Encompassing over 4.3 million acres in east-central Idaho, the Salmon-Challis National Forest is managed by seven ranger districts.

Challis Ranger District 🚶 ⛵🚤 Covering two and a half million acres of central Idaho from the Middle Fork of the Salmon River to the Lost River Sinks, the Challis forest includes the state's tallest mountain, Borah Peak. It contains more than 1600 miles of trails in the Salmon River, Pioneer, Lost River and Lemhi ranges of the Rockies, as well as the Land of the Yankee Fork Historic Area and a large part of the Frank Church–River of No Return Wilderness. There is swimming at Mosquito Flat Reservoir west of Challis and other small mountain lakes (the reservoir is at an elevation of 7000 feet; although swimming is allowed, it is very cold year-round). Excellent trout fishing is available in streams and lakes, with an important fall steelhead run in the Middle Fork of the Salmon. Facilities include picnic tables and restrooms. ~ Forest roads extend north and west off Routes 75 and 21 from Challis and Stanley, east and west off Route 93 between Challis and Mackay. To reach Mosquito Flat Campground, take Main Street west out of Challis, then turn north onto Challis Creek Road and continue for 15 miles to the campground. To reach Big Creek Campground, follow Route 93 north of Challis for 18 miles and at the end of the small town of Ellis turn onto Pahsimeroi Road. Continue for about 30 miles and then take Forest Service Road 097 three miles to the campground; 208-879-2285, fax 208-879-4199; www.fs.fed.us/r4/sc.

▲ There are 260 RV/tent sites (no hookups), plus 44 for tents only, at 26 campgrounds; $4 to $6 per night. At the gateway to the wilderness area lies Mosquito Flat Campground with ten RV/tent sites; no charge. A remote campground with access to the trail system is Big Creek Campground, which has four RV/tent sites; no charge.

Salmon Ranger District 🧍 🐎 🛖 🚣 🚤 🛶 Comprising 1.8 million acres of east-central Idaho from the Frank Church–River of No Return Wilderness to the Bitterroot Range along the Montana border, this national forest is one of Idaho's least developed. The emphasis is on Salmon River boating and rafting, fishing and big-game hunting, backcountry hiking and horseback riding (over 1200 miles of trails), and, in winter, cross-country skiing and snowmobiling. The Middle Fork and main Salmon rivers have renowned steelhead and salmon runs; trout thrive in streams and lakes. Facilities include picnic tables and restrooms. ~ A network of roads extends west from Route 93 north and south of Salmon; principal among them are the Salmon River Road (Forest Road 030) from North Fork, 21 miles north, and Moccasin Creek Road (Forest Road 021) from Williams Creek, five miles south. A few roads extend off Route 28 southeast of Salmon. To reach Wallace Lake Campground, follow Route 93 north of Salmon four miles, then turn onto Stormy Peak Road (Forest Service Road 023) and follow it twelve miles to the summit. Turn left onto Ridge Road (Forest Service Road 020), and continue for four miles, then turn left onto Forest Service Road 391 and follow it a mile to the lake and the campground. To reach Spring Creek Campground, follow Route 93 north for 22 miles to North Fork. Turn left onto Salmon River Road and continue 17 miles to the campground; 208-756-5200, fax 208-756-5225.

▲ There are 167 RV/tent sites (no hookups), plus 15 for tents only, at 17 campgrounds; $4 to $6 per night. Four A-frame cabins, open year-round for hikers, horse riders and snowmobilers, accommodate six; $15 per night. Two campgrounds that are ideal for anglers are Wallace Lake Campground and Spring Creek

Campground, with 6 RV/tent sites at Wallace Lake and 12 RV/tent sites at Spring Creek; $4 per night.

▼▼▼▼▼▼▼▼▼▼▼▼▼

Lost River Country

They're called the Lost rivers—the Big Lost and the Little Lost—because, well, they get lost. Rising in the foothills that surround Borah Peak, Idaho's highest mountain, the two streams disappear into sponge-like lowlands known as the Lost River Sinks, along the northern fringe of the Snake River Plain lava beds east of Arco. There they become part of the aquifer that weeps from the walls of the Snake River Canyon, 100 miles southwest at Thousand Springs.

In the lava lands adjacent to the Lost River Sinks are two important central Idaho locations: Craters of the Moon National Monument, whose eerie landscape trained lunar astronauts, and the Idaho National Engineering & Environmental Laboratory, a nuclear reservation of major historical importance.

If you're coming from the Upper Salmon Country, your best approach to this area is via Route 93 southeasterly from Challis. The route winds through the scenic Grand View Canyon 20 miles from Challis, then passes Borah Peak and follows the Big Lost River through Mackay.

SIGHTS

Borah Peak, 12,662 feet in elevation, crowns the Lost River Range 34 miles southeast of Challis and 18 miles northwest of Mackay. Named for Senator William Borah (1865–1940), the craggy, snow-capped alp towers above the steep, sweeping plains that surround it and is clearly visible from the highway.

One of the most powerful earthquakes to rock North America (outside California or Alaska) in recent decades occurred along a fault line at the foot of Borah Peak on October 28, 1983. Registering 7.3 on the Richter scale, it dropped the floor of the Big Lost River valley by about five feet, raised Borah Peak two feet closer to the heavens and rattled cities up to 500 miles away. An escarpment 21 miles long and as many as 14 feet high can be seen outside the **Earthquake Visitors Information Center,** 32 miles from

◆◆

AUTHOR FAVORITE

I never feel like I have enough time to fully contemplate all the strange beauty to be found at the **Craters of the Moon National Monument.** The oddities of the landscape here—cinder cones, tree molds and lava tubes—are mute testimony to the elegance of nature's destructive powers. See page 216 for more information.

Challis and a mile east of the highway. Closed weekends. ~ Double Springs Pass Road, Mackay; 208-588-2224, fax 208-588-3429.

Mackay (population 580), an 1880s copper-mining town on the Big Lost River 52 miles from Challis and 26 miles northwest of Arco, now survives primarily as a ranching center. **Mackay Reservoir**, a three-square-mile lake created by the damming of the Big Lost River in 1906, is four miles northwest of town. The **Lost River Museum**, housed in a historic Methodist church, displays turn-of-the-20th-century bric-a-brac on weekend afternoons from Memorial Day to late September, and is also open by appointment. ~ 306 Capital Avenue, Mackay; 208-588-3148.

Arco (population 1000) sits at the junction of five highways at the northern edge of the ancient Snake River Plain lava beds and directly between Craters of the Moon National Monument and the world's first nuclear power plant. That healthy glow in the faces of the townspeople is a reminder that Arco was the first city in the world to be lighted by nuclear-generated electricity. Arco's handful of motels and cafés makes it a minor oasis for travelers.

Some scientists estimate the depth of the porous Snake River Plain lava surrounding Arco to be a mile or more. On this sturdy foundation stands the **Idaho National Engineering & Environmental Laboratory**. Covering 890 square miles of desert, the facility is dedicated to developing peacetime uses of nuclear power. To that end, 52 reactors (the most on the planet) have been built at INEEL since it was established in 1949, and three are still in operation. About 7300 scientists, engineers and support personnel are employed by the U.S. Department of Energy at the site and in Idaho Falls, where it is headquartered. Tours available. ~ Route 20 West, Idaho Falls; 208-526-0050, 800-708-2680, fax 208-526-2089; www.inel.gov.

Visitors are welcome at **Experimental Breeder Reactor No. 1** (EBR-1), a national historic landmark housed in a red-brick building 18 miles east of Arco off Route 20. In December 1951, this reactor was the world's first to produce electric power with atomic energy. It ceased operation in 1964, but today guided and self-guided tours show off the inner sanctum, including four nuclear reactors (two of them nuclear-propulsion prototypes), turbines, a control room and a hot cell used for inspection and repair of radioactive materials. Free tours are offered daily from Memorial Day weekend through Labor Day. ~ Van Buren Boulevard, Atomic City; 208-526-0050, fax 208-526-2089; www.inel.gov.

Expect reactions of a different kind at **Craters of the Moon National Monument**, 18 miles southwest of Arco. The landscape here is so eerie and alien that American astronauts have actually used it as a training ground. Volcanic eruptions and lava flows that began 15,000 years ago, and continued until only about 2000 years ago, created a 60-mile-long Great Rift Zone of fissure vents and spatter cones. Some geologists predict the earth here will erupt again. Loop drive closed to vehicles in winter. Admission. ~ Route 20/26/93, Arco; 208-527-3257, fax 208-527-3073; www.nps.gov/crmo, e-mail crmo_information@nps.gov.

Explore the 83-square-mile national monument by starting at the visitors center, just off the highway. Open daily except during the winter holidays, the center features a short film describing the park's geologic, natural and human history, as well as museum exhibits and a bookstore, ranger-led walks and evening programs.

The park's seven-mile Loop Road is open from May through October. Plan on at least two hours, leaving time for several short walks. There are lava flows, volcanic vents, basaltic cinder cones, spatter cones, tree molds, lava-tube caverns and other weird and wonderful features. And the park's appearance changes with the seasons: cross-country skiers glide over snow-covered terrain in winter and wildflowers cloak the cinder fields in late spring.

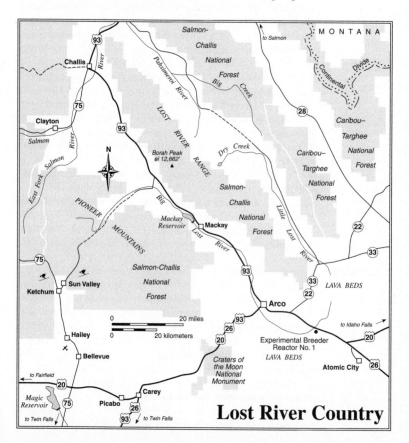

Lost River Country

After leaving Craters of the Moon, you can continue back toward Sun Valley on the main highway. Routes 26/93 branch south at **Carey** (population 300), a farming community on the Little Wood River 25 miles from the national monument, leaving Route 20 to carry you the final 20 miles to the intersection of Route 75. From there, Hailey is 14 miles north, Ketchum 26 miles.

Tiny **Picabo** (population 50) is seven miles west of Carey. Many American winter sports fans know the story of world downhill ski champion Picabo ("Peek-a-boo") Street, whose hippie parents avoided naming her until legal documents forced their hand. She was bestowed the same name as this hamlet near which they lived on a commune. Street now lives in Hailey and trains at Sun Valley.

The **Silver Creek Preserve**, world renowned since Ernest Hemingway made the creek his favorite fishing hole, is west of Picabo. The conservationist Nature Conservancy owns the area, which has a catch-and-release policy for flyfishing. The water temperature of the spring-fed stream stays between 40° and 50° year-round; its rainbow and brown trout are big and smart. Canoeists, hikers and birdwatchers are other regular visitors. ~ Kilpatrick Bridge Road, Picabo; 208-788-2203; www.tnc.org.

West of the Route 75 junction, Route 20 continues nearly due west through the **Camas Prairie**, tracing the route of Goodale's Cutoff—an Oregon Trail shortcut—nearly to Mountain Home. The economy of the Camas County seat of **Fairfield** (population 400) revolves around the farming of forage crops, upland bird hunting and fishing at **Mormon Reservoir** and **Magic Reservoir**, both of them short detours south of Route 20.

North of Fairfield is **Soldier Mountain**, a popular family ski area. It was purchased in 1996 by actor Bruce Willis with plans to make its expansive backcountry more accessible. Closed April through November and Monday through Thursday. ~ Soldier Creek Road, Fairfield; 208-764-2526, fax 208-764-2368; www.soldiermountain.com, e-mail soldiermtn@itlink.com.

LODGING A good stopping place on the road to Craters of the Moon is the **Wagon Wheel Motel & RV Park**. Sixteen rooms—including three family units (all with kitchens) and a two-bedroom cottage—feature combination shower-baths, cable TV and phones. The grounds, with a nice view of the Lost River Range, include a playground, basketball and volleyball courts, and horseshoe pit. ~ 809 West Custer Street, Mackay; 208-588-3331, fax 208-588-3334; e-mail bowhntr@net.net. BUDGET TO MODERATE.

Nearer to Craters of the Moon, the **DK Motel** satisfies budget travelers' basic requirements, and then some. The 25 rooms have queen-size beds, cable TVs and in-room coffee, and guests returning from outdoor adventures can clean their duds in the coin laundry. ~ Route 20/26, Arco; phone/fax 208-527-8282, 800-231-0134; www.dkmotel.com, e-mail dkmotel@dcdi.net. BUDGET.

Snuggled into the Pioneer Mountains off Trail Creek Road, halfway between Sun Valley and Route 93 north of Mackay, is the **Wild Horse Creek Ranch**. Guests enjoy trail riding, backpacking, fishing and hunting in summer, snowmobiling and cross-country skiing in winter. A heated swimming pool is only open in summer, but the hot tub is available in summer and winter. Four bunkhouse units share a sitting room, toilet and shower facilities; six other rooms have private baths. Smoking is not permitted in the lodge, which includes a dining room, TV lounge and game room with a bar. Reservations required. ~ Wildhorse Creek Road, Mackay; phone/fax 208-588-2575. MODERATE TO DELUXE.

DINING

Although its location in a small house probably wouldn't turn your head as you drove by, the heavenly smells emanating from **Grandpa's Southern Bar-B-Q** would likely stop your nose in its tracks. Among the offerings: pork ribs, chicken, turnip greens, peach cobbler, babyback ribs, corn muffins, sweet potato pie and pecan pie. Appreciative diners chow down at tables inside and outside on the lawn and deck. Closed Sunday in winter. ~ 434 West Grand Avenue, Arco; 208-527-3362. MODERATE TO DELUXE.

A good sandwich can be hard to come by, but **Pickle's Place** will make them deli-style before your very eyes. A casual spot also noted for homemade soups and crispy salads, Pickle's is open for three meals every day. ~ 440 South Front Street, Arco; 208-527-9944. MODERATE.

PARKS

CRATERS OF THE MOON NATIONAL MONUMENT 🏃 Fifteen thousand years of volcanic history created this 83-square-mile landscape of lava flows and cinder cones, fissure vents and tube-like caverns on the northern fringe of the Snake River Plain. Facilities include picnic tables, restrooms, hiking trails (one wheelchair accessible) and a visitors center. Loop drive closed in winter. Day-use fee, $5. ~ The park entrance is 18 miles southwest of Arco and 71 miles southeast of Sun Valley, on the south side

WILD OR MILD?

When you make reservations, consider that the time of year can be every bit as important as which outfitter; early in the season the water is higher, faster, colder and more challenging, and wetsuits may be required. Later trips can be a bit more playful; the weather is warmer and the water more forgiving. Early July is typically a good compromise between the two.

of Route 20/26/93; 208-527-3257, fax 208-527-3073; www.nps. gov/crmo, e-mail crmo_information@nps.gov.

▲ There are 52 RV/tent sites (no hookups); $10 per night. Closed early October to late May.

▼▼▼▼▼▼▼▼▼▼▼▼▼▼▼
Outdoor Adventures

FISHING

Author Ernest Hemingway made the trout waters of the Sun Valley area—particularly those of Silver Creek and the Big Wood River— famous through his writings. Southwest of Sun Valley, near Fairfield, Magic Reservoir and Mormon Reservoir are great places to troll for rainbow and brown trout.

Bill Mason Outfitters offers guided flyfishing trips throughout Central Idaho, including excursions to the Big Wood River, Magic and Mormon reservoirs, the Big Lost River, Silver Creek and the Salmon River. ~ Sun Valley Mall, Sun Valley; 208-622-9305; www.billmasonoutfitters.com. **Silver Creek Outfitters** leads flyfishing outtings to the Wood River Valley, where you can fish the Big Wood River, Silver Creek, Warm Springs Creek and the Big Lost River. ~ 500 North Main Street, Ketchum; 208-726-5282; www.silver-creek.com, e-mail silvercreek@sunvalley.net.

On the Salmon River and in the source lakes of the Sawtooth National Recreation Area, rainbow, cutthroat and brook trout are highly sought by fishermen. The tributary Lemhi River is also considered a premier trout stream. But the biggest flood of anglers hits the Salmon between September and March, when steelhead—ocean-run rainbow trout—make their annual fall and winter runs. These big fish average four to six pounds, and some 15- to 20-pound trophy lunkers have been taken.

There are many private fishing guides in the area. Among those with the loftiest reputations is **Aggipah River Trips**. ~ P.O. Box 425, Salmon, ID 83467; 208-756-4167; www.aggipah.com. Another is **North Fork Guides**. ~ P.O. Box 24, North Fork, ID 83466; North Fork Store, Route 93, North Fork; 208-865-2534; www.northforkguides.com.

BOATING

Boaters flock to Magic Reservoir, southwest of Sun Valley. In the Sawtooth National Recreation Area, boating is allowed on Alturas, Pettit and Redfish lakes. Services are not available at either Alturas or Pettit. Small fishing skiffs, canoes and kayaks can be rented at **Redfish Lake Lodge**. Allow a couple hours roundtrip for paddling to the lake's far end and the inlet of Redfish Lake Creek. This makes a wonderful picnic site and is also a trailhead for backpacking into the Sawtooth Wilderness. Day hikes are possible, too. ~ Route 75, Stanley; 208-774-3536, phone/fax 208-644-9096 (winter); www.redfishlake.com, e-mail info@redfish lake.com.

The Middle Fork of the Salmon River is Idaho's most famous stream for whitewater lovers and is ranked as one of the ten best in the world. With 100 rapids in 100 miles, it is federally protected as a "wild and scenic river," entirely surrounded by the Frank Church–River of No Return Wilderness.

RIVER RUNNING

Near Sun Valley the rivers to run are the Big Wood and Little Wood. Rafters also love the main Salmon River—from Stanley to Challis to Salmon, and all the way downstream to Riggins.

Many outfitters specialize in Salmon River trips; one of the best is **Rocky Mountain River Tours**, known for their Dutch-oven cooking (they even maintain a garden in Salmon, Idaho, so the produce on their trips is "fresh-picked"). ~ P.O. Box 2552, Boise, ID 83701; 208-345-2400; www.rafttrips.com. **Canyons, Inc.**, whose owner literally wrote the book on river safety, runs the Middle and Main Forks of the Salmon. ~ P.O. Box 823, McCall, ID 83638; 208-634-4303, 888-634-2600; www.canyonsinc.com. Or talk to **Mackay Wilderness River Trips**, which flies you into remote airstrips on the Middle Fork to begin your trip. ~ 4115 West Wright Street, Boise; 208-344-1882, 800-635-5336; www.mackayriver.com.

In 1943, when Sun Valley was closed due to World War II, the lodge was used as a hospital for wounded veterans.

Ski Idaho? What comes to mind? Two words—Sun Valley. One of the world's most famous winter resorts, opened in 1936, **Sun Valley** encompasses massive, 9150-foot Bald Mountain ("Baldy"), its 3400-foot vertical drop appealing to Olympic medalists and intermediate skiers alike, and little Dollar Mountain, geared toward beginners and intermediates. Nineteen chairlifts (14 of them on Baldy) serve 75 runs and have a total uphill capacity of 26,780 skiers per hour, making long lift lines virtually nonexistent. The resort, which usually opens Thanksgiving weekend and operates until late April, has 2054 skiable acres. ~ Sun Valley Road, Sun Valley; 208-622-4111, 800-786-8259, fax 208-622-2030; www.sunvalley.com, e-mail ski@sunvalley.com.

SKIING

For the more daring, arrangements can be made for wilderness helicopter ski and snowboard trips with **Sun Valley Heli-Ski**. Closed early April to late December. ~ 260 1st Avenue North, Ketchum; 208-622-3108, 800-872-3108; www.sunvalleyheliski.com.

A smaller family-oriented alpine destination, without overnight accommodations, is **Soldier Mountain**, 60 miles southwest of Sun Valley via Route 20 and 12 miles north of Fairfield. The Sawtooth National Forest area has a 1400-foot vertical with two chairlifts, two surface lifts, and 37 runs. Owner Bruce Willis plans a major expansion to include backcountry terrain and night skiing. ~ Soldier Creek Road, Fairfield; 208-764-2526 (snow phone).

Text continued on page 224.

Leave Those
Schussers Behind

Sun Valley, Idaho, has been synonymous with downhill skiing ever since its chairlifts—the world's first—began operating in 1936. But schussing downhill isn't the only way to travel on skis. More and more folks are exploring the backwoods on cross-country skis, leaving the slopes behind.

There are Nordic tracks near most of Idaho's ski areas, including Sun Valley, Bogus Basin, Grand Targhee, Magic Mountain, Pomerelle, Pebble Creek, Silver Mountain and Soldier Mountain. Sun Valley's proximity to the Sawtooth National Recreation Area (SNRA), and its three Nordic centers and to a well-developed riverfront system presents skiers with a variety of developed and undeveloped trails unsurpassed elsewhere in the state.

Through Ketchum and Sun Valley, the **Path and Trail System** links Ketchum and Hailey along the Big Wood River, extending about two miles north of town. Almost 25 kilometers of trails are groomed and part of the system. These also detour up Trail Creek, past Sun Valley Lodge. ~ Sun Valley/Ketchum Chamber of Commerce, corner of 4th and Main streets, Sun Valley; 800-634-3347; www.visitsunvalley.com. Near town is the **Sun Valley Nordic and Snowshoe Center**, owned by Sun Valley Resort. Forty kilometers of groomed trails follow the contours of the lodge golf course. The Sun Valley Nordic Center also offers rentals and lessons and boasts the world's first children's tracks. ~ Sun Valley Road, Sun Valley; 208-622-2251; www.sunvalley.com. Very pleasant is a warming hut 3 kilometers from the center that provides a toasty fire as well as lunch and dinner. Another option close to town is to drive up Sun Valley Road past Sun Valley Lodge (where it becomes Trail Creek Road). Continue as far as the road is open. Here you can ski along the road or follow Trail Creek as far as you like.

The Path and Trail System in Ketchum and Hailey is part of the larger **North Valley Trails** that include 100 kilometers of groomed trails criss-crossing the beautiful Sawtooth National Recreation Area. ~ Route 75 North, Ketchum; 208-788-2117; www.bcrecdistrict.com. The recreation area south of Galena Summit includes the Smoky Mountains, parts of the Boulder Mountains and the upper Big Wood River Valley, a broad U-shaped valley with rolling terrain between the mostly forested Smokies and the rocky outcrops of the Boulders.

The **Galena Lodge** sits near the northern end of the valley and offers another 56 kilometers of groomed trails. This rustic lodge nestled in a small valley is publicly owned, although operated by a private company. Ski equipment and mountain bike rentals are available, along with lessons and tours. Overnight accommodations are limited to yurts. Lunch is served every day, and dinner is provided on Thursdays and on full-moon nights. This meal schedule fluctuates with the seasons as do the days of operation; call ahead. ~ Located 24 miles north of Ketchum, Route 75 North; 208-726-4010, fax 208-726-4093; www.galenalodge.com.

Passes are required for using many of the North Valley Trails. They are priced reasonably and are available at the **Sun Valley Chamber of Commerce**. ~ Corner of 4th Street and Main Street, Ketchum; 208-726-3423; www.visitsunvalley.com.

Elephant's Perch also offers passes and rentals. ~ 280 East Avenue North, Ketchum; 208-726-3497; e-mail perchinfo@elephantsperch.com.

For those who want to really get away from it all, and have the proper skills and experience, the Sawtooth National Recreation Area affords nearly unlimited potential for backcountry touring and telemarking. Several turnouts along Route 75 are provided and the adventurous can break trail onto Galena Summit for some breathtaking telemark descents. Continue over the summit into the Stanley Basin for still more opportunities. Your imagination—and common sense—should be your guides.

For current snow reports, call 208-622-2093 or 800-635-4150.

For those who prefer exploring the outdoors on cross-country skis, the Sun Valley area has Nordic tracks. Try **Sun Valley Nordic Center**. ~ Sun Valley Road, Sun Valley; 208-622-2151; www.sunvalley.com. For passes and maps to the North Valley and Wood River trails, contact the **Blaine County Recreation District**. ~ 1050 Fox Acres Road #100, Hailey; 208-788-2117; www.bcrd.org. Maps to the Sawtooth Valley can be obtained at the offices of the **Sawtooth National Recreation Area**. ~ Route 75 North, eight miles north of Ketchum; 208-727-5013. **Galena Lodge**, 20 miles north of Ketchum, has a 56-mile trail system; dogs are allowed on a portion of them. ~ Route 75 North, 208-726-4010.

Backcountry touring is especially popular in the Sawtooth National Recreation Area (mainly around Galena Summit and in the Stanley area). For information try **Sawtooth Mountain Guides**. ~ Route 21, Stanley; 208-774-3324; www.sawtoothguides.com. **Ski Rentals** In the Sun Valley area, the leaders in downhill ski rentals include **Sturtevant's Alpine Sports**, which also carries snowboards and snowshoes. Their Hailey store has both downhill and cross-country rentals. ~ 340 North Main Street, Ketchum, 208-726-4502, 800-252-9534; www.sturtos.com; 1 West Carbonate Street, Hailey, 208-788-7847; www.sturtos.com. **Formula Sports** also rents alpine equipment. ~ 460 North Main Street, Ketchum; 208-726-3194; www.formulasports.com. **Elephant's Perch** is a cross-country specialty shop. ~ 280 East Avenue, Ketchum; 208-726-3497; www.elephantsperch.com.

ICE SKATING

Many of the world's top skaters have graced the ice in Sun Valley. But don't let that intimidate you. The outdoor ice skating rink at the **Sun Valley Lodge** has rentals available. There's plenty of free-skating time allotted, so try your spins and double axles, or just skate along to your own music. Call for public skating; some hours are reserved for hockey or private groups. ~ 1 Sun Valley Road, Sun Valley; 208-622-2194; www.sunvalley.com.

AUTHOR FAVORITE

Everyone knows about Sun Valley's downhill skiing, but for my money it also has some of the best cross-country trails around. I'm especially attached to the austere majesty of the Sawtooth National Recreation Area, home to the roaming **North Valley Trails**. See "Leave Those Schussers Behind" for more information.

The Sun Valley area boasts two 18-hole layouts designed by Robert Trent Jones, Jr., that include **Sun Valley Resort Golf Course.** ~ Sun Valley Road, Sun Valley; 208-622-2250; www.sunvalley.com. He also designed **Elkhorn Golf Club.** ~ 1 Elkhorn Road, Sun Valley; 208-622-3300; www.elkhorngolf.com. There are two nine-hole courses in Ketchum; all four courses are public. In addition, there are nine-hole courses in Challis, Salmon and Mackay and near Fairfield.

GOLF

Sun Valley has been rated by *Tennis* magazine as one of the top 50 tennis resorts in the United States. The **Sun Valley Resort Tennis Club** has 18 courts and a pro shop open daily in summer. ~ Old Dollar Road, Sun Valley; 208-622-2156; www.sunvalley.com. The nearby **Elkhorn Golf Club** has 18 courts. ~ Elkhorn Road, Sun Valley; 208-622-3300; www.elkhorngolfclub.com. For information on Sun Valley–area public courts, contact the **City of Ketchum Park Department.** ~ 900 3rd Avenue, Ketchum; 208-726-7820.

TENNIS

What better way to experience the stunning beauty of Sun Valley and central Idaho than on horseback? At the Sun Valley resort, 60- and 90-minute rides are offered daily by **The Horsemen's Center.** ~ Sun Valley Road, Sun Valley; 208-622-2391; www.sunvalley.com. Hourly, half- to full-day and overnight expeditions are available at **Elkhorn Village Stables.** Summer only. ~ Trail Creek Road, Sun Valley; 208-726-1865.

RIDING STABLES

The Sawtooth National Recreation Area is the single most popular destination for those who enjoy pack trips into the Sawtooth and White Cloud ranges. Outfitters include **Sawtooth Wilderness Outfitters.** ~ P.O. Box 81, Garden Valley, ID 83622; 208-462-3416; 208-259-3408; www.sawtoothadventures.com. **Mystic Saddle Ranch** runs overnight and multiday pack trips into the Sawtooths. Guided trail rides on old mining roads in the Galena area are also available. ~ Stanley; 208-774-3591 (summer), 208-879-5071 (fall), 888-722-5432; www.mysticsaddleranch.com.

PACK TRIPS & LLAMA TREKS

Challis and Salmon serve as gateways to the Frank Church–River of No Return Wilderness Area. Contact **Mile Hi Outfitters.** ~ Route 93, Challis; 208-879-4500; www.milehioutfitters.com. There's also **Rawhide Outfitters.** ~ 204 Larson Street, Salmon; 208-756-4276; www.rawhideoutfitters.com.

An alternative to the traditional horse-led pack trips is llama trekking. **Venture Outdoors** lets you do everything from "taking a llama to lunch" on a five-hour walk to making five-day trips into the Sawtooth and other mountains. ~ P.O. Box 2251, Hailey, ID 83333; 208-788-5049, 800-528-5262; www.venout.com.

BIKING

As elsewhere in Idaho, biking is a favorite pastime of locals. The pride of the resort community is the paved **Wood River Trail System**, which extends the length of the Wood River Valley for 22 miles from Lake Creek (four miles north of Ketchum) to Bellevue (17 miles south), mainly on a former railroad right-of-way. Administered by the Blaine County Recreation District, it is linked to the ten-mile **Sun Valley Trails** by a pedestrian underpass. Runners, walkers and in-line skaters share the trails with cyclists. ~ Hailey; 208-788-2117; www.bcrd.org.

Numerous off-road trails are also available to cyclists in the adjacent Sawtooth National Forest and the nearby Sawtooth National Recreation Area. Farther north, biking is growing in popularity in the Challis and Salmon national forests, particularly in the Land of the Yankee Fork Historic Area near Challis. **Venture Outdoors** offers guided mountain-biking trips in the Sawtooth National Forest, ranging in length from three hours to five days. ~ P.O. Box 2251, Hailey, ID 83333; 208-788-5049, 800-528-5262; www.venout.com.

Bike Rentals   Rentals and repairs are offered by such shops as **Backwoods Mountain Sports**. ~ Corner of Warm Springs Road and Main Street, Ketchum; 208-726-8818; www.backwoods mountainsports.com. **Pete Lane's** also rents bikes. ~ Sun Valley Village Mall, Sun Valley; 208-622-2279; www.sunvalley.com. **Sturtevant's Alpine Sports** rents mountain bikes and inline skates in the summer. ~ 340 North Main Street, Ketchum; 208-726-4502; www.sturtos.com.

HIKING

This region of Idaho is covered with national forests and wilderness areas, making it idyllic for hikers. All distances listed for hiking trails are one way unless otherwise noted.

Bald Mountain Trail (5 miles) offers a summer ascent of the ski resort's primary peak without the aid of chairlifts. The trail, which begins at the River Run parking lot in Ketchum and climaxes at a fire lookout, gains 3331 feet.

Craters of the Moon National Monument's **Echo Crater Trail** (3 miles) crosses ancient lava flows and passes cinder cones and petrified trees. There are campsites at the crater (bring water); a trail continues beyond. Pick up a free backcountry permit at the visitors center and stay on established trails. The smooth, ropy *pahoehoe* lava may be inviting, but *a'a* flows are fiercely sharp and make fast work of footwear.

The **Borah Peak Trail** (7 miles) is really a series of unimproved paths established by others who have climbed Idaho's highest mountain (12,655 feet). The west ridge is the route preferred by most. The Challis National Forest trailhead, on Birch Springs Road north of Mackay, is at an elevation of 7215 feet.

Sawtooth Lake Trail (5 miles) begins five miles west of Stanley, off Iron Creek Road in the Sawtooth National Recreation Area, and rises to beautiful mile-long Sawtooth Lake, the largest lake in the Sawtooth Wilderness Area. It's a fairly gentle trail until the last three-quarters of a mile, when there's a steep ridge ascent to the lake.

Bench Lakes Trail (7 miles) begins at the Redfish Lake Visitors Center and climbs to a series of small alpine lakes that stairstep down the upper slopes of 10,229-foot Heyburn Peak. There's a 1200-foot elevation gain to the first of the four lakes, 2100 feet to the uppermost.

▼▼▼▼▼▼▼▼▼▼▼

Transportation

Route 75 runs generally north and south through Ketchum and the Stanley Basin, ending at its intersection with Route 93 near Challis. Drive north on **Route 93** to Salmon, or south to Mackay and the Lost River Country. **Route 20** cuts across the southern boundary of this area between West Yellowstone and Mountain Home. The fastest way to Sun Valley from Boise will take you to Mountain Home, then east on Route 20 to Route 75. Turn left (north) on Route 75.

CAR

Sun Valley's **Friedman Memorial Airport**, on Route 75 in Hailey, is served by Horizon Air (800-547-9308) from Seattle and seasonally from L.A., Boise and SkyWest (www.skywest.com) from Salt Lake City.

Charter companies include **Stanley Air Taxi** (208-774-2276) and **Sun Valley Aviation** (208-788-9511).

AIR

Sun Valley Stages runs a charter service to Sun Valley Lodge year-round. ~ Boise Airport, Boise; 800-821-9064. Charter service from Idaho Falls is offered by **Teton Stages**. ~ 208-529-8036.

BUS

Two national agencies are ubiquitous in the regional centers. **Avis Rent A Car** (800-331-1212) and **Hertz Rent A Car** (800-654-3131) have outlets at the Sun Valley (Hailey) airport.

CAR RENTALS

In Sun Valley, **Ketchum Area Rapid Transit**, known as KART, provides free year-round service that links downtown Ketchum with Sun Valley resort, as well as Elkhorn Village and the Warm Springs and River Run communities at the foot of the ski slopes. ~ 800 1st Avenue North, Ketchum; 208-726-7140.

PUBLIC TRANSIT

Taxi and limo services are provided in the Sun Valley area by **A-1 Taxi**. ~ Ketchum; 208-726-9351.

TAXIS

NINE

West Central Idaho

So rugged and remote is central Idaho that it is crossed by more rivers than roads. A single highway, Route 95, links northern Idaho with the state's southern population centers. Running west of the granite plug known as the Idaho batholith, the road extends from the Treasure Valley through Weiser, Cambridge and Riggins en route to Lewiston and points north. Short detours lead to Hells Canyon, the deepest gorge on the North American continent, and McCall, Boise locals' favorite resort town (itself linked directly to Boise by Route 55).

Despite its importance, Route 95 is no freeway. It is a two-lane road with narrow shoulders, in places poorly maintained because of the terrain and weather. A former Idaho governor referred to it as "little more than a goat trail." That's an exaggeration, of course, but this road definitely demands pay-attention driving . . . complemented by some of Idaho's most glorious scenery.

Far more pronounced than the highway are the deep gorges of the Salmon and, especially, the Snake rivers. The Snake is a working agricultural river through much of its upper and middle course, supporting crops of potatoes, alfalfa, barley and beans, as well as sugar beets and fruit orchards below Boise in the Treasure Valley. But below (north of) Payette and Weiser, the Snake backs up in a series of reservoirs. Surrounded by sage hills, these last impoundments of the Snake River in Idaho are gathering points for boaters and anglers who proceed downriver, past the hydroelectric dams, into remarkable Hells Canyon.

East of the canyon are the former "working" towns of McCall and Riggins. Both have made the shift to Idaho's burgeoning recreational economy.

McCall was for decades a lumber town, one that had the good fortune to be situated on a long, high and pristine mountain lake. Timber companies logged the area's deep forests, and Boiseans, lured by the icy lake waters, escaped the valley's July and August heat. In winter, the surrounding mountains became a training ground for Olympic skiers. As the lumber business waxed and waned, the town's fortunes boomed and busted. After the mill closed in 1977, timber's economic role rapidly diminished. But as McCall lost the flavor of a working mill town, it adopted the atmosphere of a down-to-earth resort.

Riggins was also dependent on the area's forests, but its swan song came when the small town's mill burned to the ground. But again geography aided in recovery. Situated on a big bend in the Salmon River, Riggins had a nascent recreational economy based on river rafting and guided fishing for salmon and steelhead. Today, these pursuits have kept Riggins alive. The town can now lay claim to being the whitewater capital of Idaho—a title contested by Salmon, across the state and up-river on Route 93.

For years, Salmon and Riggins were at terminal ends of the Salmon River supply route that brought provisions to mining camps and homesteads along the river. Great "scows"—riverboats resembling wooden bathtubs, 30 feet long by eight feet wide—were built in Salmon. At either end of the boats were long sweeps: broad oars made from the trunks of medium-size trees and fitted with six- to eight-foot blades. These were so precisely balanced that one man could handle both sweeps from a platform built amidships, and with them he could ferry the boat back and forth across the river's currents, avoiding rocks and the worst of the river's rapids. In front of the platform, behind and beneath it, the boatman carried stores that he delivered along his way downriver. And when he landed in Riggins, he sold the scow for scrap lumber and made the overland loop back to Salmon to start again.

Hells Canyon Area

The Snake River from Weiser to Lewiston represents Idaho's western boundary with Oregon and Washington. Hells Canyon Dam is the last of three hydro dams on the river's Idaho border; below here, the Snake enters Hells Canyon, which in summer can feel exactly like its namesake. Its chasm penetrates aged volcanic rock, mostly basalt remnants of flattened and compressed volcanoes, and when heated by a desert sun it can be sweltering.

Through Hells Canyon, the Snake is a recreational paradise and, depending on the level of flow released from the dam, playful: the river takes a day off. A series of rapids challenge rafters, who are rewarded for their efforts by magnificent views of the canyon from river level and by the solitude of this extraordinary crevasse. These same rapids and the sheer force of the Snake River also invite jet boats to power upriver against the flow. Jet boaters come to sightsee, to fish and to hunt. But these two recreational pastimes—nonmotorized and motorized boating—are creating their own turbulence. And the adherents of both persuasions are having trouble reaching a compromise.

SIGHTS

Located 14 miles north of Payette on Route 95, **Weiser** (pronounced "wee-zer") is Idaho's gateway to the upper reaches of Hells Canyon and to the Brownlee, Oxbow and Hells Canyon dams upriver from the gorge. It's also the home of the **National Oldtime Fiddlers' Contest**, held every June since 1953 in the

Weiser High School gymnasium The festival starts on Father's Day and lasts for a week, featuring free music workshops, the National Oldtime Fiddler's Hall of Fame, Lawnmower races, outdoor dancing and, of course, the contests. Contact the Greater Weiser Area Chamber of Commerce for more information. Closed Saturday and Sunday. ~ 309 State Street, Weiser; 208-414-0452, 800-437-1280, fax 208-414-0451.

Also in Weiser is the imposing **Snake River Heritage Center and Washington County Museum**. Located in the central building of the former Intermountain Institute, a college preparatory school that operated from 1899 to 1933, it is now rebuilding after a fire in 1994. The first floor displays Indian artifacts from an on-site dig, cowboy exhibits and children's toys through the centuries, as well as vintage clothing and photographs of the area. Military exhibits are located on the second floor of this huge facility. Admission during Fiddler's Week (the third full week of June). ~ 2295 Paddock Avenue off West 7th Street, Weiser; 208-549-0205.

The village of **Cambridge**, 32 miles north of Weiser, is the junction for Hells Canyon travelers and their last chance to purchase supplies or to grab a motel bed or café meal. Worth a stop here is the **Cambridge Museum**. Intriguing displays may be of special interest to adventurers planning to travel down the canyon. Occasionally antique wooden river craft share the room with relics from Nez Perce Indians and early pioneers. Open Wednesday through Sunday from mid-June to mid-September, or by appointment. ~ Routes 95 and 71, Cambridge; 208-257-3485 or 208-257-3541, fax 208-257-3310.

Route 71 runs from Cambridge toward Brownlee Dam, 29 miles distant. The dam has created long, narrow **Brownlee Reservoir**, noted among anglers for its giant catfish, bass and crappie. Just below the dam, the highway slides across the Snake into Oregon, proceeding up the west bank of the river 12 miles to the Idaho Power Company's Copperfield Park site before crossing back into Idaho below the Oxbow Dam. The paved Snake River Road (Forest Road 454) enters Payette National Forest and traces the east bank of the Snake to Hells Canyon Dam, 22 miles from Copperfield Park.

Cross the dam to enter the **Hells Canyon National Recreation Area**. Established by Congress in 1975, the 652,488-acre recreation area protects a vast and colorful canyon that is deeper by 2000 feet and narrower by a mile than Arizona's exalted Grand Canyon of the Colorado. From the summit of Idaho's He Devil Mountain (9393 feet) to the surface of the Snake River at its foot (1350 feet), Hells Canyon has a depth of 8043 feet. ~ Headquarters at 88401 Route 82, Enterprise, Oregon; 541-426-5546, fax 541-426-5522.

The incredible scope of the gorge is apparent even to those who end their exploration at Hells Canyon Dam. But visitors who continue farther into the canyon, either by water or by land, discover more than stark and spectacular scenery. Hells Canyon was well known to prehistoric tribes and early white settlers alike, as evidenced by a 7000-year-old rock shelter, American Indian artifacts, remnants of 1860s gold mines and 1890s homesteads.

The natural history is equally impressive. The canyon is home to a plethora of unique botanical species and to a diverse wildlife that ranges from deer, elk, bighorn sheep and mountain goats to cougars, black bears and a dazzling variety of bird life.

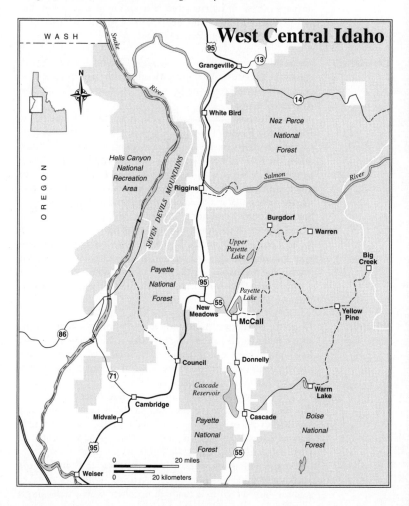

HIDDEN ► Those with four-wheel-drive may wish to travel the **Black Lake Road**, which runs 54 miles north from Council to the edge of the Hells Canyon Wilderness. The views are truly spectacular, but the route is not for everyone. While generally well-maintained, the single-lane road has only passing turnouts and is steep, narrow and unsurfaced—not well-suited for standard passenger cars and certainly not for trailers.

The Adams County seat of **Council**, 20 miles north of Cambridge via Route 95, got its name from the tribal conclaves frequently held in the region prior to the town's founding in 1878. Today, the **Charles Winkler Museum** in Council's former city hall displays American Indian artifacts from that era as well as historical ranching and mining items. Closed Monday. ~ 100 South Galena Street, Council; 208-253-4201.

LODGING The handful of small motels in the Hells Canyon gateway area includes the two-story **State Street Motel**, which has 13 modern but cozy rooms with private baths. ~ 1279 State Street, Weiser; 208-414-1390. BUDGET.

The **Hunters Inn**, poised at the junction of Route 95 to McCall and Route 71 to Hells Canyon, was a favorite hangout of the Civilian Conservation Corps after it opened in 1927. Today the restored hotel has four rustic bed-and-breakfast rooms upstairs, pine walls with mounted hunting trophies downstairs and a gourmet coffee and pastry shop. In addition to the B&B, the Inn offers nine motel units at even cheaper rates. ~ 10 South Superior Street, Cambridge; 208-257-3325, fax 208-257-3797; e-mail huntersn@cyberhighway.net. MODERATE.

In Council, the **Starlite Motel** is a comfortable ma-and-pa-type inn with all standard amenities. The 12 guest rooms have phones and televisions. ~ 102 North Dartmouth Street (Route 95), Council; 208-253-4868, fax 208-253-4883; e-mail mad@ctc web.net. BUDGET.

DINING Go to the **Homestead Café** early in the morning and you'll find where many locals like to have breakfast. This eatery also serves lunch and dinner, which includes a soup and salad bar to complement your steak and potatoes. ~ 813 State Street, Weiser; 208-414-3962. BUDGET TO MODERATE.

The **Gateway Café** is a simple place that serves three meals a day. You can sit down to eggs and pancakes for breakfast, and sandwiches and burgers for lunch and dinner; they also serve milkshakes. Closed January to mid-February. ~ 4330 Route 71, Cambridge; 208-257-3531. BUDGET.

Many outdoor sports lovers find their way to **Branding Iron Steakhouse**. Rancher-size steaks, chicken and prime rib with baked potatoes are served in a rustic atmosphere where you can get

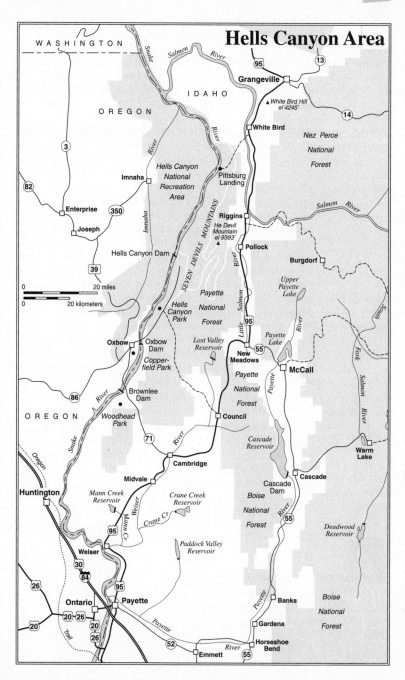

Hells Canyon Area

WASHINGTON

OREGON

IDAHO

▲ *White Bird Hill el 4245'*

White Bird

Nez Perce

National

Forest

Imnaha

Hells Canyon National Recreation Area

Pittsburg Landing

Enterprise

Joseph

Riggins

He Devil Mountain el 9393' ▲

Pollock

Burgdorf

Hells Canyon Dam

Upper Payette Lake

0   20 miles

0   20 kilometers

Hells Canyon Park

Payette National Forest

Payette Lake

Oxbow

Oxbow Dam

Lost Valley Reservoir

New Meadows

McCall

Copperfield Park

Payette National Forest

Brownlee Dam

Council

OREGON

Woodhead Park

Cascade Reservoir

Warm Lake

Cambridge

Midvale

Boise National Forest

Cascade

Cascade Dam

Huntington

Mann Creek Reservoir

Crane Creek Reservoir

Deadwood Reservoir

Weiser

Paddock Valley Reservoir

Ontario

Payette

Banks

Boise National Forest

Gardena

Horseshoe Bend

Emmett

breakfast, lunch or dinner seven days a week. ~ 103 Illinois Avenue, Council; 208-253-4499. MODERATE TO DELUXE.

NIGHTLIFE   A modicum of action is found at the **Athena Club**, which features live rock performances by Boise-area bands on Friday and Saturday nights. Occasional cover. ~ 35 East Idaho Street, Weiser; 208-549-9931.

PARKS   **IDAHO POWER COMPANY PARKS** 🚶 🏊 🛶 🚤 ⛵ Four sites in the Hells Canyon area are maintained year-round by Idaho Power. Three of the parks are on the Idaho shore of long, narrow reservoirs: Woodhead Park on Brownlee Reservoir, McCormick Park on Oxbow Reservoir and Hells Canyon Park on Hells Canyon Reservoir. Copperfield Park is located just below Oxbow Dam on the Oregon side of the Snake River. There is excellent fishing for a wide variety of species, including steelhead, trout, catfish, bass and crappie. Facilities include picnic tables, restrooms and showers. ~ Woodhead and McCormick parks are both on Route 71 north of Cambridge. Copperfield Park is on Oregon Route 86 just past the Route 71 junction. Hells Canyon Park is seven miles north of Copperfield Park on Snake River Road; 208-388-2231, 800-422-3143, fax 208-388-6902; www.idahopower.com, e-mail csorensen@idahopower.com.

▲ There are 15 tent sites and 124 RV sites (with hookups) at Woodhead Park; open-field tent sites and 34 RV sites at McCormick Park; open-field tent sites and 62 RV sites at Copperfield Park; open-field tent sites and 24 RV sites at Hells Canyon Park. Tent sites are $8 per night, RV sites $12; both are half-price November through March.

HELLS CANYON NATIONAL RECREATION AREA 🚶 🏇 🛶 🚤 ⛵ The Snake River's colorful Hells Canyon is the centerpiece of a 652,488-acre parcel, much of it wilderness, most of it in Oregon. In addition to the canyon, the Idaho portion includes the lofty 9000-foot Seven Devils Mountains. Whitewater rafters, kayakers and drift boaters put in at the mouth of Hells Canyon Creek, just below Hells Canyon Dam, for trips down the "national wild and scenic" portion of the Snake that extends 32 miles to

AUTHOR FAVORITE

If I want to get my adrenaline pumping, I brave the challenging rapids of the Snake River through **Hells Canyon**, a breathtaking (literally) journey that takes in both scenic and historical wonders. See page 248 for more information.

Pittsburg Landing, Idaho; 51 miles to Dug Bar, Oregon; and 79 miles to Grande Ronde, Washington. In the fall, steelhead-fishing trips are popular. For nonboaters, a boardwalk nature trail extends from the Hells Canyon Creek Information Station. Primary overland routes to Pittsburgh Landing and the Seven Devils Mountains start from Riggins and White Bird. ~ Take Route 95 off Route 84 at Idaho Exit 3, traveling north 54 miles to Cambridge. Turn northwest on Route 71 and continue 25 miles to Brownlee Dam; then follow the Snake River Road 38 miles via Copperfield Park, Oregon, to Hells Canyon Dam. Cross the dam to enter the recreation area. There's also four-wheel-drive access via Council and Black Lake. To reach the Upper and Lower Pittsburg Landing campgrounds, take the Pittsburg Landing exit off Route 95 in White Bird, follow the road 17 miles to the Lower Pittsburg Landing Campground, and another 1.5 miles on the same road to the Upper Pittsburg Landing Road. The gravel road is steep in places; campers should always call for road conditions before setting out; 208-628-3916, fax 208-628-3030 (Riggins) or 541-426-4978, fax 541-426-5522 (Enterprise, Oregon).

▲ There is primitive camping along the river for rafters and backpackers, and there are rustic campgrounds in the Seven Devils high country. Two campgrounds that have developed sites and minimal facilities are Upper and Lower Pittsburg Landing: there are seven tent-only sites in the upper grounds and 28 multiple-use sites in the lower one; $8 per night (mid-June to mid-September).

McCall Area

McCall may not be Idaho's best-known resort community—that honor falls to Sun Valley, with Coeur d'Alene running a strong second—but it is a favorite of many Idahoans.

Located 106 miles north of Boise on the Payette River Scenic Route (Route 55), the mountain town of 3000 permanent residents nestles at the south end of Payette Lake, a mitten-shaped, six-mile-long crystal gem surrounded by timbered 7000-foot peaks. Besides its beautiful setting, the town has a score of pleasant lodgings and restaurants, several art galleries and gift shops.

Nearly a mile high in elevation (5020 feet), McCall receives some of Idaho's heaviest snowfalls and in summer is insulated from the heat of lower desert valleys. The national forests surrounding the town boast 132 mountain lakes and 169 mountain streams, and fishing is good; anglers only must choose between them.

World-class whitewater and steelhead fishing are what draw folks to Riggins, a community of about 500. Ensconced on a bend of the mighty Salmon River at about 1800-feet elevation, Riggins is rarely beset with snow, although frost may linger on mountain peaks. Summers can be hot, which makes the river all that much more inviting. Lodgings and restaurants in Riggins are considerably sparser in number and more rustic than in McCall.

East of McCall and Riggins is the Frank Church–River of No Return Wilderness, and both communities serve as staging areas for day or extended trips into the backcountry.

SIGHTS

Traveling north from Boise, Route 55 follows the North Fork of the Payette River into **Lake Cascade**. More than 20 miles long and 4.5 miles wide, the manmade lake boasts 110 miles of shoreline, a rich bird life (including bald eagles and white pelicans) and thriving schools of rainbow and brown trout, kokanee salmon and perch. The lake was formed by a Bureau of Reclamation dam built on the North Fork in 1950 for hydropower, irrigation and flood control. Recreation is now a major use of the lake; for example, there are more than 400 public and private campsites around its

HIDDEN ▶

shores. The **Sugarloaf Camping Unit**, located on a treeless peninsula midway along the lake's eastern shore, is a wonderful place for birdwatching. ~ Stonebreaker Road, Cascade; 208-382-6544, fax 208-382-4071; e-mail cas@idpr.state.id.us.

The largest lakeside community is **Cascade**, site of a large Boise Cascade sawmill. The town of 1000 is also a recreational hub, with a Boise National Forest district ranger station, several motels and restaurants and a disproportionate number of sporting-goods stores.

A fishing resort at **Warm Lake**, 25 miles east of Cascade in Boise National Forest, draws many outdoor-sports lovers to the area. Warm Lake boasts two overnight lodges with restaurants, three campgrounds, boat ramps and rentals, a swimming beach, gas and phones. Nearby, the national forest's **South Fork Salmon River Interpretive Site** offers views of spawning chinook salmon. ~ Forest Road 474; 208-382-4271. The state Fish & Game Department's **South Fork Salmon River Fish Trap** exhibits a fish weir and holding ponds for hundreds of chinook from late June to mid-September. Get driving details from the McCall Fish Hatchery. ~ 300 Mather Road; 208-634-2690.

Halfway between Cascade and McCall is the village of **Donnelly**. To the west, Roseberry Road leads to Payette National Forest campgrounds and boat ramps at the upper end of Cascade Reservoir; to the east, the crossing road extends one and a half miles to the old town site of **Roseberry**. Most of this community's remains—several circa-1890s buildings, including its original general store and Methodist Episcopal church—now make up the

HIDDEN ▶

Long Valley Museum. The former McCall City Hall, moved to the site in 1978, houses the museum's principal exhibits on Valley County's mining, timber and agricultural history. Other buildings include a schoolhouse, a barn, three log houses, a church, and a general store that is open for business. The museum is open Sunday in May and September, Friday through

Sunday from June through August, and by appointment. ~ Farm to Market Road, Roseberry; 208-325-8383 or 208-325-5000.

A few miles north of Donnelly is **Lake Fork**, which got its start as an early-20th-century Finnish community. The simple, wooden 1917 **Finnish Evangelical Lutheran Church,** on a hilltop one and a half miles east of the village, is still a valley landmark and has been listed on the National Register of Historic Places. ~ Farm to Market Road, Lake Fork; no phone.

McCall is a town with two very distinct tourist seasons. Summer brings boaters, anglers and other water-sports lovers to Payette Lake. Hunters, horseback riders and mountain bikers head into the remote reaches of adjacent Payette National Forest, while river rafters and kayakers may be diverted by the whitewater of the North Fork of the Payette River. Originating at Upper Payette Lake, only about 16 miles north of McCall, the stream runs south for the entire 75-mile length of Valley County, nurturing

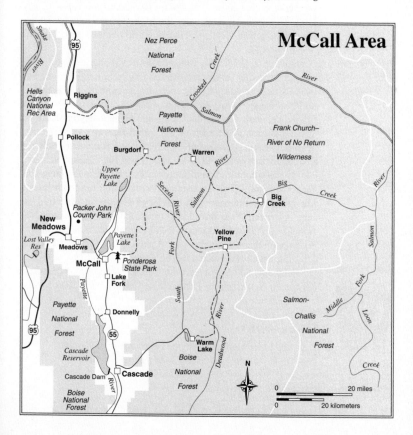

the Long Valley as it passes through Payette Lake and Cascade Reservoir.

In winter, alpine skiers frequent **Brundage Mountain Ski Area**, which ranks among Idaho's leading snow resorts. ~ Brundage Mountain Road, McCall; 208-634-4151; www.brundage.com. The McCall area also offers excellent Nordic skiing and snowmobiling as well as the McCall Winter Carnival (see "Castles Made of Snow" in this chapter), a late January tradition since 1964. Continuously scenic through the seasons is **Ponderosa State Park**, one of Idaho's prettiest parks. Its main unit occupies a two-mile peninsula just northeast of McCall; a second unit is at the head of Payette Lake. Admission. ~ North Davis Avenue, McCall; 208-634-2164, fax 208-634-5370; e-mail pon@idpr.state.id.us.

Most of McCall's attractions are of the recreational variety, but visitors are welcome to drop in at the **Central Idaho Museum**, which consists of eight buildings on the National Register; they were constructed in the 1930s by the Civilian Conservation Corps. Highlights include exhibits on the Idaho forest and McCall history and the Fire Warden's House. ~ 1001 State Street, McCall; 208-634-4497.

Northeast of McCall, forest roads of varying levels of maintenance extend to several remote and tiny communities in the Salmon River drainage. These scenic hamlets exist mainly as fishing and hunting outposts with a few summer cabins and offer only limited services. North of McCall, past Upper Payette Lake on Warren Wagon Road (Route 21), are **Burgdorf** (31 miles) and **Warren** (44 miles). East via Lick Creek Road and East Fork Road (Route 48) are **Yellow Pine** (52 miles) and **Big Creek** (74 miles).

Of these communities, Burgdorf may be of most interest to casual visitors. It has a national forest campground near a tiny hot-springs resort, originally developed as a spa in 1865 by German immigrant Fred Burgdorf. Drivers can visit the **Payette National Forest** office in McCall to borrow audio cassette tours to accompany them on their trip to Warren. ~ 102 West Lake Street; 208-634-0400; www.fs.fed.us/r4/payette.

Off Route 55 northwest of McCall, a few miles past Brundage Mountain Road, is tiny **Packer John County Park**. This former

AUTHOR FAVORITE

Even though I may be shivering in my boots, my heart warms at the sight of larger-than-life cartoon characters and mythical creatures—sculpted completely out of snow and ice—at the **McCall Winter Carnival**. See pages 240–41 for more information.

Idaho state park preserves a replica of the cabin where Idaho's first territorial convention was held in 1863. The park offers camping and fishing. Closed when there's snow. ~ New Meadows; 208-253-4561.

Route 55 connects with Route 95, the state's sole north–south highway, at **New Meadows**, 12 miles west of McCall and 25 miles north of Council. The junction town's 1911 Pacific & Idaho Northern train depot stands abandoned. ~ Route 95 South, New Meadows. Four miles north of the junction, **Zim's Hot Springs** has a mineral pool beside the Little Salmon River open to swimmers and soakers year-round. Admission. ~ Route 95, New Meadows; 208-347-2686.

◄ HIDDEN

Thirty-four miles north of New Meadows on Route 95 is **Riggins**, where it's said that the frames and walls of many houses and stores were made from the planks and beams of river scows. The Salmon River rafting capital marks the southern limit of northern Idaho; it's still a full three-hour drive from here to the state capital at Boise. A handful of small motels, cafés and bars trumpet their appeal to outdoors enthusiasts.

The **Hells Canyon NRA Riggins Office**, about a half-mile south of town on Route 95, provides full information on trails and campsites in the recreation area. ~ P.O. Box 832, Riggins, ID 83549; 208-628-3916, fax 208-628-3030. **Heavens Gate Overlook**, 19 miles from Riggins, reached via the rugged, steep, unpaved Forest Road 517 (weather permitting, generally from July to early October), affords a spectacular late-summer vista of Hells Canyon, four and a half miles west and one and a half miles down, and the adjacent Seven Devils Mountains.

One of Idaho's most remote yet luxurious guest ranches is **Wapiti Meadow Ranch**, 60 miles east of McCall in the Salmon River Mountains near Yellow Pine. The ranch was homesteaded during a 1905 gold rush; the lodge was built in 1926 and became Idaho's first "dude ranch." Trail rides and flyfishing are the favored activities at the ranch, which has four cabins and two luxury suites nestled against the 8000-foot peaks of the Frank Church–River of No Return Wilderness. The ranch features gourmet dining and a hot tub. Closed March through May and November through December. ~ 1667 Johnson Creek Road, Cascade; 208-633-3217, fax 208-633-3219; www.wapitimeadowranch.com, e-mail wapitimr@aol.com. DELUXE TO ULTRA-DELUXE.

LODGING

Since the early 20th century, the **Hotel McCall** has welcomed guests to its lakefront location in the heart of McCall. European in appearance, the hotel looks as if it would belong on the shore of Lake Geneva. All 33 rooms are decorated with country ambience, with handsome duvets and fresh flowers. A continental

Text continued on page 242.

Castles Made
of Snow

McCall is blessed with munificent amounts of winter's white gold: snow. In most years, snowplows—clearing streets and driveways—run out of places to push it, and front-loaders are called to scoop it up in their buckets and pile it higher. During heavy winters, these piles of snow can reach 15 feet and more on street corners, empty lots, as a center divider along streets, anywhere there is room. Such bounty, and the abundant snow piles, may have been the inspiration for McCall's first Winter Carnival in 1964. Or perhaps it was only serious cabin fever. Residents, in any case, turned the heaps into sculpture, the more fantastical the better. And it's been going on ever since.

The event, scheduled for one week and two weekends each year, begins in late January or early February. In recent years, the event has attracted as many as 100,000 during those nine days, and they come to see the more than 70 sculptures of snow and ice. Using shovels, hatchets, sickles, mixing spoons, even cheese graters, sculptors have created a greater-than-life-size Flintstone family dining on mammoth burgers, Humpty Dumpty, Garfield, Mighty Morphin Power Rangers, a steam locomotive made from 12 truckloads of snow and a Noah's Ark complete with monkeys, polar bears, camels and giraffes that loomed over a downtown supermarket. Other years have seen a valiant Saint George and his dragon, masks of comedy and tragedy, a flying swine called "Pigasus Ascending" and, from a modern mythology, Godzilla grasping miniature skyscrapers. And there have been attempts to build the world's largest snowman, to compete with the 86-foot Frosty built in Quebec.

McCall is about 110 miles north of Boise on Route 55. On carnival weekends the drive can take three hours; the road is very winding in places. Watch for a few sculptures in the towns of Cascade and Donnelly. Parking is available just south of McCall near the Shaver's supermarket and a free shuttle takes carnival-goers downtown. This is advisable since the streets are so filled with pedestrians that traffic crawls. Maps locating the many and scattered sculpture sites can be found in town. February weather in McCall may range from 50° to 20°F. At 5020 feet in elevation, you can safely expect temperatures below freezing. Insulated boots are helpful—even necessary—for keeping feet warm. To take away the chill, espressos and hot chocolates are served at many eateries, and most shopkeepers won't mind if you warm your toes in their stores.

McCall residents have come to think of their Winter Carnival as a kind of snow-white Mardi Gras, and they complement the sculpting with a parade, a bonfire, live music and dancing. Visitors can also compete in, or simply watch, the Men's Long Beard and the Hairy-legged Women's contests. And there is downhill skiing nearby at Brundage Mountain and daytime cross-country skiing at the Little Ski Hill and Ponderosa State Park. Accommodations can sometimes be found at the last minute, but it's a good idea to schedule ahead. For more information contact **McCall Winter Carnival**. ~ Box 350, McCall, ID 83638; 800-260-5130, fax 208-634-7752; e-mail mccallchamber@citlink.net.

breakfast is served each morning, complimentary wine or tea in the early evening and milk and cookies at bedtime. The hotel has a garden patio, a sundeck and a library with fireplace. ~ 1101 North 3rd Street, McCall; 208-634-8105, 866-800-1183, fax 208-634-8755; e-mail hotelmccall@citlink.net. DELUXE.

Less expensive accommodations are available at the **Brundage Bungalows Motel**, whose seven self-contained cabins make them especially popular with winter skiers. Colorfully painted (forest green with red doors) for a permanent Christmas season, the various bungalows sleep from two to twelve; most units have kitchen areas with refrigerators, hot plates, toasters and microwave ovens. Each room has a small TV and VCR, and a coin-op laundry is available. The cabins were built of wood in 1945, so it's not surprising they're all nonsmoking units. ~ 1005 West Lake Street, McCall; 208-634-2344, 800-643-2009, fax 208-634-4331; www.brundage vacations.com, e-mail bungalows@citlink.net. MODERATE.

Serenity reigns at the **Meadow Wood Bed and Breakfast**, situated on ten bucolic acres adjacent to Boise National Forest. Seven guest rooms, most with queen-size beds, are decorated in Western or alpine style; all have private baths. There's a hot tub on the back deck. ~ 3580 Meadowwood Lane, McCall; 208-634-3330. DELUXE.

Ten miles west of McCall, a 1911 Georgian revival–style estate has been restored as the **Hartland Inn & Motel**. There are five bed-and-breakfast rooms within the three-story brick mansion and 16 nicely kept units (four suites with fireplaces and one condo) in an adjacent motel. Rooms in the inn have private toilets but two rooms share a shower/bath; those in the motel have full private baths. ~ 211 Norris Street (Route 95 North), New Meadows; 208-347-2114, 888-509-7400, fax 208-347-2535; www.hartlandinn. com, e-mail jobethmehen@hotmail.com. MODERATE TO DELUXE.

Of several adequate lodgings in the Riggins area, I prefer the 19 units at the **Riggins Motel**, nestled among pines near the Little Salmon River. Rooms range in size from small singles to a full family suite, but all have cable television and phones. Cooking units are available on request; everyone has access to the hot tub. Pets are accepted here, and there are two RV hookups. ~ 615 Route 95 South, Riggins; 208-628-3001, 800-669-6739, fax 208-628-3524; www.rigginsmotel.com. MODERATE.

DINING   Solid home cooking, three meals a day and seven days a week, is the claim to fame of the **Whistle Stop Cafe** in Cascade's Ponderosa Plaza. Come for omelettes or biscuits and gravy in the morning, homemade chili and burgers midday, pizzas for dinner. On Friday and Saturday nights, the Whistle Stop offers a full prime rib dinner for just $8.95. ~ 109 Main Street (Route 55), Cascade; 208-382-4700. BUDGET TO MODERATE.

A Payette Lake classic is **Lardo's**, named not for a culinary additive but for a former mining town. A rustic saloon on the west side of town, it is noted for its Italian dishes (lasagna, fettuccine alfredo) and for its charcoal-grilled burgers and steaks. ~ 600 West Lake Street, McCall; 208-634-8191, fax 208-634-0515. MODERATE TO DELUXE.

Some locals call **Romano's Italian Ristorante** the best restaurant in town. They serve pastas, seafood and steaks, with entrées such as chicken picatta, veal marsala and calamari. The patio offers a sweeping view of Payette Lake. Dinner only. ~ 203 East Lake Street, McCall; 208-634-4396. MODERATE TO DELUXE.

Blackwell's Steak and Seafood Restaurant, housed in a nicely refurbished tavern, provides microbrews to wash down its gourmet dinners. Reservations recommended.~ 308 East Lake Street, McCall; 208-634-1411. DELUXE.

Mandarin spicy chicken, honey-walnut shrimp and Mongolian beef are some of the more popular dishes at the **Panda Chinese Restaurant**. They have an extensive menu of Chinese dishes, and unlike many Chinese restaurants in Idaho, this one gets by without serving American food. If the weather is good, ask to be seated on the lakeside patio. ~ 317 East Lake Street, McCall; 208-634-2266. MODERATE.

For Mexican food, you won't do better than the spacious **Si Bueno Southside Grill and Cantina** near the McCall Airport. This lively restaurant, a McCall fixture since 1978, offers steaks and seafood as well as a full south-of-the-border menu. And the cantina's margaritas are locally renowned. April and November have limited hours; call ahead. ~ Deinhard Lane, Village Square, McCall; 208-634-2128, fax 208-634-2129; www.sibueno.com, e-mail misi bueno@yahoo.com. MODERATE TO DELUXE.

Rough-hewn logs, wagon wheels, a fireplace and mountain surroundings are what you'll find at **The Mill Supper Club**, where

AUTHOR FAVORITE

Perhaps the nicest modern accommodation in McCall is the **Whitetail Club**. Spread along the south shore of Payette Lake, the handsome lodge has a fine-dining restaurant and lounge, an 18-hole championship golf course, a swimming pool, a hot tub and sauna, a fitness center with racquetball courts, a fine-dining restaurant and lounge, and even a gourmet coffee and gift shop. The lodge's 77 suites are nicely furnished with all modern amenities. Closed for renovation until fall 2001. ~ 501 West Lake Street, McCall; 208-634-2244, 800-657-6464, fax 208-634-7504; www.whitetail.com. ULTRA-DELUXE.

you can dine on prime rib, chicken and seafood. Reservations recommended. ~ 324 North 3rd Street, McCall; 208-634-7129 or 208-634-7683; www.themillmccallidaho.com. DELUXE TO ULTRA-DELUXE.

In the rafting capital of Riggins, the **Seven Devils Saloon & Steak House** keeps the spirit of outdoor adventure alive. The rustic establishment on Route 95 in the heart of town specializes in charbroiled steaks, chicken and seafood. ~ 312 South Main Street, Riggins; phone/fax 208-628-3351. DELUXE.

SHOPPING McCall is the region's shopping center. Check out **Mountain Monkey Business** for an eclectic selection of fashions and gifts. ~ 501 Pine Street; 208-634-8268.

Men's and women's fine clothing is the domain of the **Mountain Regatta Clothing Company.** ~ 304 North 3rd Street; 208-634-4710. For the literary minded, **McCall Drugs and Blue Grouse Bookshop,** has a good selection of regional-interest titles. ~ 1001 North 2nd Street; 208-634-2434.

NIGHTLIFE In an old church beside the shore of Payette Lake, the **Alpine Playhouse** hosts a variety of musical and theatrical events throughout the summer, mainly on weekends. They also put on productions in winter. ~ 1210 Roosevelt Street, McCall; 208-634-5594.

A mid-July highlight is the **McCall Folk Fest,** a series of evening concerts by folk, bluegrass, Irish and other world-music performers from around the globe. ~ P.O. Box 1839, McCall, ID 83638; 208-634-3642.

Yellow Pine hosts an old-time harmonica festival each August that recalls the days when mouth organs were the only musical instruments most miners carried.

The **Yacht Club Lounge** is a popular drinking establishment with a deck on Payette Lake. You'll find live music and dancing on summer weekends. Occasional cover on weekends. ~ 203 East Lake Street, McCall; 208-634-5649. A McCall institution is **The Foresters Club,** a tavern with deejay music Thursday night. ~ 304 East Lake Street, McCall; 208-634-2676.

When rafters are in town after several days on whitewater, things can get a little rowdy at the **Seven Devils Saloon.** There's a full bar here, and live rock or country music on weekend nights. Occasional cover during special events (about once a month). ~ 312 South Main Street, Riggins; 208-628-3351.

PARKS **PAYETTE NATIONAL FOREST** Some of the largest blocks of undeveloped wilderness remaining in the contiguous United States can be found in the 2.3 million acres of this forest. Payette National Forest covers much of west-central Idaho between the wild and scenic Snake and Salmon rivers and Boise National Forest. Outstanding recreation areas include the alpine lakes of the Salmon River Mountains, between the South

Fork of the Salmon and the North Fork of the Payette, and Lava Ridge, north of McCall and Brundage Mountain. There are large populations of game birds and big-game mammals, plus recently released wolves.There are no designated areas for swimming, but there are many small lakes. There is trout in mountain lakes and streams; steelhead and chinook salmon on the South Fork of the Salmon River. Facilities include picnic tables, restrooms and a ski area (Brundage Mountain). ~ Best access is via Forest Service roads emanating from McCall (on Route 55), Council (on Route 95) and New Meadows (at the junction of Routes 55 and 95). To reach Upper Payette Lake Campground, go north from McCall on Route 55 and turn onto Warren Wagon Road. After 16 miles you will see a sign for the campground. To reach Lake Fork Campground, take Davis Road out McCall, then turn onto Lick Creek Road and continue for eight miles until you see the sign for the campground; 208-634-0700, fax 208-634-0744; www.fs.fed.us/r4/payette.

▲ There are 215 RV/tent units plus 41 for tents only in 26 campgrounds (no hookups); $5 to $8 per night. An excellent handicapped-accessible campground is Upper Payette Lake Campground, which has 22 RV/tent sites; $8 to $10 per night. To be near great hiking trails, try Lake Fork Campground, with six tent-only sites; $8 per night. Please refer to website for fluctuating prices and conditions.

FRANK CHURCH–RIVER OF NO RETURN WILDERNESS AREA
The biggest designated federal wilderness out-side of Alaska is slightly larger than Yellowstone National Park. It extends 97 miles along the Salmon River and covers 2,353,739 acres in five national forests, including large parts of Payette and Salmon-Challis, and portions of Boise, Nez Perce and Bitterroot national forests. The Salmon River's main and middle forks are considered to offer the nation's premier whitewater experience. Swimming is possible only in a few alpine lakes. There is steel-head, trout (both catch and release only) and whitefish for fish-ing. ~ Trailheads are near Yellow Pine and Stanley; 208-634-0600, fax 208-634-0634.

▲ Primitive only.

PONDEROSA STATE PARK
Covering 1000 acres on a heavily wooded peninsula extending into Payette Lake at the edge of McCall, this stately park is one of Idaho's finest. Rich in bird and animal life—from beaver to deer and even bear—the park attracts campers and water-sports lovers in summer, cross-country skiers in winter. A second unit of the park, the 630-acre North Beach Area at the head of Pay-ette Lake, has a large sandy beach where the Payette River (a fa-vorite of canoeists) enters the lake. There are designated beaches

at both units. The small Lakeview Village has camping options. Payette Lake offers trails and trout fishing. Facilities include picnic tables and restrooms. Day-use fee, $4. ~ To reach the main unit from downtown McCall, take Lake Drive (Route 48) northeast two miles from Route 55. To North Beach, take Warren Wagon Road (Route 21) north seven miles from McCall up the west shore of Payette Lake; 208-634-2164, fax 208-634-5370; e-mail pon@idpr.state.id.us.

▲ There are 80 sites (water and electricity) at Lakeview Village and 23 at North Beach (no hookups), open approximately May 20 to October 15 (depending on the weather); $16 per night.

PACKER JOHN COUNTY PARK 🏃 ⤴ The first convention of Idaho's fledgling territorial government was held in 1863 at the log-cabin home of pioneer packer John Welch, near Meadows. Miners came from as far as the Lewiston area, to the north, and Idaho City, to the south. The original cabin was replaced in 1909 by a replica. Pine trees fill the 16-acre park, surrounded by private homes and a pasture. Trout fishing is available in nearby Goose Creek. Facilities include picnic tables and vault toilets. Closed when there's snow. ~ The park is off Route 55, ten miles west of McCall and two miles east of New Meadows; 208-253-4561.

▲ There are 25 RV/tent sites (no hookups); $5 per night.

Outdoor Adventures

FISHING

Trout—rainbow, brown, brook and cutthroat— are the primary species sought in Idaho. The Snake River and its tributaries are prime waters for catching them.

October–November steelhead-fishing expeditions originating from Hells Canyon Dam are offered by numerous outfitters including **Hells Canyon Adventures**. ~ 4200 Hells Canyon Dam Road, Oxbow, OR 97840; 541-785-3352, 800-422-3568; www.hellscanyonadventures.com.

On the Snake River above Hells Canyon, Brownlee, Oxbow and Hells Canyon reservoirs are key locations; some of the best

---

FIRE DOWN BELOW

To learn about the operations and training regimen of Idaho's firefighting parachutists, visit the **McCall Smokejumper Base**. This elite group may travel anywhere in the United States, including Alaska, to battle fires on public lands. There's no charge for tours, though tours may not be available during periods of high fire activity. ~ Mission Road, McCall; 208-634-0390, fax 208-634-0385.

catfishing in Idaho is at Brownlee, which also has crappie, bass and trout. On the Weiser River system, trout, bass and bluegill are denizens of Crane Creek and Mann Creek reservoirs, which are located off Route 95 north and northeast (respectively) of Weiser, and Lost Valley reservoir, which is just east of New Meadows.

Cascade Reservoir, on the North Fork of the Payette River, is considered one of the finest fisheries the state, with rainbow, brook and brown trout; chinook, coho and kokanee salmon; yellow perch and mountain whitefish. The 20-mile-long lake boasts more than two dozen boat launches, and in winter, there's ice fishing.

Other good fishing lakes on the Payette River system are Payette Lake and Upper Payette Lake, and Paddock Valley Reservoir east of Weiser, and Deadwood Reservoir, southeast of Cascade.

East of Cascade and McCall, on the South Fork of the Salmon River, Warm Lake is one of the few lakes in the state with a resident population of lake trout (mackinaw). Other streams in the Salmon River system, including the Middle Fork, Big Creek and Johnson Creek, have fall steelhead runs.

Flyfishing lessons are offered from June through September by **Idaho Anglers**. ~ 305 East Park Street, McCall; 208-634-4004; www.idahoangler.com.

Northstar River Expeditions leads multiday rafting and fishing trips out of McCall to Hells Canyon and the Snake and Salmon rivers. ~ P.O. Box 906, Boise; 877-610-3200; www.north star-rafting.com.

In Riggins, **Hook, Line & Sinker** has all manner of angling supplies, including licenses. ~ 112 North Main Street (Route 95); 208-628-3578. **Wapiti River Guides** specializes in steelhead- and salmon-fishing excursions on the Salmon and other rivers. ~ Route 95, Riggins; 208-628-3523, 800-488-9872; www.doryfun.com.

This region is a boater's haven. Numerous lakes and reservoirs dot the area. Cascade Reservoir, with 24 launch sites, and Payette Lake, with two ramps, are two favorites. There's also a marina, **Harry's Dry Dock & Sports Marina,** with boat rentals on Payette Lake. Closed Sunday in winter. ~ 1300 East Lake Street, McCall; 208-634-8605, fax 208-634-3272.

BOATING

The trio of Snake River reservoirs upriver of Hells Canyon Dam—Hells Canyon, Oxbow and Brownlee reservoirs—draw water-sports enthusiasts from Oregon as well as Idaho.

Other bodies of water where boating enthusiasts congregate are Paddock Valley, Crane Creek and Mann Creek reservoirs, near Weiser; Lost Valley Reservoir, near New Meadows; Upper Payette Lake, north of McCall; and Warm Lake and Sagehen Reservoir, in the Cascade area.

Gravity Sports will rent you canoes and lake kayaks. ~ 503 Pine Street, McCall; 208-634-8530. The northern end of Payette

Lake and even the final two miles of the Payette River before it enters the lake are exciting places to explore. In fall the lake's bright red kokanee salmon congregate here as they prepare to move upriver for spawning.

RIVER RUNNING

Certainly the best way to experience Hells Canyon, North America's deepest gorge, is by raft down the Salmon River. (The return trip is often by jet boat back up the river to the put-in point.) The most frequently traveled stretch is the 30 miles of moderately challenging rapids—Wild Sheep and Granite Creek rapids are both Class IV—between Hells Canyon Dam, north of Cambridge, and Pittsburg Landing, west of White Bird (see "Grangeville and the Camas Prairie" in Chapter Ten).

The season extends from April to December. **Hells Canyon Adventures** offers a six-hour jet boat trip. ~ 4200 Hells Canyon Dam Road, Oxbow; 541-785-3352, 800-422-3568; www.hellscanyon adventures.com. **Hughes River Expeditions** summer trips, ranging from Class II to Class IV, include the Snake and both the Middle Fork of the Salmon and the Salmon River Canyon. ~ P.O. Box 217, Cambridge, ID 83610; 208-257-3477, 800-262-1882; www. hughesriver.com. If they're booked, ask for a recommendation.

For Salmon River trips—which can vary in difficulty from tranquil floats to high whitewater drama—there are numerous outfitters in Riggins. **Salmon River Challenge** offers trips of one-half to six days in rafts, kayaks or dories. ~ P.O. Box 1299, Riggins, ID 83549; 208-628-3264, 800-732-8574; www.salmon riverchallenge.com.

A similar product is provided by **Exodus Wilderness Adventures**, whose experienced guides couple jet-boating excursions with rafting and kayaking. ~ P.O. Box 1231, Riggins, ID 83549; 208-628-3484, 800-992-3484. There's also **Epley's Whitewater Adventures**, which offers guided rafting trips of up to five days on the Salmon (except in winter). ~ 1512 Salmon Road, Riggins; 208-634-5173, 800-233-1813; www.epleys.com. And **Canyon Cats** offer a new twist on the sport with "catarafts"—catamaran-style inflated rafts. They also have one- to five-day trips. ~ 527 13th Street, Clarkston, WA; 208-305-1610, 888-628-3772; www. canyoncats.com.

Among the jet-boating specialists in the area is **Red Woods Outfitter**. ~ HC 2 Box 580, Pollock, ID 83547; 208-628-3673; www.redwoodsoutfitter.com. Another is **River Adventures**, who does float trips as well. ~ P.O. Box 518, Riggins, ID 83549; 208-628-3952; www.riveradventuresltd.com.

SKIING

Brundage Mountain, eight miles northwest of McCall, is located in the heart of a snow belt that brings it huge quantities of "champagne powder." With three chairlifts (including a new high-speed quad) and three surface tows, 1340 acres of terrain and an 1800-foot vertical drop, it is regarded as an intermediate mountain with several expert runs and an abundance of powder glades. There's a modern Kid's Center, a day lodge with cafeteria, a saloon, and a mountaintop restaurant in a yurt. There are full ski-school and rental facilities as well. For powder hounds who don't get enough at Brundage, guided Sno-Cat ski trips extend to two other nearby peaks, with the opportunity to stay overnight in a Mongolian yurt. Closed mid-April to July. ~ Gooselake Road, McCall; 208-634-4151, fax 208-634-4153; www.brund age.com, e-mail info@brundage.com.

> Of Payette National Forest's 2.3 million acres, only a third is accessible by road (2800 miles) and trail (2125 miles).

There's a second ski mountain at McCall, but it doesn't get anywhere near the attention that Brundage gets. Volunteers from the Payette Lakes Ski Club operate the **Little Ski Hill** where the likes of Jean Saubert, Olympic double silver medalist in 1964, first learned to ski. Located just three miles west of town, the Little Ski Hill has been in operation since 1937, a year after Sun Valley. It has vertical terrain served by surface T-bar lifts, groomed Nordic trails and a dog loop. ~ 3635 Route 55, McCall; 208-634-5691 (fax in summer).

Cross-country skiers also appreciate the roads and trails of **Ponderosa State Park** when snow blankets the ground. There are about kilometers of trails crisscrossing the park. ~ Miles Standish Road, McCall; 208-634-2164.

Ski Rentals   McCall has numerous winter equipment shops. **Home Town Sports** rents downhill, cross-country and skate skis, as well as snowboards and ice skates. ~ 300 Lenora; 208-634-2302. **Gravity Sports** offers both alpine and Nordic equipment. ~ 503 Pine Street; 208-634-8530.

GOLF

For golfers visiting this area, choices are mighty slim. **McCall Golf Course** is a 27-hole public links with varied terrain and full pro-shop facilities. ~ 1000 Reedy Lane, McCall; 208-634-7200. The **MeadowCreek Golf Resort** sports an 18-hole, par-72, 6696-yard layout. The course alternates between meadow and pine forest, while creeks and lakes present water hazards on seven holes. ~ 1 MeadowCreek Court at Route 95, New Meadows; 208-347-2555; www.meadowcreekresort.com. There are nine-hole courses in Weiser, Council and Cascade. For information on area courses, contact the **Idaho Golf Association**. ~ Boise; 208-342-4442.

RIDING STABLES

Mile High Outfitters specializes in six-day wolf education forays in the Frank Church–River of No Return Wilderness (all meals and lodging are included). ~ P.O. Box 1189, Challis, ID 83226; 208-879-4500, fax 208-879-4505; www.milehighwolf.com, e-mail info@milehighwolf.com.

Wapiti Meadow Ranch offers customized horseback rides for groups of up to four from June to late October. ~ HC 72, Cascade, ID 83611; 208-633-3217, fax 208-633-3219; www.guest ranches.com/wapiti, e-mail wapitimr@aol.com.

Meadow Creek Outfitters/Yahoo Corrals offers a variety of rides, including 90-minute, half-day and evening dinner rides. Children must be 6 years old to ride. Monday through Saturday pony rides are available. Large groups are welcome. ~ Warren Wagon Road, 2.8 miles north of McCall; 208-634-3360 (summer), 208-839-2424 (winter).

BIKING

Hundreds of miles of biking trails surround McCall, both in Payette National Forest and at local parks and ski areas. These are a few of the more popular rides (distances are one-way).

Brundage Mountain Resort (1.5 to 3 miles) has 20 miles of summer mountain-biking trails for all ability levels, served by its high-speed quad on Friday, Saturday and Sunday from July 4 through Labor Day. These single-track trails, crisscrossed by dirt roads, are the site of the Idaho state mountain biking championships on Labor Day weekend.

In an effort to bring back Idaho's native wolf population, wiped out in the 1930s, the U.S. Fish & Wildlife Service released native wolves into the Frank Church–River of No Return Wilderness Area in the 1990s.

East Fork of Lake Fork Trail (4.6 miles) begins at a Payette National Forest campground about nine miles east of McCall off Lick Creek Road. It follows the creek for a mile, climbs a ridge on a series of steep switchbacks, then levels out for three miles of single track through a pine forest.

Bear Basin Loop Ride (8.8 miles) follows gravel and dirt roads and a section of single-track trail along a ridge just west of Payette Lake. It begins on Bear Basin Road, a mile west of McCall, then follows Forest Roads 451 and 452 downhill into Warren Wagon Road, looping back uphill on a four-wheel-drive track.

Bike Rentals   There are several excellent cycle shops in McCall. **Gravity Sports** has a professionally staffed bicycle service center along with its rental department. ~ 503 Pine Street; 208-634-8530. **Home Town Sports** also has a full-service shop with a mountain-bike rental "fleet" to suit all types of riders. ~ 300 Lenora Street; 208-634-2302. During the summer, **Brundage Mountain Resort** rents mountain bikes with helmets. ~ Gooselake Road; 208-634-7462 ext. 129, 800-888-7544; www.brundage.com.

HIKING

The Hells Canyon and McCall regions offer a myriad of hiking possibilities. All distances listed for hiking trails are one way unless otherwise noted.

Snake River National Recreation Trail (27 miles) follows the Snake River through Hells Canyon from Granite Creek (with access by boat from Hells Canyon Dam, about six miles upriver) to Pittsburg Landing (accessible by Deer Creek Road from White Bird and Riggins). Hikers pass old mining sites and native petroglyphs, and wave at whitewater rafters churning past.

Seven Devils Trail (15.7 miles) penetrates the highest and most rugged mountains (up to 9393 feet) in the Hells Canyon National Recreation Area. The panoramic views to the canyon floor are sensational. The trailhead is at Windy Saddle, 17 miles from Riggins via Forest Road 517.

A perfect overnight hike for young families is to **Duck Lake** (1.5 miles), just over the Lick Creek Summit. Follow Route 48 from McCall past Little Payette Lake. This generally good gravel road winds over the summit to a developed trailhead on the left about a mile on its far side. Elevation gain is slight and the length of the walk is just far enough for youngsters to handle. The lake sits in a broad meadow and is visited by deer, elk and, of course, ducks. Bring your fishing poles.

Loon Lake Trail (15 miles) follows the meandering Secesh River, a tributary of the South Fork of the Salmon, upstream along a segment of the Idaho State Centennial Trail. The gently ascending trail begins at the Ponderosa campground on Lick Creek Road (Route 48) between McCall and Yellow Pine; it ends at the Chinook campground off Warren Wagon Road (Route 21) between McCall and Warren.

Needles Route Trail (9.5 miles) follows a long ridge of the Salmon River Mountains between Cascade and Warm Lake, providing spectacular views. This moderately strenuous and not particularly well-marked Boise National Forest hike begins off Forest Road 497 just north of Warm Lake Road (Route 22).

Indian Creek–Middle Fork–Little Loon Creek Trail (35 miles) crosses the Frank Church–River of No Return Wilderness, beginning in Boise National Forest near Yellow Pine and concluding at the Loon Creek Ranger Station in Salmon-Challis National Forest.

Transportation

CAR

West Central Idaho has two arteries. **Route 95** branches north off **Route 84**, the interstate freeway, just east of the Snake River at Payette, and runs through Weiser, Cambridge, Council, New Meadows and Riggins, where it crosses the Salmon River and continues into northern Idaho. **Route 55** begins just west of Boise and runs north through Cascade and McCall, joining Route 95 at New Meadows. Principal access to Hells Canyon is via **Route 71**, which begins off Route 95 at Cambridge and runs west to the Oregon border at Brownlee Dam.

AIR

Five major airlines fly into **Boise Airport,** the region's nearest sizable airport. See Chapter Two for more information.

There are general-aviation airports at Weiser and McCall, and smaller airstrips at Oxbow, Council, Cascade and New Meadows. Of these, McCall is considered the most important. **McCall**

Aviation (208-634-5445, 800-992-6559) runs charter service to and from the McCall Airport.

BUS

There's no transportation service through the Route 95 Hells Canyon gateway town of Cambridge; most travelers without their own vehicles will rent a 4x4 at the Boise Airport.

Boise-Winnemucca/Northwestern Stage Lines, a regional operator associated with Trailways, operates daily coach routes between McCall and Boise (southbound), McCall and Riggins, Grangeville, Lewiston and Spokane (northbound). ~ 1212 West Bannock Street, Boise; 208-336-3302; www.nwadv.com/northw.

CAR RENTALS

At the McCall Airport, **McCall Aviation** offers rentals of sedans and four-wheel-drive vehicles by the hour, day or week. ~ McCall Municipal Airport, Route 55 South; 208-634-5445, 800-992-6559.

TEN

Lewiston and the Lower Panhandle

Idaho, at its Lower Panhandle, is barely 120 miles across between its borders with Washington and Montana. At its eastern border, which is the Continental Divide, are the broad and
wild Bitterroot Mountains, and due east of Lewiston is the
Selway-Bitterroot Wilderness. This remote stretch of land almost meets the northeastern limit of the Frank Church–River
of No Return Wilderness. Lewiston, Idaho's fourth largest city, is
situated on the western boundary at the confluence of the Clearwater and Snake
rivers. Here the Snake turns west for its confluence with the Columbia River and
leaves the state.

An apparent bureaucratic anomaly has drawn the time zone boundary across
central Idaho, placing Lewiston, and all of the Panhandle, on Pacific time. In fact,
the northern and southern halves of the state have never felt close, and early in
Idaho's territorial history northern Idaho attempted to annex itself to Washington. That effort failed, but the motivation for it derives, understandably, from simi-
larities of climate and terrain between northern Idaho and Washington, and the
stark differences between the Panhandle and the Snake River Plain. As a result,
Panhandle cities and towns gravitate, both commercially and culturally—and by
proximity—toward Spokane rather than Boise.

Lewiston is Idaho's topographic low point. The Snake has dropped more than
1000 feet since Riggins, and is 2000 feet below Boise. The area is a kind of geographic and riverine terminus for the high central interior of the state; as the Snake
passes through Lewiston and leaves Idaho it carries the collected runoff of the Salmon and Clearwater rivers. Though very different in climate from the interior—
Lewiston is sometimes called Idaho's "banana belt"—the city remains intimately
connected through this water-link with the mountains.

After cutting deep through Hells Canyon, the Snake River becomes an industrial river at Lewiston. Farther inland than any other port in the West—470 miles
distant from the Pacific Ocean, the Port of Lewiston ships mostly wheat and barley, much of it grown on the Palouse Plateau north of the city. These lands are
considered to provide some of the best dry-land farming in the nation. The Palouse

is readily identified by the rounded but steeply pitched hills. Farmers here love to tell stories of their—or, more usually, their neighbors'—huge combines tipping and falling off the sides of these hills during harvest. Once you've seen the Palouse the tales are quite believable. The port also serves the enormous Potlatch Corporation sawmill and timber products plant on the banks of the Clearwater just above its confluence with the Snake.

The tributary veins of the South and Middle forks of the Clearwater River spread through all this region. Above Route 12 is the Clearwater's north fork. These streams all support important but diminished steelhead runs and attract anglers regionwide hoping for a connection with one of these powerful fighting fish. Sadly, only a few wild steelhead runs remain, and most anglers must content themselves with hatchery-run fish. Extensive runs that once followed the North Fork of the Clearwater now are stopped from reaching their historic spawning grounds by Dworshak Dam. The Dworshak National Fish Hatchery is located nearby. The fish are collected here, stripped of their eggs and milt. The fry are raised in tanks to be released below the dam. From there the smolts migrate more than 500 miles to the Pacific Ocean, returning once they mature.

The explorers Lewis and Clark, in 1805, followed the path of the Clearwater River and its tributary, the Lochsa River, on their way to the Columbia River and the Pacific Ocean. The Nez Perce occupied these lands and considered the junction of the Clearwater and Snake, and the flats that are the site of Lewiston today, to be an important meeting ground. South and east of town, between the Salmon and Clearwater rivers as they flow westward toward the Snake, is the Camas Prairie where the Nez Perce gathered in late spring to pick camas root and berries and to celebrate the new growing season.

The discovery of gold in 1860 at Pierce, in a tributary of the Clearwater River, was the catalyst that stirred the region from its relative serenity. The Union, desperate for additional revenue sources to help fund the Civil War, quickly organized the Idaho Territory in 1863. (Its first legislature met in Lewiston, 60 miles west of Pierce, before the capital was moved south to Boise.) As miners, loggers, ranchers, and farmers settled on what previously had been American Indian lands, the Nez Perce were forced onto a reservation. They did not surrender without a struggle (see "I Will Fight No More, Forever" in this chapter). The expansion of rail routes and development of hydroelectric power, both to run lumber mills and to serve upcountry lead- and silver-mining communities, contributed to the region's rapid growth thereafter.

Lewiston retains its blue-collar roots and, as one of Idaho's earliest permanent settlements, many of its fine historic buildings. Fine views can be had of the surrounding geography from Lewiston Hill—which hill that is will be obvious from anywhere in the city. This high steep bluff on the north banks of the Clearwater and Snake rivers stalled wheat commerce between Lewiston and Moscow around the turn of the 20th century—Moscow being at the heart of the Palouse—and the first good commercial road was finished in 1917. The current grade was constructed in 1975.

The University of Idaho was established in Moscow in 1889. Moscow, more than 1800 feet in elevation above Lewiston, still enjoys a mild climate. Like Lewiston, some of Idaho's finest historic buildings are here, more than enough for a day's walking tour. The Nez Perce Reservation covers 88,000 acres east of Lewiston; it is an area rich in the history of one of the West's most intriguing tribes.

Located at the confluence of the Clearwater and Snake rivers, Lewiston is an attractive town of 32,000 people, noted for its trees (hundreds of species, say urban foresters) and its mild climate. Connected via two Snake River bridges with its twin city of Clarkston, Washington, it has both

Lewiston Area

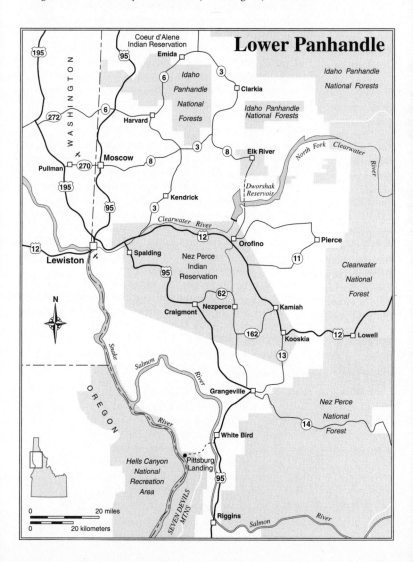

Lower Panhandle

Idaho's lowest point (740 feet) and its longest growing season (200 days).

SIGHTS

From the visitor's standpoint, Lewiston's chief virtue is as a gateway to **Hells Canyon National Recreation Area**. Jet boats depart the Lewiston-Clarkston slack water every morning for day-long and overnight excursions up the Snake to America's deepest canyon. The canyon's northern limit is about 30 miles south of Lewiston, but the area is only accessible by boat. Spectacular geology, abundant wildlife, artifacts from early settlers and prehistoric pictographs are among the attractions that await visitors.

The **Hells Canyon NRA Snake River Office** is located on the west bank of the Snake, about two and a half miles south of the Route 12 bridge that connects Lewiston and Clarkston. There are no interpretive displays here, but you'll find plenty of useful literature and park rangers to answer questions. Closed in winter. ~ P.O. Box 699, Clarkston, WA 99403; 509-758-0616, fax 509-758-1963.

Many of the area's jet-boat operators depart from **Hells Gate State Park**, four miles south of Lewiston along the Snake's east shore. There are campsites for tents and RVs. Others leave from Swallow Park on the Clarkston side of the river or from the port of Clarkston. ~ Snake River Avenue; 208-799-5015. Overnighters typically stay in guest-ranch bunkhouses below the canyon, which are provided by outfitters. See "Outdoor Adventures" for outfitters, or contact the **Lewiston Chamber of Commerce**. ~ 111 Main Street, Suite 120, Lewiston; 208-743-3531, 800-473-3543, fax 208-743-2176; www.lewistonchamber.org.

You can get a spectacular bird's-eye view of Lewiston and its two rivers from atop **Lewiston Hill** on the north side of the Clearwater. Take Route 95 to the top of the hill, 2000 feet above the city; turn off at the Vista House gift shop and follow the old Spiral Highway back down for panoramas at every switchback.

AUTHOR FAVORITE

I'm newly appreciative of the Chinese contribution to the West's development when I visit the **Lewis-Clark Center for Arts & History**, set in a historic bank building. Exhibits recall a strong late-19th- and early-20th-century Chinese presence in Lewiston. Artifacts from the old Beuk Aie Temple, built in 1890 and dedicated to the god of water, are a highlight, along with artifacts of everyday life for the predominantly Cantonese miners. Closed Sunday. ~ 415 Main Street, Lewiston; 208-792-2243, fax 208-792-2850; www.artsandhistory.org, e-mail detucker@lcsc.edu.

This route, an engineering marvel of its time, was constructed in 1917. The roundtrip drive takes less than an hour.

Lewiston has a nicely renewed **Downtown Historic District**. ~ Along Main and D streets between 5th Street and Snake River Avenue. History aficionado can learn about the city's background as a port city at the '30s art-deco **Nez Perce County Museum**, home of the Nez Perce County Historical Society. Visitors will also learn about the county's history through artifacts, photographs and interpretive signs. Closed Sunday and Monday, and from mid-December to March. ~ 0306 3rd Street, Lewiston; 208-743-2535, fax 208-743-2535.

To see the modern **Port of Lewiston**, turn west off Route 12 on 3rd Avenue North, on the north side of the Clearwater River bridge, and follow it to its end. There isn't actually a lot to see here, though—mostly massive forklifts moving containers stamped with names like Hanjin and Mitsui OSK Line.

LODGING

For visitors who plan to linger, the **Carriage House Inn** has several fully furnished guest houses available for weekly or monthly rental. ~ 504 6th Avenue, Lewiston; 208-746-4506, 800-501-4506. DELUXE.

The **Sacajawea Motor Inn** is a friendly, two-story accommodation near the Clearwater River bridge east of downtown. Its 90 rooms are comfortable and well-kept. There are some suites with whirlpools and microwave ovens. Facilities include a restaurant and lounge, an outdoor swimming pool and a hot tub, a fitness room and a coin laundry. ~ 1824 Main Street, Lewiston; 208-746-1393, 800-333-1393, fax 208-743-3620; e-mail sacajawea208@aol.com. MODERATE.

The city's finest is the **Red Lion Hotel**, on a hillside with a view toward the Clearwater River bridge. The hotel has 183 rooms, including three dozen in an all-suites wing, and executive mini-suites with microwaves and refrigerators. The city's only micro-brewery, M. J. Barleyhopper's, is in the hotel; casual meals are served in this pub, upscale cuisine at the restaurant. A swimming pool, jacuzzi and full-service athletic and racquetball club are in the suites wing. ~ 621 21st Street, Lewiston; 208-799-1000, 800-232-6730, fax 208-748-1050; e-mail lionhotel@aol.com. MODERATE TO DELUXE.

If you're looking for a clean, comfortable ma-and-pa-style motel, check out **El Rancho Motel** on the north side of the Clearwater Bridge. Among the two dozen rooms (all with TVs, refrigerators, microwaves and phones) are kitchen units and non-smoking rooms. El Rancho has a heated swimming pool, and pets are welcome. ~ 2240 3rd Avenue, North Lewiston; 208-743-8517, fax 208-798-1545. BUDGET.

DINING

For cheap eats in Lewiston, the **Anytime Tavern and Grill** offers giant-size hamburgers. Open 24 hours daily, it has six tables, a dozen barstools and an outdoor beer garden. ~ 1350 Main Street, Lewiston; 208-746-6230. BUDGET.

It's nothing fancy, but the **Golden Dragon** serves a variety of Chinese and American dishes. ~ 2402 North and South Highway, Lewiston; 208-743-1952. BUDGET TO MODERATE.

HIDDEN ►

There's nothing exceptional about the outward appearance of **Effie's Tavern**, a burger and beer joint at the working end of Lewiston's Main Street. But Effie's has turned the prosaic hamburger and fries into a test of courage and, finally, stamina. Can you manage a one-pound, plate-sized hamburger? How about a double-patty double-cheese? Want an order of fries to accompany your burger? Does it help to know that half of a small order is elsewhere considered quite adequate? The best picture on the wall shows a small boy in a high chair with a burger twice the size of his head. ~ 1120 Main Street, Lewiston; 208-746-1889. MODERATE.

For upscale dining in downtown Lewiston, try **Jonathan's**. A formal menu of steak and seafood, Continental and Cajun specialties is served; there's a small casual lounge and patio seating. Closed Sunday. ~ 1516 Main Street, Lewiston; 208-746-3438. MODERATE TO ULTRA-DELUXE.

Zany Graze is the place to head for light-hearted family fun. One of several local eateries owned by the Happy Day Corp., Zany's perpetuates a '50s diner theme in its cuisine and decor; expect good service and hearty American food. ~ 2006 19th Avenue, Lewiston; 208-746-8131, fax 208-746-1554. MODERATE TO DELUXE.

SHOPPING

The **Lewis-Clark State College Bookstore** has an extensive collection of books by regional authors and about the Pacific Northwest. Closed weekends. ~ 9th Avenue and 4th Street, Lewiston; 208-792-2242. For the city's best selection of topographic and state maps, visit **Kling's Stationers**. ~ 704 Main Street, Lewiston; 208-743-8501.

AUTHOR FAVORITE

Urban renewal in Lewiston's old town historical district has made it perhaps the busiest and most interesting place to shop in the region. Check out **Morgans' Alley**, 15 businesses, including gift, craft and antique stores and restaurants, are contained in four early-20th-century buildings linked by brick arches, stairways and passageways. ~ 301 Main Street, Lewiston; 208-750-0000.

Despite its working-class aura, Lewiston has an active cultural life. **NIGHTLIFE**
The **Lewis-Clark State College Silverthorne Series** provides the
area with professional symphony, opera, dance and theater from
September through May. ~ 415 Main Street, Lewiston; 208-792-
2243, fax 208-792-2850. The **Lewiston Civic Theater** is a community stage group offering popular productions. ~ 805 6th
Avenue, Lewiston; phone/fax 208-746-3401.

Pickings are slim for standard nightlife. Try **The Alibi** for
karaoke Sunday through Thursday and live music Friday and
Saturday. Occasional cover. ~ 1702 Main Street; 208-743-0317.
Boomers features occasional live rock music. Cover. ~ 0301 2nd
Street; 208-746-2005. **M. J. Barleyhopper's**, a microbrewery and
pub, is a good place to find a designer draft and a conversation.
~ Red Lion Inn, 621 21st Street, Lewiston; 208-799-1000.

Four miles east of Lewiston, the fun never stops at the **Clearwater River Casino**. Open 24 hours daily, this low-key casino has
more than 400 video slot machines and a 180-seat bingo parlor.
~ Route 95 East, Lewiston; 208-746-0723; www.crcasino.com.

HELLS GATE STATE PARK 🏃 🚵 🏇 ⛵ 🚤 🛥️ 🛶 Snake **PARKS**
River frontage makes this refuge a prime playground for Lewis-
ton-area residents. It's also a great departure point for boat excursions up the river into Hells Canyon, 30 miles south. There is
a designated beach in the day-use area. Fishing is especially popular when steelhead run in September and December. Facilities include picnic tables, restrooms, marina, a playground and horse
trails. Day-use fee, $4. ~ Four miles south of Lewiston at the end
of Snake River Avenue; 208-799-5015, fax 208-799-5187; e-mail
jfeider@idpr.state.id.us.

▲ There are 64 RV sites with hookups and 29 tent sites; $21
to $23 per night for RV hookups, $17 for tents.

▼▼▼▼▼▼▼▼▼▼▼
North of Lewiston, the undulating grainfields of the
rolling Palouse Hills extend for mile after mile through **Moscow and the**
north-central Idaho and across the state border in **Palouse Hills**
southeastern Washington. Besides wheat, barley and
alfalfa, farmers here produce more dry peas and lentils than in
any other part of the United States—about 500 million pounds
annually. The heart of the Palouse is the university town of
Moscow, named not for the Russian capital but for a village in
Pennsylvania.

Located just 28 miles north of Lewiston via Route 95, **Moscow** **SIGHTS**
(pronounced not "MOS-cow" but "MOS-koh") is home of the **University of Idaho** (UI). This cultured town forms half of the Palouse
Country's college row. UI students (sports teams are nicknamed
"Vandals," which should not be taken as a reflection on student

behavior) share many activities, including social and athletic events, with students from Washington State University (WSU), just ten miles across the state border in Pullman. Before Idaho raised its legal drinking age from 19 to 21 a few years ago, Moscow was the place for WSU students to spend their Friday and Saturday nights.

Of particular interest on the 450-acre UI campus are the ASUI Kibbie Dome Activity Center, a 17,500-seat indoor stadium and arena on Perimeter Drive at Rayburn Street; Shattuck Arboretum, which offers picnicking among more than 200 kinds of vegetation on Nez Perce Drive; and geology displays at the Department of Mining Engineering and Metallurgy. The UI Information Center (208-885-6111, fax 208-885-6971) is on campus at 645 West Pullman Road, a few blocks west of the city center.

Arterial highways circumvent Moscow's Main Street, which has thus remained quaint and friendly to pedestrians and buskers. The **Moscow Chamber of Commerce** is a good source of information. Closed Saturday and Sunday. ~ 411 South Main Street, Moscow; 208-882-1800, 800-380-1801; www.moscowchamber. com, e-mail chamber@moscowchamber.com.

Restaurants and bars, small shops, bookstores and art galleries like the **Prichard Art Gallery** attract students and other townspeople alike. Hours vary; call ahead. ~ 414/416 South Main Street, Moscow; 208-885-3586, fax 208-885-3622; www.art. uidaho.edu/gallery, e-mail artgallery@uidaho.edu.

The **McConnell Mansion**, three blocks east of Main, gives a glimpse of what Moscow was like a century ago. Built in 1886 by an Idaho governor, it recalls a late-Victorian lifestyle in its furnishings and decor. Revolving exhibits feature everything from black-and-white photos of families who lived here to displays of Victorian undergarments. The Latah County Historical Society offers tours of downtown Moscow. Closed Sunday and Monday. ~ 110 South Adams Street, Moscow; 208-882-1004, fax 208-882-0759; users.moscow.com/lchs, e-mail lchlibrary@moscow.com.

The **Idaho Forest Fire Museum** features displays of fire prevention and firefighting tools, as well as educational exhibits about the great burns of 1910 and the role of fire in Idaho forests. You'll also find what is claimed to be one of the world's largest collections of Smokey the Bear memorabilia. Closed Sunday. ~ 310 North Main Street, Moscow; 208-882-4767, fax 208-882-0373; www.woodlandgifts.com, e-mail woodland@woodlandgifts.com.

Horse lovers and history buffs won't want to miss the **Appaloosa Museum and Heritage Center**, three miles west of Moscow at the Washington state line. Exhibits describe the evolution of the appaloosa, its importance to the Nez Perce and its role today. Closed Sunday and Monday. ~ 2720 West Pullman Road; 208-882-5578 ext. 279; www.appaloosamuseum.org, e-mail museum@appaloosa.com.

Proceed north on Route 95 toward Coeur d'Alene, and you'll climb to **Mary Minerva McCroskey State Park**, on the Latah– Benewah county line. There are no signs announcing the primitive park, but turn left at a sign for "Skyline Drive" and you'll encounter miles of spectacular views from an unpaved road (not maintained in winter). ~ 208-666-1308, fax 208-686-3003; e-mail hey@idpr.state.id.us.

◄ *HIDDEN*

If you turn east off 95 onto Route 6 at the historic company lumber town of Potlatch, you'll find yourself on the **White Pine Scenic Route**, a marvelous wooded drive through the Idaho Panhandle National Forests to St. Maries. Farther southeast, via Clarkia on Route 3, is the **Emerald Creek Garnet Area**, one of only two places in the world (the other is India) where star garnets are found. Because the area is on National Forest land, anyone is welcome to dig for the precious stones between Memorial Day and Labor Day (for a fee). Properly equipped diggers (rental equipment available) can take Forest Road 447 eight miles off the highway, then hike another half-mile to the garnet site. St. Joe Ranger

◄ *HIDDEN*

Moscow & the Palouse Hills

District provides information. Closed Wednesday and Thursday.
~ P.O. Box 407, St. Maries, ID 83861; 208-245-2531, fax 208-245-6052; www.fs.fed.us/ipnf, e-mail slgore@fs.fed.us.

LODGING   In Moscow, the top accommodation is the **University Inn**, a Best
Western property two miles from downtown near the west end
of the University of Idaho campus. With a pool, a sauna, land-
scaped courtyard, two restaurants and a lounge, it offers more
than enough to guests in its 173 rooms; there are refrigerators and
microwaves in every room. ~ 1516 Pullman Road, Moscow; 208-882-0550, 800-325-8765, fax 208-883-3056; www.uinnmos
cow.com. DELUXE.

An alternative is the **Palouse Inn**, a former Motel 6 near downtown and the university. A continental breakfast is included with
its 110 comfortable rooms, all of which have phones and cable
TV; an outdoor swimming pool is open during warm weather. ~
101 Baker Street, Moscow; 208-882-5511, 888-882-5511, fax
208-882-9475; www.palouseinn.com. BUDGET.

DINING   For excellent Mexican food, stop by **El Mercado**. The menu features everyday south-of-the-border fare, daily specials such as
arroz con camarones, veggie options (spinach enchiladas, for instance) and superb margaritas. ~ Eastside Marketplace, 1420 South
Blaine Street, Moscow; 208-883-1169. BUDGET TO MODERATE.

The casual atmosphere and tasty pizzas at **Gambino's Italian
Restaurant** draw students and families alike. The menu includes
traditional Italian fare such as manicotti, chicken cacciatore and
eggplant parmesan. You'll also find a variety of microbrews on
tap. ~ 308 West 6th Street, Moscow; 208-882-4545. MODERATE.

The **Moscow Food Co-op** is a great place to pick up fresh,
organic picnic supplies. The bakery offers seven to ten different
kinds of bread daily, and on Friday night they serve up imaginative pizzas hot out of the oven (get there early—slices have been
known to sell out by 6:30!). ~ 221 East 3rd Street, Moscow; 208-882-8537, fax 208-882-8082; www.moscowfood.coop. BUDGET
TO MODERATE.

◆◆◆

A SLICE OF COUNTRY LIVING

Six miles out of Moscow, bird lovers flock to **Whispering Pines**,
where they can enjoy a hearty country breakfast with their downy
woodpeckers and mountain chickadees. The antique-filled accommodations range from an apartment (with satellite tv and air conditioning) to single bedrooms, but all offer views of the surrounding
hills and Ponderosa pines. ~ 1030 Crumarine Loop, Moscow; 208-882-8344, fax 208-883-8446. MODERATE TO DELUXE.

Outside Moscow, a good place to stop for a bite on Route 3 is the **Antelope Inn** beside the Potlatch River. Open daily for lunch and dinner, the inn serves hamburgers and cheeseburgers. ~ 707 East Main Street, Kendrick; 208-289-5771. BUDGET.

With more than 50 stores, the **Palouse Empire Mall**, about two **SHOPPING** miles west of downtown on Pullman Road, is the region's largest shopping center. For literature, stop by **Book People of Moscow**. ~ 521 South Main Street, Moscow; 208-882-7957; www.book people.net.

Nightlife in Moscow, though smaller than Lewiston, benefits from **NIGHTLIFE** its campus influence. The **Hartung Theatre**, on the University of Idaho campus, presents a mix of drama, comedy and musicals during the school year; in summer, the **Idaho Repertory** makes its home for five weeks in this 419-seat theater. The ticket office is closed on Saturday and Sunday. ~ 6th Street and Stadium Road, Moscow; 208-885-6465 (information), 208-885-7212 (tickets).

Among student-oriented pubs in Moscow, **John's Alley** is a favorite. Occasional cover. ~ 114 East 6th Street, Moscow; 208-883-7662. Check local newspapers as well as bulletin boards along Main Street to see who has live music and when.

MARY MINERVA MCCROSKEY STATE PARK 🚶 🐎 🚵 A wind- **PARKS** ing, 23-mile dirt and gravel road along a wooded ridgetop is the focus of this 5300-acre park, which is surprising for its lack of ◄ *HIDDEN* development. Hiking, cross-country skiing and nature walking are the main pursuits. Facilities include four picnic sites with tables and pit toilets. ~ Take Route 95 from Moscow 26 miles north to Skyline Drive, which turns left (west) off the highway just before the Latah–Benewah county line. Note that the road is not maintained for winter travel. There is no sign announcing the park; 208-666-1308, fax 208-686-3003; e-mail hey@idpr.state.id.us.

▲ No formal sites, but primitive camping is permitted anywhere. No fee; open year-round.

The Clearwater River dominates north-central Idaho, rising on the crest of the Bitterroot Mountains at the Montana border and continuing in four major **Clearwater Valley** forks to its confluence with the Snake at Lewiston. Often overshadowed by the Salmon River to its south, the Clearwater is nevertheless a stream of major importance. Its rich history made it the traditional heart of Nez Perce lands, a corridor for the Lewis and Clark expedition, and a focus of activity for 19th-century miners and 20th-century loggers.

The best way to explore the basin is via Route 12, which spans north-central Idaho from west to east. From Lewiston, the highway follows the Clearwater River upstream for 93 miles to Lowell. It then turns up the Lochsa River—a designated "wild and scenic river corridor"—to Lolo Pass, on the Rockies' crest.

SIGHTS

For much of its distance, Route 12 parallels the **Lolo Trail**, an ancient American Indian trade and hunting route also followed by explorers Lewis and Clark on their way west in 1805 and on their return in 1806. Roadside historical markers describe many points of interest; for more information, contact Clearwater National Forest. ~ 12730 Route 12, Orofino; 208-476-4541, fax 208-476-8329.

(Note: Forest Road 500 approximates the route of the Lolo Trail, but this is a primitive dirt road with virtually no facilities en route. It takes a sturdy four-wheel-drive vehicle about two days to cover its 90 miles.)

Orofino (see "Scenic Drive") is the gateway to the **Dworshak Dam** project, completed in 1973 on the North Fork of the Clearwater River. The 717-foot-high dam is the highest straight-axis, concrete gravity dam in the United States and the third highest of any type. Neither convex nor concave, but straight from abutment to abutment, the dam is an impressive structure. It creates 54-mile-long **Dworshak Reservoir**, on the western shore of which lies Dworshak State Park. Movies about the Dworshak Dam are offered at its **visitors center**, located at the top of the dam six miles west of Orofino. ~ Dworshak Dam Road, Ahsahka; 208-476-1255, fax 208-476-1262; www.nww.usace.army.mil/corps outdoors/dwa, e-mail dworshak@usace.army.mil.

Below the dam, at the foot of the North Fork bridge near the main Clearwater, **Dworshak National Fish Hatchery** is one of the world's largest steelhead trout and spring chinook salmon hatcheries. Each year, its 126 environmentally controlled outdoor ponds produce about two and a half million steelhead fry and up to one million spring chinook salmon. There are displays, self-guided tours and a viewing balcony for visitors. ~ Route 7, three miles west of Orofino; 208-476-4591, fax 208-476-3252; dworshak. fws.gov, e-mail dworshak@fws.gov.

From here, taking Route 12 south to Grangeville will put you on the **Northwest Passage Scenic Byway**, the route Lewis and Clark traversed during their search for the Northwest Passage. (See the "Scenic Drive" for more information.)

Along the way, Route 12 turns east at Kooskia and follows the Clearwater to Lowell, where the wild Lochsa and Selway rivers join to form the Middle Fork. There are few services from here to Lolo Pass on the Montana border, although numerous fine U.S. Forest Service campsites are located along both the Lochsa and (especially) the Selway. Before crossing into Montana, stop to learn about human and natural history at the **Powell Rangers**

Station, 12 miles west of Lolo Pass on Route 12. ~ 208-942-3113, fax 208-942-3311.

Orofino's best is the **Konkolville Motel** at the east end of the timber town, three miles from the Clearwater bridge. The two-story inn is prepared for anglers: it has its own fish-cleaning house! All 40 rooms have refrigerators and microwaves; all guests have access to a swimming pool, hot tub and coin laundry. You can grill your own steak dinner (all ingredients provided) for an extra fee. ~ 2000 Konkolville Road, Orofino; 208-476-5584, 800-616-1964, fax 208-476-3268; www.konkolvillemotel.com, e-mail konkol villemotel@clearwater.net. BUDGET.

The **Clearwater 12 Motel** isn't fancy, but it has everything the casual traveler needs, including a continental breakfast. The two-story motel has 29 rooms with cable TV, including a pair of efficiency units. ~ Route 12 at Cedar Street, Kamiah; 208-935-2671, 800-935-2671, fax 208-935-0378. BUDGET.

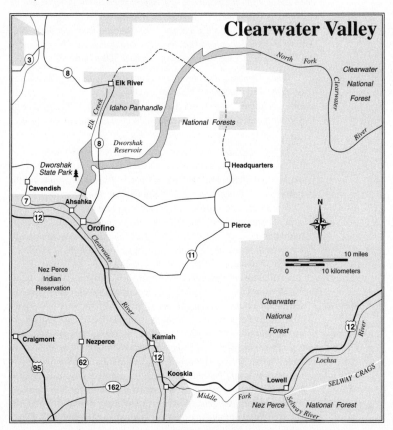

Clearwater Valley

Northwest Passage Scenic Byway

Beginning about ten miles east of Lewiston on Route 12 and continuing on Route 13 to Grangeville, the 191-mile Northwest Passage Scenic Byway essentially follows the Clearwater River, tracing Lewis and Clark's attempt to locate the Northwest Passage. The segment outlined here stretches 56 miles through bucolic prairielands, surrounded by lofty canyon walls that are a constant reminder you're in a valley. The drive itself takes about an hour, but you'll want to stop off at a number of sights for a look-see.

OROFINO Start off in the logging town of Orofino ("fine gold" in Spanish), 40 miles upstream from Lewiston on the Nez Perce Indian Reservation. With about 2800 people, this is the largest community along Route 12 in Idaho. Its **Clearwater Historical Society Museum** displays pioneer artifacts, such as old black-and-white photos from the early 20th century, antique dishes, and cooking and farming utensils. Closed Sunday and Monday. ~ 315 College Avenue, Orofino; 208-476-5033.

KAMIAH From Orofino, the byway proceeds up the gentle Clearwater River Valley. The citizens of Kamiah, responding to economic disaster when a big lumber mill closed its doors in the early 1980s, gave their downtown business district a Victorian-West facelift to attract tourism.

Nestled on the Middle Fork of the Clearwater River, just off the Lolo Pass Highway (Route 12), the **Reflections Inn** is near horseback riding, river rafting, hiking, fishing and other outdoor pursuits. There are seven rooms, each with homey decor and a private bathroom. Guests share a full gourmet breakfast, a kitchenette off a common room, and an outdoor hot tub and fire pit. ~ HCR-75, Box 32, Kooskia; 208-926-0855, fax 208-926-7860; www.reflectionsinn.com, e-mail info@reflectionsinn.com. MODERATE.

HIDDEN ▶ Beyond Lowell and near the head of the Lochsa drainage, the old-timey **Lochsa Lodge Resort** is a low-key favorite among locals. Accommodations are in ten simple log cabins and eight motel rooms set on the spacious grounds, which include a log-hewn play-and-swing set for kids. About half of the cabins have private baths; the others share showers and bathrooms in the central utility building. Fishing for cutthroat trout is reputed to be excellent, and there are many hikes in the surrounding mountains and wilderness areas. Open every day of the year, the Nordic skiing at nearby Lolo Pass is great. ~ Milepost 163, Route

It's certainly worth a few minutes to admire the work put into the city hall, fire station, library and virtually every privately owned building along a three-block stretch. On the western edge of town, keep an eye out for the sign marking Lewis and Clark's 1806 camp site.

HEART OF THE MONSTER   Two miles southeast of Kamiah, Nez Perce National Historical Park markers indicate the Heart of the Monster site where, according to tribal legend, Coyote created the Nez Perce people by squeezing drops of blood from the monster's "heart," a mound of basalt that still stands at the site.

KOOSKIA   Not far south is Kooskia (pronounced "KOOS-kee"), located at the junction of the Middle and South forks of the Clearwater River. Quench your thirst at the sarsaparilla bar of the 1912 **Victorian Opera Theatre** (Route 13), which hosts dramatic and musical performances year-round. Then follow the signs two miles southeast to the **Kooskia National Fish Hatchery**, which raises about 600,000 chinook salmon a year. The best time to visit is in May and June. ~ Clear Creek Road; 208-926-4272. From here, the Scenic Byway climbs to Grangeville via Route 13, offering views of the Camas Prairie and the South Fork canyon.

12, Powell; phone/fax 208-942-3405; www.lochsalodge.com. MODERATE.

DINING

Outside of the two main cities, you can't go wrong in the Clearwater valley at the **Ponderosa Restaurant**. This is hearty meat-and-potatoes food for hard-working loggers, who may finish up the night at the Ponderosa's Brass Rail lounge. ~ 220 Michigan Avenue, Orofino; 208-476-4818. DELUXE.

The **Kamiah Hotel Bar and Grill** is a fixture among the false facades on Kamiah's 1890s main street. Located a block off Route 12, it serves stea, seafood and pasta upstairs; its downstairs lounge has a pool table and occasionally presents live dance bands. ~ 4th and Idaho streets, Kamiah; 208-935-0960. DELUXE.

◄ HIDDEN

The windows of the **Lochsa Lodge Restaurant** look out on the crowns of two steep timbered mountains rising across the Lochsa River. The ceiling is vaulted with log beams, and bear skins, antlers and an elk skull decorate the log walls. An upright piano in one corner speaks of long winter evenings passed in community songfests, just as the flat-stone fireplace and wood stove tell of cozy winter warmth. The mountain view is that much better from tables on the wooden dining patio, comfortable usually to mid-September. Though the menu is not adventuresome—steaks, shrimp and chicken for dinner, burgers for lunch, eggs and potatoes for breakfast—it's prepared to your liking. There's a lounge and tavern here for those who crave a bit of nightlife. ~ Milepost 163, Route 12, Powell; phone/fax 208-942-3405; www.lochsa lodge.com. MODERATE TO DELUXE.

SHOPPING   For authentic Nez Perce Indian arts and crafts, such as rawhide bags and beadwork, visit **White Eagle's**. Closed weekends. ~ 3405 Route 12, Orofino; 208-476-7753.

PARKS   **CLEARWATER NATIONAL FOREST** 🏃 ⚓ 🎣 Extending west from the Bitterroot Range on the Montana border and down the tributary systems of the Lochsa River and the North Fork of the Clearwater River (with an additional parcel in the Palouse Hills), this 1.8-million-acre national forest encompasses much of the Idaho that explorers Lewis and Clark first saw nearly 200 years ago. The Lewis and Clark National Historic Trail along the primitive Lolo Motorway more or less parallels Route 12, the Lewis and Clark Highway. There are 1700 miles of hiking trails in the forest, which includes a portion of the Selway-Bitterroot Wilderness south of the Lochsa. Well-known for its elk herds, the forest has many other big-game animals, from black bear to mountain lions. There's swimming at Laird Park (on the Palouse River near Harvard) and isolated small mountain lakes. Cutthroat, brook and rainbow trout and mountain whitefish are native to the streams. Facilities include picnic tables, restrooms and a resort with a store, restaurant and lodging (at Powell, near Lolo Pass). Lolo Pass also has a visitors center. ~ Routes 6 and 8 northeast of Moscow, Route 11 east of Orofino and Route 12 east of Kooskia are the principle access highways. To reach Wilderness Gateway Campground, exit Route 12 at Mile Marker 123, about 50 miles east of Kooskia. The campground is right off the road. To reach Kelly Forks Campground, take Route 11 south of Pierce for one mile, turn onto Forest Service Road 250 and follow it for approximately 60 miles; 208-476-4541, fax 208-476-8329; www. fs.fed.us/r1/clearwater.

▲ There are 324 RV/tent sites, six for RVs only (no hookups) plus 26 for tents only at 21 campgrounds. Seasons vary, but most are open late May through September; $5 to $15 per night. A particularly good campground for flyfishing enthusiasts is Kelly Forks Campground, with 14 RV/tent sites; $7 per night. Wilderness Gateway Campground, with a playground perfect if you're traveling with kids, has 89 RV/tent sites; $8 per night.

I Will Fight No More, Forever

According to Nez Perce legend, the ancient hero Coyote slew and dismembered a monster and flung its body parts to the four winds. The different tribes of the West sprang up in all directions, but none in the land where Coyote stood. Realizing this, Coyote squeezed the blood from the monster's heart, thereby giving birth to the Nee-me-poo, "The People." History has proven them to be a people with tremendous heart.

Named *nez percé*, "pierced nose," by French Canadian fur trappers—erroneously, because only a few young men had shells in their nose—the Nee-me-poo lived for centuries in the valleys of the Clearwater and Snake rivers and their tributaries. They fished, hunted and harvested edible roots and berries. The tribe's mobility and lifestyle changed in the early 1700s with their acquisition of horses (now known as appaloosas), which they successfully bred, but they remained gracious and peaceful, as the Lewis and Clark expedition a century later would testify.

When Christian missionaries arrived in the 1830s in advance of later westward expansion, many Nez Perce adopted the white man's religion and culture. Two tribal factions emerged. Pro-American Christians acquiesced to the growing U.S. territorial presence. The discovery of gold on Nez Perce land in 1860, however, ended peaceful relations as floods of miners poured in, killing game and making gold claims on tribal lands. A new treaty was written, restricting the tribe to a reservation only one-tenth the size of the traditional lands.

A "non-treaty" faction led by young Chief Joseph of Oregon's Wallowa Valley resisted being moved onto the new reservation. Although tribe members were philosophically opposed to violence, when attempts were made to forcibly relocate them, they struck back, delivering a crushing defeat to U.S. cavalry forces near White Bird, Idaho, in June 1877. Joseph's 850 Nez Perce renegades were then pursued across Idaho, Wyoming and Montana before being captured four months later, just 40 miles short of Canadian refuge. "I will fight no more, forever," Joseph said. He and those with him were taken to Oklahoma for eight years before they were allowed to return to the Northwest; they were never permitted to return to the Wallowa Valley.

Idaho's Nez Perce have been a self-governing tribe under U.S. law since 1948. **Nez Perce National Historical Park**, established in 1965, now encompasses 38 separate sites, 29 of them in Idaho and the remainder in Oregon, Washington and Montana. Visitors who wish to tour the sites should start at the park headquarters and **visitors center**, on Route 95 about 11 miles east of Lewiston. Other sites of interest include the **White Bird Battlefield**, 10 to 15 miles south of Grangeville; the purported location of the **Heart of the Monster** myth, three miles south of Kamiah; and the **Lolo Trail**, followed by the fleeing non-treaty Nez Perce in 1877.

DWORSHAK STATE PARK 🛶 🚤 🚣 ⚓ This 1300-acre park is spread along the western shore of serpentine, 54-mile-long Dworshak Reservoir, created by the 1973 damming of the North Fork of the Clearwater River. (At 717 feet, Dworshak Dam is the largest dam ever constructed by the U.S. Army Corp of Engineers.) Idaho's most modern group retreat is at Three Meadows, where a lodge (with kitchen facilities) and cabins accommodate groups of up to 100. Swimming is good at the beach at Freeman Creek campground. The reservoir has record bass, kokanee and trout; a fish cleaning station is available. Facilities include picnic shelter, restrooms, amphitheater and a playground. Day-use fee, $4. ~ Located 24 miles north of Orofino by road, via Route P1 through Cavendish; or six miles north of Ahsahka by boat from Dworshak Dam; 208-476-5994, fax 208-476-7225.

▲ There are 46 RV/tent sites with hookups, 25 tent-only sites, plus group sites, open first weekend in April to October 1; $12 per night.

▼▼▼▼▼▼▼▼▼▼▼▼▼▼▼

Grangeville and the Camas Prairie

In the days before the arrival of the white man, Nez Perce Indians harvested the bulb of the camas lily, a starchy staple of their traditional diet, in the broad plain stretching between the Salmon and Clearwater rivers. Today this area, known to modern travelers as the Camas Prairie, is planted principally with grain.

SIGHTS

The population center hereabouts is **Grangeville**. The town of 3200 is the seat of Idaho County, which stretches from Oregon to Montana and encompasses 5.4 million acres, much of it wilderness. It is a lumber and agricultural center and an outfitting hub for trips into the Selway-Bitterroot, Frank Church–River of No Return and Gospel Hump wilderness areas of the Nez Perce National Forest.

It's ten highway miles from Grangeville to the apex of 4245-foot **White Bird Hill**, and eight miles of continual downhill grade on the south side. About halfway down the descent, at a panoramic overview, a Nez Perce National Historical Park display describes the initial battle of the 1877 Nez Perce war. The Indians routed two cavalry companies on the rambling plains below this viewpoint, but four months later the Nez Perce were forever subjugated.

Cottonwoods hang over White Bird Creek as it flows through the pretty village of White Bird, 3000 feet below the hill's summit. The creek enters the Salmon River about a mile from the hamlet. Just upriver, Forest Road 493—often too wet or icy for anything but four-wheel-drive vehicles—provides Idaho's only road access to the heart of Hells Canyon. The winding, 17-mile climb and descent to **Pittsburg Landing**, on the Snake River, is appreciated by whitewater rafters (many of whom take out here after the frightening 32-mile run from Hells Canyon Dam) and backpackers (who can begin or end their trek on the Snake River National Recreation Trail here). See Chapter Nine for rafting and camping information in Pittsburg Landing.

Northwest of Grangeville, Route 95 cuts directly across the Camas Prairie toward Lewiston. A worthwhile side trip at Cottonwood is the Benedictine **Monastery of St. Gertrude**, high atop a hill overlooking the prairie below. The building is easily visible from Route 95, two and a half miles away. Its striking twin 97-foot towers rise above the monastery, which was built of blue porphyry quarried from a nearby hill. Built in 1925, it now houses 60 Benedictine sisters. The chapel, whose high, hand-carved altar was constructed without the use of a single nail, is open to visitors. ~ Keuterville Road, Cottonwood; 208-962-3224, fax 208-962-7212; www.rc.net/boise/st_gertrude. Also open is the **Historical Museum at St. Gertrude**, which displays a potpourri of religious, Nez Perce and pioneer artifacts and quirky personal collections of the sisters. The Rhoades Emmanuel Memorial has Asian and European artifacts, some of which date to the 14th century. Closed Sunday and Monday. ~ 208-962-7123, fax 208-962-8647; www.historical museumatstgertrude.com, e-mail museum@velocitus.net.

◄ HIDDEN

Northwest about 20 miles, just outside the town of Winchester, **Winchester Lake State Park** attracts lovers of fishing and camping by summer, cross-country skiing by winter. ~ Winchester Road; 208-924-7563, fax 208-924-5941.

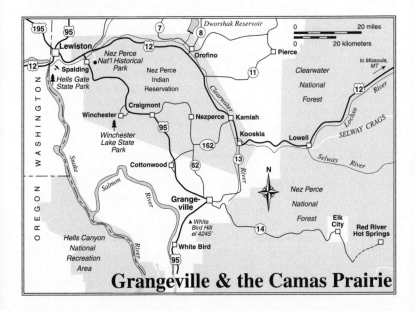

Grangeville & the Camas Prairie

Beyond Winchester, Route 95 winds through forests and canyons for about 30 miles to the **Nez Perce National Historical Park Visitors Center**. A film and museum exhibits provide an orientation to the park's 38 sites in four states, most of which are in Idaho. Most of the sites are related to the 1877 war between the Nez Perce and the U.S. cavalry. The visitors center is on a hill overlooking the Clearwater River 11 miles east of Lewiston. ~ Route 95, Spalding; 208-843-2261 ext. 199, fax 208-843-2001; www.nps.gov/nepe.

LODGING

Set back from the highway on the west end of town, the **Elkhorn Lodge** is an older inn that has been nicely remodeled. You'll recognize the buildings by their curved burgundy and gray awnings. The rooms inside are not especially large, but they are clean and airy and have in-room coffee. And there are three kitchenettes. If you prefer a bath to a shower, be sure to ask, as some of the rooms have showers only. ~ 822 Southwest 1st Street, Grangeville; 208-983-1500. BUDGET.

HIDDEN ▶

Two hours' east of Grangeville, surrounded by the forests of Selway-Bitterroot and Frank Church–River of No Return wilderness areas, are the four modern and five rustic guest cabins of **Red River Hot Springs**. Built around a pioneer spa that pours from a mountainside spring with sulfurless 120°F waters, the little resort has a steamy pool, a sauna and hot tubs. ~ Red River Hot Springs, Elk City; 208-842-2589. DELUXE.

Among the many fine B&B homes in north-central Idaho is **Mariel's Bed and Breakfast**, 20 miles north of Grangeville off Route 95. Located on a 300-acre farm with fine views across the Camas Prairie, it boasts three rooms (two of which share a bath) in a one-story farmhouse and four rooms (with private baths) in a two-story addition. Rooms have queen-size or single beds, and each is decorated differently. There's a hot tub and a large common room. No smoking is permitted indoors; children are very welcome. ~ Meadow Creek Road, Cottonwood; 208-962-5927. MODERATE.

DINING

The family-run **Palenque Mexican Restaurant** serves a varied menu of authentic Mexican dishes, including *sopitos* and flautas along with tacos, fajitas, enchiladas, burritos and chimichangas, many of them with seafood. ~ 711 West Main Street, Grangeville; 208-983-1335, fax 208-983-1710. MODERATE.

Oscar's may be Grangeville's nicest dinner house. Tack and old farm implements decorate the high walls, interspersed with antique photographs. Above the entry are the fenders and grill of a 1920s vintage car. Dinner includes steaks, seafood and prime rib. Variously embellished burgers and sandwiches dominate lunch. And as if to prove that gourmet coffees have seeped into all parts of the Northwest, you can choose espresso, latte, cappuccino and even Italian sodas. ~ 101 East Main Street, Grangeville; 208-983-2106. MODERATE.

Steak, prime rib and seafood are the specialties of the "haus" at the **Country Haus Restaurant**. A family-style restaurant whose decor pays tribute to the influence of Swiss immigrants in the Camas Prairie, the Country Haus serves three hearty meals a day. ~ 407 Foster Street, Cottonwood; 208-962-3391. BUDGET TO MODERATE.

If you're an equestrian looking for the finest for your horse, don't fail to stop at the **Ray Holes Saddle Company**. Holes' custom riding and pack saddles have been renowned since the 1930s. But don't be surprised if you have to wait a year or more for your order to be filled: There are hundreds of others in line ahead of you. Visitors are welcome to tour the workshop. Closed Sunday. ~ 213 West Main Street, Grangeville; 208-983-1460, 800-527-4526, fax 208-983-1462.

SHOPPING

Grangeville is the home of the Ray Holes saddle, one of the most venerated names in Western horsemanship.

A good selection of USGS maps, as well as new and used books and Idaho gift items, can be found at **The Book Shoppe**. Closed Sunday. ~ 227 West Main Street, Grangeville; 208-983-1248.

NEZ PERCE NATIONAL FOREST 🏃 🚣 🛥 ⤵ One complete federal wilderness area (Gospel Hump) and parts of three others (Selway-Bitterroot, Frank Church–River of No Return and Hells Canyon)—together comprising 1 million acres—make this rugged, 2.2-million-acre national forest one of Idaho's least accessible. Stretching across the middle Panhandle from Montana to Oregon in a belt broken only by the Route 95 corridor through Riggins, it's noted for its deep canyons, its fall steelhead runs, and its Nez Perce and early gold-mining history. It's bordered on the south by the main Salmon River, on the west by Hells Canyon of the Snake River; the Selway and South Fork of the Clearwater River are other major streams. This area's rivers are noted for their annual late-fall run of steelhead trout. Facilities include picnic tables and restrooms. ~ Route 14 east of Grangeville provides the best road access, serving the forest communities of Elk City and Red River Hot Springs. Another primary route is Forest Service Road 223 up the Selway River from Lowell, on Route 12. To reach Red River Campground, take Route 14 out of Grangeville and follow it to Mile Marker 46. When the road forks, bear right and go 14.5 miles to the ranger station, where the road forks again. Bear left toward Red River Hot Springs and continue five miles to the campground. To reach Wildhorse Campground, turn south off Route 14 between Mile Markers 42 and 43 onto

PARKS

Crooked River Road. Past the town of Orogrande, when the road forks, bear right onto Forest Service Road 2331. At the top of the hill, turn right and go two miles to Wildhorse Lake. The campground is one-half mile beyond the lake; 208-983-1950, fax 208-983-4099.

▲ There are 162 RV/tent sites (no hookups) plus 35 tent-only sites at 24 campgrounds. Seasons vary, but most are open from June to October; $4 to $6 per night. Located right on the Red River, and a good jumping-off point for other areas, is Red River Campground with 40 RV/tent sites; $6 per night. Hikers should check out Wildhorse Campground, which has 5 RV/tent sites; no charge.

WINCHESTER LAKE STATE PARK 🚶 🛶 🚤 🛥 ⛵ Anglers and nature lovers enjoy this pine-enveloped lake with four miles of shoreline at the edge of the Camas Prairie. With 418 acres, the park is larger than the adjacent village of Winchester. There is fishing for trout, crappie and bass; ice fishing is popular in winter. Facilities include picnic tables, restrooms and cross-country skiing trails. Day-use fee, $4. ~ Located five miles west of Winchester, which is three miles off Route 95; 208-924-7563, fax 208-924-5941; e-mail win@idpr.state.id.us.

▲ There are 49 RV hookups plus 23 RV/tent sites without hookups; $12 to $16 per night. Yurts rent for $35 to $55 per night.

▼▼▼▼▼▼▼▼▼▼▼▼▼

Outdoor Adventures

FISHING

The lower Snake, from Hells Canyon to its confluence with the Columbia in Washington, is the only place in the world where steelhead trout, catfish and ancient sturgeon share the same waters.

Other rivers, including the Salmon and Clearwater, share November-to-January steelhead runs and host rainbow trout throughout the year. In many smaller lakes, rainbow trout share the waters with bass and panfish like bluegill, perch and crappie.

River and lake expeditions are available throughout the region. Some outfitters specialize in flyfishing or power-boat fishing, steelhead or bass fishing; inquire when you book. Visitors centers normally have complete lists of outfitters.

Among the many reputable outfitters and guides is **Barker River Trips**, which offers raft excursions on the Snake and Clearwater rivers; common catches are bass and salmon. ~ 2124 Grelle Avenue, Lewiston; 208-743-7459. **Clearwater Outfitters** offers flyfishing trips to the Little North Fork of the Clearwater River for cutthroat and rainbow trout. ~ 4088 Canyon Creek Road, Orofino; 208-476-5971, 800-826-7370; www.tgi.net/clwout. Pack trips from **Triple "O" Outfitters Inc.** delve into backcountry for catch-and-release cutthroat fishing on Kelly Creek tributaries. ~ P.O. Box 217, Pierce, ID 83546; 208-464-2349; www.tripleo-outfitters.com.

Although jet boating is somewhat controversial in this area among rafters, canoeists and kayakers, it's also very popular. Unfortunately, it's also much easier to rent jet boats than nonmotorized crafts. One of the biggest Snake River jet-boat outfitters, which leaves from Hells Gate State Park in Lewiston, is **Beamer's Hells Canyon Tours.** Closed weekends from Labor Day through Memorial Day. ~ 1451 Bridge Street, Clarkston, WA; 509-758-4800, 208-743-4800, 800-522-6966. Another good one is **Snake River Adventures,** offering the same services. ~ 227 Snake River Avenue, Lewiston; 208-746-6276, 800-262-8874. Overnight stays may be in bunkhouse-style lodges, cabins, camps and such.

WATER SPORTS

When visiting the Lower Panhandle, don't miss the opportunity to fish for ancient sturgeon—prehistoric, boneless fish that can grow to 14 feet or longer.

In addition, water sports of all kinds are very popular at Lewiston's "slack water" confluence of the Snake and Clearwater rivers. No boat rentals, however, are available for waterskiers, sailors or even board sailors.

Whitewater rafting is big here, and there is no shortage of expeditioners. The most popular streams are the Lochsa and Selway rivers, tributaries of the Clearwater. In the Flathead tongue, the Selway and Lochsa rivers translate to "smooth water" and "rough water," respectively, which is appropriate given the character of each. The Selway River offers some of the most challenging whitewater in Idaho. Curiously, the outfitter with the best food and guides is based in California: ARTA. Ask to be placed on their standby list if openings aren't available. Closed weekends. ~ 24000 Casa Loma Road, Groveland, CA 95321; 800-323-2782. Also very good is **Northwest River Company.** ~ Boise; 208-344-7119; www.northwestriver.com. If you don't have time for a multiday expedition, the Lochsa River, during high water, may be Idaho's most exciting daytrip. Contact **Holiday River Expeditions.** ~ P.O. Box 86, Grangeville, ID 83530; 208-983-1518, 800-624-6323; www.bikeraft.com. Another good information source, especially for Hells Canyon trips, is the Lewiston Chamber of Commerce. ~ 111 Main Street #120, Lewiston; 208-743-3531.

RIVER RUNNING

Although this region isn't particularly mountainous, there are places where you can let gravity take its course. **Cottonwood Butte,** seven miles west of Cottonwood by way of West Lake Road, has a T-bar and a rope tow that carry skiers up an 875-foot vertical. ~ Radar Road, Cottonwood; 208-962-3624. **Snowhaven** has a T-bar. It's located about seven miles south of Grangeville. Closed mid-March to Thanksgiving. ~ Fish Creek Road, Grangeville; 208-983-2851. **Bald Mountain,** off Route 11 seven miles north of Pierce in Clearwater County, has a T-bar and a

SKIING

rope tow to serve a 975-foot vertical. Check in Pierce for more information. ~ Bald Mountain Road, Pierce.

Recommended areas for cross-country skiers are **Palouse Divide**, with 29 kilometers of groomed track 40 miles northeast of Moscow on Route 6, and **Fish Creek Meadows**, with 19 kilometers of groomed track near the Snowhaven ski area nine miles south of Grangeville on Fish Creek Road.

Ski Rentals   In the Lewiston–Moscow area, **Follett's Mountain Sports** rents downhill equipment. The Moscow Store is closed Sunday in summer. ~ 714 D Street, Lewiston, 208-743-4200; and 407 South Washington Street, Moscow, 208-882-6735. **Gart Sports** carries downhill gear. ~ 625-A 21st Street, Lewiston; 208-746-8040. **Northwestern Mountain Sports** rents both alpine and Nordic equipment. ~ 1016 Pullman Road, Moscow; 208-882-0133. Skis and boards are also available at the foot of Snowhaven ski area.

GOLF   If you want to tee off in the Lewiston–Moscow area, try **Bryden Canyon Golf Course**. ~ 445 O'Connor Road, Lewiston; 208-746-0863. There's also the **University of Idaho Golf Course**. Closed November to May. ~ 1215 Nez Perce Drive, Moscow; 208-885-6171. Two more 18-hole courses are across the Snake River from Lewiston. The **Quail Ridge Golf Club** is a public course near the Snake River south of town. ~ 3600 Swallows Nest Drive, Clarkston; 509-758-8501.

There are also nine-hole courses in Moscow, Orofino and Grangeville.

TENNIS   It's possible to hit the courts throughout much of the year in this temperate region of Idaho. In Lewiston, look for free outdoor courts at **Lewiston High School** (1114 9th Avenue) and **Sacajawea Junior High School** (3610 12th Street), or call Lewiston Parks & Recreation (208-746-2313). In Moscow, check out **Ghormley Park** (3rd and Home streets) and **Moscow Junior High School** (1410 East D Street), or call the Moscow Parks and Recreation Department (208-883-7085). The **University of Idaho** (208-885-6381) has 15 courts available for a small fee.

RIDING STABLES   Whether you're a beginner or an experienced rider, an outfitter can set you up. In the Palouse Hills try the **Appaloosa Horse Club**. Closed weekends. ~ 2720 West Pullman Road, Moscow; 208-882-5578; www.appaloosa.com.

PACK TRIPS   The Selway-Bitterroot, Frank Church–River of No Return and Gospel Hump wildernesses are wonderful areas for multiday horseback trips. **Lochsa River Outfitters** takes riders into the Selway-Bitterroot Wilderness around the Idaho–Montana border. ~ Route 12, Lowell; 208-926-4149; www.doortoidaho.com.

Lewiston's 16-mile **Clearwater & Snake River National Recreation Trail**, built by the U.S. Army Corps of Engineers, follows dikes and levees to connect a series of riverfront parks with the city center. The levees extend for five or six miles, and if you follow them south, you'll reach Hells Gate State Park, another locale where local bicyclists like to ride.

BIKING

University of Idaho students have several fine mountain-biking opportunities north of Moscow. The moderately difficult **Moscow Mountain Trail** (5 miles) follows the ridge of the Palouse Range northeast of town. **Skyline Drive** (up to 14 miles) follows a ridgeline past Mineral Mountain in Mary Minerva McCroskey State Park. The **White Pine National Recreation Trail** (5 miles), which bikers share with hikers, has spurs that extend it to an 18-mile loop off Route 6 near Emida.

Bike Rentals In Lewiston, **Pedals-n-Spokes** rents bikes. Closed Sunday. ~ 829 D Street; 208-743-6567. In Moscow, **Northwestern Mountain Sports** rents bicycles. ~ 1016 Pullman Road; 208-882-0133. **Follett's Mountain Sports** does not rent bikes, but will direct skinny-tire or fat-tire enthusiasts to bikeways and trails appropriate to the season and weather. Sales and repairs are available. ~ 407 South Washington Street, Moscone; 208-882-6735.

A widely varied choice of trails is available to visitors to the lower Panhandle. The following list is but a sampling. All distances listed for hiking trails are one way unless otherwise noted.

HIKING

The Clearwater drainage offers some of Idaho's most remote backcountry. The Middle Fork of the Clearwater is formed by the Selway and Lochsa rivers. Any number of hikes begin above their confluence.

Some of the most rugged terrain of the Selway-Bitterroot Wilderness can be found at the **Selway Crags** (8 miles). Turn from Route 12 at the town of Lowell and follow the Selway River to Fog Mountain Road. The trailhead is 12 very hard miles to the road's end. This is lovely country, but requires the verve of a mountain goat.

AUTHOR FAVORITE

A trip to the hot springs along the **Warm Springs Creek trail** (2 miles) is definitely a treat, but I like to continue past the crowded pools to the quiet cedar groves, perfect for serene contemplation. (Most foot traffic never passes the hot pools, and you are likely to enjoy the groves in solitude.) The trailhead is 55 miles east of Lowell.

A gentler trail follows **Meadow Creek** (3 miles). The upper watershed was logged heavily, but the lower end encountered by day hikers makes a wonderful walk.

Easier hikes are available from Route 12. The **Fish Creek** (9 miles) trailhead is about 23 miles east of Lowell, just over the Fish Creek bridge. For a day hike, walk only as far as Willow Creek.

Another three miles east are the **Boulder Creek Trails** (4 miles); the goal here for day hikes is Lochsa Saddle.

Northeast of Clarkia, the **Hobo Cedar Grove Nature Trail** (.5 mile) takes hikers on a very gentle gradient—suitable for senior citizens—through a dense grove of old-growth cedar and a forest floor carpeted with lady ferns. The trailhead is reached via Merry Creek Road ten miles northeast of Route 3.

Transportation

CAR

Route 95, the only north–south highway connecting Idaho's Panhandle with the Snake River Valley, is the principal artery. If you're coming from Boise, take **Route 55** north to New Meadows and from there pick up Route 95, which proceeds through Grangeville, Lewiston and Moscow. **Route 12** heads east through the Clearwater Valley and continues its scenic route to the Montana border. For road condition information, call 888-432-7623.

AIR

The **Lewiston–Nez Perce County Regional Airport** handles regional traffic. ~ 406 Burrell Avenue, Lewiston; 208-746-7962; www.lcairport.net. Horizon Air connects Lewiston with Seattle, Portland and Boise, and has connections with Alaska, American, Continental and Northwest airlines. Horizon also flies into the **Pullman–Moscow Regional Airport**. ~ 3200 Airport Complex North, Pullman, Washington; 509-334-4555.

Wheatland Express has charter and commuter bus services. ~ 509-334-2200, 800-334-2004; www.wheatlandexpress.com.

BUS

Northwestern Trailways (800-366-3830) serves cities throughout the region, including Lewiston at 3120 North and South Highway, 208-746-8108; Moscow at 120 West 6th Street, 208-882-5521; and Grangeville at Route 95 North, 208-983-0721.

CAR RENTALS

At the Lewiston airport, look for **Budget Rent A Car** (800-527-0700) and **Hertz Rent A Car** (800-654-3131)

PUBLIC TRANSIT

Valley Transit provides service in Lewiston. ~ 1424 Main Street, Lewiston; 208-743-2545. In Moscow, contact **Moscow Public Transit**. ~ P.O. Box 107, Colfax, WA 99111; 800-967-2899.

TAXIS

In Lewiston, call **Black & White Cab** (208-743-3223).

ELEVEN

Coeur d'Alene and the Upper Panhandle

 Far northern Idaho is a land quite different from the vast arid stretches of the south so dependent on the Snake River and its tributaries. Against the sometimes harsh aspect of the basalt deserts and the severity of central Idaho's terrain, the land up here seems almost accommodating, the mountain slopes more gentle, very green and punctuated by three large lakes—Coeur d'Alene Lake, Priest Lake and Lake Pend Oreille. Idaho's major northern rivers, the Pend Oreille, Kootenai, Clark Fork, Priest and Spokane rivers, are all tributaries to the Columbia. The Upper Panhandle is the only region of Idaho whose waters do not drain into the Snake.

Like Lewiston and the Lower Panhandle, Coeur d'Alene, Sandpoint and the Upper Panhandle towns look to Spokane as their commercial and cultural hub. Also like Lewiston, Coeur d'Alene is on Pacific Time. This upper reach of Idaho is the only area of the northern Rockies that does not live on Mountain Time.

David Thompson, a trapper with the Hudson's Bay Company and later the Northwest Company, was the first to do extensive exploration and mapping here. In 1809, he established a trading post near the town of Hope, about 24 miles east of Sandpoint. He called it Kullyspell House; it was the first such post in Idaho and was one of a string of forts through Idaho, Montana and Washington operated by the Northwest Company. Thompson was the first white man to see the headwaters of the Columbia. Local Indians named him Koo Koo Sint, Man Who Watches Stars, because of the time and effort he spent looking at and making calculations from the heavens. The name Sandpoint came from Thompson's journals, in which he called the locale Point of Sand. Thompson's maps were so accurate that 50 years later they were used by the Pacific Railway surveyors laying a railroad route west.

What Thompson and early settlers here saw were immense green forests, including the largest stand of white pine in the world. Most of that is now gone, replaced by second-growth stands of cedar, hemlock, tamarack and grand fir. These thrive in the moist climate drawn inland from the Pacific Northwest coast. Long

Valley, in the Selkirk Mountains of Boundary County, supports Idaho's only temperate rainforest. The Selkirks are home to the only caribou herd in the lower 48 states. The small population, numbering fewer than twenty, is part of a larger Canadian herd that has little regard for international borders. Grizzly can be found here, too, though rarely and in about the same numbers.

The timber industry has been dominant in these northern counties, as the scarred hillsides evidence, and mining had a strong local presence in the Silver Valley, now the Route 90 corridor. But agriculture, especially in the fertile Kootenai Valley, has always played a strong supporting economic role. The same is true for travel and tourism, which today are stronger than ever.

Boating and other water sports are big in Coeur d'Alene, a burgeoning resort town with a nationally acclaimed resort hotel (The Coeur d'Alene), upscale restaurants, outlet malls and theme parks. Located no more than a half-hour's freeway drive from metropolitan Spokane, the town is less than an hour from vital and historic mining towns near the Montana border. And when snow falls, Coeur d'Alene turns its attention to winter sports. Silver Mountain, about 45 miles east at Kellogg, has the world's longest gondola, and Schweitzer Mountain, just outside Sandpoint, has a new lodge and spectacular views of Lake Pend Oreille.

Pend Oreille is a mammoth body of water, 43 miles long, with record-size trout and northern pike and water so deep that the U.S. Navy conducts top-secret sonar experiments more than 1000 feet beneath the lake's surface. Sandpoint, located where Pend Oreille River flows from the lake, supports a small but growing community of artists. The wood-products industry dominates the regional economy from here to the Canadian border 60 miles away, but secluded Priest Lake, an hour's drive west and north, is one of Idaho's more beautiful—and accessible—spots to commune with nature.

Coeur d'Alene Area

Coeur d'Alene didn't make a good first impression on white visitors. Early-19th-century French Canadian fur traders, frustrated by their inability to trade cheap trinkets to indigenous tribes in exchange for valuable pelts, said the natives had *"les coeurs d'alênes"*—"the hearts of awls."

In modern Coeur d'Alene, by contrast, you *can* get something for nothing. You can get spectacular scenery and ready access to a wide variety of recreational opportunities and historic sites. Put something down, and you can stay in fine resort hotels and dine in excellent restaurants. In short, it now makes a *very* good first impression . . . and then some.

SIGHTS   Located on the northern shore of 23-mile-long **Coeur d'Alene Lake**, the city of Coeur d'Alene (now pronounced "CORE-duh-LANE") is smack on the Route 90 corridor, just a half-hour's drive east of Spokane, Washington. The centerpiece of the town of 27,000 is its widely acclaimed resort, **The Coeur d'Alene**. Even non-hotel guests can enjoy a walk on the world's longest floating boardwalk (3300 feet), which surrounds the resort's bustling marina, or play a round of golf on a waterfront course. ~ 115 South 2nd Street, Coeur d'Alene; 208-765-4000; www.cdaresort.com.

The long, narrow lake itself, most of it nestled in dense evergreen forest, was once listed among the world's five most beautiful by *National Geographic*. Home to the largest population of osprey in the western United States, the lake attracts anglers and water-sports enthusiasts from hundreds of miles away. **Lake Coeur d'Alene Cruises** depart in summer from Independence Point, just west of the resort. There are 90-minute afternoon cruises three

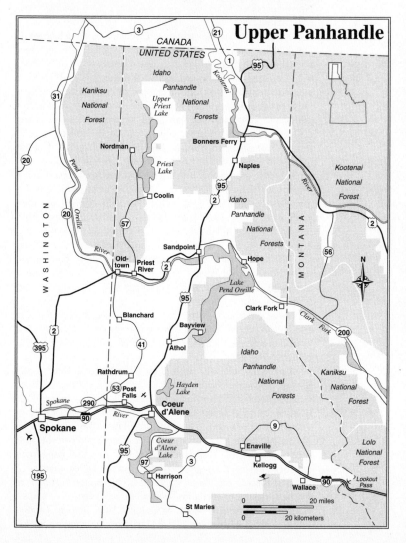

times daily, as well as dinner and Sunday brunch cruises. On Sunday and Wednesday, six-hour length-of-the-lake cruises head up the tributary **St. Joe River**, which at 2200-foot elevation is said to be the highest navigable stream in the United States. Fare. ~ 208-765-4000, 800-365-8338; www.cdaresort.com, e-mail resortinfo@cdaresort.com.

Sherman Avenue is the quaint main street of downtown Coeur d'Alene. For information and suggestions on the best way to explore, stop by the **Coeur d'Alene Chamber of Commerce**. ~ 1621 North 3rd Street, Suite 100, Coeur d'Alene; 208-664-3194; www.coeurdalene.org.

Opposite the visitors center, at City Park, is the **Museum of North Idaho**, with extensive exhibits on the region's logging, transportation and agricultural history, and native culture. Admission. ~ 115 Northwest Boulevard, Coeur d'Alene; 208-664-3448. A few blocks farther west, on the campus of North Idaho College, the **Fort Sherman Museum**, housed in the powderhouse of a late-19th-century military fort, has displays that depict life in Coeur d'Alene in that era. Nearby, now owned by the college, are the former Fort Sherman officers' quarters and chapel. ~ College Drive and River Avenue, Coeur d'Alene; 208-664-3448.

There are great places for cheap recreation on either side of the resort: **City Park** (West Lakeshore Drive), with a lifeguarded swimming beach and broad grassy tracts for sunbathing, picnicking and Frisbee playing; and **Tubbs Hill**, a 150-acre natural park that juts into the lake and offers, among other trails, a three-mile loop beginning from the 3rd Street boat launch on the resort's east side.

Kids a little too tightly wound? Shuttle them over to the waterslides of **Wild Waters**, just off Exit 12, open daily in summer. Admission. ~ 2119 North Government Way, Coeur d'Alene; 208-667-6491.

Coeur d'Alene has recently become a mecca for classic-car and motorcycle enthusiasts, with several shows held locally each year. Chief among them is "Car d'Lane" during the last weekend of June.

A pleasant half-day's drive is the **Lake Coeur d'Alene Scenic Byway**, a 95-mile loop along the eastern shore of Coeur d'Alene Lake (via Route 97) and back on Route 3, past a chain of nine small lakes, to the interstate. The byway exits Route 90 about ten miles east of Coeur d'Alene at **Wolf Lodge Bay**, noted for its November gathering of bald eagles. It meanders down the photogenic shoreline to **Harrison**, an old lumber and shipping town with several structures still standing from the 1800s, then turns north on Route 3 past Black, Care, Medicine, Rose and other lakes whose surrounding wetlands delight birdwatchers.

An alternative route back to Coeur d'Alene follows Route 3 south to the lumber town of **St. Maries** on the winding St. Joe

River. Beginning in the late 1880s, logs that floated down the St. Joe were processed here before cross-lake shipment to the railhead at Coeur d'Alene. But in 1910, the wild-and-woolly river town became the hub of activity for firefighters battling northern Idaho's Great Fire. Fifty-seven of them died before the 4600-square-mile blaze burned itself out after raging for more than a month. Their graves are set in a ring at **Fire Fighters' Circle** at ◀ *HIDDEN* Woodlawn Cemetery. ~ 23rd and Main streets, St. Maries; 208-245-4609. Reminiscences of St. Maries' turn-of-the-20th-century heyday can be seen at the **Historic Hughes House Museum**. ~ 606 Main Avenue, St. Maries; 208-245-1501.

West of St. Maries on Route 5 is **Heyburn State Park**, Idaho's second largest; it encompasses the channel of the St. Joe and several lakes created by its silt deposits as it flows toward Coeur d'Alene Lake. Route 5 joins Route 95 at Plummer, in the heart of the **Coeur d'Alene Indian Reservation**, notable to visitors mainly

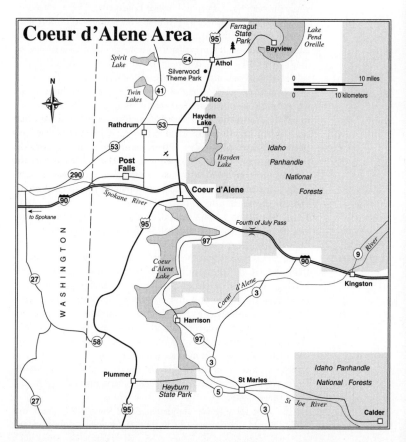

Coeur d'Alene Area

Farragut State Park

Lake Pend Oreille

Bayview

95

54   Athol

Spirit Lake

Silverwood Theme Park

0   10 miles

0   10 kilometers

N

Twin Lakes

41

Chilco

Hayden Lake

Rathdrum   53

Hayden Lake

Idaho

53

Panhandle

Post Falls

National

290

Forests

90

Spokane River   Coeur d'Alene

to Spokane

Fourth of July Pass

WASHINGTON

95

97

90

River

9

27

Coeur d'Alene Lake

Kingston

3

Coeur d'Alene

Harrison

97

58

3

Idaho Panhandle

Plummer

St Maries   National Forests

27

Heyburn State Park

5

St Joe River

95

3

Calder

for its bingo parlor at Worley and its grand plans to launch a National Indian Lottery in 38 states. The city of Coeur d'Alene is 34 miles north. ~ 800-523-2464.

West from Coeur d'Alene on Route 90 toward Spokane is the town of **Post Falls**, built around a Spokane River sawmill in 1880. A huge Louisiana-Pacific lumber mill now stands beside **Falls Park**, which overlooks a narrow canyon that provided a spillway for that early mill. Nearby **Treaty Rock Park** preserves pictographs said to have sealed an 1871 treaty between a Coeur d'Alene Indian chief and Post Falls founder Frederick Post. The tribal chief granted Post the right to 200 acres along the upper falls of the Spokane River. The two parks are connected by **Centennial Trail**, a paved path for walkers, runners and bicyclists that extends for 63 miles and links Coeur d'Alene with Spokane.

Hayden Lake, about five miles north of Coeur d'Alene, is often portrayed as a stronghold of the white supremacist Aryan Nation; while the neo-Nazi group did have a headquarters here, a successful lawsuit shut it down. The land has been donated to Northern Idaho College, with plans to create a peace park and human rights education center. It's important to note that the overwhelming majority of area residents, many of whom live in secluded lakeside estates, repudiated the hate group's activities.

Located 15 miles north of Coeur d'Alene is the **Silverwood Theme Park**, a worthy destination for families. You'll find over 60 carnival rides and family-oriented attractions, as well as a Victorian main street and a transportation theme. A train runs continuously on a three-plus-mile track around the park throughout the day. Be sure to experience *Tremors*, a wooden roller coaster that plunges underground five times during the ride. The park is open daily from Memorial Day weekend through Labor Day, weekends for a month after those dates. Admission. ~ North 27843 Route 95, Athol; 208-683-3400, fax 208-683-2268; www.silverwoodthemepark.com, e-mail info@silverwood4fun.com.

LODGING   There's no question that the 18-story **The Coeur d'Alene** is something special. Its lakefront location in downtown Coeur d'Alene and high standard of friendly service deserve their reputation. The resort has 337 rooms and suites that range from standard to luxury penthouse in style, as well as four restaurants, three lounges, a shopping plaza, a large indoor fitness center, a marina, lake cruises and a golf course—the latter featuring a floating green on the 14th hole. Ask about seasonal packages. ~ 115 South 2nd Street, Coeur d'Alene; 208-765-4000, 800-688-5253, fax 208-664-7276; www.cdaresort.com, e-mail cdabus@cdaresort.com. DELUXE TO ULTRA-DELUXE.

If you're looking for convenience and low prices, check out **El Rancho Motel**. Several blocks from the freeway, this old-timey motel offers 14 rooms with knotty pine walls. There are a couple two-bedroom units, and each room is equipped with a microwave, a refrigerator and a coffee pot to make getting up a little easier. ~ 1915 Sherman Avenue, Coeur d'Alene; 208-664-8794, 800-704-8794. MODERATE.

For a cozier experience, the Craftsman-style **Baragar House Bed & Breakfast** has three air-conditioned rooms with cable TV and VCRs. The Country Cabin room, which features realistic wall and ceiling murals that create an outdoorsy ambience, shares a bath with the charming Garden Room; the Honeymoon Suite, brimming with Victorian touches, has a private bath. Give the common room's piano a whirl, or relax in the indoor hot tub and sauna. There's also a guest laundry and high-speed internet access. Full breakfast is served in the dining room; complimentary snacks are available all day. ~ 316 Military Drive, Coeur d'Alene; 208-664-9125, 800-615-8422; www.baragarhouse.com, e-mail stay@baragarhouse.com. DELUXE TO ULTRA-DELUXE.

Family heirlooms, lace and chintz imbue **Gregory's McFarland House** with a sense of an English B&B. The five antique-filled suites of this 1905 home are lovingly decorated; all have private bath. You'll find a pool table, TV and VCR, books and games in the comfy family room, as well as a piano in the living room. No children under 14 allowed. Full breakfast included. Reservations recommended. ~ 601 Foster Avenue, Coeur d'Alene; 208-667-1232, 800-335-1232; www.bbhost.com/mcfarlandhouse. DELUXE TO ULTRA-DELUXE.

Looking for a "city slicker" opportunity at a guest ranch? The **Hidden Creek Ranch**, near Coeur d'Alene Lake, may fill the bill. Horseback riding, fishing, hiking and other activities fill the days, campfires and cookouts the evenings. Up to 40 guests stay in six log cabins, all with traditional lodgepole furnishings and

AUTHOR FAVORITE

Canopied beds, plush carpeting and antique-filled accommodations are reason enough for me to book a room at **The Roosevelt Inn**; the gourmet breakfast is just an added bonus to a night's stay at this B&B, whose 15 guest rooms have taken over the classrooms of a fully refurbished 1905 elementary school. The hosts, one of whom is a former student of the school, have furnished the three-story red-brick building with European antiques, and their breakfast fare includes Belgian waffles, fruit-stuffed crêpes and fluffy omelettes. ~ 105 East Wallace Avenue, Coeur d'Alene; 208-765-5200, 800-290-3358, fax 208-664-4142, www.the rooseveltinn.com, e-mail info@therooseveltinn.com. DELUXE.

private baths. Gourmet meals are served daily in the main lodge. All meals and activities are included in the price. Six-day minimum stay in July and August; single-night stays in May, June and September. ~ 11077 East Blue Lake Road, Harrison; 208-689-3209, 800-446-3833, fax 208-689-9115; www.hiddencreek.com, e-mail hidden creek@hiddencreek.com. ULTRA-DELUXE.

The Coeur d'Alene resort boasts the world's first and only floating golfing green.

On the banks of the Spokane River about eight miles west of Coeur d'Alene is **Red Lion Templin's Hotel.** This property has a marina and offers cruises aboard the *River Queen.* The hotel has 167 rooms with standard amenities and river view, a restaurant and lounge, a pool, a hot tub and a fitness center. ~ 414 East 1st Avenue, Post Falls; 208-773-1611, 800-283-6754, fax 208-773-4192; www.redlion.com. MODERATE TO DELUXE.

DINING

For true Mexican food prepared by a Mexican family, skip the chain joints and drop in at **Toro Viejo.** The menu for the most part looks familiar, with tacos and enchiladas, but the preparation is way beyond Tex-Mex. Decor is festive and colorful. ~ 117 North 2nd Street, Coeur d'Alene; 208-667-7676. BUDGET.

You can choose sidewalk seating or the dining room at **Brix,** a dressy nightclub and restaurant housed in a 1906 landmark building. The menu offers mostly steaks, including a bison T-bone, as well as seafood, entrées such as southern-spiced king salmon, and farm-raised sturgeon with lobster brandade. ~ 317 Sherman Avenue, Coeur d'Alene; 208-665-7407; wwwbrixrestaurant.com, e-mail info@brixrestaurant.com. MODERATE TO ULTRA-DELUXE.

Takara Japanese Restaurant and Sushi Bar has some of the best Japanese cuisine in the Rocky Mountains, served in an atmosphere more typical of Tokyo. There's a full sushi bar here as well as a noodles/teriyaki/tempura menu, and tatami rooms are available for private parties who want a more authentic Asian experience. ~ 309 Lakeside Avenue, Coeur d'Alene; 208-765-8014, fax 208-765-2825. MODERATE.

For a romantic night out, the place to go is **Beverly's,** overlooking Coeur d'Alene Lake from picture windows on the seventh floor of The Coeur d'Alene resort. Try to be there for the sunset view. The menu features Northwest cuisine, and service is impeccable. ~ 115 South 2nd Street, Coeur d'Alene; 208-765-4000, 800-688-4142; www.cdaresort.com. DELUXE TO ULTRA-DELUXE.

For a down-home night out, Coeur d'Alene locals drive ten miles east to the **Wolf Lodge Inn,** at the far end of Coeur d'Alene Lake's Wolf Lodge Bay. Beef and more beef dominate the menu at this rustic lodge, which grills its enormous steaks (the *smallest* is 16 ounces) on a hand-built stone barbecue. Decor is straight from the ranch. Reservations are highly recommended. Closed

Monday in winter. ~ Wolf Lodge Road at Route 90 Exit 22; 208-664-6665, fax 208-777-8727. DELUXE TO ULTRA-DELUXE.

Coeur d'Alene visitors can find most of what they want in the shops that line **Sherman Avenue** between 2nd and 8th streets. The Coeur d'Alene resort operates **The Shops**, a two-story mall, between 2nd and 3rd. Look also for **Northwest Artists**, a cooperative venture of 30 regional artisans, which offers such goods as pottery, jewelry, stained glass, fused glass, fine arts and watercolors. ~ 217 Sherman Avenue, Coeur d'Alene; 208-667-1464; www.nwartists.net.

On the north end of town, **Silver Lake Mall** is anchored by three major department stores and includes a range of boutiques, jewelers and specialty shops. ~ 200 West Hanley Avenue, Coeur d'Alene; 208-762-2112. Also popular is the large CDA **Antique Mall**, with a wide choice of early-20th-century *objets* and collectibles from any era. ~ 3650 Government Way, Coeur d'Alene; 208-667-0246.

For those who must, just inside the Washington state line, flanking either side of the Route 90 frontage road, are the **Factory Outlets at Post Falls**. There are over 50 stores, including Bass Apparel, Van Heusen and American Tourister. ~ West 4300 River-bend Avenue, Post Falls; 208-773-4555.

The **Lake City Playhouse**, Coeur d'Alene's community theater, performs musical comedies, dramas and other plays during the year, and holds children's workshops during the summer in its renovated neighborhood church. ~ 14th and Garden streets, Coeur d'Alene; 208-667-1323, fax 208-667-6328.

When Coeur d'Alene residents want to dance or listen to contemporary bands, they head to the **Shore Lounge**. ~ The Coeur d'Alene resort, 115 South 2nd Street; 208-765-4000; www.cdaresort.com. Jazz and blues lovers can dine on bistro fare like shrimp pizza and cassoulet while they get their fill of music on a nightly basis at **The Wine Cellar**. ~ 313 Sherman Avenue; 208-664-9463; www.coeurdalenewinecellar.com.

The **Iron Horse Bar & Grill** has pool tables and a pinball machine; a menu offers breakfast, lunch and dinner. ~ 407 Sherman Avenue, Coeur d'Alene; 208-667-7314.

On weekend nights, regional bands play country music at the **Slab Inn**. There's plenty of room to dance in this 1934 building. Weekend cover. ~ 800 West Seltice Way, Post Falls; 208-773-5440.

HEYBURN STATE PARK 🚶 🚲 🐎 ⛺ 🎣 🚤 ⛵ Idaho's second-largest state park (created in 1908) embraces three smaller lakes and the bayou of the St. Joe River as it flows into Coeur d'Alene Lake. Heyburn's 7800 acres offer fishing, camping and nature watching along the forested shores of Chatcolet, Benewah and Hidden lakes. Hawley's Landing is the most modern of several use areas. There are beaches at Plummer Point and Rocky Point. You can fish year-round for bass and panfish; row boats are available for rent. Facilities include picnic tables, restrooms, showers, an amphitheater and a store. ~ Located below the south end of Coeur d'Alene Lake, 10 to 14 miles west of St. Maries on Route 5; 208-686-1308, fax 208-686-3003; e-mail hey@idpr. state.id.us.

▲ There are 85 RV/tent sites and 15 for RVs only (57 hookups) plus 33 for tents only in three campgrounds, open from mid-April through October; $16 per night for RV hookups, $12 per night for tents.

IDAHO PANHANDLE NATIONAL FORESTS 🏃 🚲 ⛰ ⬅ About half the land in the upper Panhandle is contained within this 2.5-million-acre forest, consisting of the former St. Joe, Coeur d'Alene and Kaniksu national forests, and extending into neighboring Washington and Montana. The Coeur d'Alene division of the national forest consists of over 300,000 acres. Hunting, fishing, hiking, cross-country skiing and snowmobiling are popular pursuits. Seven big-game species make their homes amid the rugged peaks, canyons and valleys. You can catch and release for trout in the north fork of the Coeur d'Alene River. Facilities include picnic tables and restrooms. ~ Numerous roads extend into the national forest, including Route 268 (Fernan Lake Road) east of Coeur d'Alene. To reach Bell Bay Campground, take Route 90 seven miles east of Coeur d'Alene to Exit 22. Travel south on Route 97 for 25 miles and turn west into the park when you see the sign for the campground; the campground is three miles farther from this point. To reach Beauty Creek Campground, take Route 97 south for about two and a half miles to Forest Service Road 438, which leads into the forest. The campground is located about one mile down this road; 208-769-3000, fax 208-769-3062; www.fs. fed.us/ipnf.

▲ There are five campgrounds in this area with RV/tent sites (no hookups); no charge to $12 per night. Most campgrounds are open from May to September and have potable water. Only 30 miles south of Coeur d'Alene is Bell Bay Campground: There are 26 RV/tent sites (no hookups); $8 to $10 per night. A good jumping-off point in the forest is Beauty Creek Campground: There are 16 RV/tent sites; $12 per night (no hookups).

▼ ▼ ▼ ▼ ▼ ▼ ▼ ▼ ▼ ▼ ▼
Silver Valley

The Silver Valley, which flanks the Route 90 corridor east of Coeur d'Alene, is the largest silver-producing area in the world as well as a major player in the mining and smelting of lead and zinc. Though an 1882 gold strike first brought miners scurrying to this western slope of the Rockies, it was the other three minerals that made their fortunes (three violent labor strikes in the 1890s notwithstanding). More than one billion troy ounces of silver have been drawn from the slopes above the Coeur d'Alene River in the century-plus since mining activity began. A string of atmospheric mining towns—Kellogg, Osburn, Wallace, Mullan—climb to the Idaho–Montana border at 4725-foot Lookout Pass, a half-mile in elevation above Coeur d'Alene.

SIGHTS

The traveler's first vision of the valley, however, is of a far less frenetic nature. Twenty-four miles east of Coeur d'Alene, look for a hilltop church near the town of Cataldo. The Mission of the Sacred Heart, the oldest standing building in Idaho, is preserved within **Old Mission State Park**. Erected in 1850–53 by members of the Coeur d'Alene tribe under the direction of Jesuit Father Antonio Ravalli, the Greek revival–style structure still contains its original artwork, which has been restored. The neighboring parish house and nearby cemetery are also open. The mission's significance is interpreted by a park visitors center. There is an annual Feast of Assumption pilgrimage by Coeur d'Alene Indians on August 15. Admission. ~ Route 90 Exit 39, Cataldo; 208-682-3814, fax 208-682-4032; e-mail old@idpr.state.id.us.

Kellogg, 11 miles east of Cataldo, was always a company town whose heart and soul belonged to Bunker Hill, one of the world's largest lead-mining firms. When the company downscaled and laid off hundreds of workers in the 1970s, city fathers pro-

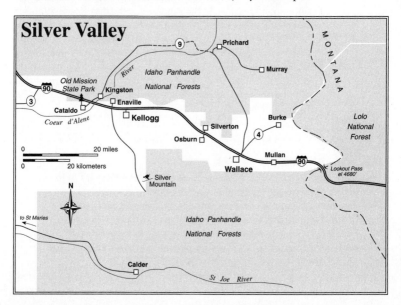

Silver Valley

moted a Bavarian theme in Kellogg's downtown architecture, without a lot of success. But in 1990 they opened the world's longest gondola (3.1 miles up 6295-foot Kellogg Peak) and, suddenly, the once-tiny Silverhorn ski hill put on a whole different face as Silver Mountain.

Silver Mountain cannot yet be called a world-class resort, but a lodging and dining infrastructure is already developing around it. In summer, when there's no snow for skiers, bikers can rent two-wheelers at the gondola and enjoy the mountain trails. A concert series in July and August attracts some of the top contemporary names in popular music and jazz to an open-air amphitheater near the gondola's upper terminal, and sightseers can ride the gondola most winter and summer days just to enjoy the view. ~ 610 Bunker Avenue, Kellogg; 208-783-1111, 800-204-6428, fax 208-783-9201; www.silvermt.com.

Elsewhere in Kellogg, the **Staff House Museum** houses the collection of the Shoshone County Mining and Smelting Museum. Open daily in summer; closed in winter. ~ 820 McKinley Avenue, Kellogg; 208-786-4141.

The **Sunshine Mine** is one of the world's biggest single-lode producers of silver. But a **memorial** is a sober reminder that mining remains a dangerous profession. A sculpture of a hard-rock miner commemorates the 1972 Sunshine Mine disaster in which 91 men perished. Eighty-two miners escaped the tragic fire four miles south of the memorial—and 3700 feet below the earth's surface. It remains the worst mining disaster in the United States since about 1920. ~ At the Big Creek exit from Route 90, three and a half miles east of Kellogg.

The best preserved of the Silver Valley mining towns is **Wallace**, deservedly a designated National Historic District. A small town, Wallace covers about 15 city blocks and is home to only 1000 people. Take time to walk its streets and look at the turn-of-the-20th-century downtown buildings and Victorian- and Queen Anne–style homes.

sights

AUTHOR FAVORITE

When in Wallace, a tour of the **Sierra Silver Mine** is not to be missed. A 16-passenger trolley takes visitors from the downtown ticket office on a narrated journey to the entrance of the depleted mine, where they are fitted with hardhats. An experienced miner discusses mining history and techniques during the one-hour walking tour through a 1000-foot, descending U-shaped tunnel. Tours are offered daily, May through September. Admission. ~ 420 5th Street, Wallace; 208-752-5151.

Wallace is a town of museums. The **Wallace District Mining Museum** recalls the history of the Silver Valley in artifacts, photographs and a video presentation. Here lies—in a coffin—what was once the only stoplight on Route 90 (the town gave it a huge funeral when it was taken down). Limited winter hours; call ahead. Admission. ~ 509 Bank Street, Wallace; 208-556-1592.

The elegant and historic **Northern Pacific Depot Railroad Museum,** with its château-style architecture, recounts the district's railroading past with a re-creation of a turn-of-the-20th-century train office, railroad memorabilia and old photos. Closed October 15 through April 1; closed Sunday in October and April. Admission. ~ 219 6th Street, Wallace; 208-752-0111, fax 208-753-9361.

The **Oasis Bordello Museum** offers tours of a brothel that operated in Wallace—along with three others—until federal officers finally closed it down in 1988. The brothel still looks exactly as it did when it was vacated. Wallace was the last U.S. city outside of Nevada to allow bordellos. Admission. ~ 605 Cedar Street, Wallace; phone/fax 208-753-0801.

Continue up Route 90 toward **Lookout Pass,** 13 miles distant on the Montana state line. There's a small downhill ski area here, but the pass appeals as much to cross-country skiers, snowmobilers and snowshoers in winter, backpackers and mountain bikers in summer. Many of these adventurers make their headquarters in tiny Mullan, five miles back toward Wallace.

Off-highway adventurers can exit Route 90 at Wallace (to Route 4) or Enaville, near Cataldo (to Route 9), and take all-weather gravel roads through the last major gold-rush area in the lower 48 states. Steamships once plied the Coeur d'Alene River as far as Enaville, where passengers then boarded trains to the mining district. Little remains except the rustic Enaville Resort.

Route 9 continues up the river valley to tiny Prichard and ◄ *HIDDEN* Murray, which today serve mostly anglers and hunters. A century ago, these towns were a focal point of the Silver Valley mining rush. The entire region remains rife with remnants. Be sure to stop into the **Spragpole Saloon and Museum** to see thousands of artifacts and historic photographs, and to learn the story of Maggie "Molly B'Damm" Hall, the proverbial saloonkeeper/ madam with a heart of gold. ~ Prichard Creek Road, Murray; 208-682-3901.

The old mining town of **Burke,** seven miles from Wallace up Canyon Creek on Route 4, has a main street that *Ripley's Believe It or Not!* described as so narrow that merchants had to pull in their awnings to let trains go by; trains, in fact, ran through the middle of its one hotel, which straddled the tracks. The entire area is within the Idaho Panhandle National Forests, which includes the **Settlers Grove of Ancient Cedars** about 30 miles north of Wallace on Forest Road 805 near Eagle. The 183-acre grove of western red cedars comprises century-old trees as much as eight feet in diameter.

LODGING

A welcoming front porch and a warm fireplace greet you at **The Mansion on the Hill**, a gracious bed and breakfast that sits on land homesteaded by Noah Kellog, the man who discovered silver in these parts. The main house offers two spacious suites, both with balconies that overlook sweeping mountain views; there are also two private cabins on the surrounding property as well as a hot tub and a restaurant. A full breakfast is included in the rates. ~ 105 South Division Street, Kellogg; 208-786-4455, 877-943-4455, fax 208-786-0157; www.mansionbnb.com, e-mail stay@mansionbnb.com. DELUXE TO ULTRA-DELUXE.

HIDDEN ►

The **Historic Jameson Saloon, Restaurant and Hotel** will appeal to history buffs with a taste for the offbeat. Situated in a lovingly restored, corner brick building—most of the town's wooden structures were destroyed in a 1910 fire—hotel guests have a choice of six upstairs rooms that were once a Wallace brothel. The rooms are reached by a fairly steep staircase leading up from what is now the dining room. At the top of the stairs is a large greeting room where, one presumes, the ladies met their guests. Airy, high-ceilinged rooms line either side of a narrow hallway. Each is decorated with beautiful period furniture and shares a bath down the hall. A continental breakfast, cooked to order, is included. ~ 304 6th Street, Wallace; 208-556-6000. MODERATE.

The tiny town of Wallace is where the movies *Dante's Peak* and *Heaven's Gate* were filmed.

For modern, standard lodging, the **Stardust Motel** has 42 quiet rooms. Situated right downtown in Wallace, the somewhat dated '50s-ish building has had a good facelift. Inside are tasteful furnishings, light walls and dark woods. The all-tile bathrooms, including the floors—a holdover from its earlier life—add a nice touch. One suite has a full kitchen. ~ 410 Pine Street, Wallace; 208-752-1213, 800-643-2386, fax 208-753-0981. MODERATE.

DINING

Along 6th Street in Wallace are several small diners. Locals seem to favor **Sweet's Cafe**. The decor is a bit fussy, with dainty sheer curtains and wood wainscoting, but pleasant, and large enough for about a dozen tables and an equal number of counter seats. The unassuming menu is what you'd expect: basic breakfasts, burgers, steaks, fresh seafood and chicken. The hallway back to the restrooms is lined with historic photographs of the Silver Valley and a wonderful panorama shot of old Wallace. ~ 310 6th Street, Wallace; 208-556-4661. BUDGET.

HIDDEN ►

A good dining choice—one in tune with the turn-of-the-20th-century mining flavor of the district—is the **Historic Jameson**

Saloon, Restaurant and Hotel. It occupies a 19th-century hotel and saloon and perpetuates its original Victorian ambience. Hamburgers and deli sandwiches highlight the lunch menu, while dinnertime offerings are strictly of the steak-and-seafood variety. ~ 304 6th Street, Wallace; 208-556-1554. MODERATE TO DELUXE.

The **Enaville Resort**, also known as The Snake Pit, dates from 1880, when this settlement was at the head of the steamship route to Coeur d'Alene. The old log building, where miners once stocked up on provisions, liquor and women, today serves such frontier favorites as Rocky Mountain oysters and buffalo burgers. ~ 1480 Coeur d'Alene River Road, Kingston; 208-682-3453. MODERATE.

◀ *HIDDEN*

Shoppers and history buffs will want to walk Bank Street in historic Wallace. All manner of shops along here sell antique silver, collectibles and Western handicrafts.

SHOPPING

Two shops in Wallace specialize in jewelry made from the local silver. At **Victoria's Antiques**, Vickie Field designs many of the pieces in her store, detailed representations of flowers set with Idaho precious stones. She has also brought in tea services and candelabra. ~ 618 Bank Street, Wallace; phone/fax 208-556-1500. **Idaho Silver** has a broader selection of work by contemporary silversmiths. Especially elegant are the geometric earrings and pendants by Rob Harper. ~ 606 Bank Street, Wallace; 208-556-1171.

The **Wallace District Art Center** displays painting, sculpture and crafts from area artisans. ~ 510 Bank Street, Wallace; 208-752-8381.

You can boo the villain and applaud the hero in summer performances by **Sixth Street Melodrama**. The mining-town ensemble, which play in a delightful little Victorian theater, offers more serious productions in fall, winter and spring. ~ 212 6th Street, Wallace; 208-752-8871, 877-749-8478.

NIGHTLIFE

OLD MISSION STATE PARK 🏃 Idaho's oldest building is the imposing Mission of the Sacred Heart, sitting on a hilltop between the Coeur d'Alene River and the freeway. Built by Jesuit priests and Coeur d'Alene Indians in the early 1850s, the mission still offers services by special arrangements. The 18-acre park also includes a restored parish house. Facilities include picnic tables, restrooms, a visitors center and short trails. Day-use fee, $4. ~ Take Route 90 east from Coeur d'Alene for 27 miles. Take Exit 39 (Cataldo) and follow directional signs to the park; 208-682-3814, fax 208-682-4032; e-mail old@idpr.state.id.us.

PARKS

IDAHO PANHANDLE NATIONAL FORESTS 🏃 🏕 ⛷ 🚤 🚣
⤵ The 350,000 acres that make up the Coeur d'Alene River

Ranger District of the national forest offer miles of hiking and cross-country skiing trails, along with historical mining areas and important stands of old-growth cedars. Whitewater-rafting enthusiasts love the Coeur d'Alene River, which offers many species of trout for anglers. Facilities include picnic tables, restrooms and two ski areas. ~ Numerous roads extend into the national forest, including Route 50 east of St. Maries and Route 9 north of Cataldo. To reach Kit Price Campground, take the Kingston exit off Route 90 east of Coeur d'Alene. Take Coeur d'Alene River Road north about 18 miles to Babins Junction where you will turn left. Continue to Prichard where the road turns into Route 208. Eight miles farther you will see a sign for Kit Price Campground on the right side of the road. Three more miles on the right is Devil's Elbow Campground. Big Hank Campground is six miles beyond, on the left side of the road; 208-752-1221, fax 208-556-5154; www.fs.fed.us/ipnf.

▲ There are four developed campgrounds and many undeveloped tent/RV sites (no hookups); no charge to $10 per night. Most campgrounds are open from Memorial Day to mid-September. Situated on the Coeur d'Alene River are the Big Hank, Devil's Elbow and Kit Price campgrounds: There are 30 RV/tent sites at Big Hank, 20 tent sites at Devil's Elbow and 52 RV/tent sites at Kit Price; $10 per night.

▼▼▼▼▼◇▼▼▼▼▼▼▼▼

Lake Pend Oreille Area

About 1200 feet deep with 111 miles of shoreline, Lake Pend Oreille is the monster of the north. Named by early French Canadian trappers, who claimed to have seen native tribes wearing pendant ornaments in their earlobes, (the name is pronounced "pond-or-RAY"), Lake Pend Oreille is a major draw for anglers seeking trophy-size freshwater fish, and for other outdoor sportsmen. The town of Sandpoint, at its northern outlet, is the regional center; isolated Priest Lake, to its northwest, and the forest country surrounding Bonners Ferry, a logging town just below the Canadian border, are other attractions.

SIGHTS   At the southern end of the lake, four miles east of Athol, is **Farragut State Park**. The U.S. Navy had a major training base here during World War II, and the huge park later became a popular venue for Scout jamborees. A visitors center near the main (west) entrance has park information. Mountain goats and other surprising wildlife can often be seen through binoculars on the rocky cliffs below Bernard Peak, across Idlewilde Bay from Farragut. The navy still operates a deep-water acoustic testing facility (closed to the public, of course) for electronically controlled submarines at the little fishing-resort town of Bayview, just north of Farragut. ~ Route 54, Athol; 208-683-2425, fax 208-683-7416; e-mail far@idpr.state.id.us.

Sandpoint is on the lake's north shore where the Pend Oreille River leaves the lake. The town's population of 5500 swells during the summer and winter with people taking advantage of the numerous outdoor activities. Festivals also lend a celebratory air to the streets much of the year, and the popular waterfront is always bustling.

Route 95's two-mile **Long Bridge**, which enters the town from the south, crosses between the two, flanked by a bicycle path. There's also the annual summer **Festival at Sandpoint,** a top-drawer

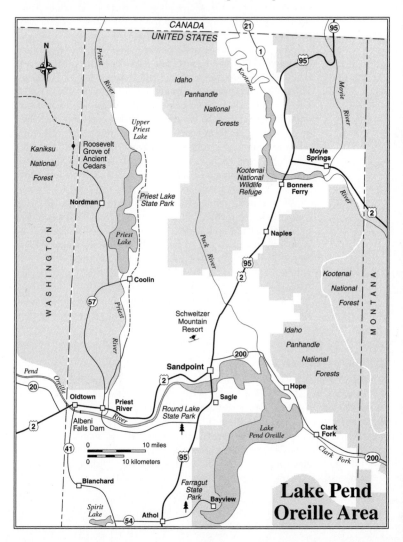

concert series. ~ P.O. Box 695, Sandpoint, ID 83864; 208-265-4554; www.festivalatsandpoint.com.

Sandpoint has a couple of small museums. The **Bonner County Historical Museum** recalls the area's native and pioneer cultures. Exhibits on logging, mining and agriculture in this town are highlighted. Admission. ~ 611 South Ella Street, Sandpoint; 208-263-2344.

Lake Pend Oreille Cruises offers lake trips everyday during the summer; spring and fall trips are also available. Private charters available too. Fee. Closed January through March. ~ Sandpoint City Beach; 208-255-5253, 888-726-3764, fax 208-265-9217; www.lakependoreillecruises.com.

Sandpoint's leading attraction may well be the burgeoning **Schweitzer Mountain Resort.** Just 11 miles uphill off Route 95, the four-decade-old ski resort is Idaho's second largest (after Sun Valley). It's no exaggeration to say that the view from here across Lake Pend Oreille is truly magnificent. But only in recent years, with the opening of the luxurious Selkirk Lodge and the White Pine Lodge at the foot of the lifts, has the resort's growth really taken off. Summer business has taken off, too: Mountain-bike rentals are now available at Schweitzer from July to September. ~ Schweitzer Mountain Road, Sandpoint; 208-263-9555, fax 208-263-0775; www.schweitzer.com.

West from Sandpoint, Route 2 follows the Pend Oreille River for 29 miles to the Washington border town of Newport. Six miles east of the boundary is **Priest River**, whose chamber of commerce occupies part of the late-19th-century **Keyser House Museum.** The restored wood-frame home is furnished with period antiques and boasts a special "timber education" room. ~ 301 Montgomery Street, Priest River; 208-448-2721.

Plans are being drawn to have a tour train operate along the Pend Oreille River between Priest River and Newport. The train

THE HOPE PENINSULA

A good portion of Lake Pend Oreille's shoreline is inaccessible by road. But an interesting stretch of highway for campers and boaters is the 34 miles of Route 200 along Pend Oreille's northeastern shore, between Sandpoint and the Montana border. The **Hope Peninsula**, a large promontory extending into the lake about halfway to the state line, has several resorts, campgrounds and boat launches around its shores. Clark Fork, located where the river of the same name empties into Lake Pend Oreille, is a fishing and lumbering center on the main Northern Pacific Railroad line.

will pass the **Albeni Falls Dam,** which offers public tours and has an adjacent recreation area. Built in the early '50s, this small dam controls the water for Lake Pend Oreille. It's located 20 miles west of Sandpoint on Route 2. ~ Route 2, Newport; 208-437-3133.

The Priest River flows out of **Priest Lake,** Idaho's least developed and most pristine large lake. Including scenic Upper Priest Lake, it is 25 miles long; its southern end is 30 miles north of the town of Priest River via Route 57. Only two tiny hamlets lie near its shores, and National Forest and other federal and state lands surround more than 75 percent of it. Most casual visitors approach the lake through the three separate units of **Priest Lake State Park.** The Indian Creek site, halfway up its eastern shore, has the widest range of facilities. Northern segments of the Idaho Panhandle National Forests surround Priest Lake. ~ 314 Indian Creek Park Road, Coolin; 208-443-2200, fax 208-443-3893; e-mail pri@idpr.state.id.us.

Fourteen miles northwest of Nordman, one of those Priest Lake hamlets by the Idaho–Washington state line, is a unique old-growth-forest area, the **Roosevelt Grove of Ancient Cedars.**   ◀ HIDDEN
Some of the giant trees in the 20-acre upper grove are estimated to be at least 2000 years old. This has been a protected area since 1943. The cedars, in the Washington portion of Idaho Panhandle National Forests, are two miles off Forest Road 302 via the Granite Falls Trail. ~ Priest Lake Ranger District; 208-443-2512.

North from Sandpoint toward the Canadian border is the lumber town of **Bonners Ferry.** This is the seat of Boundary County, which is unique in the nation in that two of the county's sides are state boundaries and the third is an international border. About ten miles east of Bonners Ferry, where Route 2 crosses the Moyie River, an overlook affords a memorable view of scenic **Moyie Falls** and the Big Moyie Canyon Bridge, 600 feet above the river. The 100-foot falls, which cascade over jagged rock outcroppings, are best seen in the spring; they often slow to a trickle during the dry summer and autumn seasons.

Kootenai National Wildlife Refuge, five miles west of Bonners   ◀ HIDDEN
Ferry on the south shore of the Kootenai River, provides 2774 acres of wetland wilderness for migratory birds and a variety of native mammals. There are well-maintained trails for observation within the refuge. Entry is limited from October to December (bird-hunting season). ~ West Side Road; 208-267-3888, fax 208-267-5570; kootenai.fws.gov.

Near Lake Pend Oreille in downtown Sandpoint, **La Quinta Inn**   **LODGING**
has 68 comfortable and well-maintained rooms. Facilities include a restaurant/lounge, a swimming pool, a fitness room and a hot tub. ~ 415 Cedar Street, Sandpoint; 208-263-9581, 800-282-0660, fax 208-263-3395; www.laquinta.com. DELUXE.

Ski and snowboard aficionados will enjoy Schweitzer Mountain's **Selkirk Lodge**, a WestCoast hotel. Built in elegant alpine style at the foot of two chairlifts and the top of another, the lodge has 82 rooms with private baths and modern wood decor, fine dining in a bar and grill, stone fireplaces in the wood-appointed lobby area, and even outdoor hot tubs. Also part of the Schweitzer Mountain complex, the **White Pine Lodge** offers fully furnished condos. ~ Schweitzer Mountain Road, Sandpoint; 208-265-0257, 800-831-8810, fax 208-263-7961; www.schweitzer.com, e-mail stay@schweitzer.com. ULTRA-DELUXE.

On Priest Lake, **Hill's Resort** has 53 housekeeping units, all with kitchens and private baths, that range from rustic cabins to luxury chalets. The latter boast picture windows that look out upon the pristine lake and the Selkirk Mountains beyond. A year-round family resort with 12 acres of lakefront, it also has an award-winning restaurant and a lounge. A wide range of outdoor activities are offered, with water-sports rentals, tennis courts and an 18-hole golf course on site. There's a one-week minimum stay in July and August. ~ Luby Bay Road, Priest Lake; 208-443-2551, fax 208-443-2363; www.hillsresort.com, e-mail desk@hillsresort.com. DELUXE TO ULTRA-DELUXE.

DINING

In the Pend Oreille district, there's good Italian food at **Ivano's**. The emphasis here is on classic Northern Italian styles, including veal, chicken, pasta and fresh seafood. Diners enjoy the outdoor patio of the renovated home, located two blocks west of Route 95. ~ 102 South 1st Avenue, Sandpoint; 208-263-0211. MODERATE TO ULTRA-DELUXE.

Swans Landing is a delightful alternative at the south end of the Long Bridge over Lake Pend Oreille. Sweeping views and tasty steak, seafood and homemade pasta specialties make this modern lodge-style building a favorite waterfront hangout. All soups and desserts are homemade. ~ Lakeshore Drive at Route 95, Sandpoint; 208-265-2000, fax 208-265-2011; www.swanslanding.com. DELUXE TO ULTRA-DELUXE.

HOSTEL ENVIRONMENT

The **Naples AYH Hostel**, eight miles south of Bonners Ferry in northernmost Idaho, is lodged in an old dance hall with beautiful hardwood floors. There are 16 beds, mainly in dormitories but 4 private rooms are available; guests share a kitchen and toilet and shower facilities. Located a block west of Route 95, the hostel features its own old-fashioned general store and laundromat. Unlike most hostels, it's open to guests during the day. ~ Route 2, Naples; 208-267-2947, fax 208-267-4118. BUDGET.

Every table in the fine dining room at **Hill's Resort** has a view of Priest Lake and the Selkirk Mountains beyond. Nature's bounty, from morel mushrooms to wild huckleberries, are combined in many of the recipes, which feature chicken, beef and native trout. Open daily in summer, weekends the rest of the year. ~ Luby Bay Road, Nordman; 208-443-2551, fax 208-443-2363; www.hillsresort.com. DELUXE TO ULTRA-DELUXE.

SHOPPING

◀ HIDDEN

There is no finer collection of photographs depicting Idaho the way it was—which was not so long ago—than at **Hallans Gallery**, a charming green-on-green cottage beneath a grand old cedar right off Sandpoint's main drag. Ross Hall toted his camera around Idaho with an instinct that the rough-and-tumble era of the old logging and mining camps, and of ranching, was ending, and so there is a documentary feel to much of his work. He captured the slippery work of loggers in cork boots riding logs down the Clark Fork River, and the mood of cattle roundups in western Montana and a beautiful exposure of Memaloose Island in Lake Pend Oreille, a spiritual site for native tribes. ~ 323 North 1st Avenue, Sandpoint; 208-263-4704, 888-448-4255; www.rosshallcollection.com, e-mail dannhall@sisna.com.

NIGHTLIFE

There is a major summertime concert series at Sandpoint. The **Festival at Sandpoint**, which is held for ten days in mid-August, has featured such big names as Willie Nelson, Maureen McGovern, the Robert Cray Band, the Temptations and the Neville Brothers. Performances are held at Memorial Field. ~ P.O. Box 695, Sandpoint, ID 83864; 208-265-4554; www.festivalatsandpoint.com.

Sandpoint's **Panida Theater**, a historic Spanish mission–style landmark, presents a wide range of plays, concerts, dance events and films to Lake Pend Oreille–area folks. ~ 300 North 1st Avenue, Sandpoint; 208-263-9191; www.panida.org.

PARKS

FARRAGUT STATE PARK 🏃 🚴 ⛴ 🚤 🛶 ⛵ Established in 1942 as an inland U.S. naval training station, the base was decommissioned in 1946 but became a 4000-acre park in 1965; it later gained fame as a venue for national and world Scout jamborees. The park has more than four miles of Lake Pend Oreille shoreline and offers many recreational opportunities. There's a small beach but no lifeguards at Beaver Bay. You can fish the lake year-round for game fish, including trout, bass and perch. Facilities include picnic tables, restrooms, showers, a visitors center, an amphitheater, a shooting range and more than 30 miles of trails for hiking and mountain biking. Day-use fee, $4 per vehicle. ~ Take Route 95 north from Coeur d'Alene for 20 miles, then turn east on Route 54. It's about four miles to the park entrance; 208-683-2425, fax 208-683-7416; e-mail far@idpr.state.id.us.

▲ There are 45 RV sites (all with hookups) in one campground and 63 tent sites in another; six group camps by reservation; $16 per night for RV hookups, $12 for tents.

ROUND LAKE STATE PARK 🏃 🏊 ⛵ 🎣 This 142-acre gem is a great place for families. Nature trails weave through the evergreen forest that surrounds a small lake carved by an Ice Age glacier. Campfire programs describe the lush plant, bird and animal life found here. The handsome visitors center dates from 1926. There is a designated beach for swimming and you can fish year-round for trout, bass and panfish. Facilities include picnic tables, restrooms, a visitors center and an amphitheater. Day-use fee, $4. ~ Located two miles west of Route 95 on Dufort Road, ten miles south of Sandpoint; 208-263-3489, fax 208-255-5569; e-mail rou@idpr.state.id.us.

▲ There are 53 RV/tent sites (no hookups); $12 per night.

PRIEST LAKE STATE PARK 🏃 🏕 🏊 ⛵ 🚤 🎣 Three separate units offer myriad recreational opportunities along the shore of Idaho's most pristine large lake. Dickensheet, 46 acres on the banks of the north-flowing Priest River just south of the lake, is popular with whitewater rafters and river anglers. Indian Creek, 295 acres on Priest Lake's eastern shore, is the most developed site; open year-round (and attracting winter snowmobilers and Nordic skiers), it has a small store as well as the park headquarters. Lionhead, 415 acres at the lake's north end, draws nature lovers. Lionhead and Dickensheet are open May through October (or until they're snowed shut). You'll find sandy beaches at Indian Creek and Lionhead. There is excellent trout fishing in the lake and river. Facilities include picnic tables, fire grates, showers, restrooms and a store (at Indian Creek). Day-use fee, $4. ~ Take Route 57 north from the town of Priest River for 22 miles; then turn east on Coolin Road. It's one mile to Dickensheet, 16 miles to Indian Creek, 28 miles to Lionhead; 208-443-2200, fax 208-443-3893; e-mail pri@idpr.state.id.us.

▲ There are 11 RV/tent sites (no hookups or water) at Dickensheet, 93 RV/tent sites (11 full hookups) at Indian Creek, and 47 RV/tent sites (no hookups) at Lionhead; $16 to $18 per night for RVs, $9 to $12 for tents. Indian Creek has five cabins that sleep up to six; $35 per night, by reservation only; 208-443-6710.

IDAHO PANHANDLE NATIONAL FORESTS 🏃 🏕 🏊 🎣 The Bonners Ferry district of the national forest consists of over 400,000 wooded acres. It contains the highest mountain range in the entire forest, the Selkirk Range, with a crest of 7500 feet, and the Moyie River, which is well known for its flyfishing and whitewater rafting. The forest is also popular with cross-country skiers and offers over 300 miles of hiking trails. Swimming is possible, but cold, in the mountain rivers and lakes. Fish for

Kokanee salmon, northern pike and many species of trout in the Kootenai River and the high mountain rivers and streams. Facilities include picnic tables and restrooms. ~ Route 57 north of Priest River and the Moyie River Road north of Bonners Ferry extend into the national forest. Robinson Lake Campground is located south of Eastport on Route 95. Take Forest Service Road 273 one-half mile to the campground. To reach Meadow Creek Campground, continue north past Robinson Lake approximately one and a half miles to Good Grief junction, and take a right onto Moyie River Road into the campground; 208-267-5561, fax 208-267-6754; www.fs.fed.us/ipnf.

Two endangered species, the grizzly bear and the caribou, reside in the Bonners Ferry area of the Idaho Panhandle National Forests.

▲ There are up to 22 RV/tent sites (no hookups); free to $8 per night. Most campgrounds are open from May to October. Situated on a high mountain lake is Robinson Lake Campground, with 10 RV/tent sites; $6 per night. Fly-fishers love Meadow Creek Campground on the Moyie River, with 22 RV/tent sites; $6 per night.

KOOTENAI NATIONAL WILDLIFE REFUGE 🚶 ⤵ This 2774-acre refuge on the Kootenai River provides a resting ground and a feeding and breeding area for migratory birds such as tundra swan (in spring) and various ducks and Canada geese (mainly in fall). Bald eagles may also be seen, as well as deer, moose, black bear and coyote. Three observation areas have been designated along a 4.5-mile automobile route through the refuge. During bird-hunting season, from October to December, entry to the refuge is limited. Fishing is allowed in designated areas along some of the refuge's creeks. Facilities include picnic tables and restrooms. ~ Take Westside Road (County Road 18) west five miles from Bonners Ferry along the south bank of the Kootenai River; 208-267-3888, fax 208-267-5570; kootenai.fws.gov, e-mail aaron_drew@fws.gov.

◀ HIDDEN

Outdoor Adventures

FISHING

The large lakes of the far north—Coeur d'Alene, Pend Oreille and Priest—are home to trophy-class kamloops, cutthroat, Dolly Varden and rainbow trout, kokanee salmon and northern pike. Spirit and Hayden lakes, near Coeur d'Alene, are also outstanding for kokanee salmon.

Other rivers share November-to-January steelhead runs and host rainbow trout throughout the year. In many smaller lakes, rainbow trout share the waters with bass and panfish like bluegills, perch and crappies.

River and lake expeditions are available throughout the region. Some outfitters specialize in flyfishing or power-boat fishing, steelhead or bass fishing; inquire when you book your reservations. Visitors centers normally have complete lists of outfitters, as well as information on fishing derbies in Coeur d'Alene Lake and Lake Pend Oreille.

Among the many reputable outfitters is **Diamond Charters**, which offers half- and full-day charters on Lake Pend Oreille. ~ P.O. Box 153, Hope, ID 83836, Hope; 208-265-2565, 800-487-6886; www.diamondcharters.com. **Priest Lake Outdoor Adventures** will take you out on Priest Lake for mackinaw lake trout. ~ 400 Fairway Drive, Priest River; 208-443-5601. Ask at marinas about lake charters, or at the **Fins & Feathers** tackle shop, whose guides will show you their favorite trolling grounds on Coeur d'Alene Lake. ~ 1816 Sherman Avenue, Coeur d'Alene; 208-667-9304; www.fins1.com.

WATER SPORTS

There's plenty of water in northern Idaho for all types of watersports enthusiasts. Motorboats are easily rented at the northern lakes, especially in Coeur d'Alene and Sandpoint and on Priest Lake. **Coeur d'Alene Watersports** rents paddleboats, kayaks, canoes, aqua-cycles and small electric boats for use along the lake's northwestern shore. ~ Independence Point; 208-765-5367. Private concessionaires at the lake may also offer waterskiing and parasailing. **Red Lion Templin's Resort** has paddleboats for rent. ~ 414 East 1st Avenue, Post Falls; 208-773-1611.

On Lake Pend Oreille, **Windbag Marina** rents sailboats, paddleboats, canoes and other seaworthy vessels. ~ City Beach, Bridge Street, Sandpoint; 208-263-7811; www.windbaymarina.com. About four miles south of Sandpoint, **Bottle Bay Resort** rents kayaks, canoes, paddleboats and fishing boats; it also has a restaurant and cabins, and a beach for swimming and fishing. ~ 115 Resort Road, Sagle; 208-263-5916; www.bottlebayresort.com.

RIVER RUNNING

Popular rafting rivers in the area include the St. Joe, the Coeur d'Alene and the Priest. **River Odysseys West** runs the St. Joe,

---

SCUBA DIVING IN COEUR D'ALENE LAKE

Here's a surprise: Scuba divers *love* Coeur d'Alene Lake. No fewer than 28 wrecks of old steamships can be found beneath the lake's surface. Two full-service dive shops, with sales and rentals, can be found in Coeur d'Alene. **Divers West** has snorkeling and dive gear for rent; certification classes are also available. ~ 1675 Lee Court, Coeur d'Alene; 208-664-0751; www.diverswest.com. In addition to sales, **Tom's Diving** leads customized dive trips to Coeur d'Alene Lake. ~ 500 North Marine Drive, Blackwell Island, Coeur d'Alene; 208-664-0852.

Coeur d'Alene and Moyie rivers. ~ P.O. Box 579, Coeur d'Alene, ID 83816; 208-765-0841, 800-451-6034; www.rowinc.com. Or contact the **Idaho Outfitters and Guides Association** for an exhaustive listing. ~ P.O. Box 95, Boise, ID 83701; 208-342-1438; www.ioga.org.

Northern Idaho has two major destination resorts, both in the Coeur d'Alene area, as well as a handful of smaller day areas.

SKIING

Schweitzer Mountain Resort, in the Selkirk Mountains 11 miles north of Sandpoint, has a vertical drop of 2400 feet, the second longest in Idaho, and 2500 acres of skiable terrain. The 6400-foot peak has spectacular views of sparkling Lake Road Oreille—and is served by six chairlifts and two tows. Cross-country trails (25 kilometers) are available. This is a full destination resort with ample slopeside lodging, ski shops, restaurants and expert instruction. Snow conditions permitting, Schweitzer opens for Thanksgiving and remains open into April. Average annual snowfall is 300 inches. ~ Schweitzer Mountain Road, Sandpoint; 208-263-9555, 800-831-8810, fax 208-263-0775; www.schweitzer.com; e-mail ski@schweitzer.com.

Silver Mountain, in the Silver Valley 35 miles east of Coeur d'Alene, has blossomed since the world's longest single-stage gondola (3.1 miles) opened in 1990. The vertical drop here is 2200 feet to the Mountain Haus at 5700 feet; five chairlifts serve the rest of the mountain, which peaks at 6300. Skiable terrain is 1500 acres. Silver Mountain's season is similar in length to Schweitzer's, and it also offers full rentals and instruction. ~ 610 Bunker Avenue, Kellogg; 208-783-1111, 800-204-6428, fax 208-783-9201; www.silvermt.com, e-mail cathyj@silvermt.com.

Here are other, smaller northern Idaho ski areas:

In the Coeur d'Alene area, 15 miles east of Wallace on the Idaho–Montana state line, **Lookout Pass** has a chairlift, a rope tow and an 850-foot vertical. Cross-country skiing is available. ~ Route 90 Exit 0, Mullan; 208-744-1301; www.skilookout.com. **Fourth of July Pass**, 13 miles east of Coeur d'Alene in the Idaho Panhandle National Forests, has groomed cross-country trails for all ability levels. ~ Route 90 Exit 28, Coeur d'Alene; 208-769-3000. **Ski Rentals** Skis and snowboards are available from **Silver Edge**. ~ 610 Bunker Avenue, Kellogg; 208-783-1111. You can rent alpine and Nordic gear as well as snowboards and snowshoes at **The Alpine Shop**, located in the lodge of Schweitzer Mountain. ~ 800-831-8810. Grangeville's **Holiday Sports** offers ski repair. ~ 126 West Main Street; 208-983-2299.

There's no shortage of public and private golf courses in northern Idaho. The most famous is **The Coeur d'Alene Resort Golf**

GOLF

Text continued on page 306.

Northern
Idaho Hikes

A favorite hike in northern Idaho's Selkirk Mountains is to the head of Long Canyon Creek. Barely five "crow" miles from the Canadian border, Long Canyon Creek joins the Kootenai River as it meanders northward in wide slow bends. Much of the Selkirk Range, rising to the west, has been logged of its white pine forests, as have the Cabinets and Yaak mountains to the east. That makes Long Canyon an anomaly as one of only two major old-growth basins remaining in the Selkirks.

The Selkirks also support the only officially acknowledged grizzly population in Idaho. The griz are drawn here by the remoteness of the high terrain and the solitude. When hiking in bear country it is advisable to make some noise, which seems unfortunate since the quiet is an important reason for seeking out remote places. Nevertheless, a surprised bear is the worst kind of bear to meet, and so conversing loudly every now and again or, better yet, banging on a tin cup, is a good idea. Remember that the qualities allowing griz to survive here are the very qualities you, too, are seeking. There still will be room for the sweet quiet.

The path for hiking Long Canyon is known officially as **Trail 16** (18 miles). To find it, pick up Route 1 traveling north approximately 15 miles above Bonners Ferry and follow the signs to Copeland, continuing through town until the intersection with Westside Road. Turn right and look for the trailhead sign at about ten miles. A gated road leads from the parking area to the trailhead. The top of the drainage is the goal, but much shorter excursions and day hikes can be made.

The first couple of miles are easy going, but the next mile is steep, perhaps a 35-percent grade in the steepest sections. The trail levels off a bit for the next mile across an open slope before dropping back to Long Canyon Creek and a streamside campsite. Depending on what time of day you started, this might make a good first night's camp or a turnaround for day hikers. A mile farther is an unmaintained trail tending southeast to Parker Ridge. A loop hike can be made by following Parker Ridge back down to the Kootenai Valley, landing you less than three miles south of your car at the trailhead for Trail 14. But if you've the time and energy, the best of Long Canyon lies ahead—views of the long, green basin from the high ridges at the top of the drainage, and of northern Idaho's and southern Alberta's highest peaks.

The **Upper Priest River Trail (Trail 308)** (8 miles) wends through miles of deep and enchanting western cedar forest. The very easy, almost flat, trail ends at American Falls, a 20-foot roar of white tumbling river, which is about eight miles in, so this goal should be considered only if you intend to camp overnight. Overnighters are advised to look for a campsite before arriving at Malcolm Creek at about seven miles—after that the trail steepens. Day hikers can extend as far as they wish into the hush of these magical cedar groves. To find the trailhead, you first must find Nordman, a tiny town north of Priest Lake. Continue north on Forest Service Road 302 (Granite Creek Road) for 14.75 miles to the Granite Pass Junction. Take Forest Road 1013 and after 11.5 miles you will find the trailhead sign.

The nearby Upper Priest Lake Scenic Area affords some of northern Idaho's most stunning scenery. Many consider this country to be northern Idaho's most beautiful. Day hikers can take the **Upper Priest Lake Trail** (5 miles) to reach the lake at Trapper Campground. What awaits you are spectacular views of Snowy Top Mountain in the Selkirk Range. This area is home to the only caribou herd in the lower 48 states. To find the trailhead, follow the directions above to Forest Service Road 1013. After about five miles, turn right on 655. Continue for half a mile or so; the trailhead is on your right.

Two day hikes can be made from the highly glaciated Pack River Valley. The Pack River Road leaves Route 95 about ten miles north of Sandpoint and continues for 20-some miles; the scenery from the road makes the drive alone worthwhile. **Harrison Lake** (3 miles) and the **Beehive Lakes** (4.4 miles) hikes wind through this intricately sculpted mountain crest, perhaps the state's most exotic example of glacial carving. The Beehive Lakes trailhead begins at the Trail 279 signpost off Pack River Road; the Harrison Lake trail leaves the road about a mile farther on; both are fairly difficult hikes.

Course, once voted "America's most beautiful resort course" by *Golf Digest.* Its signature hole, the 14th, has the world's only floating (and movable) green. ~ 900 Floating Green Drive, Coeur d'Alene; 208-667-4653; www.cdaresort.com.

Other 18-hole public links in the area include **Coeur d'Alene Golf Club.** ~ 2201 South Fairway Drive, Coeur d'Alene; 208-765-0218; www.clubproshops.com/dlowe. You can also tee off at **The Highlands Golf & Country Club.** ~ 5600 East Mullan Drive, Post Falls; 208-773-3673. **Avondale-on-Hayden Golf & Tennis Club** is a semiprivate course. ~ 10745 Avondale Loop, Hayden Lake; 208-772-5963. North of Coeur d'Alene, there's a tight 18 at the **Twin Lakes Village Golf Course.** ~ 5416 West Village Boulevard, Rathdrum; 208-687-1311; www.golftwinlakes.com. The **Stoneridge Golf Course** is nearby. ~ Route 41, Blanchard; 208-437-4682. In Sandpoint, play at **Hidden Lakes Golf Resort.** ~ 151 Clubhouse Way, Sandpoint; 208-263-1642; www.hidden lakes.com.

The region has nine-hole municipal courses at Coeur d'Alene, St. Maries, Kellogg, Chilco, Sandpoint, Priest River, Priest Lake and Bonners Ferry.

TENNIS

If Idaho's odd shape reminds you of an upside down tennis racket, you had better head for the courts. In Coeur d'Alene, there are courts at **McEuen Field** (Front Avenue) and **North Idaho College** (West Lakeshore Drive); in Sandpoint, at **City Beach** (Bridge Street). Or call city parks departments in Coeur d'Alene (208-769-2250) or Sandpoint (208-263-3158).

RIDING STABLES

Many guest ranches in the region offer rides as part of lodging packages or rent horses to day visitors. The **Rider Ranch** features horse-drawn hay rides year-round, trail rides from April through October, and chuckwagon dinner rides in the summer. ~ 6219 South Wolf Lodge Creek Road, Coeur d'Alene; 208-667-3373; www.riderranch.com. **Western Pleasure Guest Ranch** leads horseback trips from April through October; sleigh rides are offered in the winter. ~ 1413 Upper Gold Creek, Sandpoint; 208-263-9066; www.westernpleasureranch.com.

PACK TRIPS

If you want to duck out of civilization (like most of the locals seem to), try hopping on a wayward mule. Outfitters offering back-country adventures include **Idaho Outdoor Experience,** which offers trips ranging from a few hours to a few days. ~ 548 Cabinet Gorge Road, Clark Fork; phone/fax 208-266-1216; www.idaho outdoorexperience.com. **St. Joe's Outfitters and Guides** leads trips to their rustic, backcountry lodge or into the high country of the Bitterroot Mountains. ~ 8311 Windfalls Pass Road, St. Maries, ID 83861; 208-245-4002; www.stjoeoutfitters.com.

Northern Idaho offers extensive opportunities for mountain bikers, as well as on-road bikers.

So widespread are biking opportunities that the Silver Valley claims the world's largest system of mountain trails. Formally known as the **Silver Country 1000 Mile Trail System**, it caters heavily to ATVs and snowmobiles, but it's also a great network for mountain bikers, hikers and cross-country skiers who don't mind sharing their outdoors with motorized vehicles.

While it's a stretch to say there are 1000 miles of trails here, it is no exaggeration to say there are hundreds. Among favored shorter links are the **Slate Creek Run** (15 miles), which extends around Gibson Point off Moon Pass Road southeast of Wallace, and the more challenging **Red Oaks Run** (6.5 miles), which follows a ridgetop above Placer Creek Road, also southeast of Wallace.

Elsewhere in northern Idaho, **Centennial Trail** extends for 63 miles, following the Spokane River from Wolf Lodge Bay, east of Coeur d'Alene, to Spokane, Washington.

In Sandpoint, the **Long Bridge** south on Route 2 across Lake Pend Oreille is flanked by a two-mile bicycle and jogging track.

Like Silver Mountain, **Schweitzer Mountain Resort** converts its slopes and provides uphill chairlifts. ~ Schweitzer Mountain Road, Sandpoint; 208-263-9555; www.schweitzer.com.

Biking opportunities are almost limitless in other mountain areas such as **Lookout Pass** on the Idaho–Montana border, where rentals and guided tours are available. ~ Route 90 Exit 0, Mullan; 208-744-1301; www.skilookout.com.

Farragut State Park, at the south end of Lake Pend Oreille, also has a series of marked bike trails. ~ Route 54, Bayview.

Many rafting outfitters also lead mountain-biking expeditions. Contact the **Idaho Outfitters and Guides Association** (see "River Running") for a listing.

Bike Rentals The **Alpine Shop** at Schweitzer Mountain Resort rents mountain bikes. ~ 800-831-8810. In Sandpoint, **Alpine Designs** offers rentals of dual-suspension mountain bikes developed

AUTHOR FAVORITE

For me, there's nothing finer in summer than an exhilarating bike ride down **Silver Mountain**, especially when I'm spared the uphill climb by the resort's gondola! This Kellogg ski area turns its slopes into biking trails by summer, converting ski shops to bike shops and providing uphill transportation by gondola. Silver, in fact, boasts 59 miles of biking trails. ~ 610 Bunker Avenue, Kellogg; 208-783-1111; www.silvermt.com.

and built on the premises. ~ 312 North 5th Avenue, Sandpoint; 800-263-9373.

HIKING

A widely varied choice of trails is available to visitors to northern Idaho. The following list is but a sampling; see "Northern Idaho Hikes," in this chapter, for more. All distances listed for hiking trails are one way unless otherwise noted.

Tubbs Hill Trail (3.4 miles) loops around the circumference of a 150-acre city park that juts into Coeur d'Alene Lake. En route are three-story high caves, sandy beaches and scenic overlooks.

Caribou Ridge Trail (4.6 miles) descends 1800 feet from a lookout and picnic area atop 4000-foot Mount Coeur d'Alene to a National Forest campground at Beauty Bay, one of the easternmost spurs of Coeur d'Alene Lake. The upper trailhead is on Forest Road 439, off Route 97.

Navigation Trail (10 miles) begins at Beaver Creek campground at the north end of Priest Lake, 12 miles north of Nordman via Forest Road 2512. It passes through forest, meadow and bog, beaver ponds and an old trapper's cabin, with many scenic views of Upper Priest Lake, before ending at Forest Road 1013.

▼▼▼▼▼▼▼▼▼▼▼▼

Transportation

Route 95 is the primary north–south highway through Idaho's Panhandle running north from Boise via Lewiston to Coeur d'Alene, Sandpoint and on to Canada.

CAR

The main east–west highway in the Upper Panhandle is **Route 90**, the interstate that runs east from Seattle and Spokane through Coeur d'Alene and the Silver Valley, and on through Montana to Chicago and Boston. Farther north, it is vaguely paralleled by Route 2, a U.S. highway that cuts northeasterly from Spokane to Sandpoint and Bonners Ferry before turning sharply southeasterly toward Kalispell, Montana.

AIR

The **Coeur d'Alene Airport** handles regional traffic. Empire Airlines flies roundtrip from Boise to Coeur d'Alene via Lewiston four times every weekday. Empire also flies to Coeur d'Alene from Spokane.

In addition, **Spokane International Airport** is served by Alaska, Delta, Horizon, Southwest and United. The **Airport Shuttle** offers shuttle service between Seattle and Coeur d'Alene. ~ 888-622-3400.

A number of smaller airports handle charter and private flights, including sightseeing excursions.

BUS

Greyhound Bus Lines services the region, including Coeur d'Alene. ~ 137 East Spruce Avenue; 800-231-2222; www.greyhound.com.

TRAIN

Sandpoint has the only passenger rail service in Idaho. **Amtrak's** (800-872-7245; www.amtrak.com) northernmost line, the "Empire Builder," cuts across the Panhandle here, providing daily westbound service to Seattle and Portland, Oregon; eastbound to Chicago. The depot is on Railroad Avenue.

CAR RENTALS At the Coeur d'Alene airport, look for **Thrifty Car Rental**. ~ 800-367-2277.

PUBLIC TRANSIT **North Idaho Community Express** provides service in Sandpoint. ~ Sandpoint; 208-263-7287.

TAXIS In Coeur d'Alene, contact **Taxi by Hall**. ~ 208-664-2424. In Sandpoint, call **Bonner Cab**. ~ 208-263-7626.

Index

Lodging Index

Dining Index

HIDDEN GUIDES

Adventure travel or a relaxing vacation?—"Hidden" guidebooks are the only travel books in the business to provide detailed information on both. Aimed at environmentally aware travelers, our motto is "Where Vacations Meet Adventures." These books combine details on unique hotels, restaurants and sightseeing with information on camping, sports and hiking for the outdoor enthusiast.

THE NEW KEY GUIDES

Based on the concept of ecotourism, The New Key Guides are dedicated to the preservation of Central America's rare and endangered species, architecture and archaeology. Filled with helpful tips, they give travelers everything they need to know about these exotic destinations.

PARADISE FAMILY GUIDES

Ideal for families traveling with kids of any age—toddlers to teenagers—Paradise Family Guides offer a blend of travel information unlike any other guides to the Hawaiian islands. With vacation ideas and tropical adventures that are sure to satisfy both action-hungry youngsters and relaxation-seeking parents, these guides meet the specific needs of each and every family member.

Ulysses Press books are available at bookstores everywhere. If any of the following titles are unavailable at your local bookstore, ask the bookseller to order them.

You can also order books directly from Ulysses Press
P.O. Box 3440, Berkeley, CA 94703
800-377-2542 or 510-601-8301
fax: 510-601-8307
www.ulyssespress.com
e-mail: ulysses@ulyssespress.com

HIDDEN GUIDEBOOKS

____ Hidden Arizona, $16.95
____ Hidden Bahamas, $14.95
____ Hidden Baja, $14.95
____ Hidden Belize, $15.95
____ Hidden Big Island of Hawaii, $13.95
____ Hidden Boston & Cape Cod, $14.95
____ Hidden British Columbia, $18.95
____ Hidden Cancún & the Yucatán, $16.95
____ Hidden Carolinas, $17.95
____ Hidden Coast of California, $18.95
____ Hidden Colorado, $15.95
____ Hidden Disneyland, $13.95
____ Hidden Florida, $18.95
____ Hidden Florida Keys & Everglades, $13.95
____ Hidden Georgia, $16.95
____ Hidden Guatemala, $16.95
____ Hidden Hawaii, $18.95
____ Hidden Idaho, $14.95
____ Hidden Kauai, $13.95

____ Hidden Los Angeles, $14.95
____ Hidden Maui, $13.95
____ Hidden Montana, $15.95
____ Hidden New England, $18.95
____ Hidden New Mexico, $15.95
____ Hidden Oahu, $13.95
____ Hidden Oregon, $15.95
____ Hidden Pacific Northwest, $18.95
____ Hidden Salt Lake City, $14.95
____ Hidden San Francisco & Northern California, $18.95
____ Hidden Seattle, $13.95
____ Hidden Southern California, $18.95
____ Hidden Southwest, $19.95
____ Hidden Tahiti, $17.95
____ Hidden Tennessee, $16.95
____ Hidden Utah, $16.95
____ Hidden Walt Disney World, $13.95
____ Hidden Washington, $15.95
____ Hidden Wine Country, $13.95
____ Hidden Wyoming, $15.95

THE NEW KEY GUIDEBOOKS

____ The New Key to Costa Rica, $18.95

____ The New Key to Ecuador and the Galápagos, $17.95

PARADISE FAMILY GUIDES

____ Paradise Family Guides: Kaua'i, $16.95
____ Paradise Family Guides: Maui, $16.95

____ Paradise Family Guides: Big Island of Hawai'i, $16.95

Mark the book(s) you're ordering and enter the total cost here ➡ [_____]

California residents add 8.25% sales tax here ➡ [_____]

Shipping, check box for your preferred method and enter cost here ➡ [_____]

☐ BOOK RATE   **FREE! FREE! FREE!**

☐ PRIORITY MAIL/UPS GROUND   cost of postage

☐ UPS OVERNIGHT OR 2-DAY AIR   cost of postage

[_____]

Billing, enter total amount due here and check method of payment ➡ [_____]

☐ CHECK   ☐ MONEY ORDER

☐ VISA/MASTERCARD _____EXP. DATE_____

NAME _____PHONE_____

ADDRESS _____

CITY_____ STATE _____ ZIP_____

MONEY-BACK GUARANTEE ON DIRECT ORDERS PLACED THROUGH ULYSSES PRESS.

ABOUT THE AUTHOR

RICHARD HARRIS has written or co-written 31 other guidebooks including Ulysses' *Hidden Colorado, Hidden Cancún & the Yucatán, Hidden Baja, Hidden Belize, Weekend Adventure Getaways: Yosemite Tahoe* and the bestselling *Hidden Southwest.* He has also served as contributing editor on guides to Mexico, New Mexico, and other ports of call for John Muir Publications, Fodor's, Birnbaum and Access guides. He is a past president of PEN New Mexico and currently president of the New Mexico Book Association. When not traveling, Richard writes and lives in Santa Fe, New Mexico.

ABOUT THE ILLUSTRATOR

CLAUDINE GOSSETT is a freelance illustrator living in the San Francisco Bay area. She has done work for a wide range of projects, from health books to skateboard and snowboard graphics to album covers to children's books.